5/1u

THE LADY
WITH THE BORZOI

THE LADY WITH THE BORZOI

BLANCHE KNOPF,

LITERARY
TASTEMAKER EXTRAORDINAIRE

LAURA CLARIDGE

FARRAR, STRAUS AND GIROUX

NEW YORK

Farrar, Straus and Giroux
18 West 18th Street, New York 10011

Library of Congress Cataloging-in-Publication Data
Names: Claridge, Laura P., author.
Title: The lady with the Borzoi : Blanche Knopf, literary tastemaker extraordinaire / Laura Claridge.
Description: First edition. | New York : Farrar, Straus and Giroux, 2016. | Includes bibliographical references.
Identifiers: LCCN 2015034660 | ISBN 9780374114251 (hardback) | ISBN 9780374709730 (e-book)
Subjects: LCSH: Knopf, Blanche W., 1894–1966. | Publishers and publishing—New York (State)—New York—Biography. | Women publishers—United States—Biography. | Editors—United States—Biography. | Alfred A. Knopf, Inc.—History. | Knopf, Alfred A., 1892–1984. | Literature publishing—United States—History—20th century. | Authors and publishers—United States—History—20th century. | Books and reading—United States—History—20th century. | BISAC: BIOGRAPHY & AUTOBIOGRAPHY / Editors, Journalists, Publishers.
Classification: LCC Z473.K72 C58 2015 | DDC 070.5092—dc23
LC record available at http://lccn.loc.gov/201503466

Designed by Abby Kagan

www.fsgbooks.com
www.twitter.com/fsgbooks • www.facebook.com/fsgbooks

To the original four, plus the two they've brought to the journey,
and to the only one who could navigate such
a brilliant but disparate crew.

Without you, nothing.

Books succeed,
And lives fail.

—ELIZABETH BARRETT BROWNING

Odi et Amo. (I hate and I love.)

—CATULLUS

CONTENTS

CONTENTS

PART THREE

❧

PART FOUR

❧

THE LADY
WITH THE BORZOI

INTRODUCTION

EFT OFF HER COMPANY'S MASTHEAD but called by Thomas Mann "the soul of the firm," Blanche Knopf—the name she would always prefer to Mrs. Alfred A. Knopf—began her career in 1915 as cofounder of the company that just celebrated its hundredth anniversary. She quickly began scouting for her fledgling publishing house quality French novels she'd get translated, such as Flaubert's *Madame Bovary* and Prévost's *Manon Lescaut*. Soon she would help Carl Van Vechten launch the literary side of the Harlem Renaissance, publishing works by Langston Hughes and Nella Larsen, while she also nurtured and often edited such significant authors as Willa Cather, Muriel Spark, and Elizabeth Bowen. Through Dashiell Hammett, James M. Cain, Raymond Chandler, and Ross Macdonald, she legitimized the genre of hard-boiled detective fiction. H. L. Mencken was among her writers and closest friends. She acquired momentous works of journalism such as William Shirer's *Berlin Diary*, John Hersey's *Hiroshima*, and the work of the investigative reporters James "Scotty" Reston and Edward R. Murrow. She introduced to American readers international writers whom she met and had translated into English, among them Thomas Mann, Sigmund Freud, Albert Camus, and Simone de Beauvoir.

Intelligent, voracious, seductive, and hardworking, the petite woman who dressed in designer clothes and oversized, colorful jewelry was determined not to be overlooked or easily categorized. A "mongrel," she joked, like her frequent companion George Gershwin, who mixed "the vocabulary of serious music with that of the dance halls," she was seen by her friends as witty, loyal, and straightforward.[1]

Her career spanned the years from World War I to the 1960s. In 1915, when she started the company with Alfred Knopf, her twenty-two-year-old fiancé, Blanche, two years younger, believed her future as a publisher to be guaranteed through a prenuptial verbal pact she made with Alfred that they would be equal partners. (As the literary historian John Tebbel has said, "In 1915, Alfred A. Knopf and Blanche Wolf, later his wife, founded the firm that bears his name.")[2] But once they married, the "mutual understanding" was disregarded. Eventually Alfred would explain unconvincingly that because his father planned to join them at the firm, her name could not be accommodated: three names on the door would be excessive. Moreover, she would own just 25 percent of the company while Alfred owned the rest.

Blanche realized that the promise of parity she'd been made was false: she would have to rely on herself. It's unlikely that in 1915 she was aware of any other women who were part of her profession. There were a few, such as Caro M. Clark, who in the early twentieth century breached the prejudice against advertising in the book world; and Elizabeth Peabody, who published Transcendentalist authors, including Nathaniel Hawthorne and Henry David Thoreau. Neither Clark nor Peabody, who died the year Blanche was born, was active by the time Blanche began her career. But the start of World War I would further the changes already under way in the publishing world, as the field was evolving from a gentleman's occupation into a business enterprise. Less obviously, but at least as significant, "in an age when white men controlled the narrative," Blanche stood at what Stacy Schiff, in *Cleopatra*, calls "one of the most dangerous intersections in history: that of women and power." Closer in time to Blanche were Rebecca West and Dorothy Thompson, who exemplify, according to their biographer, Susan Hertog, the dangers of "speaking truth to power."[3]

At the beginning of the war, due to a scarcity of high-quality paper, the patrician houses Macmillan, Houghton Mifflin, Doubleday, and Little, Brown, as well as Henry Holt and Scribner's, two of the oldest, turned from releasing trade books to promoting textbooks, with their greater profit margin. Blanche and Alfred began acquiring previously published works from England (often translations of Russian and German books), reprinting them (under loose early-century copyright laws), and spending their money on hard-to-find fine paper instead of on authors. The Bolshevik Revolution, followed by Russia's withdrawal from World War I, allowed Knopf's Russian books, cheap to obtain, to accrue some small cachet. Russian authors dominated the new company's first five years, proving important to the publishers because they helped establish Knopf as "one of the very few American publishers interested in European books."[4] Yet, as the historian Richard Hofstadter has said, "it was not republishing the Russians which was to distinguish the firm, but bringing to America the work of writers like Mann . . . Sartre, Camus and others"—all three Blanche's authors.[5] The Langston Hughes biographer Arnold Rampersad claims, "A brilliant woman living somewhat in the shadow of her lordly husband, Alfred, she signed up most of the writers, especially the foreigners, who made Knopf a prestigious as well as a profitable imprint."[6]

Still, by the time Alfred died in 1984, Blanche had somehow disappeared from Knopf's history. Asked seven years after her death about Blanche's role in their company, Alfred lamented that she'd never been properly recognized: "She had, as I realize more and more, a very big finger in the pie."[7] Continuing, he admitted that "she had a very considerable influence on the list, [even signing Knopf's books by musicians] . . . I realize it more now than when she was alive."[8] He was not the only one to recognize Blanche after her death: the highly regarded defense lawyer in the Scottsboro case, Osmond Fraenkel, whose wife had known Blanche since they were both children, acknowledged that he hadn't liked Blanche particularly and had failed to take her seriously. Upon late-life reflection, however, the defender of civil liberties who fought more than one battle for the publishing world realized that "she was indispensable to the business."[9] The essayist Joseph Epstein has written, "I've long been fairly certain that Blanche was the more interesting character."[10]

Indeed. She made up for being kept on the sidelines—in part by turning her husband's lack of sexual interest into her own liberation. She ripped through the Roaring Twenties, partying with friends like the Fitzgeralds and Sinclair Lewis, whom she thought too unreliable to publish in spite of their genius (they would go to more established publishers with less to lose than the Knopfs), and sleeping with the most prominent conductors and musicians of the age. She maneuvered through World War II by flying into, not away from, battle. The writer and Knopf publicist Harding "Pete" Lemay, who knew Blanche during the last ten years of her life, remembers that "she was an extraordinary person, a woman against all odds of her time and her specific place. She invented herself so early, when she was so young."[11]

PART ONE

1

HUNGRY FOR ADVENTURE

FROM HER LATER ACCOUNTS, she only pretended to be calm, smiling graciously as she boarded the C-47. The slight sway of her walk gave her an aura of confidence, though it came from a shot of bourbon she'd secretly swallowed before takeoff. Saluted by the handsome young lieutenant about to lift her over the gap between the plane's body and its metal steps, she was taken aback until she remembered that she wore a uniform.[1] It was 1943, and for this flight, the army had designated Blanche a lieutenant colonel. The alcohol and a set of earplugs allowed her to fall asleep despite the noisy engine, and she was in Newfoundland before she knew it. Once in London, she changed into her civilian clothes. Routine bombing had been occurring nightly in the aftermath of the Blitz, and only hours after she'd arrived, an air raid siren blasted the air. She was having a drink at Claridge's, just a few blocks down from the Ritz, where she was staying, "both places miraculously intact." Blanche wrote that she "crossed the road and went upstairs to my room. I sat all dressed up in a wool dress, my handbag and my papers at my side, and worked with a splitting headache. Heard a lot of noise . . . About a quarter to twelve there was a siren, and I [went downstairs where the reporters were gathered and asked], 'Is the air raid starting now?'" Everybody laughed, Blanche's mistake providing the most levity the reporters had known in weeks. "The siren was the all clear . . . After that I never paid any attention to the raids. What I did was pull the blankets up over my ears and go back to sleep."[2]

Though it was supposedly fully booked, the Ritz, where half the war correspondents were staying, somehow made room for Blanche. The day of her arrival she had rushed through the lobby during a blackout, accompanied by a British literary agent carrying flowers that an anonymous admirer had left for the publisher at the front desk. In the week that Blanche remained in London, she would share drinks and dinners (early, "because no buses ran after nine") with journalists, writers, and friends, including Edward R. Murrow, the CBS broadcast journalist. She would later publish a collection of his broadcasts that included his wartime coverage, but for now she was pleased that he had agreed the previous year to provide a blurb for a first book, *Prelude to Victory*, by Blanche's young author the reporter James B. "Scotty" Reston. At Reston's request, she had edited the book personally instead of handing it over to one of the first-rate house editors, and Knopf published it in 1942.

Born on July 30, 1894, in a pleasant but unprepossessing Upper West Side brownstone, she spent most of her premarital life on the Upper East Side at 40 East Eighty-Third Street, where the family moved after her birth—or at the Gardner School, on Fifth Avenue between Forty-Eighth and Forty-Ninth Streets. Founded in 1860 by a Baptist minister, Gardner was aimed primarily at well-off Jewish girls, as well as at non-Jews lacking the social clout to attend the more exclusive all-girls schools, such as Chapin or Brearley. The writer Mary

Craig Kimbrough, who in 1913 married Upton Sinclair, author of *The Jungle*, had attended Gardner a few years before Blanche. Such an alliance for a southern girl from Mississippi suggests that Gardner was liberal leaning.

Like other young ladies being groomed for marriage, Blanche followed her well-meaning parents' agenda: taking piano and riding lessons in the mornings and studying French after school, when she was tended by a German nanny. Gardner allowed Blanche to escape a dull home, her pleasant but somewhat distant mother and father not being particularly interested in books or cultural life. Her brother wasn't much company, either. Eight years older, Irving was rarely around, except, as he matured, to persuade their father to back his latest business venture.

But at Gardner, Blanche entered an enchanted universe. A six-story French Renaissance building with modern conveniences, from electricity to elevators to its own filtration plant, Gardner thrilled Blanche with its winding white marble staircase that led to an endless array of grand bookcases.[3] These were filled with books that fed all sorts of fantasies, in particular nineteenth-century novels by Jane Austen, George Eliot, Victor Hugo, Gustave Flaubert, and other literary masters. Her classmates would remember her as well liked but primarily a loner—some thought her shy, others a snob.[4] While giggling classmates ran up and down the school stairs, Blanche stationed herself at the bottom, reading. Through her brother's wife, Irma, Blanche met Paula Herzig, Irma's cultivated sister, who taught her to value French literature in particular. Soon Paula was speaking French with Blanche and taking her to concerts to hear the Impressionist music of Claude Debussy, Maurice Ravel, and even Frederick Delius.[5]

Blanche's childhood friend Rita Goodman Bodenheimer told an interviewer that after graduation from Gardner, Blanche changed, her "thoughts now only in the book world," but in reality such preoccupation was hardly a swerve from her interest while in school. Bodenheimer recalled that until Blanche met Alfred Knopf, she was "satisfied with being alone or with a few friends," but then "she decided her old friends were frivolous." She resolved to "improve herself," and she refused all beaux and walked her Boston terrier by herself, often reading along the way.[6]

Such stories were told—often by envious schoolmates—fifty years after the fact. In addition to the primacy of reading, however, they do suggest themes that would define Blanche throughout the years, from her penchant for living alone to her love of dogs. She liked to make up parts of her life, too, later recounting little of her family that proved true—her fantasies and embellishments still glimpsed in Knopf's house histories and reference books today. One of the publisher's oft-repeated tales referred to her father, Julius Wolf, as a "gold jeweler from Vienna," though his immigration papers reveal that he was a farmer or day laborer ("*Landmann*") in Bavaria. Blanche's father abandoned farming during the immigration waves of the 1870s, a few years before yet another decree against Jews occurred. At the behest of a relative already settled in the New World, in 1877 Julius holed up in steerage and traded Hamburg for New York City. Through distant cousins working in a small Manhattan business, the clever newcomer mastered the making and selling of cloth and before long became a major manufacturer of caps and baby hats. By 1882 he was part owner of Sonn and Wolf, a millinery company that designed and made ruffles and trimmings. Julius left the business only months before it went bankrupt, luck or instinct determining his fate once again.

Bertha Samuels, Blanche's mother, had inherited money just in time to offer a solid dowry to Julius, following the custom of the day. Bertha's father, Lehman Samuels of Manhattan, along with his brother, was the country's largest exporter of beef and live cattle until 1877. That year, even as Julius Wolf sailed to America, Samuels Brothers became a casualty of the country's "Long Depression," one of the eighteen thousand American businesses and banks—and ten states—that went bankrupt, caught in the financial debacle of 1873–

79.[7] *The New York Times* reported that the demise of the Samuelses' firm, held in the highest esteem, shocked its customers.[8] But, working ceaselessly, by 1885 Lehman Samuels had made his fortune back.[9]

When Blanche was born in 1894, family finances were again on solid ground. The Wolfs soon moved into their home on the refined Upper East Side. There Julius, with his noticeable accent, habitually deferred to Bertha, who, as a first-generation American, cheerfully dominated the household. "Julius looked very jolly," Blanche's cousin remembered: "short, round, with ruddy cheeks and dancing brown eyes," even though he was also "austere—a typical German," she added.[10] The few surviving photographs suggest a cheerful if rotund adult, the parent who, according to one of Blanche's breezy and improbable stories, would gladly take Blanche and a cousin to Paris for their high school graduations.

Bertha Samuels Wolf was a stout, self-possessed matriarch who proudly told Blanche that no one would have guessed her own father had run a slaughterhouse. Pictures of Blanche and her mother show two women laughing together heartily, not the stark family image recalled by those interviewed after Blanche's death. One of Blanche's early friends, Helene Fraenkel, dismissed Bertha Wolf as "exceedingly pretty but little and so fat that she was square." The Wolfs' lack of interest in the arts led Blanche, Fraenkel maintained, to seek "someone intellectual to marry."[11]

Though Bertha, like her husband, at times could be remote, she managed to teach Blanche the importance of self-presentation. Bertha dressed well, favoring what would later be called "the Jewish uniform": smart, tailored black suits (in the 1920s made to order by the emerging couturier Sally Milgrim), always adorned with a string of pearls. One relative thought that Bertha looked like Lillian Russell when she was young and that Julius looked like "a typical butter-and-egg man."[12] Whatever their appearance, the egg man's determination, as well as his wife's inheritance, enabled his daughter, years later, to adopt the attitude of those who came from wealth. Still, neither Julius nor Bertha was inclined to support a college education for either of their children, especially their daughter. Blanche does not seem to have considered going beyond high school, though Barnard (along with other colleges) had been available to women since the late 1880s. In her case, the conjugal wait after she finished Gardner would deliver her a profession, if male-inflected from its beginning. As one scholar notes, "Blanche would launch an esteemed career in literary publishing," guided by a man whose male professors were trained in a canon that emphasized male authors.[13]

By the time she graduated from Gardner, Blanche had already set her sights on marrying the muscular, olive-skinned Alfred Knopf. Blanche found him attractive not least because, like her, he preferred books to people, reading voraciously at Columbia University and, during college breaks, at beaches on the South Fork of Long Island. Blanche had occasionally spoken to the athletic boy in Lawrence, on Western Long Island, where he lived on his father's estate.

Blanche, Jewish but secular, was relieved that Alfred proved no more religious than she. An agnostic, he showed even less interest in his Jewish identity than did his father, Sam, who had at least joined Temple Emanu-El, Manhattan's fashionable congregation, for the sake of appearances. Alfred's indifference meshed with Blanche's adult convictions and impatience with religion, which she increasingly believed did the world more harm than good. She and Alfred both disdained what was called Jewish society. Shopping on Rosh Hashanah, when she believed Manhattan stores to be less crowded, Blanche told disapproving friends that she had read too much about different cultures to believe in one spiritual authority.

The somewhat reserved adolescent girl nonetheless managed to charm much of the Jewish community of Woodmere, near Lawrence on Long Island's South Shore. In the 1970s, Elsie Alsberg, who before their marriage had known both Alfred and, less well, Blanche, recalled that the usually "solitary girl" occasionally "invited everyone" to her summer rental, supplying food, then joining in the singing and dancing, with a friend's father driving some of the guests home in his luxurious seven-passenger Pierce-Arrow.[14] The summer after graduation, in 1911, the seventeen-year-old made her debut at the Lawrence Athletic Club, where, at a party, she was formally introduced to Alfred Knopf. Despite her friends' unkind whispers that they thought him unattractive and pedantic, Blanche enjoyed talking with him. A girl whose head was filled with exotic fables, she was drawn to his intellectual manner and self-possession. According to that young man's memories, it took "another year or so" before they became "seriously interested in each other."[15]

Louis Davidson told his friend that if he himself didn't already have a girl, he'd go after this "beaut" himself.[16] With medium-length copper-red hair, opaque gray-green eyes, and a curvaceous body, Blanche looked like a pre-Raphaelite beauty.[17] Another friend remembers her perfect manners, and that she "rarely spoke . . . absolute silence"—but that when she did, she had a "warm speaking voice."[18] Eventually she would become, when necessary, an artful speaker but an even more astute listener, her fluid, elegant low voice and her ability to concentrate major assets throughout her career.

Years later, Blanche recalled how quickly she and Alfred became friends that summer of 1911. Alfred was delighted to keep company with such a practical girl, who, instead of "chatter," liked to talk about books—or, more accurately, to listen to him talk about them. But she'd have to forgo his tutelage for a while: after graduating from Columbia University in early 1912, Alfred took off for Germany for a six-month tour. He had arranged an introduction in England to the distinguished writer John Galsworthy, who in 1921 was to become the first president of PEN (Poets, Essayists and Novelists), the writers' organization that would eventually spread worldwide. Galsworthy was the subject of Alfred's senior thesis—their fateful meeting going on to inspire the acolyte to publish great writing.

As soon as he returned in June, the couple became an item, with Alfred working as an office boy for Doubleday. "Blanche knew exactly what I had been doing [figuring out the publishing world] when I started work at Doubleday's; and she was an avid reader, filled with enthusiasm for and vitally interested in whatever involved books and the people who wrote them . . . And so [our] little firm was [soon] established," Alfred would recall succinctly of the couple's professional beginnings, entwined with the personal from the start.[19] Blanche lauded Alfred's decision to scuttle law school, his original plan, one he had not found exciting even when considering it before graduation. Publishing, Blanche felt sure, would allow a place for her, while the law would require a college degree followed by further professional training.

Later she remembered how from its conception her relationship with Alfred was about books. Alfred "had [realized] I read books constantly and he had never met a girl who did. He was earning eight dollars a week [the equivalent of around $170 in 2015] . . . I saw him and [all we did was] talk books, and nobody liked him— my family least of all. But I did, because I had someone to talk books to and we talked of making books . . . We decided we would get married and make books and publish them."[20] Some girls dreamed about making babies, but Blanche and Alfred wanted to make books.

"We never talked anything but books and music, music and books," she recalled nostalgically in later interviews.

> I rode horseback with him occasionally, which was the only thing I had ever done all my life apart from playing the piano and studying . . . I talked to my parents seriously [about marrying Alfred] and they wouldn't hear of it. There were twelve other men around I could marry but not this one. Not only because he was a Russian Jew [Alfred was in fact born in the United States] but, according to my family, his family of poor reputation, [was] not [meant] for me . . . [Still I was determined to] marry him and publish books.[21]

If Blanche brought to the table a life that lacked excitement, Alfred supplied all the drama anyone could want, his harrowing childhood and history affecting Blanche's future as much as his own. Sam Knopf, born in a Warsaw suburb in 1862, had reason to be proud, and seeing the esteem in which Alfred clearly held him, Blanche, too, admired the father. By the time she met him, he had become director of one of New York City's small mercantile banks.[22]

But Alfred knew, firsthand, that life had been hard for Sam, the youngest of seven children. In spite of its longtime anti-Semitic policies, Poland enjoyed a liberal period when the *Haskalah*, a Jewish form of the Enlightenment, enabled a good life for Sam's parents: Abraham Knopf taught English at the University of Warsaw, while his wife, Hannah, earned a chemistry degree.[23] By the late 1860s, however, anti-Semitic abuse prompted the Knopfs to flee the country and move to America. From the ship's arrival sprang the first of many probably apocryphal stories about the Knopf family, forming a legend both Alfred and Blanche encouraged: in what would be his five or six incomplete autobiographies, Alfred would consistently record that Abraham and Hannah, departing from the eastern frontier of western Russia, traveled by way of Manchuria to San Francisco, where they stopped to visit friends, the grandparents of Jascha Heifetz, the future violinist (later to become Blanche's lover), then sailed a wildly out-of-the-way route around the Horn to reach New York City in 1873.[24]

When Abraham Knopf died a year after arriving in America, like his wife unable to find a teaching job, their daughters agreed that even the youngest in the household would have to earn money to help support the family. By the time Sam was twelve, he had dropped out of school to be raised by his married sister in Houston, where he would become the quintessential entrepreneurial American of the late nineteenth century. Formal education was out of the question. Alfred would say of his father that Sam had taught himself "everything," including the history of Judaism. His son admired his father's homage to the "people of the book," an identity associated with Jewish people that had been passed down by Sam's parents. "With very little schooling he became a literate and . . . civilized adult," said Alfred, "buying sets of the French and Russian classics illustrated with full color plates galore and bound in three quarters red morocco," an aesthetic the son would replicate.[25]

Sam Knopf got his citizenship papers in 1893, shortly after Alfred Abraham Knopf, the first child of Sam and Ida Japhe, was born on September 12, 1892, at the Knopfs' home at 234 Central Park West. Alfred's mother was from a Latvian Jewish family that had settled in Manhattan in time for Ida's own birth, making her a first-generation American. A former student of the schoolteacher would write Alfred in 1949 that although "plain," she was "splendid" in personality and "had that wonderful facility of being able to impart [her knowledge] to the immature mind. I loved her."[26]

His friends all agreed that Sam deserved a good wife, and the canny man knew that marriage to Ida would ensure his American citizenship. A natty dresser with a stickpin always in his tie and suits "a shade too well-cut," as an aristocratic friend confided, the man was "a little sharp."[27] At five feet, ten and a half inches, the exact height his son Alfred would reach, Sam was proud of his trim physique. As an adult, Alfred would imply that his father had been one for the ladies, whom he easily met and befriended while plying his trade. Sam had become a salesman, traveling the Northeast by stagecoach, in which he carried samples of clothing and miniature models of furniture supplied him by eight or ten manufacturers.[28] By working nonstop, he would become well-off, through the connections he curried as much as the social skills he honed. He was so successful that he was hired as the manager of a large Manhattan clothing store, Bierman, Heidelberg & Co., and near the time of Alfred's birth was offered the chance to open a branch in Cincinnati. Alfred, who throughout his life idolized his father, called him "a very strangely remarkable person." He never understood how Sam became accepted in gentile circles, an influential financial counselor to important businesses.[29] Nor how he became a member of clubs that usually didn't admit eastern European Jews, who were not members of "our crowd," the term the author Stephen Birmingham coined in describing the prejudice among Jewish society, including millionaire magnates such as the Guggenheims, the Loebs, and the Belmonts. But such mystery only encouraged Alfred to hold his father in awe.

In 1894 the Knopfs decamped for the Midwest, where, the local paper reported, Sam quickly became "a social favorite." They lived in a smart area of town, Walnut Hills, their elaborately landscaped Victorian home on Lincoln Avenue a scene of swank gatherings. Alfred's first memory was of walking along a bluff over the Ohio River "with a Negro manservant." On March 17, 1895, Ida gave birth to a daughter, Sophia Celeste, usually called Sophie.[30] In Cincinnati, Sam's mounting prosperity allowed him to open his own wholesale clothing business, Samuel Knopf & Co., at Fifth and Race Streets. Increasingly he found reasons to travel, leaving the young Ida alone in their large house with the babies. Sam dismissed her complaints about boredom and loneliness, deserting her (as she saw it) for months at a time.

In July 1896, Sam sent Ida, Alfred, and Sophie, together with a servant, to the Shenandoah Valley in Virginia. A Jewish family, even a wealthy one, couldn't or wouldn't vacation at the new Homestead Resort in Hot Springs, or at the Greenbrier in White Sulphur Springs, West Virginia, but there were desirable places available to the Knopfs just the same. Sam lodged Ida and their young children at the Grand Hotel in Rockbridge Alum Springs.

Though it proved almost as warm in Virginia as it was back home, Ida wrote brightly to Sam that at least "the air is always fresh and pure." In a letter to a Cincinnati friend the young woman confided that "the place is full of Southerners . . . A very refined class of people extend the courtesies of the day, and that is all."[31] Despite the cheerful countenance she presented to her husband, Ida was depressed among the throng of vacationers. From Sam's reputation as a ladies' man, Ida must have worried about his fidelity to her even before their marriage, but she adored him. Now, nine days after she wrote both Sam and a friend that she was terribly lonesome, she finally got the attention she craved.

On July 25, 1896, according to *The Cincinnati Enquirer*, friends at the summer camp summoned Sam: "Come immediately." That morning, a servant maintained, "there was a man in the cottage, and he was in Mrs. Knopf's room." Believing him to be a burglar, the maid had run shrieking from Ida's bungalow.[32]

According to a second newspaper, *The Commercial Tribune*, almost from the day that Sam Knopf delivered his family to the springs and then went his way, guests at the resort had been aware of a Peoria businessman spending an unseemly amount of time with Mrs. Knopf. To all admonitions, she "turned a deaf ear, and pursued the folly of her way." Upon Sam's arrival at the camp, the *Tribune* claimed, the husband's inquiries quickly resulted in "a confession signed by [Ida] in which she admitted her guilt . . . He also obtained the statements of the man in the case" regarding Ida's infidelity, which caused "[Mr. Knopf] to send his wife and their children to New York, where they have been ever since. Mr. Knopf and his wife have not lived together since that occurrence," the reporter noted.[33]

Ida took Alfred and Sophie to her parents' modest house in Brooklyn's Bensonhurst neighborhood, while Sam remained in Cincinnati. He sold his business, gave up the elegant house on Lincoln Avenue, and went to live at his clubs. According to the *Enquirer*,

He ordered a sale [at auction] of the effects in his magnificently furnished home. Everything in it was sold at prices that did not represent one fiftieth of its real value. Previous to the sale, he had forwarded an ad of household effects to his semi-divorced wife . . . From almost the very hour that the separation took place Mrs. Knopf did everything in her power to effect a reconciliation. Scarcely a day passed in which a letter was not received begging forgiveness. Some of them were pathetic in their pleading. The disgraced wife offered to come back as a menial and scrub his floors. "I will be your dog if you will only let me remain under your roof," she wrote. He was obdurate and steadily declined to answer any of the letters.[34]

At 11:20 on the morning of February 12, 1897, Ida Knopf went to A. F. Underwood's drugstore on Bath Avenue, where she bought two ounces of carbolic acid, a sweet-smelling clear liquid, for use, she assured the druggist, as a disinfectant. At 2:00 the next morning, Dr. E. H. Mayne was called to the house. All the doctor could do was to tell the woman screaming in pain that it would be over soon.

Into his old age, Alfred was troubled by the memory of that night. Not yet five, the child knew there had been difficulties between his parents since the previous summer, when he witnessed the tensions at the Virginia retreat. On this freezing February night, he had awakened to hear loud voices and servants running in the hallway outside his room. When he realized something terrible was happening, he hid under the covers. The *Brooklyn Sunday Eagle* reported that Dr. Mayne "found Mrs. Knopf suffering great internal pain. The physician resorted to all known remedies, but at 11:30 p.m. yesterday the woman died." Ida was thirty-three years old; her agony had ended in death the evening before Valentine's Day.[35]

An anonymous source told the police that "Ida had been suffering for a long time from an incurable disease; believing she would never be well again, she killed herself." The story held for three days, and when inquiries were made to Sam, back in Cincinnati, he feigned shock: he had visited his wife in her Bensonhurst home the Friday she bought the acid, finding her as happy as ever, with "everything her heart could wish for."

Mr. Knopf neglected to mention to the reporter that on the prior Monday in the Cincinnati Court of Common Pleas, he had filed a suit for divorce from Ida on grounds of adultery. He had not informed Ida until Friday morning, when he briefly visited her Brooklyn apartment. She then walked to the pharmacy and bought the poison. The Cincinnati papers, which stressed the prominence of the Knopfs in "Jewish society," printed the full story as soon as Ida's suicide was revealed: Sam's wife had been named in the divorce papers as an adulteress who was expected to yield custody of her children and to relinquish her husband's name. Ida Japhe was buried at the Union Fields cemetery in Bath Beach on February 17, 1897. Neither Alfred nor his sister, Sophie, would remember their mother very clearly, and Sam would not speak of Ida again. Alfred spoke directly of her to Blanche just once, early in their marriage, and she would never forget the expression on his face as he told her the story.

Sam moved back to New York City, remarrying a year later. Lillian Harris would prove a loving stepmother. The family lived in a large wood-frame house in Washington Heights, in the upper reaches of Manhattan, considered in the last years of the century to be the "country." Its solitude and relief from what happened in Brooklyn left their mark on Alfred forever, creating a lifelong desire to live outside New York City. Lillie, however, would go unappreciated by both her husband and her stepchildren, who later complained that she was "not very smart" (but, Sam always added, very sexy). The family became quite a mixed brood—Bertha, a girl from Lillian's previous marriage, who took "Knopf" as her last name, together with Alfred and Sophie, and a child, Edwin, born of Sam and Lillie's marriage.

In different combinations, the children were farmed out to friends and relatives during summers and holidays, allowing Sam and Lillie to take vacations on their own. Sam often combined work with play, a routine Alfred would replicate when he became a parent. When the children did accompany their parents on car trips, Lillie in particular would gently chastise young Alfred for focusing on a book instead of looking at the scenery. But the boy formed his own opinions and kept on reading *Tess of the D'Urbervilles* or his "lowbrow" favorite, Sherlock Holmes—books being the safest, most soothing world he could imagine.

2
_____

THE BOOK LOVERS

ECADES AFTER SHE AND ALFRED WED, Blanche would tell
her sister-in-law Mildred Knopf that her marriage had
hinged on a pre-engagement promise she extracted: Alfred
had to make Blanche an equal partner in the publishing company
they'd dreamed of creating from the start of their courtship.[1] Unusual for its time, such an arrangement was especially gutsy for a
girl just figuring out what she wanted from life—let alone knowing
how she would achieve it. But for all her prenuptial savvy, Blanche
was crazy about the very well-read twenty-two-year-old Alfred Knopf.

Throughout their courtship, Alfred assumed the unofficial role
of Blanche's tutor, his way of expressing his love for her, she decided. He had derided the modern art that secretly interested her—
especially the Fauvism, Futurism, and Cubism that were promoted at
the city's early-winter exhibit at the 69th Regiment Armory. Officially
titled "International Exhibition of Modern Art," the 1913 show,
organized by the Association of American Painters and Sculptors,

would come to be known as "the Armory Show." Though the exhibit would be in New York City for only a month, its outsize impact had conservative critics howling at what they considered the preposterous loss of the traditional figure that had grounded almost all art to this point, with Marcel Duchamp's *Nude Descending a Staircase (No. 2)* usually deemed the show's most revolutionary piece. The brochure featured part of an earlier abstract "poem" by Gertrude Stein called "Portrait of Mabel Dodge at the Villa Curonia," which the flamboyant Dodge, who had befriended Stein in Paris, distributed at the show. Admired for the weekly salon she held in her new apartment at 23 Fifth Avenue, Dodge counted among her crowd Carl Van Vechten, soon to become one of Blanche's closest friends. Van Vechten would introduce Blanche to Stein and to Max Eastman, a Greenwich Village radical who financed the journalist and activist John Reed's trip to Russia. (The loss of Reed, Mabel Dodge's lover, caused Dodge to eat figs studded with glass and to swallow laudanum, from which the sturdy woman promptly recovered.)

Feeling uncomfortable around such know-it-alls, as he saw them, Alfred told Blanche they were a bunch of poseurs—their art, except for Eastman's, lightweight. Many critics took the same view, one writing in *Harper's Weekly*, for instance, that there were "still laws in art as in physics . . . If your stomach revolts against this rubbish it is because it is not fit for human food."[2] Van Gogh, Rodin, and Matisse were basically unskilled or mentally ill, such detractors maintained. Blanche was uneasy at the censure the Armory Show inspired, sensing it was akin to how books were censored in her world, the world of words. But she remained silent, believing that she lacked the education and experience to make such judgments. Her instincts were right, however: American art would change forever after the exhibition.

For a while, the closest the couple would get to the avant-garde was their reading of a well-respected progressive novel, Henry Sydnor Harrison's *V.V.'s Eyes*, an early endorsement of women's and workmen's rights. Soon Alfred began calling Blanche "VV," for the book's broad-minded male physician with famously piercing blue-gray eyes—the doctor's sympathy for women making him appear advanced. Alfred would use "VV" as Blanche's nickname erratically throughout their lives, an acknowledgment of the gulf between his wife's independence and the world of the traditional Victorian housewife that had been left behind.

For her part—and in place of his school nickname, "Knoppie"—Blanche was regularly calling Alfred "Reuben," inspired by a popular song of the day, "Reuben and Rachel," originally published in 1871 and resurrected during World War I.[3] A children's song recounting a gentle battle of the sexes, its new, slightly altered opening line, "Reuben, Reuben, I've been thinking," was ready-made for Blanche's coquetry. Her suggestive notes to her suitor accelerated, proper yet more intimate by the month. Coyly rejecting Alfred's invitations to spend the weekend in Lawrence, she also found ways to signal that "this was the man she wanted."[4] At the end of 1913, she sent him a message that was clearly a flirtation: "Funny thing, this morning, when I was still in a very sleepy state I reached out my hand for a letter"; she was disappointed to find she'd been dreaming.[5]

To Blanche, her head filled with literature, Alfred was a glamorous suitor—and he was interested in her, despite all that she needed to learn.

Pleased, she noticed how he sought to impress her, taking her the next summer to an intercollegiate rowing regatta on the Hudson, where he could boast of Columbia University's standing. He would brag about running track in college: "My interest lasted a long time, and before we were married Blanche and I went frequently to the New York Athletic Club Games at Travers Island and to the Pennsylvania Relays at Philadelphia." The couple also enjoyed attending polo matches at Garden City, where they sat close to each other on the grass, Blanche packing the picnic lunch and Alfred explaining how the game worked.[6]

As an old man, Alfred would recollect their courtship as a series of affectionate moments, even calling their first years "romantic": "I would walk under her windows at night and whistle the Scheherazade. A sort of signal. She wouldn't come out. Just to know I was there."[7] In the middle of 1914 she wrote him: "Words are—almost impossible for me but I want you to understand that I know [how much you are helping me] always, what a bully friend you are and sometime, perhaps, I can tell you better . . . how much you are appreciated."[8] Her parents, meanwhile, were getting nervous about the relationship's obvious direction. The courtship progressed, and by the end of the year Blanche wrote her beau: "You are a bad child. I was reading after I spoke to you when suddenly it entered my head that you said your folks had gone to Woodmere for the day—so I asked information your number, she told me—and then I phoned to ask you here to dinner—and—you would return at six—they told me. Well, that is too late for Sunday dinner. I'm disappointed."[9]

Though they didn't know the details, by 1915 the Wolfs had heard enough about what seemed Sam Knopf's dark marital history and his unstable finances that they wanted their daughter to look elsewhere for love. They asked their son's educated mother-in-law to take Blanche to the Panama-Pacific International Exposition in San Francisco that March; maybe its wonders would cause her to forget the insistent boyfriend at home. Though the trip did nothing to undermine Alfred Knopf, the exhibition was even more fantastic than promised by the newspaper accounts Blanche had devoured—especially its dazzling Tower of Jewels, a 435-foot construction covered with more than one hundred thousand "gems." The three-quarter-inch to two-inch pieces of variously colored faceted glass were loosely suspended, shining day and night and swinging in the breeze, depending upon sunlight or a searchlight for illumination. The gem palace and the fair's massive neutral-colored buildings, in shades of white and gray, seeded in Blanche a dual aesthetic she would exploit as she grew older: a love of extravagant color when she wanted to draw attention, usually as bold accents to her first love, arctic white, the color identified with her name and one that allowed her to stand out on her own terms. She came to love extremes that played off one another, teaming long-sleeved white cotton blouses from Woolworth's with elaborate couture skirts by Elsa Schiaparelli, mixing fine gold bijoux with Seaman Schepps's bold semiprecious stones.

Eager to write to her beau about the fair's splendors, Blanche nonetheless held to her promise not to contact Alfred while she was away. As soon as she returned in mid-1915, however, the two became engaged, keeping their wedding plans secret until early 1916: Blanche assumed that the less notice, the less fuss their relatives would make. Years later, in a short-lived effort to write a memoir, she would recall her efforts to dispel her parents' reservations about their prospective son-in-law: "I spent a day with my mother in the automobile, going upstate for lunch and sold her."[10] Surely Bertha found the Knopfs' domicile impressive, its garage with the chauffeur-driven car placed, Blanche would tell her, at Alfred's disposal by the handsome patriarch, Sam. "Having been sold [my mother] proceeded to sell my father, which was easy for her. As we proceeded to become engaged, Mr. Knopf's pap offered to give me stock amounting to $50,000 (which never was seen or heard of thereafter)."[11]

In spite of paper shortages in 1915, the war was proving a propitious moment to start a publishing house devoted to high-quality fiction and nonfiction, if only because older firms were curbing their production. Blanche and her fiancé worked tirelessly while most established publishers put their publication schedules on hold. Often she worked from home, while Alfred operated out of a small corner of his father's nineteenth-floor office in the recently built neo-Renaissance Candler Building at 220 West Forty-Second Street.

That spring, the couple began compiling their initial list, aimed at a fall release. They secured the French author Émile Augier's *Four Plays* as their first book (for which they ordered a print run of 1,500 copies). That the plays were no longer under copyright outweighed their' tedium and poor organization. A month or two later, Alfred took Blanche to meet his friend the newspaperman Henry Mencken, the "Sage of Baltimore," who would help them launch Knopf. Blanche and Mencken took an instant liking to each other. Before the Knopfs returned to New York, "Menck" insisted that they allow him to ask his acquaintance, the well-regarded scholar Barrett Clark, to translate *Four Plays*. Henry knew that in order to have a chance, the French text would have to be rendered in first-rate English. (One of the earliest significant orders Knopf received was from the Chicago department store Marshall Field and Company, which ordered the Augier on Mencken's recommendation alone.) Energized by the visit, Blanche and Alfred commissioned the well-respected Plimpton Press to bind the book in a vivid orange and blue. To embolden their imprint further they used the American typeface Cheltenham, inspired by the British Arts and Crafts movement and highly successful in the early 1900s, largely due to the variety of widths and styles it offered. A favorite among newspapers, it was adopted as a headline typeface by *The New York Times* around 1906.[12]

Especially since few Americans were interested in the obscure French dramas, such eye-catching design proved to be clever marketing. Soon the couple imported Nikolai Gogol's *Taras Bulba: A Tale of the Cossacks*, a Russian *Romeo and Juliet* that had been translated into English years before. For the novel's cover, the Knopfs hired Claude Bragdon, a highly regarded architect and book designer, who stayed with the firm its first year, tracking down translators for the Russian books the company leaned toward. Americans were eager to read about Russia's current unrest, and the new publishers knew how to seize the moment. Bragdon helped them gain an aesthetic reputation that quickly drew in other prestigious designers.[13] England provided most of the domestic versions at first, but Blanche especially wanted Knopf to have its own slate of linguists and not depend on the motherland to translate for their developing company.

Although most of the selections to land on that initial list in 1915 dealt with early Russian history and politics (little read then and soon forgotten), at least three (also obscure) books could be taken seriously by educated American readers: *Taras Bulba;* Stanislaw Przbyszewski's *Homo Sapiens,* a novel; and Guy de Maupassant's *Yvette, a Novelette, and Ten Other Stories,* translated by the Knopfs' friend Mrs. John Galsworthy. If the Knopfs had few widely recognized authors, their careful selection of literature caused people to take notice. As their firm developed, they made a decision to value quality over quantity, and soon their average yearly publications would number around one hundred.

By October they had rented, through Sam's connections, their own thirty-by-ten-foot space on his floor, and they hired a "bookkeeper and errand boy and a stenographer" by the end of that first year. As Blanche recalled, "I worked very hard every day at this publishing business. We both did."[14] Still, "Could we possibly be more crowded?" she complained when they and the office help they paid seven dollars a week (roughly a fourth of what Alfred had made doing the same work at Doubleday) seemed always to be bumping into one another. Several months later, they added two more employees, still operating out of one room, for which they paid forty-five dollars a month in rent.[15] Soon they would occupy a small row of offices with shipping rooms behind.[16]

Blanche was pleased to get to the office on her own: almost five years earlier, Penn Station had opened, Grand Central following a few years later, already supplemented by the burgeoning subway lines. Organized by nature, she managed the fledgling business, signing contracts with writers she'd found or approved, checking out translators, deciding upon bindings (occasionally even using stained tops, "dyeing the thin upper edge of the pages in a color that complements the binding or stamping"), as well as choosing the printing company best suited to the book at hand.[17] She quickly absorbed the rudiments of what would prove her life's work. Studying typography, paper, ink, and the mechanics of printing presses, she found every facet of publishing fascinating. Above all, her love of reading was gratified by the hours she spent devouring manuscripts delivered by her growing network of writers.

Blanche proved a superb editor of fiction and poetry: she listened to the rhythm of the language on the page and reacted to phrases, vocabulary, even punctuation, as she considered who might be right for Knopf. After deciding upon a manuscript, she typically turned it over to trained editors who would accomplish what she instinctively knew needed to be done. Although she would express her wishes to those editors without hesitation, she never seemed to feel educated enough to talk knowingly to scholars such as the Yale graduate Wilmarth Lewis, a rare-book collector published early by Knopf (he would later edit forty-eight volumes of Horace Walpole's letters for Yale University Press). Those close to her, however, recognized her intelligence and sure literary sensibility. Lewis himself trained with the Knopfs for ten weeks in 1921 to learn the differences between commercial and academic publishing, and in 1922 he published his novel *Tutors' Lane* with them. He found Blanche "terribly keen, full of business, very much on her toes."[18]

Alfred seemed to have inherited his father's passion for sales. He discovered that he enjoyed selling books more than actually working on them—or even reading them, though he remained a history buff. From his various sales trips (at first confined to the Northeast), he irregularly sent work-related postcards and telegrams to Blanche while he traveled by train, befriending bookstore owners.

From their initial meetings with Blanche and Alfred, even before the couple had started their business, both Joseph Hergesheimer, by 1914 a (temporarily) bestselling novelist, and H. L. Mencken wanted to have a role with the new publishing firm. Alfred had made his first contact with Hergesheimer the year before at the publisher Mitchell Kennerley's office, where he worked briefly, and from which he managed to poach the author, who still owed Kennerley two books before Knopf could sign him. In late 1913, the ambitious newcomer had met Mencken at *The Baltimore Sun*, where the two men shared their enthusiasm for Hergesheimer and Joseph Conrad, one a chronicler of supercilious society and the other a creator of dark, layered tales. Mencken, keen and discerning and a well-established journalist, would become the Knopfs' go-to man. His support would allow them to take editorial risks, including adding his acquaintance Carl Van Vechten to their roster, and he would serve as a confidant to Blanche, someone with whom she could speak honestly about the business and about Alfred as well.

Somehow the couple—or, more likely, Sam Knopf—found the time to announce their engagement in *The New York Times* in early January 1916 and to plan for a wedding held four months later. From the beginning, the event was fraught, mostly because of Sam Knopf's overbearing nature. Blanche often felt harassed by Sam, who tried repeatedly to force his future daughter-in-law into a wedding spectacle that went against her grain. She preferred a small family affair or simply to elope at City Hall. Though she implored her fiancé for his support, Alfred said he couldn't intervene. He could not risk upsetting his father.[19]

Blanche recalled, "I wanted no formality, no ceremony . . . As I remember, I begged my family not to do it . . . and their saying 'Anything you want,' and I begged the very-very curiously correct [young Alfred], whom I admired, to stop the whole thing and just go off and get married. He was frightened and wouldn't do it. I have never been particularly conventional, but he always is."[20]

Ultimately, Blanche acquiesced; how could she hold out, especially in view of the tragic story Alfred had recently confided about his mother? The story of Ida's suicide had hardened her against Sam; he had behaved as a monster to someone Alfred had clearly loved. Afterward, to lighten the mood, Alfred had shared with Blanche what he assumed was an unrelated story, one he would repeat throughout his life. Laughing, he recounted how he'd become a "kleptomaniac" when he attended the Horace Mann School, where the wealthy young man had been expelled for stealing—books, of course. In his later passion for distant histories or tales of western mountain terrain, he ensured that he had stories other than his own to think about. His avoidance of his past moved Blanche, who was inspired by her enthusiasm for Freud and French philosophy. She knew all about avoidance, both in theory and in life, and she readily discerned the family trauma that Alfred sometimes claimed not to remember, though he had re-created it for Blanche in excruciating detail.

At 1:00 p.m. on April 4, 1916, at New York's St. Regis hotel, in the second-floor suite overlooking Fifth Avenue (in what would later be called the Versailles Room), Blanche Wolf wed Alfred Knopf. Though the event was paid for by Blanche's family, its every detail was orchestrated by Sam Knopf. If Blanche felt the typical bridal jitters and even shared an occasional giggle with her single attendant, Alfred looked the part of the proper groom, stiff and almost military in his bearing. From later behavior it would seem that both the bride and the groom lacked a deep affection for each other from the start. What should have been said at the brief ceremony, as H. L. Mencken suggested often in the coming years, was how anyone could see that until one of them died, books would be at the center of the Knopfs' marriage.

At Sam's insistence, Blanche wore Sophie Knopf's wedding gown from the year before. Shiny white satin trimmed on its bodice with embroidered point lace, "like frostwork on the windows," the dress had a tulle veil tucked and gathered by sprays of orange blossoms, their scent blending with Blanche's lilies of the valley. The bride worried that the lush fragrance filling the room was too rich, making it hard for those around her to breathe. Though neither was religious, the couple had been implored by Sam to be married by a man of God. Blanche and Alfred would both remember fondly the officiating justice of the peace, a former rabbi whose skepticism had encouraged him to enter a secular profession.[21]

The newlyweds' honeymoon was organized and paid for by Sam, just as he had done for his daughter. Refusing to allow Blanche the privacy she sought, he sent the wedding announcement to *The New York Times*, citing White Sulphur Springs, West Virginia, the same place that Sophie had gone, as the honeymoon location. Alfred would remember his nuptials hazily, at times getting the date wrong by a week or more. He recalled that he and Blanche were only interested in books and music.

The couple left their wedding reception quickly, catching a train to Washington, D.C., where they would spend a few days, and then, deviating from Sam's itinerary, taking a train to Hot Springs, Virginia, where an April snowstorm kept them inside. They ended up at a resort in Southern Pines, North Carolina.[22] Writing of her wedding night, Blanche would recall, "Both of us were virgins and very badly mated in the first place. My mother had told me nothing about life and sex, so on my own I [had gone] around to an old family doctor and asked him what happened and he told me. My sister-in-law gave me a ring [more commonly called a pessary, a contraceptive diaphragm] and put it in my suitcase when we left without telling me what to do with it, and I had no idea what to do with the damn ring. So for weeks we were very unsuccessful and very unhappy."[23]

Initially, Blanche assumed they'd work out their "beginners' problems," given time and patience. She was more upset about still finding herself under others' control. Her mother expected her daughter's trappings to convey a certain Edwardian aura, while her husband sought the life of an English squire: "The gentleman [Alfred] wanted very much to live in the country and I wanted to have Russian wolfhounds and books and didn't care where they were, so we were on the verge of renting a house in White Plains for seventy dollars a month [the equivalent of about $1,600 in 2015]. Unwisely I took my mother up [to see it] before signing the lease. She had hysterics at the thought of her daughter living in such a hole." Brooking no protest, Blanche's parents rented for the newlyweds a house in Hartsdale, an attractive, modest hamlet next to Scarsdale in Westchester County, less than thirty miles from Manhattan, and furnished it in "satins and velvets and what not."[24]

But it wasn't finished when the bride and groom returned from their honeymoon, so the newlyweds lived in a Manhattan hotel and went to work—there and at the Candler Building. In May, when their home was ready, they moved into the incongruously opulent place where they would live for two and a half years. Embodying her mother's taste, instead of Blanche's preference for an up-to-date, streamlined look, it was outfitted with a boudoir, guest room, study, living room, and dining room, "bedrooms, bathrooms, [and] maid's room." One "little Finnish maid" took care of it all.[25]

The Hartsdale house, oddly named "Sans Souci" ("carefree"), was small for entertaining, but Blanche gave elaborate Saturday parties "up there," as she called life in the suburbs, once a month. Perhaps because in later years she ate so little, she would recall the meals prepared by the maid as sumptuous, though guests thought them mundane. And when Sam and Lillian Knopf came for dinner, Blanche was inevitably told "where to get off: nothing was right for them ever. They would go into the pantry and into the kitchen and say the chicken was being cooked wrong, this is not right, why don't you have butter before, or after, or whatever." Compared with the relatively laissez-faire parents who had reared Blanche, the Knopfs "made for a very strange [visit]." At times it seemed Sam had no manners, honking loudly as he spewed his tobacco into a spittoon, even in front of guests. Nonetheless, she frequently asked her in-laws to spend the night.[26]

Blanche and Alfred often hosted weekends at their home for Knopf's burgeoning list of writers as well. A month into their marriage, through Mencken's contacts, the couple met at least a few of Greenwich Village's cosmopolitan circle of artists. Encouraged by their recently signed poet and Harvard graduate Witter Bynner, they would soon add to their list the leftist writer Floyd Dell, whose 1916 satire *King Arthur's Socks* had been the first production of the transplanted Provincetown Players, in their new home in the heart of the Village.[27]

More important to Knopf's future, Bynner also helped the Knopfs sign the Village's Lebanese-American poet Kahlil Gibran, a purely commercial gamble that cost them little. In reality, much of their business was a risk, and Blanche knew they couldn't wait too long to hit the mark. The ever-practical Alfred Harcourt was right: to thrive, publishers had to release a highly successful book within their first year. Noisily heralding themselves as willing to tackle all sorts of books as long as they were good, the novices had aspirations. Other publishers gossiped, and if many wished the new kids on the block success, others were unsettled by their mild air of superiority. The young Knopfs were ready to compete.

Early in 1916, even before they wed, Blanche and Alfred had repackaged W. H. Hudson's *Green Mansions: A Romance of the Tropical Forest*, first published in England in 1904.[28] When Alfred had visited John Galsworthy during his graduation trip to Europe in 1912, the writer gave him an old copy of *Green Mansions*, which Blanche later read. Excited to discover that the book was in the public domain, the publishers issued a new edition with a foreword contributed by Galsworthy. Timing proved crucial to the revived success of *Green Mansions*: the novel, an ill-fated romance, was ideally positioned for American publication during World War I. Its European hero seeks refuge from battle in Venezuela's virgin forests, where he stumbles upon the last of an aboriginal race, a clawed bird-girl, whose ethereal presence enthralls him. The couple fall in love, but their radical differences preordain them for sorrow. Blanche would remember the story fondly until she died, even possessing during the last half of her life nails (from illness and malnutrition) like the talons of the book's dying heroine and, like her, often restricting her diet to lettuce leaf lunches. The Knopfs' surprise hit created a vogue for Hudson's other novels, enabling the publishers to share their windfall with the elderly writer, who was as shocked by the Knopfs' generosity as by the sales.[29] *Green Mansions* would go through nine printings by 1919. Their first book to sell twenty thousand copies, its sales ensured the company's survival, for a while at least.

Not all their decisions that year were farsighted: they'd been offered the chance to publish George Moore's *The Brook Kerith*, which had been brought to them by Hergesheimer. At the time, the Knopfs felt that Moore's work—based on the premise that Jesus didn't die but had survived by taking natural medicines, then traveled to India in pursuit of enlightenment—"shouldn't be published by a Jew." Their authors didn't want to see the new publishers harassed by the period's zealous censors. The Knopfs would regret their caution, since John Sumner, heir to the oppressive Anthony Comstock as head of the New York Society for the Suppression of Vice, allowed the book to pass.[30]

The Anglo-English novelist Elizabeth Bowen would write of her American publishers that there was "an effrontery in their early lists," which were soon notorious for their variety.[31] The 1916 list, for example, advertised a book called *Eat Well and Be Well* next to thick

Russian literary works by the Marxist writer Maxim Gorky and the nineteenth-century poet Mikhail Lermontov. *Music and Bad Manners* would prove central to Knopf's future because of its author, Carl Van Vechten. Today considered a minor novelist but a gifted portrait photographer, Van Vechten had strong instincts about others' writing that would serve the Knopfs well. He encouraged Blanche to include James Weldon Johnson's *The Autobiography of an Ex-Colored Man* amid a cache of otherwise second-rate novels the couple had collected for their short-lived "Blue Jade Library." Later, Van Vechten would direct additional significant African-American writers to Blanche, including Langston Hughes and James Baldwin.

In 1916, Van Vechten was behind Blanche's insistent wooing of Dorothy Richardson, by several overly enthusiastic accounts the first stream-of-consciousness novelist in England. His efforts resulted in Knopf's publishing an early section of Richardson's fictional autobiography, *Pilgrimage*, which eventually ran to thirteen volumes. In its day, *Pilgrimage* was significant enough to be discussed by Virginia Woolf and Katherine Mansfield—though Richardson would quickly vanish from the public eye.

In light of such early success, Blanche felt that she and Alfred were building a book company second to none. Happily entrenched in her work, she realized that the older firms weren't interested in signing original works by unknown authors, or in translating European books into English—both of which would become Blanche's specialties. When the newly popular poet Vachel Lindsay wrote the year before, "I wish you Godspeed in your publishing enterprise," the couple had taken his attention as a sign that they would make it, especially when they saw Lindsay's P.S.: he'd like to dine with them.[32]

Even as their business expanded, publishing was still virtually closed to Jews. Houghton Mifflin, Charles Scribner's Sons, and Doubleday, all with solid WASP credentials, held the advantage. But between the two world wars, Viking, Simon & Schuster, Random

House, the Literary Guild, and the Book-of-the-Month Club, together with the Knopfs, would remake the literary landscape.[33]

Blanche and Alfred often found themselves in competition with a nice but "dreary" man, Ben Huebsch, or with his opposite, Horace Liveright, whose firm, Boni & Liveright, opened in February 1917 (Boni would drop out a year and a half later). Both Knopfs bristled at being associated with Liveright, whom they considered a playboy. But Alfred and Blanche heeded the publisher's lessons on selling books. Liveright sent circulars advertising his authors to three hundred major bookstores every week, and he gave away books along with articles about them and their authors to newspaper editors, in addition to using celebrity endorsements.

Some of Alfred's disdain for Liveright must have derived from envy: with Albert Boni, Liveright in 1917 had founded the Modern Library, which became the industry standard for printing inexpensive editions of classic works. While Liveright didn't interest Blanche, his pal Carl Van Vechten did. Carl was an anomoly, with a shock of prematurely silver hair, knowing blue eyes, a usually closed mouth (to hide his buckteeth), and thin bangles encircling one delicate wrist; the husband of the beautiful, respected stage actress Fania Marinoff was rumored to like men at least as much as women.

Van Vechten had been one of New York's "recognized eccentrics" even before World War I. A Ph.D. in humanities from the University of Chicago had ensured him a wide range of subjects to write about. Even the erudite Mencken sought his opinion on the writers he and George Jean Nathan found for their magazine, *The Smart Set*. As suggested by his almost instantaneous friendship with Gertrude Stein (whose unfinished work he edited after her death, as well as becoming her literary executor), Van Vechten could talk knowledgeably about anything to anyone. It was from Van Vechten that Blanche heard about the "extraordinary" Paris debut of *Le Sacre du Printemps* that provoked the French audience's hissing; the Salon des Indépendants show in Paris where Duchamp's *Nude Descending a Staircase (No. 2)* was refused; and the Armory Show in New York City a year later, where the painting was boldly displayed.[34] From his multitude of lovers to his apartment decorated in "all the colors of the rainbow" to the raunchy diary he kept of his friends' misbehavior, the charming, sometimes overbearing Van Vechten seemed to fit in everywhere—his guidance compensating, often, for the formal education Blanche lacked.

From the start of their friendship, Carl's brilliance nourished Blanche's creativity, his whimsical book on cats motivating her to find a singular logo for Knopf. An animal implied motion, she decided, even more than the windmill used by London's William Heinemann. After Blanche suggested that they use one of their borzois, or Russian wolfhounds, on the spine and title page of their books, the elegant dog that looked perpetually on the move quickly became the Knopf colophon, perfect for a house resounding with Russian literature. The couple would eventually hang a three-foot-long wooden borzoi on Knopf's reception room wall.

As Blanche had hoped, connections begat connections, and with fiction and poetry being her departments (Alfred preferred to stick with history and music), she was pleased when Van Vechten brought Wallace Stevens and Elinor Wylie to Knopf. Stevens would never relinquish his Hartford, Connecticut, insurance job, even after he had become one of the country's most celebrated modern poets. The ethereal Elinor Wylie, who envisioned herself an avatar of Percy Bysshe Shelley, would soon publish in the prestigious *Poetry* magazine, and Knopf would release her first volume of poems a few years later. Now, in 1916, the first full year of publishing at the thinly staffed Alfred A. Knopf, twenty-nine books came out, twelve of them translated from the Russian. Such books helped open Americans to an exotic country, also evoked by their richly dyed book covers, frequently designed by Blanche and Alfred themselves. In addition to the Russian literature, there were nine American, six English, and two German books on the 1916 list. Carl Van Vechten and Henry Mencken, and occasionally Joseph Hergesheimer as well, served as informal scouts, the threesome knowing that the publishers' list of books would make them look good, too: the Knopfs sought only the best of any genre they published. Still, it was Mencken whom Blanche would use as her go-to reader, asking him for a second opinion after she finished evaluating a manuscript, which he would give only after it had passed muster with the publisher: "Don't try it out on me!" he once told her.[35]

Knopf's 1917 list would contain thirty-seven books, including such topical volumes as *The Book of Camping* and *Meatless and Wheatless Menus* (a nod to the war), alongside the novice poet T. S. Eliot's first prose book, *Ezra Pound: His Metric and Poetry*, published anonymously, with British rights sold to the London publisher John Lane. Knopf also published Van Vechten's *Interpreters and Interpretations*.[36] From the very beginning of their venture, the young publishers tended to choose books for what they considered their inherent value, rather than sales possibilities, assuming that in the long run quality would win out. The principle would not always prove providential: though it would earn the firm a formidable reputation, the Knopfs got used to their best talent often moving on to publishers with a larger purse. (Alfred would always lament passing on *The Waste Land* when he thought Eliot wanted too much money.)

Knopf expanded rapidly, assuring Blanche that this was her calling. If only the churlish Sam Knopf would disappear. Her father-in-law seemed to enjoy undermining her, as if to prove she should be a homemaker rather than a career woman. Reassuring herself as well as Alfred, who was selling books in Boston, Blanche began 1917 by telegraphing him, "Monkey dear I've this moment said goodbye to you and I'll be a good woof just be an old Reuben and have a good time your partner is at the office everything is going to be perfect."[37] Just like Alfred's mother, who had heard enough stories about Sam Knopf's dalliances with women to make her leery, her young husband's adoration of his father demanded her attention—like father, like son, her mother had warned her.

On January 6, 1917, Blanche's father, sixty-two-year-old Julius Wolf, who by now owned the second-largest children's hat company in the country, died of a sudden heart attack.[38] His daughter, though never close to her father, was surprised to feel a great sadness at losing him, and she stayed home from work for several days to care for her mother. Bertha, however, convinced her son, Irving, and his wife to come live with her and urged her daughter to resume her normal routine. Blanche had little choice: the young publisher had to deal with government censors who were ready to pounce on writers for the least infraction.

In the country's patriotic wartime climate, Mencken's eighty-page *A Book of Prefaces* included the essay "Puritanism as a Literary Force," in which the Knopf writer attacked iconic American writers of the nineteenth century, including Henry James and Mark Twain. He believed that they had fallen prey to a Puritan spirit "that encouraged them to wrap themselves in the cloth of righteousness." The Knopfs were at the ready, they assured Mencken, if the government's censors came after him. A suit was initiated, but Mencken wasn't worried: he liked nothing better than fighting stupidity. Fortunately for everyone, the suit was dismissed.

Turning to Joseph Hergesheimer, the Knopfs would now publish their first original American fiction, two years after they opened their doors for business. Hergesheimer's moderately successful novel *The Three Black Pennys*, a generational chronicle of ironmasters who rise in society, wasn't expected to bring in much income. Blanche was just relieved that she and Alfred no longer had to physically bind the individual book sheets sent back from the printers.

Until now, even Sam Knopf had occasionally helped with the tedious process.

Alfred's cousins and their families often served as assistants in the office, where their bosses were demanding and their wages low. Working for the new publishing company already carried a modicum of cachet; still, the salaries, minimal even by industry standards, ensured a fast turnover. Whenever a young worker complained, he was immediately fired, despite being Alfred's kin, the publisher disgusted that money was so important to people in such a noble profession.

By the end of 1917, with her husband taking the sleeper train to Chicago at least quarterly and traveling the Northeast Corridor as well, Blanche was handling the Candler office by herself, except for the times Sam would stop by to advise her on how to do things. Between December 12 and December 17, she wired Alfred daily: "Dearest so sorry I couldn't get letter off to you but this will have to do. Everything is splendid in town and here at Sans Souci are you being careful and successful. Do take the best care of Reuben because I love him and come back soon V." If her notes had begun to sound syrupy, the tone was a veiled apology for tensions at the office, especially on occasions when Alfred blithely dismissed Blanche's concerns about an author, while hardly registering her complaints about his father.

According to Alfred's childhood friend Elsie Alsberg, Blanche seemed uneasy. "At the beginning of the marriage, in the house in Westchester before Pat [the Knopfs' son] was born, I sensed the marriage was not too good. [Blanche] was a little on the snippy side, not this nice sort of flow that exists between young people who care about each other." Even when they entertained together at home, Blanche seemed uneasy.[39]

Perhaps Alsberg failed to remember what had upset Blanche when they last dined together: her husband flirting with Elsie, to whom the young wife thought Alfred was seriously attracted. Soon

Blanche had the meager solace of getting back at Elsie: Marjorie Henley, a "new girl" in the same Westchester community, had taken Elsie's place.[40] The recent bride was confused that her husband already seemed interested in other women, though he seemed uninterested in making love to her.

As a woman in an era immersed in Freudian psychology, Blanche already seems to have realized how incomplete the sexual side of her marriage was destined to be, and she more or less gave up on it, though she continued to show Alfred affection. She loved to ride horses with him in Central Park, before they went into the office.

During their courtship, when he realized how important riding was to her, Alfred had enlisted in the National Guard, the First Field Artillery based in the armory at Broadway and West Sixty-Sixth Street. He was given free riding lessons in case the war across the ocean needed him. Now he could please his wife with his new prowess while receiving credit for national service. He even regaled Blanche with stories of being thrown from his horse and suffering his sergeant's ire.

If Alfred rode in part to satisfy Blanche, he more often found himself in the role of teacher, tutoring her in classical music, about which she knew little. When playing the piano as a child, she had been an indifferent student. In contrast, she paid attention when she and Alfred attended concerts several times a week, usually at Carnegie Hall or at the Philharmonic Society of New York (now the New York Philharmonic), or even in Philadelphia or Boston. A young virtuoso who impressed everyone, including Blanche, was the violin prodigy Jascha Heifetz, descendent of those acquaintances of Alfred's grandparents, now making his Carnegie Hall debut at age sixteen.[41]

At her mother's insistence, concertgoing was cut short for decorum's sake when Blanche became visibly pregnant. On May 19, 1918, eight months along, she wrote her peripatetic husband about being in the office without him: "Babe—I'm counting the nights—four—that you're still to be away—and then I'll have you back with me

Reuben for a little while." Blanche continued, almost frantically: "Goodnight my precious Reuben or Good morning. All my heart is with you. Your ownest V.V. in the world."[42] From various comments throughout the years, it appears that Alfred had been stricken with the Spanish flu and barely recovered before embarking on his latest sales trip.[43] Worried about his health, Blanche didn't seem concerned about her own susceptibility, though she must have been nervous about the baby.

She was of two minds about the forthcoming event (her maternal grandmother had died in childbirth), and almost certainly she sensed her husband was ambivalent about such matters. The age itself seemed unsure. Margaret Sanger had recently dared to link contraception and women's rights, arguing that women no longer had to become mothers: it was a matter of choice.[44]

Blanche's self-consciousness about her appearance, particularly the excessive weight she seemed to be gaining during the pregnancy, convinced her to accept her mother's offer to have a corset made— "a very elaborate affair which I wore one day and discarded." Soon after, she stopped going into the office, but she was willing to encounter people who didn't know her. She simply had too much energy to allow her appearance to override all her activities: "I took stenography [courses] in White Plains. I had no car so I had to take a trolley up to White Plains . . . When I came home I would take the Russian wolfhound for a walk. Then I would do everything which was sent up from town. I read the manuscripts, which were all routed to come straight to Hartsdale instead of 220 West 42 St. At night [Alfred and I] would work on advertising and we would discuss the manuscripts I had read. It was quite a busy life."[45]

From her difficulty wearing the pregnancy corset, to the insult of a neighbor's asking for her due date—after the baby had been born— the experience caused Blanche to go on an essentially lifelong diet. She would also contrive birth narratives to suit the needs of the moment. In her most fantastic version, neither she nor her doctor even realized she was pregnant. One day, after Alfred went to work, Blanche, allegedly surprised by stomach pains, went to the hospital, where, to everyone's amazement, Pat was born. In another version, one she told a fully grown Pat in the midst of an argument, she shouted at the nurse holding her newborn son, "Take him away and don't bring him back again. And they took 'this thing' away."[46]

The reality was more mundane. In his diary entry for June 17, 1918, Alfred wrote that "V.V. woke me with pains at 6. Pretty bad by 7 when she phoned Ryan [their driver] to come around. To town on 8:01 [train]. Worried and still feeling rotten from my cold." Blanche, apparently believing herself to be in false labor but acknowledging she couldn't be sure, had told Alfred to go to work: she was leaving for White Plains Hospital but would be back within the day. Instead, after a five-hour labor their child, Alfred A. Knopf, Jr. ("Pat"), was born.[47] Years later, Alfred's editorial corrections to Blanche's nine pages of notes she wrote when Pat was an adult—subtly changing "took 'this thing' away" to "took 'the thing' away"—perhaps cloaked his uneasiness with his wife's seemingly unmaternal sentiments by not even allowing a demonstrative pronoun to stand.

In keeping with the times, Blanche stayed in the hospital for nearly two weeks after Pat's birth. Like other "modern women" of her era, she considered nursing a child a "disgusting physical act," but she tried it anyway, only to give up when Alfred blamed Pat's crying on her nervousness. Typical of men in this period, Alfred participated little in the baby's care, later remembering only a few anecdotes about the mother and son's first night home: the father went to bed at 11:10, according to his diary, with Pat wailing in the guest room, where Blanche slept. In his next entry, he reported that "Pat, they say, cried till 1 a.m." On July 4, three weeks after his son's birth, Alfred, before heading off for a nine-mile hike alongside their new boxer and the single borzoi they had trained, watched Blanche give Pat his first bath.[48]

More than fifty years after Pat's birth, Angeles "Toni" Pasquale, an office worker and sometime personal assistant to Blanche, told the writer Susan Sheehan that once, when Alfred was out of town, he forgot the "little diary" that he kept on his desk, and, snooping, the employee read it. After Alfred described giving "the baby its 2 A.M. feeding," he wrote, "Blanche says I don't love her but I do." Perhaps Alfred deliberately left his journal where he knew Blanche would see it, his poignant if tortured way of saying "I love you."[49]

3

———————

A THIRD KNOPF

BLANCHE RETURNED TO WORK within weeks of Pat's birth, fearing that Sam might try to push her out of the company if she took much time off. She hired a baby nurse, Fraulein Hanover, whose qualification for child care appears to have been her position as wardrobe mistress to the stage actress Katharine Cornell, who had no children.

For the most part, Alfred seemed unmoved by the infant's presence, acknowledging his newborn son through journal entries such as "Blanche up much of night with the baby." He assumed, since the couple had hired more staff, that Blanche's load at the office would be manageable. Still, the new mother found herself going to work each day angry, tired, or depressed. She seemed unable to convey such emotions except when she'd write Alfred from a distance, while he was on a train and she at her desk. Irritating Blanche further, Sam had become a presence at the company, often suddenly appearing without notice. As the Knopf historian Amy Root Clements has remarked, Alfred's founding a publishing house had become "a way of 'staying home' with his father and relishing the traits they shared . . . an affinity for salesmanship, a desire to be connected to affluent circles, and a taste for expensive travel, housing, dining, and tailoring."[1]

Blanche's telegrams to Alfred were affectionate and tense by turns: the company needed her, she wanted to remind him, and her instincts said to rein in Sam, however intimidating he could be. Sam's subordinates would remember how he shouted at them one minute and uttered platitudes the next: "Never raise your voice to a person who is dependent on you," and "Do unto others."[2] Clifton Fadiman, later the radio host of *Information, Please!* and a judge at the Book-of-the-Month Club, began his literary career as the Knopfs' stock boy, and he remembered that the brusque "Sam Knopf scared me to death."[3] Another employee said he was "aggressive and insensitive [and he] displayed little consideration for people's feelings."[4] As Blanche maintained, "There was no way of disagreeing without a row and probably being thrown out."[5]

Especially challenging for the young mother and publisher was the sweeping disregard with which her father-in-law treated not only her professional observations but her ideas in general. Even the birth announcements she sent out met with Sam's disdain. Their vibrant aquamarine in place of baby blue announced the infant's arrival along with his mother's distinctive aesthetic and her inclination to flout convention.

The year Pat was born, Blanche and Alfred decided to give up the spacious suburban house rented for them by Blanche's parents. Concerned about the distance from her widowed mother, who was living in the city, and worried that she and Alfred needed to be closer to their office anyway, Blanche convinced her husband to move to Manhattan, where it was much easier for Bertha to see her grandson and the couple's commuting expenses would be reduced. They found a great deal on the rental of the two upper floors of a converted brownstone at 44 West Ninety-Fifth Street, which was owned by Alfred's childhood dentist, who still maintained a practice on the first floor.[6]

The dentist made a generous arrangement with them, keeping the rent at seventy-five dollars a month for the six or seven years they lived there, after renovating the building so that the top floor was a combined living-dining room, perfect for entertaining, with a maid's room and a kitchen in the rear. The master bedroom and bath were at the front of the second floor, with a room and bath for the baby and his nurse in the back.[7] Friends recall that "Blanche chose everything for the house with great care," with one longtime acquaintance, Beatrice Leval, saying that she'd "never met anyone who was as much a perfectionist and paid so much attention to detail as Blanche"— even "folding her bills going the same way in her billfold."[8]

These days, when Alfred was away, Blanche was expected for dinner at her mother's or her brother's on the Upper West Side, where Irving now had his own place with his wife, Irma; or even with Alfred's family, which included Alfred's sister, Sophie, and other in-laws. She disliked such gatherings intensely, feeling again the sensation she had as a child, of being the odd girl out due to her bookishness. Too often Blanche found herself "tongue-tied" with all the relatives, believing they had little interest in anyone's ideas but their own. "Nothing," she wrote Alfred after dutifully executing her family obligations, "was good" while he was on the road.[9] But things were just as bad at the office, where Alfred devoted his time to Sam rather than to his wife.

Given that Blanche's own father had died within a year of her wedding and that Alfred was frequently gone selling books, the young woman often felt she had no one but her mother on her side. Meanwhile, she had to gather her courage and stand up to Sam. "I'm not your secretary," she'd briskly remind him when he stopped by the office and asked her to make him coffee. "Just who do you think you are?" Sam would bellow back. After a particularly violent shouting match, Blanche ran down to the lobby to hide in the phone booth and cry, scared that upon her return the apoplectic Sam would be dead of a stroke and that Alfred would blame her.[10]

A few months after Pat's birth, in a hired car whose chauffeur drove them through the countryside, Alfred told Blanche, after several false starts, that his father wanted to "come into the business with us." Sam Knopf, until now informally part of Knopf, hoped to expand the company and "put much money into it."[11] Arguing, the couple drove around Manhattan for two hours, and Blanche lost.

Blanche had reminded Alfred that his father was not a publisher and that if they took his money they'd be beholden to him. But Alfred, she would later recall, was "subjugated" to his father's will. "Had I said then, 'I will leave you if you do this,' he still would have gone ahead. It was my moment to have left him. But I had neither the background nor the sense to know that this was what I needed to do because from there, it was never anything but trouble and unpleasantness for me. I was working under two strong wills and would have to lose out for the rest of my life, and have. That was my last gasp."[12]

Rather than confronting the role Sam played in his wife's unhappiness, Alfred defended to the last the father he chose to remember as always being there for him. As a child, Alfred had twisted everything he had seen and heard into evidence of Sam's valor. In the age of psychoanalysis, the notion of a "reaction formation" neatly summed up Alfred's defense against his father's cruelty to Ida. Instead of admitting his rage, the boy exaggerated its opposite: he overlooked Sam's complicity in his wife's death, but reveled in his role of savior to his son. After all, Sam, unlike Ida, had stuck around.

As Blanche came to understand her husband's demons, she realized she should carefully consider whether to try for more children, as she had originally planned. She knew that the scarring from her gynecological problems, including her severe endometriosis with resultant D & Cs (dilation and curettage, a procedure to remove tissue from inside the uterus), made future pregnancies improbable, yet she preferred to think she was making the decision to have only one child. Unwilling to acknowledge her sadness at having no such choice, she made up her own account. Decades after Pat was grown, she told a friend that when she started working again, "Mr. Knopf's stepmother [Lillian] came to see me and said to the baby, 'When are you going to have a sister?' I said, 'No sister or brother for this young man. There is a war coming [in fact, the war was nearing its end] and one is enough. There are not going to be any more. And that is that.' And there weren't any."[13] As an adult, her son would imply that Blanche just didn't like being a mother, possibly getting this idea from hearing how repelled she'd been by him as an infant.[14]

Three months after Pat's birth, in September 1918, the Knopfs, hoping to sign the popular southern novelist James Branch Cabell, visited Cabell at Dumbarton Grange, his estate near Richmond, Virginia. Cabell was working on his eighth book, *Jurgen: A Comedy of Justice*, to be published in 1919, and Blanche wanted the titillating novel for Knopf. Disappointed when the couple discovered it was already committed to the respected publisher Robert McBride, Alfred later believed they had narrowly avoided a disaster when *Jurgen* was prosecuted for obscenity. Denounced by the New York Society for the Suppression of Vice due to its immoral eponymous hero, *Jurgen* was about a man who took wicked trips to heaven and hell, where he dared seduce the devil's wife. All copies of the novel were quickly seized by the vice squad and withheld until a ruling two years later, which vindicated Cabell and created exponentially higher sales for *Jurgen* than it would have earned otherwise. The publicity also encouraged his friends to form the whimsical "James Branch Cabell School," which included Mencken, Van Vechten, and Elinor Wylie.

During her initial trips to Richmond, the usually confident Blanche sometimes felt out of place; she once joked that the magnolia trees with their overpowering scent reminded her of the flowers at her wedding.

On October 18, 1918, a month before the war ended, Mencken finished the manuscript of *The American Language*, a book about the differences between America's national language and England's. The next year, the book would sell 1,370 of the 1,500 copies printed, and the remainder would be gone in early 1920, a superb record for a reference book. One of the young company's proudest achievements, *The American Language* would be revised three times during Mencken's lifetime and would be seen as a declaration of linguistic independence. "No more would America suffer the oppression of literary colonialism. A new day had dawned on American literature. American writers were finally able to take flight from the old tree and to trust for the first time their own dialect," Edmund Wilson observed.[15] The book's reception pleased Blanche, who believed that only Mencken had the authority to tell Americans that their language made the United States more up-to-date than the motherland.

Although such success buoyed her, Blanche disliked it when Alfred struck out on the road alone. She occasionally sensed "currents" between him and his old girlfriends, puzzling in part because he seldom wanted to have sex with her. Her daily updates on the office and her love notes suggest she was worried about his distance—both physical and psychological. On November 2, 1918, she wrote: "Honeybake, Everything has been going wrong. I tried to go to

Sofie's today and after 45 minutes in the underground found myself just where I had started—so I didn't go . . . Give my love to all the boys & girls. What are you doing every minute and seeing? Honey, I've only had four penciled lines today [Alfred rarely wrote her]— and I'm lonesome. I want you."[16]

Only three years into their marriage, Blanche was beginning to see how difficult—and lonely—a partnership it was. Often, she sparred with her husband even as she lavished him with affection: "I went to a shop on Sixth Avenue and sold junk of mine for only $1200 which I'm promptly spending. So there are my troubles—do you see why I'm lonesome—ma honey—I love you too much—you darling. Your letters—well, you don't say anything—what do people say to you and do?—ok for Heaven's sake keep me close to you. My lover—and don't love me."[17] Surely she meant to say "don't forget"— or, even, "lose me."

When Blanche wasn't busy with the office or the baby, she was buying things: "All I seem to do is spend money. Pat's a wonder—he went to Carl's [Van Vechten] today and to see mother. Mother Knopf went to Sofie's. [Much] love darling—I wish you were here to hug me. Be good, and careful." She ended with: "Woof woof."[18]

Throughout 1918, Blanche worked long hours, reading manuscripts at home or in the office, evenings and weekends included. By the end of the year, Knopf had published thirty-seven books, though none of them produced high profits, mostly due to the rise in manufacturing costs in the last year of the war. But Knopf authors were making strides. Joseph Hergesheimer was fast gaining a reputation for being the novelist of the rich and dissolute, his life increasingly imitating his art: "fantastic in dress, extravagant in conversation: more, he was brilliant." Alfred, who shared Hergesheimer's self-regard (along with his penchant for bright cravats), had noted humorously that the author "worked at being a conscious artist," with his "loudly checked tweeds" and country house in West Chester, Pennsylvania. There the "local celebrity," as if landed gentry, held court and read

"Vogue, the *Gazette du Bon Genre,* and the *Memoirs of the Court of Louis XIV."*[19] Blanche put a smile on her face for the novelist, who made her squirm with what he thought were clever suggestive comments; privately, she found Hergesheimer an unbearable coxcomb, especially when she heard that he'd told James Branch Cabell the two men were the "only real artists in America."[20]

Doing her part to develop their publishing list, Blanche now invited at least a dozen guests to her home on weekend afternoons, "every kind of person," though at the beginning she could offer only cheap wine and cucumber sandwiches.[21] The Knopfs' ledger shows that by the end of December the new mother had added regular weeknight dinners to her entertaining schedule as well, and these were even more elaborate than those served on the weekends. Blanche's dinners would accelerate through the 1920s, when she found the best of Prohibition liquor to pair with the caviar she had begun to serve. Before long, with Sam's help, the firm came up with a hundred thousand dollars, and Blanche was appointed vice president, Alfred president, and Sam treasurer.[22] But though Blanche and Alfred had dreamed up Knopf together, she would never convince her husband that she belonged to his world. Speaking with Simon & Schuster's editor in chief Jack Goodman, Alfred said, "Looking back to the days when I was on the board, the idea of a woman being part of it is something that I simply cannot become reconciled to."[23]

To the Knopfs' relief, in 1919 Joseph Hergesheimer's *Java Head* was off to a good start, unlike *The Three Black Pennys* two years before. Its subjects miscegenation and opium addiction, the novel was narrated from multiple perspectives and proved to be both a commercial and a critical success. Its success only made Hergesheimer more insufferable, as far as Blanche was concerned. She nonetheless threw the requisite book parties on his behalf. Hergesheimer, soon identified with stories of debauchery among the wealthy, would prove a major author for Knopf through the early thirties, with what critics now think of as melodramatic, overwrought prose. In its time, however, his writing was considered elegant, part of the aesthetic school in favor throughout the 1920s. Sinclair Lewis's *Babbitt* (in which George Babbitt reads a long passage from *The Three Black Pennys*) borrowed from the older author. And Hergesheimer's themes of high-society decadence inspired novels such as F. Scott Fitzgerald's *The Great Gatsby*. In 1922, a poll of critics in *Literary Digest* voted Hergesheimer "the most important American writer today."[24]

The initial success of *Java Head* and the financial assistance it provided did much to buoy the Knopfs. Throwing stylish cocktail parties on those evenings when Alfred was home, or tending to fretful authors and their contracts while he was away, Blanche played to strengths her husband lacked. By now the Knopfs were accumulating an impressive stable of authors, both in English and in translation. Hugh Walpole, a wildly popular British novelist between the world wars, pronounced Knopf "a very intelligent publisher—the best in America there's no doubt."[25] Encouraged to travel more to increase book orders, Alfred seemed, to Blanche's delight, to appreciate any time when she could join him, or even meet him at the station upon his return.

In September 1919, a police strike in Boston unnerved the couple, who were staying downtown at their favorite hotel, the old Parker House. Opened in 1855, and the first in Boston to feature running water and elevators, the hotel boasted famous guests. Charles Dickens gave his premier reading of *A Christmas Carol* on American soil there, and half a century later, John F. Kennedy proposed to Jacqueline Bouvier. Ho Chi Minh would work as a baker in its kitchen and Malcolm X as a busboy in the restaurant. On this visit, however, when the Knopfs called on Ellery Sedgwick, editor of *The Atlantic Monthly*, he looked terrified, sitting behind his desk with a revolver in his hand. The night before, lawless mobs had looted the neighborhood, its plate-glass windows crashing around him. Finding the excitement intoxicating, Blanche wanted to stay. But Sedgwick urged her and Alfred to leave town and meet again at a more hospitable time, so the couple returned to New York, posthaste.

4

A NEW WORLD OUTSIDE HER DOOR

JUST AS SAM DID during his marriage to Ida, Alfred was leaving his wife alone with a young child for weeks at a time. But Blanche, unlike Ida, aspired to become an indispensable part of the family business.[1] After realizing she could leave the office in capable hands after all, she accompanied Alfred increasingly over the next three years. She connected with ever-more-powerful book buyers at department stores, who were able to afford larger purchases than the smaller shops, and listened carefully to their concerns. She made arrangements for the couple to visit Rich's in Atlanta, Kaufmann's in Pittsburgh, Wanamaker's in Philadelphia, and, of course, Marshall Field's in Chicago, all of which had expanding book sections.

Blanche's tact often compensated for Alfred's temper when he felt insulted. Once, when Wanamaker's book buyer and general manager, Walter Cox, belittled the local Philadelphia author Joseph Hergesheimer to Alfred, the publisher stormed out of the store, leaving Blanche to smooth things over, a job she often assigned herself.

The Knopfs realized what loyalty, sometimes requiring a delicate touch, meant in their business—and that it paid to reward repeat customers. A few years earlier, when one book buyer had ordered 250 copies of *The Three Black Pennys*, the couple, though short on cash, took him to lunch at the elegant Sherry's restaurant on Fifth Avenue, its popular social gatherings to come to an end in the following years due to Prohibition.

As the publishers' well-orchestrated efforts took off, their success encouraged their competitors. George Oppenheimer, who had worked at Knopf for a few early years, founded Viking (with Harold K. Guinzburg) in 1925. Having learned the trade from Blanche and Alfred, Oppenheimer now annoyed them with his irritating chatter whenever he ran into them. In contrast, they welcomed the news that the reliable Ben Huebsch was joining Viking; maybe he would temper its founder's silliness. Publishers of various persuasions were coming to market in those days, outpacing the older ones still recovering from the ravages of World War I. But however modern the publishing world looked, Blanche wasn't a real part of it to most people's thinking: she was, she repeated sardonically throughout her life, Alfred's wife.

Shrewdly, she fought back, making her gender work for her. Throughout 1919, she promoted her favorite French novels in the unexpurgated form now allowed in the United States. Over the next five years, the respected critic Burton Rascoe would write introductions to several of the Knopf reissues, among them *Madame Bovary*. In 1920 the house published Prévost's *Manon Lescaut* (about the costs of upper-class—and illicit—love), and in 1922, Émile Zola's *Nana* (the story of a once-poor courtesan, destroyed by her appetite for luxury). A Knopf shipping clerk remembered how he tried to stem "the crisis caused by women in the book bindery who were cutting out for their friends' juicy pages from a nineteenth-century French novel describing a love scene with details rarely printed in those days."[2] In 1925, when she felt sure American readers were ready, Blanche commissioned a translation of Théophile Gautier's

Mademoiselle de Maupin, a semihistorical love triangle involving ambiguous sexual identities.

While Blanche was getting the stories of her fictional lovers translated, she listened to tales of actual sexual misconduct that she found
more shocking. Van Vechten told of running into George Gershwin
(whom he'd met in 1919) at T. R. Smith's apartment. Smith, an
editor at Liveright and a friend of Mencken's, owned an extravagant
pornography collection. The four men were already frequenting
Harlem, enjoying music and dance as white people rarely had, with
Gershwin profoundly affected. He was witnessing the blues give
birth to jazz, producing sounds he'd never heard before. Impossible
to define, jazz delighted Blanche with its improvisation, its novel
syncopation, its moments borrowed from African, European, and
homegrown traditions. Not only the French knew how to misbe-
have, she would decide, and Harlem undoubtedly beat the Village
hands down for creating a scene. When she stepped north of Ninety-
Sixth Street, a place ready-made for anyone inclined to flout convention, she must have sensed she was going to become someone new.

Indeed, by 1920, change was the constant of the age. Within a
year or so of the boys returning home from the war, the scent of money
permeating the air was but one suggestion that Prohibition would
not cost Americans their liquor after all. The boozy city, egged on by
officials banning liquor from the land, delighted Blanche, who, like
many others, looked forward to rebelling against (rather than com-
plying with) the impractical new sanction ruling New York City
along with the rest of the country. Referred to most often as the
Volstead Act (the legislation had been handled by Andrew Volstead,
chairman of the House Judiciary Committee, though the Anti-Saloon
League's Wayne Wheeler had created the bill), the Eighteenth
Amendment's ratification was certified on January 16, 1919, and it
took effect on January 17, 1920. As if to announce "out with the old,
in with the new"—but in its own way, not through prohibitions—a
skyscraper arose in place of the seemingly immortal Delmonico's,

where Blanche's relatives had taken her twice. The restaurant had been celebrated as Manhattan's finest for almost a century, its ballroom the site of countless society debuts.

In part because of the accounts of Harlem that Carl Van Vechten shared with her, the formerly apolitical Blanche had become aware of the exclusion of "colored people" from the polls now open to white women. As worrisome, the Ku Klux Klan had teamed with local suffragettes to oppose drinking. Against such madness, Carlo (a name, along with "Carlos," that Van Vechten often used) and Henry Mencken would prove Blanche's stalwart companions and protective friends throughout the decade. It was on their arms that she entered the unmarked doors of Manhattan speakeasies (usually staffed with the finest chefs), and it was in their company that she sought even wilder clubs in Hoboken, New Jersey. "Meet you in Hoboken" had acquired new cachet, the phrase appearing in messages between friends who had introduced Blanche to the raciest social circles of the age.

She was also close to Sinclair Lewis, who sought to be published by Knopf but whom Blanche reluctantly turned down: a daring writer, Lewis was notorious for the extravagant demands he placed on his publishers—always wanting more money, more publicity, more love (the money a sticking point with Alfred). When Blanche finally convinced her husband to buy an almost finished manuscript by Lewis for Knopf, she petitioned the author too late. *Main Street*, a novel that lacerates the hypocrisy of small-town life, was signed to Harcourt, Brace and Howe and published on October 23, 1920. It would be number one on *Publishers Weekly*'s annual bestseller list (compiled from bookstores) for 1921, within the first six months of its release selling 180,000 copies and within a few years reaching two million.[3] Though there are no records of Blanche's frustration, it is hard to believe that the Knopfs failed to "have words."

Lewis, who would remain a lifelong friend of the Knopfs, was just one of the new literary lights who had emerged from Greenwich Village (and then moved on). Willa Cather would move to, not from, the Village: born in Virginia, raised in Nebraska, and transported briefly to Pennsylvania, Cather would nonetheless identify in her fiction most strongly with the Great Plains. One day, having been interested in Knopf ever since they'd published Hudson's *Green Mansions* four years earlier, she left her apartment at 5 Bank Street and took the subway to the Candler Building. Though the company history maintains that she showed up at the office unexpectedly, she had in fact called Blanche for an appointment.[4] (In later years Cather would claim to have moved to Knopf from her longtime publisher, Houghton Mifflin, because of "how different" Knopf books looked from others.)[5] She was impressed by the young company's obvious support of its authors, conveying through their prominent, well-designed ads that writer and publisher shared goals. In contrast, Houghton Mifflin had barely eked out notices for her novels, including her latest, *My Ántonia*, published two years earlier, in 1918. Complaining to Houghton Mifflin about their weak advertising, Cather referred to Knopf's promotion of Hergesheimer's *Java Head*: even before the novel was officially released, Knopf had reprinted early positive reviews to build an audience. Now, surprised at the modesty of the Knopfs' office—Blanche was working the switchboard at lunchtime—Cather was nonetheless pleased when the publishers offered her a chance to try them out: they would quickly publish a book of her short stories, even while she was still under contract to Houghton Mifflin for her novels.[6] So it was that in September 1920 the Knopfs released *Youth and the Bright Medusa*, advertising it to the hilt.

Of course, Cather knew that when a book sold well, the house was willing to spend more to advertise the next one. In 1915, Houghton Mifflin had allotted Henry Sydnor Harrison's *V.V.'s Eyes*, read by the Knopfs during their courtship, more than six thousand dollars for publicity because of strong sales for the author's first novel, *Queed*. The advertising funds assigned to Cather's books had been puny by comparison (though not insignificant in those years): in 1915 *The*

Song of the Lark received a budget of one thousand dollars, and in 1918 *My Ántonia* was given three hundred dollars, this last an insulting vote of no confidence. Its initial sale made only thirteen hundred dollars for Cather, and it earned her only four hundred in the second year. Though not insignificant to many writers, the figures were below Cather's expectations.

Looking at the numbers, Cather believed she couldn't write the kind of book that would sustain Houghton Mifflin's commercial appetite.[7] The Knopfs, however, made her feel welcome. From the September 29, 1920, advertisement for *Youth and the Bright Medusa* in *The New Republic* (with Alfred's exhortation to those in the know) to Blanche's addressing the daily needs of the author—sending her her favorite foods and assurances of being available day or night—Cather knew her home was with Knopf. She proved it with the sixteen books she proceeded to publish with them.[8]

"Life was simply no longer a battle," Cather's companion and biographer, Edith Lewis, noted. "She no longer had to feel apologetic or on the defensive."[9] Cather wanted her books published in August, for instance, to tap the summer vacation trade, and Knopf obliged. It wasn't about finances: Cather was interested in the sales primarily for what they said about her worth as a writer. She had a private income, which caused Knopf to treat her with even more respect, directing their accountant, Joe Lesser, to do her income taxes yearly. In 1923, their faith in her would be vindicated when *One of Ours*, a story of a midwesterner's journey to the front in World War I, won Knopf's first Pulitzer Prize for "novels." Meanwhile, *Youth and the Bright Medusa* kept selling as well, and her royalties topped nineteen thousand dollars on the two books that year alone.

Alfred's top-of-the-page, stentorian advertisement in *The New Republic* read:

There are not many living writers from whom a new book commands the attention with which each successive volume of Miss

Cather's is now awaited. There seems to be no disputing the fact that she is our foremost living woman novelist. In the stories in the present volume she deals with youth's adventures with the many-colored Medusa of art. Each tale is marked by the amazing ardor and restless energy of imagination which is peculiarly Miss Cather's; by a quick, bold cutting into the tissues of human experience and emotion that makes each of them a new discovery about character and life.[10]

Four years after winning the Pulitzer, Cather would publish *Death Comes for the Archbishop*, the story of two priests offering Christianity to the Hopi and Navajo Indians who'd recently become part of the United States territory of New Mexico. The novel would be included among *Time*'s one hundred best English-language novels from 1923 to 2005 and on the Modern Library's list of the hundred best English-language novels of the twentieth century.

The Cather connection boosted Blanche's confidence to a new level. Alfred was impressed by her gift for discerning whom to publish, and she felt she had finally gained her husband's respect. Such certainty allowed her to be more relaxed, even playful with Alfred. Now, when the two were at home together, he took to working nude at his desk, in obeisance to the summer heat—and he even allowed his wife to snap a picture of him without his clothes.

Around this period, Blanche increased the number and size of the parties she gave. For the most part, the guests still came from Knopf's roster of writers, though often the invitations were supplemented by Van Vechten. He encouraged Blanche to include interesting figures emerging onto the Harlem scene, such as Paul Robeson and A'Lelia Walker, who had just inherited her mother's fortune, making her the richest black woman in America.[11] Blanche, impressed by strong women, was especially taken by A'Lelia's story: her mother, Madam C. J. Walker, a former laundress who became a brilliant businesswoman, had built an empire on a secret hair formula. Selling it to black women to straighten their hair, Walker, upon her recent death, had ceded the "beauty empire, an Italianate villa overlooking the Harlem River, and several elegant townhouses" to her only child.[12]

By October 1920, Blanche was able to take a break. As a result of their recent hire of the solid Joe Lesser as their bookkeeper/accountant, she could relax and enjoy the kind of genial family life she'd often envied. Together, she and Alfred took Pat to Atlantic City on several weekends; Alfred's photographs show Blanche smiling broadly, delighted to watch Pat roll his hoop or dig near the water's edge. Bundled against the autumn breeze, she sits in a sand chair, contentedly reading a manuscript while her husband and son throw a ball.

Within a mere five years of Knopf's incorporation, Alfred and Blanche had published a list of early work by authors who would later become well-known (though the majority with other, better-paying houses): T. S. Eliot, Robert Graves, Wyndham Lewis, H. L. Mencken, George Jean Nathan, Ezra Pound, and Carl Van Vechten. Mencken and Van Vechten continued scouting other writers, who in turn recommended their acquaintances. After Floyd Dell spoke of his friend Susan Glaspell's one-act play *Trifles*, his enthusiasm caused Blanche to regret having passed when she'd had an opportunity to see it a few years earlier. The story of a woman so battered by her husband that she eventually kills him became an instant stage hit after it premiered in Provincetown, Massachusetts.

These days, when Willa Cather invited the Knopfs to her large, old-fashioned, but comfortable apartment on Bank Street for her Friday "at homes," the couple might also stop by to visit Dell, who since January 1918 had been deep into a torrid affair with Edna

St. Vincent Millay.[13] After "Vincent" and Floyd parted, Millay briefly turned to Knopf's author the famously homosexual poet Witter Bynner. For now, however, Blanche was not greatly interested in Dell's love affairs or anyone else's: she was preoccupied with launching Dell's autobiographical novel *Moon-Calf*, set in the Midwest, as was Sinclair Lewis's *Main Street*. The books appeared within days of each other that September, and of the many important postwar novels published in 1920 by midwestern authors (including Fitzgerald's *This Side of Paradise*), Lewis's and Dell's novels presented the most complicated attitudes about small-town living.[14]

Though Dell's protagonist Felix Fay's journey to adulthood would be seen in years to come as predictable and prosaic and Dell himself as a minor figure, during the early decades of the twentieth century his name appeared in newspapers and book reviews almost daily. By the time he finally hit it big with *Moon-Calf*—a bildungsroman (as was Fitzgerald's novel)—he had already been popular for ten years, among the first exodus of midwestern writers to Greenwich Village. As of October 20, 1920, the novel had sold 38,500 copies and gone through eleven printings. In December, *Publishers Weekly* claimed that Dell's novel was written "for readers who think."[15]

An innovative advertising campaign had jump-started the book, with Knopf reintroducing the "sandwich man," used before the turn of the century and now deployed to sell books as well as other products. In September, a temporary phalanx of Knopf sandwich men had swarmed over the financial and theater districts, their sandwich boards advertising *Moon-Calf* (and other forthcoming titles). According to a contemporary report in *Publishers Weekly*, the men were "dressed in bright colored artist garb with smock, Windsor tie, and tam-o-shanter. A copy of [all books being] advertised was attached to the sign, for passersby to glance through. At the bottom of each sign the names of the nearest stores were listed. Arrangements were made with retailers in the canvassed neighborhoods to install window displays of the books advertised." The placards were rotated from place to place so that each bookstore got its "full benefit . . . Retailers reported substantial sales."[16]

In 1920, the Knopfs prepared to celebrate their fifth publishing anniversary. But despite Alfred's early promises that they would be equal partners, when he arranged for an homage to be printed honoring "the Borzoi's five years of publishing," Blanche was instead omitted entirely. After her death, Alfred told an interviewer that from the start he'd always intended to use his name alone for the company's moniker, whatever Blanche had assumed.[17]

In his foreword to the 1920 homage, its 140 shiny trimmed pages bound in a vivid red-and-gold brocade cover, Alfred wrote that he was approaching "the conclusion of my first five years' publishing," and that "my authors" are loyal, as were his "loyal staff."[18] The volume consisted, essentially, of accolades from Knopf authors praising only Alfred as the leader of the Knopf enterprises. Alfred even commissioned a dedicatory piece from Carl Van Vechten. In an age of statistics, numbers were abundant in this "detailed record," meant to show, one contributor explained, "just what five years of publishing means." Such authors as Dorothy Richardson, Dell, Mencken, and Hergesheimer expressed their indebtedness to Alfred Knopf for their "recognized place in letters."[19] In his postscript, Alfred—who begins and ends the volume—made the only allusion to Blanche as he passingly noted a promising book currently under consideration. *Letters of a Javanese Princess*, written by "probably the first feminist of the Orient," was a manuscript, he implied, "found by Mrs. Knopf."[20]

After his wife's death, Alfred would begrudge any suggestion that she had been key to their business from the start and would instead assign her to a secondary role. To Susan Sheehan eight years after Blanche died, he said, "I wouldn't quarrel if she wanted to be on record as saying she helped found the business in 1915." Sheehan doggedly continued: "She said that she was 'in publishing' since your official opening on October 15, 1915." At this Alfred became impatient:

"Well, that's stretching it a little. But she was insofar as she knew every single thing I was doing."[21] The disregard for her equal part in creating Knopf, reflected in the anniversary brochure, infuriated Blanche and wounded her deeply. She found herself dreading rather than welcoming the trip abroad that the couple was already planning for the following summer, to sign authors around the world while promoting Knopf's current books as well. Suddenly, she felt herself not only Sam's but the company's servant. As if restaking her maternal role, she spent a good deal of time ensuring that everything was set for Pat's care at the hands of relatives and hired help.

In May 1921, when Blanche and Alfred sailed upon their first joint business trip to the Continent, few American publishers had preceded them, except to stop occasionally for meetings in London and even less frequently in Paris, before or after vacationing elsewhere in Europe. Blanche was plagued with a variety of physical ailments during the crossing, not least debilitating abdominal cramps from endometriosis. She was ambivalent, too, about following an agenda set exclusively by Alfred. They would stay with the Galsworthys, outside London, and would meet Joseph Conrad, known to Alfred through letters if not yet in person. Meanwhile, she worried about leaving her toddler at home with their nanny.

She had enrolled him in nursery school for the fall, the brand-new Birch Wathen School (to become in 1991 the Birch Wathen Lenox School) at West Ninety-Third Street between Amsterdam and Columbus, not far from the Knopfs' Ninety-Fifth Street home.[22] Ten years after Blanche died, Pat told an interviewer that around this time, when he was three, Blanche went abroad with Alfred to do business for the first time, and she made sure he would hardly notice, with loved ones always at hand. But it wasn't only ambivalence about leaving her son that preoccupied her; Blanche was wondering for the first time about her importance to Knopf.[23]

For their trip, Alfred chose the Cunard Line's ocean liner the RMS *Carmania*. Only recently returned to passenger service, the

Carmania had served as a troop ship during the war. Two years later, when the Knopfs sailed, it was not the most luxurious ship, having been refitted and its passenger size cut in half, with trips across the Atlantic taking between five and seven days. But Sinclair Lewis, his wife, Grace, an editor at *Vogue* magazine, and their young son were on board, and "Red's" nightly presence at their table guaranteed an exciting, at times even harrowing, voyage. After Lewis sided with the ship's crew over a pay dispute, the captain was indignant when the writer appeared at dinner in a white dress shirt smeared with coal dust. He also created a drunken spectacle, gloating that he had gone down to the engine room to help the stokers and had urged the men on in their rebellion.[24]

After disembarking in Liverpool, the Knopfs saw more of the Lewises in London. The couples were scheduled to meet in Bath, about one hundred miles from the city, for the Derby Day dinner at the Bath Club, one of the region's major social events. Unfortunately, the event was less than exuberant, since the regional football team had performed worse than ever.[25] Blanche wrote friends, with a hint of amusement, that Lewis arrived very late to the dinner, and "Old Sydney Pawling" (partner to the English publisher William Heinemann, the Knopfs' friend) refused to wait to begin the meal. When the ever-voluble Lewis finally presented himself, Pawling punished the garrulous man by not letting him say a word throughout the dinner.[26]

After another round of nonstop appointments in London with publishers and agents, the Knopfs were staying at the country house of the publisher Sir Newman Flower, with whom they were acquainted, and his notoriously haughty wife, Lady Evelyn. There, for reasons that remain undisclosed, Blanche attempted suicide. The incident is shrouded in secrecy to this day, and it is only because of the Flowers' son Desmond's memoir that we know of the incident at all.

As Desmond recalled, upon Blanche's "endeavor," Lady Evelyn Flower had "stamped up and down the corridor, fuming, 'I don't care a damn whether she commits suicide or not, but I won't have her doing it in my house.'"[27] Apparently, Blanche took an overdose of pills. A doctor was called and Blanche's stomach was pumped, which is the only record that remains of what was surely a terrifying experience, especially as it must have evoked for Alfred the memory of his mother's death. It seems possible, at least, that the episode expressed Blanche's despair at having been omitted from the Knopf five-year celebration, an omission that reverberated with industry people she met on this trip. It isn't hard to imagine Alfred accepting Newman Flower's assumption that "Knopf" meant Alfred alone, and Blanche feeling powerless to correct their British host. From his engagement promise, she had trusted Alfred to ensure that she played an equal part in building and running Knopf, and she had believed he would add "Blanche Knopf" to the firm's name eventually. Instead, he had betrayed her, and, now suspecting he didn't plan to ever include her name, she became despondent.

A week or so later she set off with Alfred to meet Mencken's friend Thomas Mann in Germany. There, just as Mencken had predicted, Blanche decided Knopf must publish *Buddenbrooks*. Through an interpreter, she appreciated Mann's clear writing at once, though she underestimated the translation difficulties of his sometimes trying Germanic syntax. Regardless, in 1995 his biographer Ronald Hayman would say that "never again will it be possible to produce such a corpus of great novels and reach such a wide audience. Unlike other masters of modernism . . . [Mann] was never obscure, never demanded too much of the reader for his books to be bestsellers."[28]

A novel about the decline of a wealthy North German merchant family, *Buddenbrooks* would be the first of Mann's novels printed in English and published in the United States. Blanche hired the respected scholar Helen T. Lowe-Porter to do the translation. (Lowe-

Porter would translate Mann's complete works, except for the later fiction *The Black Swan* and the unfinished *Confessions of Felix Krull, Confidence Man*.)[29] When the two-volume English version of *Buddenbrooks* sold unexpectedly well in 1924, the Knopfs sent Mann an end-of-year bonus, though nothing in his contract demanded it. Throughout the decade, Blanche would be dealing with Mann and arranging for translations—and in the late thirties she helped him and Katia, his wife, relocate to America, along with several of their children. Though close to the Manns from the start, observing the elderly author's old-world formality, Blanche always signed herself "Mrs. Alfred A. Knopf."

Back home, her depression firmly at bay, Blanche resumed her work with all phases of the company: she solicited authors (including the poets John Crowe Ransom and Edith Sitwell), wrote follow-ups to those she'd met in Europe but had been unable to sign, located translators, read manuscripts, approved book designs, and developed advertising copy. She reprinted world classics, especially novels, having them set in Suburban French type, which imitated script, on paper specially manufactured with an Indian (red-brown) tint. The trip to Europe, although Alfred had chafed to return to the States, had made her appreciate how large the world was that she'd always wanted to explore.

Before she'd gone abroad, Blanche had even taken a peek at the changes outside her own door, where peace and prosperity encouraged many Americans to believe that "injustice, oppression and exploitation . . . had been swept away."[30] In May 1921, the musical revue *Shuffle Along*, beginning its run at Daly's 63rd St. Theatre, proved a perfect fit for a brave new age. (The show's hit, "I'm Just Wild About Harry," would be used in Harry Truman's 1948 presidential campaign.) Blanche was thrilled at the play's message: the Negro was here to stay—allowed to sit in the orchestra seats, not just the balcony. The musical would run for more than five hundred performances, and within a year several of its singers were appearing regularly at Blanche's parties, most often Paul Robeson. Part of the show's barbershop quartet, he was unfailingly accompanied by his wife, Essie, who feared (correctly, it turned out) that he would have affairs with white women if Essie wasn't always at his side. *Shuffle Along*, however, the first financially successful Broadway show to use African-American writers and cast, broke the taboo not on miscegenation, but on the even greater illogic forbidding depictions of romantic love onstage between African-Americans.

Visiting Europe, Blanche had realized that the new American writers—the group of expatriates such as Ernest Hemingway and F. Scott Fitzgerald—were the talk of the Paris cafes. Anything featuring African-Americans was the most popular stage ticket to snag, and Blanche recognized that she herself inhabited the "hottest" city in the world. Manhattan was undergoing dramatic urban transformation (from sixty thousand African-Americans ten years earlier to what would, in Harlem alone, become a community of more than two hundred thousand people in 1930).[31] When she arrived home from her first trip abroad, Blanche saw that Harlem had become the "intellectual and artistic capital of the Negro world"—and from there, of New York City.[32]

Carl Van Vechten would guide Blanche through this new scene—which he had documented much earlier, in December 1913, when he wrote for the *New York Press* about the current all-black Harlem production of *My Friend from Kentucky*. More recently, in 1922, he had published a short essay about Bert Williams, one of the most famous (to mixed audiences) black entertainers of the late nineteenth and early twentieth centuries. It was published in *The Reviewer*, the literary quarterly recently established in Richmond. Carl had been fascinated by African-American culture since his youth in Cedar Rapids, Iowa, where, in spite of its paucity of African-Americans, his father, an insurance salesman, had helped Laurence Jones, a black educator in Iowa, found (with Van Vechten's funding) the Piney Woods

School for Negro Children in Mississippi. Carl grew up assuming that African-Americans were not only like him but more deserving because of their disadvantages. Thus the family was instructed to address their yardman as "Mr. Oliphant" and their cook as "Mrs. Sercey."[33]

Van Vechten would become Blanche's personal guide into a world new to her but well trodden by her friend. As James Weldon Johnson would claim, "In the early days of the Negro literary and artistic movement, no one in the country did more to forward it" than Van Vechten.[34] Carl could easily move between advocating fair treatment of African-Americans to championing their culture, exhorting the twenties "speakeasy intelligentsia" of New York City to pay attention to them.

And his omnivorous nature made him a perfect scout for Knopf. Van Vechten was eager to make his acquaintance with the southern white literary scene in Richmond that Blanche had described and promised to present to her friend. The small Virginia circle was the equivalent of the artist groups of the Midwest and later the West as well, contingents of writers, painters, and sculptors of the early twentieth century. But that November, Carl and Blanche were both otherwise engaged, so when Blanche sought to sign the Knopfs' southern friend James Branch Cabell, she sent in their stead her other regulars, Hergesheimer and Mencken. The men would meet at Cabell's imposing residence in Richmond under Blanche's behind-the-scenes direction. They went to dinner at the home of the editor Emily Clark before they discussed business the next day. The thirty-five issues of Clark's *The Reviewer*, the Richmond-based experimental literary magazine that would last for four years, counted Van Vechten among its first contributors by virtue of the Bert Williams essay he'd written.

Blanche worried aloud about the men coming off as pushy Yankees, her concern causing Mencken to guffaw. Admittedly, Clark made things a bit awkward when she brought up Mencken's recent article declaring the South a desert of literary production. Her magazine meant to dissect both the Old and the New South, with controversial social issues addressed and submissions encouraged from new and established writers, including Allen Tate, Robert Penn Warren, John Crowe Ransom, and others. Blanche had urged Mencken to rethink his homegrown prejudice. She herself found the South's newly complicated culture easier to relate to than she had the old, even three years earlier.

But no matter how well Mencken behaved, or the good feelings he and Hergesheimer generated, the visitors couldn't secure the deal Blanche sought. Though he was too much the gentleman to discuss money, Cabell made it clear that he was offered much better terms elsewhere. It was a theme to be played out throughout Knopf's existence as an independent publisher, Blanche disagreeing with Alfred's penurious assessments that prevented paying higher advances. She chafed from afar while the negotiating with Cabell ensued: How could she acquire the best if she couldn't compete? She sent a telegram to her husband's Chicago hotel that assured him he was missed even as it conveyed her real interest, the deal she sought with Cabell: "Dearest there is no news but that I am beastly lonesome for you."[35]

Smoking two packs of Chesterfields a day, she was deflected from focusing on Cabell while she waited eagerly for reaction to Van Vechten's whimsical yet philosophical novel *Peter Whiffle: His Life and Works*. A paean to prewar Paris, *Peter* had been midwifed by Blanche, who'd prodded Carl to finish it. Though the Knopfs had published several books by Van Vechten, he'd not yet had a real success, and Blanche felt sure this would be his breakthrough. She was right: *Peter* won high praise, its initially slow sales picking up momentum. The Knopf catalog quoted the literary critic Carl Van Doren's advance review in *The Nation*: "A biography of an imaginary person," he claimed, "makes possible at once the freedom of the novel and the sober structure of the biography. *Peter Whiffle* crosses two literary forms fascinatingly."[36] A blend of the new and the conventional, *Peter Whiffle* mixed fantasy and realism while positioning the author himself as if present. Not only was Van Vechten the first-person narrator, but many other characters were also presented as real. Perhaps it struck Blanche that she and Peter Whiffle, with their mutual experience of inventing themselves, at some level shared the theme of being someone other than they seemed. After all, Blanche would always pretend that her father was a goldsmith from the Old World.

Soon after the novel's publication, Gertrude Stein, Hergesheimer, and Cabell, as well as the arts entrepreneur Mabel Dodge (portrayed as the character Edith Dale in *Peter Whiffle*), sent Carl their praise. By August the novel had sold more than 5,700 copies, a respectable number for fiction. The designers had created ninety-seven variations of batik papers to appear on the endpapers, but after *Peter Whiffle* went through eight printings this first year, it was consigned to plain cloth bindings: the fancy versions were no longer needed to attract an audience.

Blanche still hoped, however, to secure a first-rate designer for several other novels. According to his memoirs, Alfred noted that during the previous year the Knopfs had "become acquainted with the splendid artist George Bellows. I was laboring under the delusion that we could get, and could afford to pay . . . a really first-rate man for some of our fiction." He first took the well-respected illustrator C. B. Falls, and then Bellows, to lunch. In any case, Alfred remembered, "George, his wife Emma, Blanche and I" became very close friends, "and we used to exchange meals, our going to the house on East 18th Street and the Bellows coming to us at West 95th. It wasn't long before I became a great admirer of his lithographs, so many of which are absolutely perfectly American. We had precious little money," but somehow Alfred arranged a deal with Bellows to do his father's portrait, though the artist never did a book jacket for Knopf.[37] To no avail, Blanche protested their commissioning the painting. She at least got a new friendship out of it, enjoying for years to come the Bellowses themselves.

On New Year's Eve, as 1922 came to a close, a firecracker detonated just as Edwin Knopf, Alfred's younger half brother, reached for it. After several days in the hospital, Edwin was forced to have his right hand amputated. Sam Knopf was distraught, and kept "weeping to the point where his desk blotter was wet," though he told Ned, as Sam called him, that he would simply have to make do with one hand.[38] The story would be embroidered over the years, until Edwin had saved a child by falling on a live grenade.[39] Fortunately, Edwin was left-handed. Blanche mentioned the accident in a brief letter to Mencken, but she had to shift gears rapidly, helping Alfred prepare for a trip to Chicago in a few days. He would solicit large orders from the ever-faithful Marshall Field's and from Carson Pirie Scott & Co., a department store, he'd told her more than once, whose building was designed by Louis Sullivan (with a later addition by Daniel Burnham). Blanche felt she needed to talk with Mencken before then, so that he could help her decide which of her books Alfred should push.

In 1922 and '23, it seemed at times that their business, their child, and the couple's mutual friends, Mencken and Van Vechten, were what held the Knopfs together: there appeared little personal bond between them. During this period, their young son became a bed wetter, his soaked linens usually discovered by the housekeeper after his parents had left for work. When Alfred was informed of the mishap on his return home, he would hit Pat with a belt or razor strap. Once, the desperate boy placed his wet bedding on the floor and tried to dry it with an iron, thereby burning holes in the sheet, carpet, and floor.[40]

Alfred would also strike Pat if the boy failed to eat everything on his plate. "I always feared my father," the adult son recalled almost nostalgically, his fear converted into admiration. Only when Pat got his pilot wings in World War II would he stop being afraid of Alfred and bask in his praise, having become the war hero Alfred had never been.[41]

When, after his father's death, Pat was asked by the writer Peter Prescott about rumors that Blanche had been struck, too, Pat replied that "Alfred beat her from the beginning." He also told William Koshland, eventual president of Knopf, that Alfred pummeled his mother, claiming that he could "remember his mother yelling because his father was beating her up."[42] Given Pat's complicated personality, it is hard to know what to trust. According to Frances Lindley, Blanche's friend and a Knopf editor until she became a publicist and later an editor at Harper & Row, Pat was a very loud, crude person. "He's not as insensitive [sic] as he makes himself sound. He's very vehement; Pat's capacity for self-awareness is as limited as his father's. He always overacted antagonism to his mother."[43] The boy usually ran out of the room when the adults fought. "[My father] had the makings of a violent man," he asserted.[44] Later, Pat asked Prescott to strike his comments from the record.

According to the sociologist Stephanie Coontz, an upper-class man physically abusing his family in the early part of the twentieth century wasn't unheard-of, but it was nonetheless considered a disgrace, something to be hidden from public view.[45] Blanche surely felt the shame of the battered wife, the sense that she had done something wrong, along with a growing rage she worked hard to suppress.

She tried to develop interests in common with her husband, outside of work, if only to present a unified front to Pat. But everywhere she zigged, he zagged: she liked the East, he the West; she light meals, he stick-to-your-ribs food; she spirits, he fine wines. They recognized that their literary interests remained distinct as well: Blanche sought fiction, poetry, and nonfiction adventure, while Alfred still valued world histories and books on classical music. They had in common one enthusiasm: a passion for dogs. Even though it was a rushed spring in 1923, with both publishers leaving for London by mid-March before heading for Berlin, Alfred suddenly seemed preoccupied with buying a dog. Blanche at least understood his eagerness, one of the infrequent moments they agreed on anything these days: dogs loved you unconditionally.[46] As Emily Dickinson had written, "Dogs are better than human beings because they know but do not tell."[47]

5

WILD SUCCESS

BEFORE THEY LEFT FOR EUROPE, the couple visited a country kennel owned by a well-respected breeder of a rare British bloodhound. The friendly, calm animal so impressed them that they crossed the Atlantic Ocean discussing the pros and cons of a purchase. Finally deciding the hound cost too much, they reluctantly wired the breeder, "Not now."[1] When Alfred won money gambling on the way home, however, they immediately cabled that they had changed their minds.

Blanche loved the hound, which was exceptionally large yet "extremely gentle and very shy." The breed's reputation for "ferocity" was ill-deserved, she decided.[2] Photographs show her sitting with a dog almost as big as herself lolling half in her lap. Marlow, named after Conrad's narrator Charles Marlow, was the nervous sort, once so afraid of the racket he made by kicking over a few milk bottles that he ran off and hid for several days. The hound slept in Blanche and Alfred's bedroom, sighing loudly as he fell asleep at night, a sound

Blanche found soothing. Nonetheless, she worried that he was confined, the large dog getting too little exercise. After spending time in Port Washington with the Daniel Guggenheims, and returning home at the end of the summer, Blanche and Alfred decided to board Marlow during the week in Westchester County, where he'd have more room to run. They'd take him home on weekends to Ninety-Fifth Street, which had a backyard. But Marlow developed distemper, and within a few days of his first trip home, the dog was dead.

His replacement was paid for by the seller, but this did little to comfort Blanche, who had already become deeply attached to Marlow and worried that somehow they were to blame for his death. Nor was she reassured by the traits the new bloodhound exhibited when he was delivered to the office. Far from friendly, as the breeder had assured them he was, the growling dog gnawed the furniture, causing Alfred to run across the street to buy him food. Too rambunctious for the Knopfs' needs, Marlow II was put up for sale, Blanche commenting that "Marlow" seemed an accursed name for their dogs.

Just before selling Marlow II, however, Blanche and Alfred entered him in a large competition on private grounds in Mount Kisco, New York, where he was the only English bloodhound to show and therefore was awarded the blue ribbon. Not surprisingly, the Knopfs were motivated to take the bloodhound to more dog shows, where he inevitably won first place by default.

Hoping to tame Marlow further and find a way to keep him in spite of his weaknesses, the couple bought him a companion, a scruffy young Irish terrier, a "gay rascal" who loved to annoy "the huge boy." When the hound fell asleep on the sofa, Alfred wrote in his memoirs, the "little one exercised himself enormously, trying to make sexual contact but never coming within twelve inches of touching the big dog."[3] Reluctantly, they sold Marlow II and for the immediate future stayed with the terrier, who required little outdoor exercise.

For some months the couple's usual battles stayed at bay. Their decisions on which writers to add to the Knopf roster were in sync, and Blanche especially appreciated the way Mencken and Van Vechten played to the Knopfs' individual strengths, acting as unpaid, informal scouts, ensuring both Blanche's and Alfred's loyalty. Poets and novelists who came to the company through such links inevitably led to further connections. In this way, the publishers had included chapbooks by Kahlil Gibran on their early lists, the poet brought to them by Witter Bynner—who had in turn been delivered to them by Carl. So far sales of Gibran's few books had been disappointing, but Blanche insisted that they keep the writer on their list: she had a hunch about him. *The Prophet* proved her right.

At 51 West Tenth Street, where he lived from 1911 till his death in 1931, the "moony Lebanese mystic" wrote his long prose poem, over the years to be translated into forty languages.[4] In print since its publication in 1923, *The Prophet* was written in Arabic and then translated into English—and it proved a major moneymaker for Knopf throughout the company's history. (Johnny Cash even recorded a spoken-word version of the book in 1996.) Though they reveled in *The Prophet*'s success, the publishers were bewildered by the book's popularity. They finally decided that the story's simplicity, despite its supposed intricacy, made readers, especially young adults, feel intelligent. And there was the ever-popular theme of a journey of self-discovery.

Almustafa, a prophet and the story's protagonist, boards a ship that will carry him home after twelve years in a foreign city. Beseeched by fellow travelers, he discusses subjects encompassing the human condition, the narrative forming a kind of gentle *Canterbury Tales*, divided into chapters whose subjects range from joy and sadness to talking and drinking—with life and death undergirding everything. Typical of the poem is "On Love":

> When love beckons to you follow him,
> Though his ways are hard and steep.

And when his wings enfold you yield to him,
Though the sword hidden among his pinions may wound
you.
And when he speaks to you believe in him,
Though his voice may shatter your dreams as the north wind
lays waste the garden.
For even as love crowns you so shall he crucify you. Even as
he is for your growth so is he for your pruning.[5]

A few years too late for Blanche, in 1968 John Lennon used a line (with a slight alteration) from Gibran's 1926 collection of parables and aphorisms, *Sand and Foam*, in the Beatles' song "Julia," on *The White Album*: "Half of what I say is meaningless, but I say it so that the other half may reach you." In its first year of publication, forty-five years before the book had become "cool," Knopf sold 1,159 copies (of an ambitious first printing of 2,000). Demand for *The Prophet* doubled the following year—and doubled again the year after that. From the mid-twenties, annual sales rose almost exponentially throughout Blanche's life: 12,000 in 1935, to 111,000 in 1961, to 240,000 in 1965. One of the country's bestsellers of the twentieth century, *The Prophet* still sells more than 5,000 copies a week in the early twenty-first century.[6]

From his various journal accounts of their work as well as public references, it seems as if Alfred never mentioned Blanche's wisdom in holding on to the poet (who died of cirrhosis and tuberculosis at age forty-eight). He did point out, however, that Knopf hadn't spent more than a few thousand dollars advertising what he considered a screed. In his 1980 book *In Quest of Music*, Irving Kolodin, the *Saturday Review* music critic, wrote that he clearly remembered the place Kahlil Gibran held "in the life and fortunes of Alfred A. Knopf, Inc."[7] A majority of the 150 books on music that Knopf eventually published would be subsidized by *The Prophet* (and later by Julia Child's *Mastering the Art of French Cooking*).

Gaining confidence in her professional decisions, seeking reassurances from Mencken and Van Vechten far less frequently, Blanche breathed easier. Her professional life had fallen into a complex rhythm that felt right, and Blanche relished the range of demands her job entailed—even her interactions with her husband, when he was civil. Unlike the heads of today's major houses, the Knopfs, in Alfred's office, met with everyone, roughly ten people each morning. Alfred was in charge of beginning and ending the meetings, and he did most of the talking as well. At 10:00 a.m., Blanche, Alfred, and their accountant, Joe Lesser, saw the manufacturing and sales staff and the senior editors, two or three by now, who were expected to report any problems and be gone by 10:15. Then the executive committee convened. On Tuesdays, again with the Knopfs present, a group of five or so assembled in the library to discuss book jackets, and on Wednesdays, an editorial meeting with three or four in attendance lasted less than twenty minutes.

Often Blanche went to Elizabeth Arden afterward to get her hair and nails done, preparing for her evening work: acting the socialite, attending endless parties and musical events on the arms of friends, making sure she was seen while she herself was always on the lookout for a book idea that could come from anywhere or anyone. Her husband usually preferred staying at home and hooking up with his private bootlegger, afterward drinking alone. At least Alfred's devotion to the best in anything culinary kept Blanche's parties supplied with first-rate liquor, unlike New York's less fortunate. The common folk generally stuck with two drinks: gin and lemon, which tasted like sulfuric acid, or a martini so dry it seemed like a "concentrated solution of quinine." Both tasted so bad that they were regarded "as purely medicinal and swallowed at one gulp." On the rare occasions when she accepted either, the drink made Blanche gag.[8]

Paradoxically, Prohibition ensured that fashionable urbanites would drink more than ever, misbehaving flagrantly in the process, though Blanche wasn't as wild as her friends, if only because of the manuscripts she had to read in the morning. Sometimes she'd give in to the chance to go out for a taste of the wild life that was the buzz of the day. Carl, especially, repeated outrageous stories, causing Blanche to join his party crowd more often than she should. At dinner, for instance, in the apartment of the actress Carlotta Monterey and the popular *New Yorker* cartoonist Ralph Barton, Van Vechten had listened for three hours to the couple's debate over whether or not they should continue to live together. Upon their inconclusive finish, they ripped off their clothes and gave "a remarkable performance. Ralph goes down on Carlotta. She masturbates and expires in ecstasy. They do 69, etc.," after which Carlo, bored, "finally left."[9] Blanche tried to listen as if nothing fazed her, but she was aghast and her friend knew he had impressed her.

Though her attire in the office was impeccable, Blanche undeniably had become showier in the jewelry and makeup she wore, even at work. She connected with Knopf's women novelists—and many of the men—far more naturally than Alfred did, if only because she seemed to dress up for everyone, thus flattering them all. This was the year Willa Cather confirmed her hunch that Knopf was the right place for her, in large part because she bonded with Blanche, who knew enough to tone down her appearance when the stolid writer came to visit and to let Cather take the lead as they talked.

As promised, the Knopfs energetically advertised her novel *One of Ours*, a slow but deliberately paced story about a desolate young man lonely on his parents' Nebraska farm, then finally finding himself through the battles of World War I far from home. Its near glorification of war's potential to bestow purpose earned some negative reviews, but sales kept climbing. Cather had hoped for ten thousand advance orders for *One of Ours*; instead, Knopf's aggressive marketing led to twelve thousand early sales. They initially printed fifteen thousand copies, but immediately ordered another ten thousand to meet demand.

When *One of Ours* earned Cather the Pulitzer Prize in 1923, the unimpressive sales of *My Ántonia* soared, as did those of all of the author's previously published books. The Knopfs had signed Cather at just the right moment.

Cather remained a favorite of the house for decades—as much, Blanche would only half joke, for requiring no advance as for her novels. Blanche invited her to the Knopfs' dinners when Gershwin was playing, and Cather remained grateful to the couple until her death in 1947, especially to Blanche, for whom she would autograph one of her author photos: "For you, with love, dear Blanche, Willa Cather." Her inscription to Alfred was less affectionate: "For Alfred Knopf from Willa Cather."[10] Many decades later, Phyllis Robinson, Cather's biographer, would conclude that those who wanted to stay important to the writer had to realize the "fond attention that was so necessary to her."[11] Blanche's authors responded not only to her magnanimity, but also to an attractive vulnerability she often hid, announcing as it did her wish to be liked.

In 1923, when *Publishers Weekly* began tracking such figures, Knopf would release one hundred titles. Additional statistics for the same year showed 150 publishers averaging 39.27 titles (including textbooks and manuals) per house. In 1930 the average was nearly the same, at 40.69 titles a year, a number that would drop during the Depression, though not dramatically. Books, it seemed, were a commodity readers would find a way to afford, and publishing in those days appeared robust.[12] However briefly, the period fed a diet of optimism to English-language authors, especially those eager to be published in the United States. Carl Van Vechten would recall how "no one born after World War I could have any faint concept of the epoch during which so much writing blossomed," both at home and abroad.[13]

He was speaking of a group each of whom in some respect had

confronted a world war—now more than a few preternaturally aware of life's end—including F. Scott Fitzgerald, Ernest Hemingway, William Faulkner, and Virginia Woolf, alongside Theodore Dreiser, Sinclair Lewis, James Branch Cabell, Elinor Wylie, W. Somerset Maugham, and Hergesheimer and Mencken. Some would be forgotten within a few decades, but for now, often connected in part through their various gatherings at Manhattan's Algonquin Hotel, the writers thrived on the vibrancy they lent one another. It was as if the intellectual acuity of the Round Table—Alexander Woollcott, Heywood Broun, Robert Benchley, George S. Kaufman, Harold Ross, and at least one woman, Dorothy Parker—sharpened all those who encountered it.[14] Parker, for instance, challenged to use the word "horticulture" in a sentence, produced the memorable line "You can lead a horticulture but you can't make her think." Blanche thought that wonderful, wishing she herself had the wit (and confidence) to shoot off such one-liners.[15]

The publisher made sure that her social calendar always accommodated Van Vechten's Algonquin parties. Anytime his brother, Ralph, was in town, the Algonquin became the center of Midtown's attention. One time the brothers hosted a "very wet party" in Ralph's hotel rooms, the throng of guests threatening to burst into the hallway. With a young actress perched on his knee, Mencken fell asleep, letting the girl slide to the floor while he "snored loudly enough to rouse the guests in the neighboring suite." Awakening, he was astonished at the entirely new set of guests, including Tallulah Bankhead. Total strangers wafted in and out of conversations that Blanche, staying most of the night, soaked up: talk about sex, Freud, Prohibition, "kissing parrots," and more outlandish topics the later it got. This was now her territory, one she relished having to herself, her husband wanting no part of it.[16]

Not all was revelry. From entries in Alfred's diary, its binding studded with diamonds, by late August the Knopfs were disappointed in the sales for *Java Head*, which, expected by now to be earning well, was grossing only 25 percent of their earlier projections. Hergesheimer remained in good spirits, though Joe Lesser had already alerted the publishers to trouble selling the author's next novel, *Cytherea*, to the movies, as they'd hoped—not due to nonexistent censorship issues, they gently disabused their disappointed author, but because of the rapid decline of *Java Head* sales.[17] At least others on the Knopf list were selling well: Van Vechten's books were doing better in Philly these days than Hergesheimer's, even though Joe was a native. Later that week at lunch with Carl, Alfred estimated sales of twenty-five thousand for *The Blind Bow-Boy*, Van Vechten's novel about a boy who, when grown, is summoned to New York by his wealthy father and given an education in life. Critics considered it a latter-day *Great Expectations*, but even the self-assured Van Vechten thought that comparison overblown.

In fact, the image in *The Blind Bow-Boy* of "absinth served in goblets" came to Van Vechten at a Knopf dinner party, a few of whose guests were thereafter used as models for his novel's key female characters. A kind, liberal socialite shouts "with laughter" when her beautiful mother announces that she's about to marry "a Jew." Amused, the upper-crust woman declares that you "will not be received," then continues on, merrily, with other matters.[18] A bestseller, the novel, which Sinclair Lewis delightedly called "impertinent, subversive," tracks a young man's education in the Seven Lively Arts and Seven Deadly Sins. With its snake charmer from Coney Island and its musician named Bunny, it was a mix of the fantastic and the real, including a character based on the fabulously wealthy and now openly bisexual Mabel Dodge Luhan, who in life married an "Indian," a Native American, who wooed her with a drum and a teepee.

Wagering that the novel would sell, the Knopfs used the first-rate Vail-Ballou Press in Binghamton, New York, as typesetter for their exacting friend, and esparto (strong fiber) paper manufactured in Scotland and furnished locally by W. F. Etherington and Co., New York. These details of bookmaking, which followed a note describing "the type in which the book is set" as Caslon, wowed not only Knopf's readers but other publishers as well. Their artisanal attention pleased Van Vechten, who in turn vowed to send more strong authors Knopf's way. Earlier, at Blanche's behest, Carl had convinced Wallace Stevens to sign with her. Now, in 1923, along with *The Blind Bow-Boy*, Knopf published Stevens's first book of poetry, *Harmonium*, which some critics believe to be the second most important volume of twentieth-century American verse, after *The Waste Land*.[19] Of the original edition of fifteen hundred, only a hundred copies of *Harmonium* were sold, with Filene's in Boston selling their remaindered books for eleven cents each the following December. Often you had to wait a long time for a book to emerge as a classic, something Blanche understood. Spotting talent before the public was ready for it was part of her job.

The year 1923 proved providential in many respects. Upon her first New York City recital a year earlier, the London concert pianist Myra Hess had been provided with an introduction to the Knopfs by Ada Galsworthy. Now the raucous young musician, after hitting it off with Blanche at their first meeting, had become her good friend.[20] Myra loved to sing "The Rosary" a half tone flat at subsequent dinners with the Knopfs, exactly the kind of mischief Blanche enjoyed, though she rarely showed this side of herself before people who might criticize her.[21] Myra's friendship would prove rich and easy to maintain, particularly since the Knopfs had decided to open a London office: they, especially Alfred, wanted to create a greater presence in the English-speaking countries and, at least as important, to ensure they'd be among the first to bid on Britain's books as soon as they were to be signed to American publishers.

The new office would have to wait, however, while Blanche submitted to the hysterectomy she'd long been delaying. Young for such a procedure, she had been fighting gynecological problems since Pat's birth. Alfred and Pat both told Peter Prescott that she had strongly wanted to get pregnant again, which her five-year postponement of the surgery supports. Too frail to go to her friend George Gershwin's recital in New York, she did manage to attend when it was repeated in Boston. After the performance, Gershwin took her aside to share his news: Paul Whiteman, a noted American bandleader and orchestral director, had commissioned him to write a special composition for a program to be held in six weeks. Whiteman wanted to try a concerto for piano with jazz band, Gershwin said, in what was probably his first allusion to *Rhapsody in Blue*.

But the end of 1923 would involve Gershwin in more than his music, the chaos of the era and his personal life powering his energetic composition on the horizon. He and Edwin Knopf retreated to the Grove Park Inn in Asheville, North Carolina, in order for the musician to finish the symphony he had begun.[22] Their visit would be memorable enough in its solitude for Gershwin to consider briefly, thirteen years later, casting Fred Astaire in a film based on the hotel's "enforced sepulchal silence . . . with its squeakless guests."[23] A few days after the men returned to Manhattan, Gershwin let it slip that the actress Mary Ellis, Edwin's bride of one year, had been sleeping with him before Edwin's wedding and was doing so still. After a few weeks of intrigue and turmoil that January—the extended Knopf family offering advice, and Gershwin attending dinner at Blanche's as usual—"Eddie" and Mary Ellis settled down, though everyone gossiped about how she was mad about Gershwin (who, it turned out, was in love with Pauline Heifetz, the already famous violinist's sister). Gershwin, though not yet Jascha Heifetz, was usually present at Blanche's typically intimate parties (due in part to their house being of modest size but large enough for the always perfectly tuned piano), where the slightly cocky young composer developed a characteristic stance of holding a fat cigar between the second and third fingers of his right hand while he tickled the piano keys.[24] One night Stravinsky attended, sitting stony-faced throughout Gershwin's performance, and Paul Robeson continued to show up, occasionally singing with the younger Broadway tenor Taylor

Gordon. At some parties, Gershwin, eager for feedback, started playing at 9:00 p.m. and didn't stop until 3:00 a.m., grateful that such casual evenings allowed him to rehearse his compositions.

Finally, in Midtown Manhattan, on the afternoon of February 12, 1924, across from Bryant Park at the 1,100-seat Aeolian Hall, Gershwin presented *Rhapsody in Blue* in front of a sold-out audience. After listening to a seemingly endless program performed by the Palais Royal Orchestra, the audience, which included Rachmaninoff, Heifetz, Leopold Stokowski, Victor Herbert, Walter Damrosch, Heywood Broun, Fannie Hurst and her lover, the Arctic explorer Vilhjalmur Stefansson, Mencken, and Van Vechten, started to exit. Then Gershwin, the twenty-second and penultimate performer on the program, dashed to the piano. Whiteman, the conductor, signaled for what would become the single most famous clarinet glissando ever played, his baton lingering in the air even as Gershwin began his downbeat. At the conclusion of *Rhapsody in Blue*, there was a near stampede to congratulate its composer on what would be a defining moment of the Jazz Age.

Provoked in part by the clear signs that the age was only getting grander, nine years after Knopf opened its doors Sam decreed that Blanche and Alfred and their current staff of forty employees leave the Candler for Midtown's Heckscher Building (today the Crown Building). Designed by Warren and Wetmore, the firm that built Grand Central Terminal (and Aeolian Hall), the building at 730 Fifth Avenue was one of the most prestigious sites in Manhattan. The expensive quarters were nonetheless configured so that Blanche and Alfred would share an enormous office, an arrangement she found impossible. "The old man," however, had huge, imposing quarters to himself, and "he pounded the table at meetings and made a noise and wanted everything done his way."[25] Sam subsidized their mahogany-paneled five-thousand-square-foot office and, more important, maintained his contacts with the advertising and banking firms who'd employed him years before.

The Heckscher offices positioned Knopf at the center of activity, announcing the company's modernity. The building was the first affected by the new zoning law, whereby at required intervals, skyscrapers had to be "set back" in layers from the street, the structure allowing light among the juggernauts that otherwise blocked the sun. Blanche thought the Heckscher's resultant series of cantilevered boxes boring, except for the golden ornament on top, and she believed that paying for space in the $25 million building absurd.

The family tensions were as hard on her as her slow surgical recovery, which caused her to turn down Van Vechten's invitation to accompany him to Richmond in the early spring of 1924. She was also preoccupied with launching what she considered Carl's best novel, *The Tattooed Countess*, to be released in June. In many ways, as Sinclair Lewis wrote, his own *Main Street* as well as Sherwood Anderson's *Winesburg, Ohio* and Willa Cather's *O Pioneers!* influenced *The Tattooed Countess*, while Van Vechten, "often compared to Mr. Aldous Huxley . . . has gone beyond Huxley."[26] An aging and widowed countess, a midwestern girl who had married European money, returns to her provincial community and takes as a lover an adolescent boy (thought by Van Vechten's sister Emma to be based on Carl), and the two flee to Paris.

Gertrude Stein told Van Vechten, enigmatically, that "after having been tender to everyone else you are now tender to yourself." Scott Fitzgerald wrote from Europe that the view of Iowa was "unbeatable," and Knopf's poet Elinor Wylie called it a "cruel little masterpiece of analysis." Many readers found the novel lacking. The critic Joseph Wood Krutch lamented in his review for *The Nation* that the characters "had no gift of life," while the *Literary Review* and *The New York Times* deemed it "easy reading" and light entertainment, respectively.[27] In any event, sales of *The Tattooed Countess*, along with his income from his first two novels, allowed Carl to move to a choicer location, a spacious double apartment at 150 West Fifty-Fifth, leaving behind 151 East Nineteenth Street—and, to his dismay, his neighbors, Theda Bara, George Bellows, and (the sporadically present) Elinor Wylie among them.[28]

During the novel's release Blanche missed what turned out to be a "perfectly riotous dinner party at the Cabells." Still, Van Vechten promised Blanche that he would share all the best gossip, which inevitably came from Wylie (an honorary southerner, since she had spent her adolescence in Washington, D.C.), Ellen Glasgow, and Emily Clark, who gave "dinner parties galore."[29] Blanche's earlier assumptions about Virginia had hinged on images of slavery as well as critical remarks that the Baltimorean Mencken had made about "his people," and she now realized that she had taken Mencken too seriously.

She possessed, it seems, a genuine feel for equality, extending even to her friends' children, who, when they accompanied their mothers for lunch with Blanche, were often confused by the serious questions she asked them.[30] The young weren't used to such frank interest. Respect and a sense of social justice were important to the publisher, perhaps due to her early awareness that the "right kind" of Jew had pale skin, an illogical formula that left her cold. She had fought with her mother when Bertha declared the dark-skinned family Blanche was marrying into inferior to the lighter Ashkenazi Jews. The publicist Harding "Pete" Lemay, well into his nineties, still remembers Blanche sorrowfully recounting to him that before he arrived at Knopf in 1958, when Blanche felt backed against the wall by her husband, she'd haughtily repeat something that supported her mother's silly position of racial superiority based on skin shade.[31]

Exhausted by the recent office relocation, a few months later Blanche was forced into another move as well, this one personal, also dictated by her father-in-law. Upon Sam's insistence that they "have a residence worthy of their company," she and Alfred moved from their two-floor rental at the dentist's house on West Ninety-Fifth Street to a new, modernist two-bedroom apartment at 1148 Fifth Avenue, where they would live for the next four years. Overlooking Central Park on the Upper East Side, their third-floor apartment was filled with light. It was a "long, long apartment," Pat would recall as an adult, with a "huge, grand room." Running the full length of the corridor with bookcases on either side, "as you turned to your left, my mother's room . . . [had a door] that led into a twin-bedded room that my father and I shared."[32] Blanche had been just fine at West Ninety-Fifth Street, which she knew the "old man" found too humble, thereby compelling his son to "move into much more elegant quarters."[33] Clearly Blanche's disgust wasn't over aesthetic issues, but over her father-in-law's unremitting control and Alfred's unfailing acquiescence.

Blanche brooded that Alfred's family had too much control of Pat as well, who was "frightfully spoiled by his grandparents and not by me."[34] She worried about Alfred's nastiness to their son, and about Pat observing his father's nastiness to her. By the end of the summer of 1924, she had resolved to put the boy out of harm's way by enrolling him in Columbia Grammar School at 5 West Ninety-Third Street on the Upper West Side, a full-time program preventing her child from spending much time with Sam and Lillie—or Alfred. The following year, Pat would attend the Riverdale School for Boys in the Bronx, which five years earlier had begun to take in boarding students. Alfred was attracted to its strong athletics, and Blanche to a riding program that she wanted for her son.

In her late-life personal notes, Blanche wrote that "time went on until it all became impossible and Mr. Knopf wanted to move back to the country which he had always cared more about than anything else. I warned him if he did I would not go with him as the business of working in an office all day long and taking a train to the country was physically impossible."[35] Perhaps in retaliation, Alfred made his father an official part of the company.

During the year that Sam Knopf was voted a board member and

shareholder, Blanche believed that he had "little money but gave the impression of being a millionaire." Somehow he put money into Knopf and brought in outside interests, so that in 1924 Knopf was incorporated. "From then on our troubles began and from then on I started to run away," Blanche said.[36]

She felt herself constantly criticized by "the old man," the "unremitting stress" leading to an affair with a Frenchman sustained over three years.[37] It is possible, given the distance from which Blanche told this story and her penchant for combining facts, that her Frenchman was Hubert Hohe, a lover not to come into her life for another fifteen years.

During this period, the thirty-year-old Blanche came up with evershrewder ways to have a real sex life. Their stronger income allowing her to throw lavish parties for her favorite musicians, she appreciated the ability to have an occasional (and sometimes long-lasting) liaison with whichever famous conductor or instrumentalist was in town, or even nearby, in Philadelphia or Boston. These men exuded the passion she felt penned up inside her, along with the music she had grown to love, even as she listened with her eyes shut. Leopold Stokowski, Jascha Heifetz, and Benno Moiseiwitsch would all become regular lovers, but it was the Russian conductor Serge Koussevitzky who would have the strongest hold on Blanche. In 1924 Koussevitzky was beginning what would be a twenty-five-year tenure as music director of the Boston Symphony Orchestra, and from the start, Blanche would sponsor a celebration for him after the BSO's first New York concert of each season. As one admirer commented about "Koussie," as his friends called him, "His sartorial splendor, his beautiful carriage, his reserved but dramatic gestures on the podium, all of these endeared him immediately to the . . . ladies."[38]

Leopold Stokowski, director of the Philadelphia Orchestra, guest conducted the New York Philharmonic each year as well. After seeing him on the podium for the first time in 1924, Blanche began holding an annual mid-December lunch for him. Stokowski was a physical conductor who, with his "twist of a wrist or an eyebrow," elicited a musician's maximum effort on the maestro's account.[39] From 1923 to 1926, the charismatic playboy was between famous lovers and wives (to include Greta Garbo and Gloria Vanderbilt), and the local women found him "free and unbridled" in bed—though controlling and cold outside the sheets.[40] Stokowski, with his Olympian detachment, liked to be in command—much like Alfred. The conductor's first rehearsal in Philadelphia was legendary: *"Guten Tag,"* he had called out almost before reaching the podium. "Brahms! First movement!" Slashing his baton downward, he caught most of the orchestra off guard, and they struggled to catch up with what is usually a "monumental opening." Stokowski stopped and started again, without a word. A member of the orchestra recalled, "It was if we'd been given some magic potion—[we] had never played so well."[41]

Stokowski was a musical showman of the first degree, from throwing the sheet music on the floor to prove he didn't need a score, to experimenting with lighting in the dark concert hall, to finding ways to cast dramatic shadows of his hands and head. Soon after arriving in Philadelphia, he began conducting without a baton, with his freehand style becoming his trademark. Blanche enjoyed his showmanship, while Alfred was more of a traditionalist. By the time William Koshland was hired in 1934, Knopf's well-heeled office manager (later to be Knopf's president and chairman) would notice how the Knopfs no longer arrived or departed together from Stokowski's performances in Manhattan, and Koshland alone would often take Blanche to Philadelphia, where she attended the maestro's early season instead of waiting for his Manhattan concerts.

The quiet girl at the bottom of the stairs turned out to enjoy not only the symphony hall but the nonstop social engagements that her husband disdained. A ceaseless party shored up with booze and endless conversation circulated through New York City in the twenties, and Blanche's increasing access to important social figures made her one of the era's fixtures, appearing wherever the action was—including throwing her own parties, occasionally up to four times a week.

Certainly she looked the part: she had become thin enough that her racy, above-the-knee flapper "rags" hung straight down, just as they were meant to, no undergarments necessary. She loved her pale lavender chiffon, its sequined cloth like the fluid jewels she'd seen long ago at the San Francisco world's fair, its color shifting as night turned into day. With vermillion lipstick that harmonized with her short reddish hair, her sultry eyes lined in kohl, Blanche reminded more than one spectator of the exquisite covers of a Knopf book. Moving among her guests, she trailed the scent of Caron's dirty-sweet perfume Narcisse Noir, a one-two-three punch of the most "deviant and reprobate of all smells"—orange blossoms and civet, sanctioned for either sex to wear. Carl Van Vechten had even perfumed the air of his 1923 novel *The Blind Bow-Boy* with the "odour of Narcisse Noir."[42] The period's best young writers, no matter their current publishers, continued to be at the center of Blanche's parties. A usually drunken William Faulkner was repeatedly ushered into a taxi in front of her apartment during the small hours. During the fall of 1924 Blanche herself was drinking hard, at least for her, substituting shots of whiskey for food: the previously slender and well-proportioned petite woman suddenly began to look as abnormally thin as the Chanel models abroad had become.

However much Blanche enjoyed traveling to scout books for the company, she also was exhilarated at the clothes the trips enabled her to buy in Paris salons. At home, good-looking ready-made dresses were easily obtained at stores such as B. Altman's and Henri Bendel (Saks Fifth Avenue would open in 1924), but she had started yearning for clothes made just for her (though an off-the-rack theater dressing gown created by the stage designer Erté would become a lifelong favorite). She envied the elegance and self-possession of Parisian women, and, having left her measurements with French couturiers, she allowed herself the luxury of buying bespoke clothing for the first time in her life. Narcisse Noir would give way to the more astringent and costly My Sin, when it premiered in 1925, a bouquet of lemon, clove, jasmine, vetiver, civet, and musk, with its flacon designed by Baccarat. During the twenties and thirties, Blanche commissioned fashions from Elsa Schiaparelli, replaced by Christian Dior in the forties. Occasionally, since at times she fit a size 2 perfectly, she'd buy a sample reserved for her by the designer, something previously worn to publicize the season's collection.

Blanche's determination to "go French" and become thinner than ever was aimed at least in part at Alfred: she might run off if he continued to mistreat her, or maybe she'd waste away altogether. With Pat in boarding school, she became the complete focus of Alfred's erratic rages, which were too violent to call temper tantrums. At this juncture, Alfred was furious that she was devoting so much time to her new passion, foxhunting, for which she woke at dawn if she'd not been partying the night before. It's unlikely that he considered his own role in her resolve to drive to Greenwich, Connecticut, or to Goldens Bridge in northern Westchester. There she joined in the camaraderie and exhilaration of the hunt, returning to the office in time for meetings and to work through the afternoon into the night, all alone, this peaceful, solitary work compensating for the time she spent riding to hounds.

Blanche seemed unwilling to pause long enough to think hard about her life. Living episodically, bouncing from one moment to the next, she was assured an endless run of excitement bereft of much contemplation. If she ran fast enough, life would take care of itself.

Her foxhunting was yet another way to avoid seriously confronting her personal life. It was also the extent to which Blanche wished to engage with the country. Alfred would recall that "when we had an opportunity to rent an almost ideal house, quite near the stables where she kept her horse, she decided against our taking it if it meant, as it would have meant, giving up the New York apartment." Blanche's "excess sociability," wherein Alfred sometimes didn't even recognize the gate-crashers at his own party, furthered her husband's determination to leave urban life behind. When he was offered the perfect property by his lawyer friend Jim Rosenberg, he couldn't resist and was soon planning his grand country house.[43] By the end of the decade, Alfred would be comfortably ensconced at 63 Purchase Street in Purchase, currently in Harrison, New York, his daily commute to Grand Central Terminal around forty-five minutes by train. He would read *The New York Times* while he rode the train to the city and sometimes look over manuscripts, though not voraciously as he had before.

Once again, Sam was there for the financing. He made an unspecified but undoubtedly large down payment on the Purchase house, an investment that over time would include money for lush landscaping and Italian tile for the pool—as well as the pool itself.[44] Blanche had agreed with Alfred that she would occasionally entertain their authors at the estate, though she was put out at its rough interior. A local designer whom she approached for decorating ideas sniffed and declared it a hovel. Bennett Cerf, hearing Blanche's story (and knowing how much both Knopfs liked Random House's signature design), convinced the artist Rockwell Kent to draw them an ironic colophon based on Random House's logo, with the Knopfs' house captioned "the Hovel." Nothing about the home said "Blanche," and she never enjoyed staying in its dark environs, the lack of light remarked on by countless visitors.

In Manhattan, as though to counter what she complained to Mencken was Alfred's near obsession with leaving the city altogether—possibly even moving Knopf's offices as well as his residence to the suburbs—Blanche worked on making ever more contacts and solidifying the old ones. By late 1924, she was routinely holding parties at the Knopfs' apartment for her musical friends, in particular the pianists Arthur Rubinstein and Benno Moiseiwitsch, Jascha Heifetz, of course the conductors Serge Koussevitzky and Leopold Stokowski, and, always, George Gershwin. No doubt she meant to impress New York society and to dazzle her husband with her quick success in "his" field, great music.[45]

But aside from using the celebrities to enhance her own stature, Blanche felt comfortable with such men. Even with their oversized egos, they possessed a passion for something outside themselves. Their ardor was fixed on their music, just as hers was centered upon publishing. Sex with such men must have suited her perfectly: they all thrived on her praise and expected little else but an hour of her lovemaking.[46] Without fail, as if marking them, she gave each of her lovers a solid-gold Dunhill cigarette lighter and case, monogrammed, though there is no record of Blanche having received such gifts from the men. As sensitive as they were to the unspoken, perhaps they realized that she preferred holding the upper hand.[47]

Given the era she inhabited, Blanche's affairs were not as shocking as they might have been earlier or even later in the century. After Blanche's death, the still beautiful retired actress Florence Vidor Heifetz, divorced in 1946 from Jascha Heifetz, told interviewers that she had realized her husband (a notorious womanizer) and Blanche were having an affair, even as all three remained close. Assuming Alfred's coldness had practically propelled Blanche into Jascha's arms, Florence was disgusted that the publisher had never given his wife "the credit she deserved. Alfred had a power complex . . . Blanche was an enormously clever woman . . . [but] she denigrated her own achievements, would talk discouragedly about them." Florence encouraged her friend by saying, "Blanche, all you have to do is go into Brentano's and look at your publishing [feats]."[48]

The people Blanche really admired, however, were women like Florence Heifetz and Mildred Oppenheimer, the soon-to-be second wife of Alfred's brother, Edwin. To Florence, Blanche praised the "wonderful" women who "blended home, family and career, instead of just being a career woman," like herself. She wasn't fishing for a compliment but acknowledging aloud the failure of her family life.[49]

At the office the couple's professional separation served them well. Both Knopfs stuck to subjects that interested them, with Alfred's enthusiasms ranging from geology and history to fine wine, to which Blanche paid as little attention as her husband did to fiction and poetry and current events. Nor did Alfred share his wife's growing obsession with Van Vechten's Harlem scene. Carl had explained how an earlier set of African-American writers and their works— James Weldon Johnson's *Autobiography of an Ex-Colored Man*, Paul Lawrence Dunbar's poems, and the writings of Booker T. Washington and W.E.B. DuBois—were crucial to the energy currently circulating. Authors past and present seemed to speak to one another comfortably, as the canon was relatively small.

Certainly Blanche had been quick to appreciate the "Negro revues," starting with *Shuffle Along* in 1921, and she agreed with Van Vechten that Gershwin's music had its roots in black culture.[50] For people like Blanche, *Shuffle Along* had been a cultural turning point, alerting New Yorkers to the African-Americans' new status. Carl knew intuitively that his friend would surely find the day's "Negro talent, Negro beauty, [and] Negro humor" rejuvenating, so long as the nonstop revelry did not wear her out.[51]

Unlike many middle-class white women of her generation, Blanche felt no hesitation about mingling with people of various races and sexual orientations: for her, this was part of the very definition of being modern. Her clothes and maquillage grew ever more extreme, with her bob slightly wavy and still vampish red-brown, a style that remained her signature for decades, and her makeup as dramatic as Marie Antoinette's: her red lipstick became glossier, her rouge more obvious, and her eyebrows plucked more severely into the popular pirouette arch. She wore an amethyst stone that matched her perse eyeshadow. Blanche was "sexing up" her look, as the magazines called it. Everyone, including Blanche, was electrified over sex.

Manhattan's 1924–25 theater season continued the trend of sex everywhere—after the autumn shock of Paul Robeson's performance in Eugene O'Neill's play about miscegenation, at the Provincetown Playhouse in Greenwich Village. Blanche was impressed by *All God's Chillun Got Wings*. The drama had created plenty of steam during its previews when a black man kissed a white actress's hand, an action that caused police to guard the playhouse on opening night. Van Vechten, determined to help break down the color barrier, confided that he was trying to convince George Gershwin to cowrite a serious jazz opera for African-Americans, but that the composer insisted he wasn't ready for the challenge. As if working out issues of his own sexual identity, gossiped about for some years, at one of Blanche's parties the composer played his song "The Girl I Love," which he now retitled "The Man I Love," rendering gender as variable as race was starting to seem.

6

BOOKS OF THE TWENTIES

I N 1924 D. H. LAWRENCE ACCEPTED for a second time Mabel Dodge Luhan's invitation to the writers' colony she had established in Taos, New Mexico, in 1919. The Knopf poet Witter Bynner, who had moved to Santa Fe in 1922 when Lawrence first visited the colony, now encouraged the Englishman to contact Blanche. After all, Thomas Seltzer, Inc., Lawrence's six-year-old American publishing house, was already shutting down—primarily for having published Lawrence's *Women in Love.* The New York Society for the Suppression of Vice had pursued Seltzer relentlessly, driving him into bankruptcy.

Though Lawrence was sorry for his doting publisher, he thought Seltzer unbusinesslike, a worrisome trait in a publisher who now owed his author five thousand dollars in back royalties. Storm Jameson, the Knopfs' agent in London, was on top of things, ensuring that Blanche knew when to step in and make an offer. Upon the urging of Bynner, and with the encouragement of Lawrence's friend

Aldous Huxley, in 1925 Lawrence signed with Knopf as his new American publisher.[1]

Lawrence's third novel, *Sons and Lovers*, appeared in 1913. Though the novel and its successor, *The Rainbow*, would eventually be voted among the hundred most important novels of the twentieth century, the third of the triumvirate, 1920's *Women in Love*, was denounced soundly by at least one reviewer: "I do not claim to be a literary critic, but I know dirt when I smell it, and here is dirt in heaps—festering, putrid heaps which smell to high Heaven."[2]

While Blanche had appreciated Lawrence's earlier novels, she believed his prose was too often self-aware: when describing mine workers, for instance, the author felt always present, Lawrence's ofttimes feverish emotion calling attention to itself instead of to the story. However, she found the novel's frankness about previously unspoken sexual relationships between men and women invigorating.

By May 2, 1925, Blanche and Lawrence were already corresponding about the proofs for his novel *St. Mawr*, the publisher reassuring the tense writer that "the *St. Mawr* proofs did very well, and all that had to be done was done by you."[3] Lawrence had moved to Del Monte Ranch in Questa, approximately sixteen miles from the writers' chatter at Taos and from Mabel Dodge Luhan's determined friendship as well: "Please tell your clerk that the address is Questa, not Taos," he would write Blanche toward the end of the month.[4] Living in New Mexico for two years, Lawrence completed three books for Knopf: in 1925, *St. Mawr* (with Luhan the model for Mrs. Witt, "who destroyed all the men she met"); in 1926, *The Plumed Serpent* (with Lawrence's take on Mabel's "degrading marriage" to the Taos Pueblo Indian Tony Luhan); and in 1927, *Mornings in Mexico*, a series of short essays about the colorful life of New Mexico and Mexico in the 1920s.[5]

Barely noticed by American readers, with reviewers for the most part uninterested (though often praising Lawrence's graceful style), the books gained no traction in England, either. The novel that would prove legendary, however, was *Lady Chatterley's Lover*, the story of a gardener and his rich lover—which Blanche dared not publish. She had delicately gone back and forth with Lawrence about the cuts *Lady Chatterley's Lover* must undergo in order to appease the government censors, but he, equally polite, refused. Finally Lawrence published it in 1928 with a small Italian press, the Tipografia Giuntina. Italy approved of the author's sexual bounty, and the novel's sales were higher than those of any of his previous works, earning the writer more than he'd ever made in his life, "more than all his other books combined."[6]

Also in 1925, even as Blanche tended to the demanding Lawrence, she was competing hard with other publishers to sign Clarence Darrow to Knopf, imploring him to write a book about the upcoming Scopes "Monkey Trial." She invoked Mencken's name as an enticement, aware that Darrow knew the literary crowd (including Blanche herself) from all the parties the lawyer had attended in Manhattan. Though the book never came to fruition—"[It] is a long way off," Darrow wrote her—he promised to stop by and see her when he was "down again" from Chicago. He closed his warm response by commending the Knopfs for the literature they were "getting out" and for the "good work" being published in *The American Mercury*.[7] With Knopf's financial backing, in February 1924, Mencken and the writer George Jean Nathan had printed the first copy of their new high-toned monthly, born of Mencken's conviction that since the Armistice, the country had undergone extreme changes. The Ku Klux Klan, for instance, had increased from a few hundred members before the war to more than four million by the 1920s.[8] If the "Jazz Age had no interest in politics at all," as Fitzgerald claimed, then *The American Mercury* was conceived by Mencken as an antidote. The nation's blustering confidence, "a veneer on top of confusion and conflict," called out for redress.[9]

Even though Blanche usually kept her editorial distance from the dense monthly—she already had too much on her desk to assume an entirely new project—its thoughtful editing caused her to value Mencken even more, as she observed her friend's engagement with what he considered matters of principle. These days, Blanche found herself seeking Mencken's advice on her personal life as well as his professional opinion. The publisher's other best friend functioned similarly, though he was one for literary chitchat as much as serious counsel. In mid-February, Carl brought Blanche up to date on Horace Liveright's latest shenanigans and told her how when Carl recently had tea with Gertrude Stein, she had proclaimed Liveright disgusting, "a mass of obvious and cheap sensuality."[10]

As if emboldened by the louche image, Blanche stunned her friend by suddenly throwing "all discretion aside" . . . and informing Van Vechten that she was "tired of sleeping" with Alfred. "What is the world coming to?" Van Vechten asked his wife, Fania.[11] Carl was known to be a purveyor of salacious secrets, but he didn't usually speak of his personal sexual encounters to others, and he assumed that friends like Blanche behaved more conventionally than he, however current they tried to appear. He'd forgotten that he had described in great detail the machinations of Ralph Barton and Carlotta Monterey only months earlier.

No couple's intimate habits can be known by anyone other than themselves. But from comments repeated throughout the years after Blanche's death (and later, after Alfred's as well), Blanche's reluctance to sleep with her husband was fueled not only by their sexual incompatibility, but also by her anger over his violent temper and his acquiescence to Sam. From appearances, at least, Alfred seemed oblivious or perhaps indifferent to her feelings. In late-life interviews, despite his awareness of Blanche's published articles supporting open sex, along with the gossip of friends, Alfred answered questions about Blanche's extramarital love life by saying, "I don't think she was unfaithful except with Heifetz, with whom she had an affair."[12] "In the beginning and for a while," he said, "Blanche's distinguished friends were virtually all musicians. And there I'm sure I played a large part. But I never pursued it as far as she did. Koussevitzky, for instance: she'd go back during intermission every concert. We'd know the concert wasn't going to resume until you'd see her come walking down below the stage taking her seat . . . They were very devoted friends. She had Heifetz, she had Gershwin."[13] To pair Heifetz, a longtime lover, and Gershwin, with whom Blanche was in no way sexually involved, while omitting "Koussie," was an extraordinary confirmation of Alfred's ability to deny reality.

That reality included downstairs talk, the butlers and housemaids telling tales: Mrs. Knopf misbehaved for sure when the mister was away, while his own visitors never seemed to be there for sex but just for dinner with fine wine. Though there would be suggestions through the years that Alfred infrequently turned to other women for sex, more often his friends and colleagues assumed he was "asexual." Given the times, when "aberrant" behaviors weren't seemly to advertise, his chilly reserve toward Blanche might make more sense if he'd been homosexual. Instead, it seems that Alfred simply lacked a physical need to connect emotionally with anyone, so he procured prostitutes instead.[14]

Fortunately, there never was a better time than the 1920s to be all over the sexual map. It sometimes appeared that romantic relationships everywhere were turning barmy. As Scott and Zelda Fitzgerald, with their well-publicized drinking and depressions, exemplified a marriage gone mad, so did couples even closer to home. In March, barely settled down from the Gershwin affair, the singer Mary Ellis took up with the British actor Basil Sydney, causing Alfred's brother, Edwin, to threaten suicide. (Ellis, who would marry five times before she proclaimed herself a lesbian, later wrote that she'd married Edwin only out of pity when he lost his hand while they were dating.) The drama continued through mid-April, but matters finally came to a head and the couple divorced amicably.[15]

Blanche and Alfred were delighted to be completely disentangled from Mary Ellis and Knopf's competitor Horace Liveright, Edwin's brother-in-law (through Liveright's marriage to Ellis's sister). Liveright was turning out books at least equal to the Knopfs', including early Faulkner and Hemingway and Eliot's *The Waste Land*. (Alfred, for whatever reason not soliciting Blanche's opinion, had turned down Eliot's masterpiece.) Goading Alfred at publishing events, the lanky (married) libertine called him "coz" while he openly disported with the women inevitably surrounding him. Increasing his animosity, Alfred knew that Liveright's father-in-law of a few years, the owner of International Paper, had supplied all the money Liveright could ever want.

Thus news of Edwin's divorce was gratifying to the Knopfs from a professional and personal point of view: when Liveright managed to overspend even his father-in-law's robust endowment and struggled to meet his payroll, the Knopfs, always disdainful of the publisher, surely shared a private conjugal laugh, especially when their twenty-seven-year-old friend the independently wealthy Bennett Cerf, partnering with Donald Klopfer, bought Liveright's Modern Library in 1925 for $210,000. (In 1927, with Klopfer, Cerf would found Random House and eventually make the Modern Library its subsidiary.)

And there was more: when he heard of the Modern Library sale, Alfred, believed by Cerf to represent "publishing at its best," invited him and Klopfer to the office for a talk. There he "launched into a tirade about Horace Liveright," who had dared put *Green Mansions* into the series. Though the book had no copyright, Alfred considered it Knopf's property by now. Worst of all, the arrogant Liveright bragged that it was "the biggest-selling book in the whole Modern Library." Bennett Cerf told "Mr. Knopf" truthfully that he'd known nothing about this, to which Alfred replied, "Well, what are you going to do about it?" Cerf suggested his Modern Library pay Knopf six cents per copy sold, which Alfred thought "very fair, since legally he [Alfred] had no case."[16] Thus began a friendship between Knopf and Cerf that would ultimately change the publishing world.

More modestly, the Knopfs were expanding their enterprise, too. *The American Mercury* now featured a monthly advertisement for Knopf, *The Borzoi Broadside*, which would evolve into *The Borzoi Quarterly*. A pamphlet accompanied by a personal message written by Alfred, the *Quarterly* promoted Knopf's new books. *The American Mercury's* launch under Mencken had proved good timing, with the journalist's popularity at an all-time high in the summer of 1925. Harvard students regarded him as a defender of the logical versus the fantastic, of evolution versus creationism, a brilliant sardonic voice, much as today's audience views Jon Stewart. Mencken's scathing eyewitness coverage of the Scopes "Monkey Trial," in which Clarence Darrow went up against William Jennings Bryan, would see him emerge a kind of national hero. Filed with *The Baltimore Sun*, his reports had even provided pretrial advice to the ACLU, a gutsiness that Blanche admired. Scopes himself, forty years later, suggested that "in a way it was Mencken's show," with the journalist's "lacerating critique" of the Bible Belt (a term Mencken coined) and the "booboisie" (also his) winning lasting attention.[17]

That public affection was not, however, lasting: within a year after the trial, five hundred newspaper editorials about Mencken were published, 80 percent of them unfavorable. He had let loose with such "withering scorn" that much of the population felt personally attacked.[18] Blanche was determined to support Mencken through this period, though her time with him was newly limited, due to her mother's serious distress. When she had noticed Bertha acting "unlike herself," Blanche postponed her spring buying trip to Europe. On May 17, Bertha had a massive stroke. Belatedly, Blanche realized why the fifty-nine-year-old woman had insisted on traveling to

Europe earlier that year to see distant friends and relatives, a trip whose ever-changing plans Blanche had found exhausting. Bertha had been battling arteriosclerosis at least since her husband's death seven years earlier, so the cerebral thrombosis in her right hemisphere couldn't have been a complete surprise. For sixteen days she lay unconscious, having suffered a "bleed in her brain," and on June 3, 1925, with her daughter at her side, she died.[19]

As a final gesture of respect, Blanche honored her mother's wishes (the costs having been covered in her will) to be buried at Salem Fields Cemetery in Brooklyn, alongside Julius (as well as the Guggenheims and other well-known Jewish families).[20] Her mother left "no less than" five hundred thousand dollars to Irwin and Blanche, to divide equally, with Belmont Garage left to her son exclusively.[21] Though financially taken care of, Blanche was otherwise on her own now, without protection, psychologically, against Alfred and his father.

On the night of the funeral, Blanche cheerlessly dressed for Sam's birthday party. Barely pausing to process the loss of her mother, she prepared to depart for Europe with Alfred, Pat, and his governess, their ship disembarking the next morning. Little information exists about the family's journey. Once they were ashore, the three set off for different destinations, Alfred to London and Pat to join Edwin on an Alpine vacation. Blanche made her typical rounds. Her longest stop was in Paris, a city flush with American as well as foreign writers. In spite of recently giving birth, her French agent Jenny Bradley was continuing her weekly gatherings for authors at her dual home/office on the Île Saint-Louis. The guests might include such current figures as Ernest Hemingway, James Joyce, André Malraux, Gertrude Stein, Alice B. Toklas, or F. Scott Fitzgerald. With the Knopf writer André Gide, Blanche attended Natalie Barney's salon as well, where the atmosphere was less casual but especially welcoming of women.

The publisher returned to New York several months later displaying a new confidence, as if losing her mother had driven her to take a new tack. At board meetings, when Alfred resumed talking over her as if she weren't even at the table, she began interrupting him. Sometimes going too far when nothing seemed to blunt her husband's rudeness, she deliberately nettled him: she'd turn to the man on her left, then her right, speaking softly until Alfred shouted at her to be quiet. Everyone knew what was coming: Alfred went into high dudgeon with whatever Knopf worker was at hand, surrounded by those who looked into their laps in embarrassment. At times, the volatile Alfred antagonized Blanche at editorial meetings, swooping down on her just as she thought there was an all-clear. Ralph Colin, a member of the board for thirty years (he resigned the year Blanche died) and an important figure in New York City's music and arts community, remembered how personal the Knopf fights had become by the time he was there, neither allowing anything to pass. "They were lying in wait for the other to make a misstatement." Yet, Colin added, "we were always sure Alfred was absolutely crazy about Blanche."[22]

Continuing, Colin said that the Knopf marriage wasn't "broken up by her one serious lover, Hubert Hohe. It would have broken up anyway: the hopelessness of Blanche's competition with Alfred. No matter what she could do, he could do it better. He was the name."[23] As Pete Lemay said, "The audience Alfred desperately needed nourished a streak of cruelty in him."[24]

Blanche understood that no one, including her son, dared cross Alfred. She became tense when she and Alfred took authors to lunch and he ordered expensive wine for those guests he was trying to woo, and lesser selections for others at the table. More than forty years later, after Knopf published Julia Child's *Mastering the Art of French Cooking*, Alfred went to dinner at his author's home. When her husband, Paul Cushing Child, proudly picked a wine from his carefully collected cellar, Alfred said not a word, but he "surreptitiously turned his back to him and took notes on the labels." He refused to compliment his host, "and as soon as he was in the living room, he whipped out a cigar." Paul "never got over it."[25] An earlier time, when the Knopfs took the University of California, Berkeley, law professor Farnham Griffiths to lunch, Alfred nudged Griffiths to tell Blanche to put out her Chesterfield: the smoke would ruin everyone's palate for the wine. A gallant man, Griffiths declined, and Alfred signaled the waiter to remove the guest's wineglass.[26]

As William Koshland said of his boss, "He ruled as a potentate" and was "monumentally insensitive."[27] Often it seemed as if Alfred totally forgot about feelings. But not everyone cared. In an interview with the writer Susan Sheehan, the longtime editor in chief of *The New York Times Book Review* Francis Brown praised Alfred, with whom he dined at Purchase a few times a year and could "ask for bourbon or scotch and get it." He hailed his host as a "great publisher," in part because the two men connected without any effort. Blanche had adopted the opposite strategy of Alfred's: she listened intently (her MO obvious in photographs) to her writers, and those she respected from other houses, encouraging them to do all the talking. While such intensity invited easy confidences, it could also imply, to the careless observer, that she was by silent decree inferior to her husband, who was never willing just to listen.[28] Anyone with powers of observation knew that such an assumption about Blanche was as far from the truth as Alfred's would-be omnipotence.

PART TWO

7

HARLEM

I N 1925 KNOPF WAS CELEBRATING ITS TENTH YEAR. The nationally syndicated *Brooklyn Daily Eagle*, one of the nation's top-ten newspapers, sent the reporter Cecelia Garrard to interview Blanche in her office for their Sunday magazine section. Garrard exclaimed over Blanche's unusual position; women had become more common in business, but never as married partners. The reporter asked Blanche how the Knopfs settled differences over acquisitions, for instance. "Smiling," Blanche replied that they discussed their feelings with each other and came to an agreement—or yielded to the spouse better versed in the literature at hand. Often, however, "We compromise . . . and if we couldn't agree, we wouldn't take it."[1]

Though Knopf's current anniversary pamphlet mentioned Blanche more often than the version created five years before, it was still primarily an homage to Alfred. Blanche was determined to insert herself into the story now, creating a mythical confluence between her wedding anniversary and the start of Knopf. "You mean . . . that you took on a husband and a business at the same time? That you said 'I do' to two things at once?" the incredulous reporter asked. "I didn't marry the business," Blanche replied. "I helped start it. I feel far more like a mother than a wife to it."[2]

A confused Garrard switched tactics and pursued the "mother" reference, asking Blanche about Pat, but Blanche kept pushing Knopf publishing. As the alarmed interviewer sensed that Blanche might prove stubborn after all, Garrard assured her audience in a parenthetical comment that the publisher was "no Lucy Stoner." (Lucy Stone, an American suffragist and abolitionist, fought for women to keep their "maiden" names after marriage—her followers were referred to as "Lucy Stoners.") In near frantic prose, Garrard told her readers that Blanche not only shared her husband's name, but was also dressed to dazzle—she didn't even "look bookish. Not a bit— and she had a child as well." Despite Blanche's maneuvers to make her equal status with Alfred clear, the article's title read "Man and His Wife Chief Officers in Publishing Firm."[3]

Sam Knopf seems to have ignored the interview, possibly chagrined that Blanche came off as fearless. During the years the patriarch had been serving as treasurer of Alfred A. Knopf, Inc., he had also continued working as merchandising adviser to the American Exchange-Pacific National Bank and as business manager of *The American Mercury*. To Blanche's suggestion that perhaps Sam had too much on his plate (her worry proved prescient), her father-in-law growled. As the literary agent Lurton Blassingame would remark after Sam's death, he was a man "with a tremendous store of crude, nervous energy, an active, practical mind, and strangely enough, an outcropping vein of sentimentalism."[4] Such sentimentalism was meant to compensate for his petty meanness to underlings—or to those around whom he felt insecure, such as Blanche.

Toward the end of 1925, when Blanche recognized that she needed a distraction from Alfred and his father, she convinced Van Vechten to find her a first-rate teacher of modern dance to prepare for holiday parties. Soon she and five women friends, including the actress Helen Hayes and the author Anita Loos, who had written the bestselling *Gentlemen Prefer Blondes* that year for Liveright, were taking weekly lessons. Working hard to master the Charleston and the newer Lindy Hop at the studio of Charles David, who had co-choreographed *Shuffle Along,* the group soon added the more difficult Black Bottom, which had originated at the Harlem music hall that would later become the Apollo Club. Blanche reveled in the chance to have fun among women she trusted. Emboldened at one dinner party that she gave in her apartment, she mysteriously disappeared, to return in top hat and cane, play a 78 on the Victrola, and perform a medley of all three dances with heady confidence. Alfred applauded vigorously, even as the guests seemed unsure what to think. She knew that Alfred was baffled as well, and that he admired her.

Increasingly, Harlem felt like Blanche's world, not least because she was receiving a steady stream of poetry and prose from writers directed her way by Van Vechten. Only a few months before the year ended, while appearing at a cabaret organized by the National Association for the Advancement of Colored People, Carl had been introduced to the twenty-two-year-old poet Langston Hughes. Later, when an African-American periodical, *Opportunity,* sponsored a literary contest that Hughes won, both Carl and Vachel Lindsay urged him to send his poems to Blanche.

Wowed by the bold originality of the work, she immediately arranged to publish *The Weary Blues*, whose first printing in 1926 would become emblematic of its times. As Hughes's biographer Arnold Rampersad recounts, sales of his books over the years would vary, "from a few hundred when *The Dream Keeper* appeared in 1932 to several thousand on the publication of his *Selected Poems* in 1959. Volumes such as *Fields of Wonder* [1947] and *One-Way Ticket* [1949] did poorly, which probably led Knopf to pass on his *Montage of a Dream Deferred* [Holt, 1951]."[5]

Steadfast, both Blanche and Van Vechten supported Hughes's career throughout his life. (When nine black youths were accused of raping two white women in the infamous Scottsboro case of 1931–37, for instance, Hughes recalled that it was Van Vechten who "encouraged me in my efforts to help publicize [it]." Blanche knew that, more than anyone's, Carl Van Vechten's interest in African-American culture was genuine. In the latter half of the 1920s, she worked with him to bring recognition to black writers. She quickly realized that Langston Hughes spoke to her through his references to a "black man's soul" and as a "Negro" who "ain't got nobody in all this world, / Ain't got nobody but ma self." Such estrangement from "his people," his belief that he was alone, resonated with the still-young woman, well acquainted with loneliness through her own loveless marriage.[6]

Always be true to yourself, Blanche urged Hughes, when he was ambivalent about a novel he wanted to write. In Hughes, Blanche recognized a kindred spirit who depended on books to lead his way, just as she had most of her life. "Literature is a big sea full of many fish. I let down my nets and pulled." Books had been Hughes's salvation when his family dispersed by the time he was six: "I believed in books more than people," he wrote.[7]

For some years Alfred, egged on by Sam, had talked about the London office he felt Knopf should pursue. Now, looking to 1926, the Knopfs geared up to create their physical presence in London. Blanche, who initially thought that Paris would be a more strategic move, became more enthusiastic after she hired the perfect couple to run the new office: the English author/agent Storm Jameson (who had ensured that D. H. Lawrence went to Knopf, and with whom Blanche had bonded upon first meeting several years earlier) and Storm's soon-to-be husband, the historian Guy Chapman. In January 1926, Knopf London officially launched. A year and a half later, at

Sam's insistence on a grander edifice, the company rented a five-story building nearby, at 37 Bedford Street, in the heart of the Bloomsbury district.

Unfortunately, the London office proved to be, as one Knopf employee would later call it, a "folie de grandeur."[8] Storm and Guy resigned within a few years, and though the Knopfs hired someone else to keep the office going, they would shutter it completely in 1931. Sam had been enthusiastic about the office from the beginning, "certain that his son's company would flourish." Once again, he invested in the location's appearance, pouring money into the Bedford Street building while castigating Guy Chapman for his failure to send regular financial statements.[9] But Knopf U.K. was a money pit: by 1928, the publishers had already lost $48,000 on an initial investment of $72,000; ultimately, their net loss would be more than $100,000, as Alfred conceded, not counting the "wasted time and effort."[10] (The subsidiary, officially opened January 4, 1926, was not legally dissolved until 1950.) In Alfred's words, "we had succumbed to the virus of wanting somehow to operate in England."[11] And, he might have added, for allowing Knopf Ltd to be outbid by various British publishers for foreign rights to Knopf's own American books! It was hard, the Knopfs would discover, to run a business from afar, its bosses too many and too often at odds.

In February 1926, however, prospects for doing business in London looked strong, and Blanche was pleased to acquire the popular English novelist Warwick Deeping's *Sorrell and Son* at Storm's recommendation. Her faith in Storm was rewarded straightaway: the book appeared on *Publishers Weekly*'s bestseller list at number three for 1926, and number four for 1927. (Between 1915 and 1934, Zane Grey led the number of bestsellers with nine titles, followed by Deeping and Sinclair Lewis with seven each.)[12] Deeping's novel, based in part on the author's experiences during World War I, portrayed a man who devotes himself to making his son's life a success. Reviewing *Sorrell and Son*, *The New York Times* said that the novel included "pedestrian pages" as well as "pages of power." As its sales figures rose, the *Literary Review* wrote that *Sorrell and Son* was "an absorbing story. Its characters are Dickensian. Mr. Deeping has made it as fascinating as excavation work for a skyscraper."[13]

To advertise the British novel, Blanche, usually in charge of their fiction campaigns, encouraged Sam, whose best instincts in advertising had usually paid off, to take the lead. Having worked his way into yet another job as executive, this time with the advertising agency Barron Collier, Sam convinced that company to donate to Knopf unsold space on the car-card concession Collier owned on the Long Island Railroad and the New York City subways. ("Car cards" are advertising cards mounted inside the passenger cars of trains, subways, and streetcars, at the ends of the car or above the windows, running lengthwise on both sides.) Sam also managed to rent space on an upper Broadway billboard to market the novel. *Sorrell and Son* was Knopf's first book to sell more than a hundred thousand copies, and though Blanche thought the publicity lowbrow, she held her tongue, instead congratulating Sam for his ideas—success was a goal they all endorsed.[14]

Eager to acknowledge Knopf's strong year so far, Blanche threw an early-spring celebration at home. The racially mixed party—in large part due to Van Vechten's "trend-setting articles" in *Vanity Fair*—included such figures as James Weldon Johnson; the novelist Walter White; Serge Koussevitzky; the twenty-five-year-old Aaron Copland; the "it" girl of the day, Aileen Pringle, a quick-witted, glamorous movie star with whom Mencken was having an affair; and Kahlil Gibran. Blanche went all out, even hiring someone to sing songs written by Eskimos.[15] To the publisher's delight, Fannie Hurst showed up: the year before, after being introduced by Van Vechten, Blanche and Hurst had become fast friends.[16]

In June, Blanche and Alfred returned to London to check on the new office. Blanche was pleased that Storm was about to acquire André Gide's "novel within a novel" *Les Faux-Monnayeurs*, or *The*

Counterfeiters.[17] The book's myriad points of view evoked the Cubist art of the era, with numerous homosexual relationships central to the story. Clearly, Storm was in touch with the times, and the Knopfs left for the Continent relieved that their London gamble was proving worthwhile. But Blanche failed to realize how difficult it would be for the three strong Knopf personalities to operate from afar as a team, the future confusion already suggested by the two letterheads they often used interchangeably, the English version lacking the Knopfs' names and positions, substituting instead Guy Chapman and Storm Jameson as managers of the company.[18]

The couple undertook individual whirlwind trips to Paris, Berlin, Leipzig, Munich, Dresden, Vienna, Salzburg, Prague, Budapest, and Biarritz, barely making it to Alfred's brother's wedding on June 24. Just twelve months earlier Edwin had gotten divorced from Mary Ellis, to whom he'd been married for two years; now he wed Mildred Oppenheimer at Les Charmettes, an extravagant villa Mildred's aunt had rented for the summer. A promising playwright herself, Mildred would quickly cede her profession to her husband.

Blanche was eager to return home so that she could concentrate on the "foreign" talent sweeping Harlem. Van Vechten, the "undisputed downtown authority on uptown night life," along with Langston Hughes, had convinced Blanche that the best current writing was being done by those in the New Negro Movement (later known as the Harlem Renaissance).[19] Though ultimately involved in every decision Blanche made concerning "her" Harlem writers, Van Vechten asked that his advisory role be kept confidential. He had too many friends—among them James Weldon Johnson, Countee Cullen, Ethel Waters, Paul Robeson, and even Langston Hughes—who might compete for his attention.

By the fall, Blanche had signed books by Johnson and Nella Larsen, whose short stories addressed the contradictions of class, race, and gender. When the publisher learned that African-Americans still found it hard to buy orchestra seats in theaters and meals in restaurants, she was shocked. She had believed (from the mixed company at her friends' parties and her own) that such rank separation had more or less vanished, at least in Manhattan.

She learned instead that the ugly phrase "nigger heaven," an allusion to the balcony where black audience members sat while whites were seated below, said it all. She decided to thwart Sam Knopf and to support Carl's determination to use the phrase for the title of his new novel, thereby bringing the reality into the open.[20] She knew Sam was scared of offending Knopf's readers or getting pulled into court, but her father-in-law was not supposed to interfere editorially. As for "Henn," as Blanche sometimes now called Mencken, even his fears about the book's "orgy passages" failed to dissuade her.[21] The final decision was Blanche's.

Certainly everyone was abuzz over *Nigger Heaven*, which was released that August and was selling well by October. It was variously reviewed, though Edwin Clark's reaction in *The New York Times* was typical: praising the book and reminding the reader how Van Vechten seldom failed to entertain, he nonetheless suggested that the novelist was not one to go deep.[22] Countee Cullen and W.E.B. DuBois were furious at what they considered the perpetration of vicious stereotypes.[21] Important black leaders and artists were split in their response: some, including Langston Hughes, Nella Larsen, and Wallace Thurman, thought the novel told an essential truth, though Hughes wrote Carl that "the word nigger to colored people of high and low degree is like a red rag to a bull"—regardless of the author's intent. As the scholar Emily Bernard says, "For black Americans, language . . . is a territory." Language is also one's homeland, as the writer Czesław Miłosz, displaced for over forty years, maintains.[24]

In just four months, the book went into ten printings and sold a hundred thousand copies. *Nigger Heaven* rejected concepts such as the "natural primitive," even as it exploited a decadent and exotic

Harlem, celebrated by hip white folks. The front of its dust jacket claimed that "Carl Van Vechten continues to act as historian of contemporary New York life, drawing a curious picture of a fascinating group hitherto neglected by writers of fiction"—the overly refined description probably Alfred's.[25]

The novel focuses on a quiet coffee-colored librarian and the young man who loves her, a hopeful writer, determined to sustain their relationship despite society's racism. They feel lucky to be able to pass as white if they so choose—which they don't. Van Vechten was bold in calling blacks on internecine racism—the ranking of family and friends on their skin tone even as they seemed to value white professionals more than those of color. At a dinner party, a guest claims scornfully that Harlem residents prefer to "go to white lawyers . . . white banks and white insurance companies." *Nigger Heaven*'s heroine, Mary, wearing Narcisse Noir (Carl's inspiration from Blanche) dabbed behind her ears, protests that she gets along fine with all colors and believes everyone in Harlem is treated the same whatever the shade of their skin. The hostess disagrees, and someone seconds her, saying, "A white prostitute can go places where a coloured preacher would be refused admittance . . . Why, even in the Negro theatre they won't engage dark girls."[26]

Clearly, *Nigger Heaven* was meant as a polemic. In Harlem the book was loudly denounced by crowds gathered in libraries, and Van Vechten was hung in effigy at 135th Street and Lenox Avenue. The instant bestseller, despite or because of its press, became a pocket guide to Harlem. Published when Harlem was in vogue for people in the know, its popularity caused Blanche, on her trips to speakeasies, to become annoyed at the tourists she considered déclassé. Carl, who alone could rib Blanche for her hauteur, started addressing her in letters as "Grand Duchess, Sweet Puss" or, using Mencken's invention, "Dearest Grand Duchess Cunegunde Wilhelmina Schwartz."[27]

That Thanksgiving, while Alfred was in Chicago, Blanche threw a splendid autumn party with many of her usual crowd. The Robesons were there, along with the Knopfs' French literary agents, William and Jenny Bradley, and the writer Rebecca West. West and Blanche understood each other instinctively: they both believed in the importance of one's appearance. Back home, West's interactions with the defiantly plain Bloomsbury group made her uncomfortable with their smug rejection of middle-class convention. Like Blanche, Rebecca believed that dressing well showed respect for others, while flaunting plainness was a form of arrogance.

A few days after the social gathering, West wrote Blanche a detailed response to a book by Elinor Wylie and to an article by Mencken, both given her by her new friend. West explained that at times she still found Mencken self-indulgent, going on too long as if "a lazy dawg." Regarding Wylie's first book with Knopf (the December 1926 Book-of-the-Month selection), West loved *The Orphan Angel*, a novel that reimagined the death of Wylie's phantom lover, Percy Bysshe Shelley. In Wylie's version, the Romantic poet, instead of drowning, immigrated to America. Though West ordinarily admired Wylie more for her fine writing than for the almost eerie atmosphere she sometimes created, she found the harsh beauty of at least one of the characters in *The Orphan Angel* as persuasive as a cruel Mayan sculpture.

At yet another late-night party that Blanche gave, West, who eventually wrote that she found the drunken scene dominating Manhattan in those days wearisome, accompanied Carl to Harlem, where the intrepid pair convinced the blues singer Clara Smith to return with them to Blanche's party and sing "Dinah" and "St. Louis Blues." Later they persuaded the tenor Taylor Gordon to perform a round of spirituals. His absence by now no longer conspicuous, Alfred preferred to travel and avoid the frivolous parties of the day, or simply to risk being labeled a misanthrope when he was home. At times almost a recluse, he understood that socializing with the likes of

Van Vechten furthered Knopf connections, but he usually left Blanche to serve as hostess while he went to bed.

For the most part, Alfred dismissed partygoers like Zelda Fitzgerald, who was too agitated to interest him, and whom Blanche also found irritating. Mencken protested, insisting that the Fitzgeralds, introduced to him by Van Vechten, were, when sober, highly intelligent—even though Scott was signed to Charles Scribner's Sons. Dutifully, Blanche invited them to several preconcert parties, but she continued to find the couple lacking: Scott was often morose, she felt, the writer having decided their generation had "grown up to find all gods dead, all wars fought, all faiths in man shaken." Privately, she worried that he might be right.[28]

8

MENCKEN

IN JANUARY 1927, Blanche was in Hollywood. Like other writers and publishers, she was eager to get in with the movie crowd, which was buying up novels for the big screen, it seemed, even before they were reviewed. Back east, Mencken waited impatiently for Blanche to return. Menck had convinced Alfred, who needed a tonsillectomy and minor "internal nose repair," to forgo New York hospitals and seek treatment at cozy Saint Agnes Hospital, near Mencken's Baltimore home (and, though a charity facility, a bastion of Johns Hopkins fellows). Now he found himself called to the phone repeatedly to answer questions from Sam, who was minding the New York office while the other Knopfs were away.[1] Blanche arrived home by the end of the month, in time to relieve her father-in-law of his duties and still get to Boston for the world premiere of Copland's Piano Concerto, conducted by her beloved Koussie.[2]

Back in East Coast working mode by mid-February, she was eager to see the company's poetry list released in early spring. With the first book's title, *Fine Clothes to the Jew*, its author, Langston Hughes, seemed to be (good-naturedly) paying Knopf back for approving Carl Van Vechten's incendiary *Nigger Heaven* the year before. But the same critics who had flinched at Van Vechten's title now also disdained Hughes's. They were offended by the phrase that referred to those who, pressed for cash, sold their best clothes to Jewish pawn shops.[3] Critics generally disliked Hughes's new work, finding it insulting to virtually everyone: the headline for the *Pittsburgh Courier* review was "Langston Hughes' Book of Poems Trash," while the *New York Amsterdam News* went with "Langston Hughes—the Sewer Dweller."[4]

Eventually even Hughes regretted the title, deciding that "it was confusing and many Jewish people did not like it." Not surprisingly, Sam Knopf had vehemently objected to it. Van Vechten, still indignant at Sam's earlier argument against his own *Nigger Heaven*, called Sam's interference "a pretty piece of impertinence"—and Blanche deferred to her friend; thus *Fine Clothes to the Jew* stuck.[5] Though not particularly successful in sales or critical reception, this collection, along with *The Weary Blues*, would make Hughes's reputation. Arnold Rampersad has equated *Fine Clothes to the Jew* with Walt Whitman's *Leaves of Grass* in its significance "within the Western canon."[6]

That spring Blanche hoped to listen to the radio with Alfred as Charles Lindbergh, on May 21, landed at Le Bourget Airport outside Paris, following his two-day flight from New York City. Blanche thought that being together while history was made would be a rare occasion that the couple might celebrate. But Alfred had planned his Berlin business trip for mid-May and was out of town for Lindbergh's triumph. Blanche instead heard the news and watched the subsequent ticker tape parade on Fifth Avenue with Van Vechten. She would arrive in France a few weeks later, where she had managed to schedule a few days with Alfred at Cap d'Antibes, not too far from Jenny Bradley's vacation home. The Knopfs had been civil to each other of late, though Blanche was aware that their lack of time together underwrote such courtesy.

In New York, there were separate living arrangements for the couple, allowing Blanche her freedom. The Purchase house was in no way to her taste, its dark wooden interior reminding her just how much she disliked its design. She saw that it could be a great spot for overnight guests, however, especially city writers thrilled at the prospect of a weekend in the country. Now she thought about furnishing both domiciles. To her surprise, Cap d'Antibes turned out to be a perfect place to initiate the process: "Arthur Versay," much respected by wealthy Americans for his expertise in fine paintings and porcelain, happened to be in nearby Cannes, advising a select group from New York about furnishing their homes with antiques. Blanche believed his taste impeccable and hired him at once. Roaming the shops in the coastal villages, she found a few white French provincial chairs to mix with her prized modern ones, and some sturdy side tables for the heavy look Alfred preferred for the Purchase house, an odd blend of stolid Jacobean and Early American furniture. "Versay" would sit quietly in a corner and, with a subtle movement of his chin, signal his approval or rejection of the piece Blanche was examining.[7]

Still abroad in July, Blanche was relieved when raves appeared for the two-volume translation of Thomas Mann's *The Magic Mountain* she'd commissioned, using Helen T. Lowe-Porter again. (As usual with translations, one reviewer lauded Lowe-Porter's rendition, while another faulted it.) Though a difficult novel with long philosophical digressions, the story of a temporary home for consumptives, set in the small Alpine valley of Davos, fascinated critics. Even when Edwin Muir of *The Nation* complained of its "wearisome passages," he admitted they often proved "the most fascinating"—if one had the energy to read the sometimes interminable sentences. The *Boston Evening Transcript* called *The Magic Mountain* "one of the greatest and most moving books of our time." *The Times Literary Supplement* claimed that "not one sentence of this vast corpus is insignificant or irrelevant," with Mann possessing "the true epic form." Indeed, Mann could have titled it *An Anatomy of Melancholy*, according to *The Saturday Review of Literature*, if Robert Burton's book about the woes of the world hadn't "preempted the title" in 1621.[8]

Though she had immediately recognized the book's power, Blanche confessed to Mencken that she found its style tedious. He agreed, acknowledging that no matter how gifted the translator Blanche hired, certain rhythms and repetitions, especially Mann's, weren't meant for English.

When they returned home, Blanche drove out to Purchase to see the progress on the house, where she was particularly impressed by the grounds. Alfred's friend Frank Bailey had advised him on landscaping and had donated a near forest to the property as well, counting on Knopf's assistance in return, when Bailey needed advice on his business pamphlets. Frank dispatched three designers to plant trees and geometrically spaced shrubs on Alfred's seven and a half acres. Though Blanche was fond of Frank, she knew his generosity was connected to Sam Knopf: Frank, a major real estate agent in the boroughs, had become friends with Sam when Alfred's father tried but failed to emulate Frank's business tactics in real estate.

Unlike Jim Rosenberg, who had helped Alfred finance the property and whom Blanche disliked because of his conservative politics, Frank impressed her. An amateur horticulturist with his own arboretum in Locust Valley, on the North Shore of Long Island, he also had a magnificent residence in Essex House, on Central Park South. Its expanse, on a rare day, allowed a view from the Statue of Liberty to West Point. Blanche also enjoyed joking about the unusual pantry of medicine bottles she and Frank each maintained. Frank, who had bequeathed millions to his alma mater, Union College, would also be a great help if Pat, not much of a student, wasn't admitted to Princeton, his first (and unlikely) choice.

Anticipating the need for a quid pro quo, Alfred had offered to publish Bailey's diatribe against current income tax laws.

Soon Blanche was tending to two September 1927 publications, whose disparity, she commented, only proved Knopf's flexibility. Willa Cather's *Death Comes for the Archbishop* was released to great critical praise. Blanche, enthusiastic about Cather's novel from the first, appreciated that the seemingly old-fashioned author was experimenting with a new form for her book, the deft inclusion of historical figures within her fiction. Two years earlier, *The Professor's House* had also shown Cather attempting, if not successfully, to move her fiction from its traditional mooring to something that mixed past and present. Her subsequent novel would reap the rewards of her earlier efforts. *Death Comes for the Archbishop* portrays two well-meaning priests, one French, one from the Midwest, sent to help the Vatican create parishes in the territory recently ceded to America. A cadre of priests has been living among and supposedly tending to the Native Americans, especially the Hopi and Navajo. But many of the religious figures fear, correctly, the end of the free reign they've been given to take advantage of the population instead of caring for the people.

Cather based the tale on the life of a priest who founded a Santa Fe church—but she populated it with the fictional presence of Kit Carson, Stephen Foster, Saint Augustine, and James Fenimore Cooper, among others. "In the first place, this is not a novel. In the second place it is one of the most superb pieces of literary endeavor this reviewer has ever read regardless of language or nation," one reviewer wrote. *The Nation* said that "it is a book to be read slowly, to be savored from paragraph to paragraph." A less enthusiastic reader complained of the book's "perplexed . . . intention." The very ambiguity of genre applauded elsewhere was criticized here: "It is not really a novel; and since it seems left in a halfway condition, one wishes it were."[9] Cather was stretching herself and her readers, refusing to submit to strict genre requirements. And for some readers,

Death Comes for the Archbishop was even a love story about two men, Bishop Latour and Father Vaillant.

If Cather's novel had been a commercial risk, the other big autumn book was a sure hit—at least in retrospect, Blanche said wryly. Logan Clendening's *The Human Body*, a forthright exploration of physiology, was instantly popular. Throughout the twenties, studies of the brain and anatomy had filled the marketplace, though the majority were centered on psychoanalysis or women's reproductive systems. *The Human Body* instead gave a straightforward overview of both male and female anatomy. Several years earlier, Mencken had read Clendening's medical textbook and felt sure that the physician could distill his professional knowledge into a book for the layperson. With Mencken serving as Knopf's ambassador, the doctor had quickly agreed.

Blanche decided now to build on Knopf's early, barely activated Borzoi Mystery Stories, to encompass dark, stylish detective fiction. She was impressed by manuscripts that had reached her of late, often through their beginnings with the magazine *The Black Cat*. Before she could discuss with Alfred her plan to rejuvenate the series, however, the couple was again at odds, and she put the project on hold. Alfred, complaining that the Publishers' Lunch Club discriminated against Jews, prepared to sponsor his own "Book Table" in 1928—and proceeded to exclude Blanche or any other woman from joining. Humiliated and fuming at her omission, Blanche chain-smoked her Chesterfields, as she uncharacteristically snapped at a reporter that she had no desire to be inside with all those cigars anyway. Nor with the spittoons, which even Alfred kept in his office, copying his father. Joe Lesser tried to distract her with strong financial figures—sales of $1,213,000, putting the company's profits at $61,595 (approximately $800,800 in 2015 currency)—but Blanche's anger was unappeased.

The timing was perfect when she received a letter from her friend the pianist Myra Hess, with her irresistible joie de vivre, about a possible trip to the States. To Mencken Blanche jested that maybe Myra could marry him when she arrived; he had been taken with her during her earlier visit. At the very least, Blanche expected to dine with him by herself before Myra arrived and captured his attention. It was time for her and Menck to get some more fabulous chicken paprikash, which she had enjoyed the last time the two had been out together. Blanche wanted to stem rumors that she wasn't eating.

Such gossip, however, wasn't far from the truth. Continuing to keep her weight down to that of the young flappers, Blanche played with her food rather than downing it. By 1928, she was on her cleansing diet again, a part of her regimen for several more years. Often she ate only a few celery stalks and olives in a day, and the occasional piece of fish. When Myra Hess confirmed that she was indeed coming, Blanche decided to fast for the next week, then eat normally with Hess. The publisher loved looking like one of the gaunt Parisian women who frequented the Café de Paris or Café de Flore.

By the 1930s, if she didn't count every calorie, Blanche sensed the ghost of her overweight parents and the memory of herself as a zaftig high school girl always on a diet. Within a few years she would visit Mencken's doctor, Benjamin Baker, at Johns Hopkins, whom she told, "Keep me in good health and keep me from getting fat." Decades after Blanche's death, the ninety-year-old physician would remember using words like "crazy" and "ridiculous" in response to her requests, including reducing her weight to seventy-five pounds, which would have caused her "to throw her arms around" him if he'd succeeded.[10] Mencken suspected that her newest diet aid (probably an amphetamine) was agitating her, and that such concern about her weight was exacerbated by living in the metropolis.

Half teasing, he suggested to Blanche that Knopf move to Baltimore, a much more reasonable place than New York, where commerce was becoming impossible and where "in five or ten years not a publisher will be left."[11] In contrast to New York, he joked, "there is plenty of music in Baltimore, but not too much. The beer is good. A sound house, with plenty of room, costs less than half as much as a New York flat. There are no subways or elevated lines. The taxis are clean and cheap. New York is only four hours away. I throw out the idea!"[12] But Baltimore was a southern city, and Henry knew that Blanche would never leave Manhattan. She thrived on modernity, and the energy of Manhattan revitalized her. Others might have bemoaned the innovative builders whose visions of the new included demolishing the "old"—including Mrs. Cornelius Vanderbilt's Fifth Avenue mansion—but Blanche couldn't wait to see what rose in its stead.

9

A WELL OF LONELINESS

IN THE MIDST OF PREPARING THE FALL 1928 LIST, Blanche received from Scott Fitzgerald a "full conjugation" of the verb "to cocktail."[1] Scott had heard from Mencken that she was downing a few too many Manhattans meant to pass for lunch, and cleverly passed on the concern—of both men. On February 10, when Blanche was suddenly seized by a stabbing abdominal pain, she figured the alcohol had caught up with her. Sidney Jacobs, Knopf's recently hired production manager, urged her to eat something to stave off what he felt sure was hunger, but the knife-like sensations only grew worse. Finally, she took a cab to Lenox Hill Hospital, where doctors performed an emergency appendectomy and found a large tumor that, fortunately, turned out to be benign.

Her spirits were briefly revived by a letter brought from the office that had been plucked from the slush pile. Blanche was struck by the name Dashiell Hammett, having heard of him before, though she couldn't recollect where. Soon she remembered: Hammett, an ex–Pinkerton detective, had published short stories in Mencken's *The Smart Set*, coedited with George Jean Nathan for a few years, and, more recently, in *The Black Mask*, the pulp fiction magazine Mencken and Nathan had begun in 1920 (and sold two years later). Boldly accompanied by a manuscript, Hammett's letter to Blanche explained that he wanted to prepare two novels for Knopf's release. The timing was perfect, given Blanche's plan to revive the Borzoi Mystery Stories. Reading the submissions while she was propped up in her hospital bed, she was quickly convinced of the treasure she had just been delivered. With Hammett's confidence further motivating her, Blanche revitalized Knopf's mystery fiction line, creating the "tough-guy crime novel." As the two-time Edgar Award winner Andrew Klavan writes, novelists including "Hammett, James Cain, and Raymond Chandler [all Blanche's finds] . . . made one of our nation's most significant contributions to world literature, an enduring genre as American as jazz."[2]

Her excitement was short-circuited, however, by a bout of depression when she returned from the hospital after her abdominal surgery. Perhaps, as friends suspected, her erratic eating habits had worn her down. But Carl Van Vechten, while visiting her at Lenox Hill, had discovered the probable reason for her intense sadness, though he was pledged to keep it a secret. The pianist Benno Moiseiwitsch, with whom Blanche was having a passionate affair, had called on her at Lenox Hill to say he was leaving on a yearlong concert tour. Blanche cried for an entire day, Van Vechten remembered. It was only after she phoned him several times, going on at great length about the pianist's upcoming trip, that he had realized Benno was Blanche's lover.[3]

Deliberately provocative, Blanche would eventually name two dogs after Moiseiwitsch and Jascha Heifetz—supposedly for the animals' attempts to "harmonize" with the men's recordings. Although Blanche's handsome musicians were physically ardent and enthusiastic lovers, they were emotionally cold. Like the future CIA head

Allen Dulles, who once demanded that he and his lover, Mary Bancroft (a friend of Blanche's through her Washington connections), make love hastily on a sofa to "'clear his head' before an important meeting," so Blanche's musicians expended their primary passion on their music, using what was left over on women other than their wives.[4]

Now Benno, during a hiatus between marriages that had allowed him to pay especial attention to Blanche, would be gone.[5] When Alfred visited her in the hospital, Blanche had rallied, modeling her floppy flower hair bow for the photograph her husband took.[6] Dressed in a pale robe, she held to her chest two white stuffed animals, a unicorn and a cat, given to her by Moiseiwitsch.

Blanche rarely admitted discomfort, physical or emotional, no matter how bad she felt. At the same time, she was a soft touch for any sign that someone—especially Alfred—cared about her. He was so seldom affectionate that it took but the smallest gesture for Blanche to stop her sniping. Showing off her gifts to her husband was meant to suggest to him how much she enjoyed receiving presents, and how others—specifically lovers—liked giving them to her. For all her marital disappointments, Blanche still wanted Alfred's heart.

In May 1928, the publisher's depression culminated in a "nervous breakdown," resulting in a hospital stay at Dr. Dengler's Sanatorium in Baden-Baden. She shared her "situation" with the Mann translator Helen Lowe-Porter, with whom Blanche had become friends. Lowe-Porter wrote her, "You had been doing too much and had too much on your mind. Don't wear yourself out."[7] But there seemed no other way: Knopf depended on her. While Alfred was able to ignore the business when he needed to relax, Blanche seemed afraid to appear anything but indispensable. The entire time she was at the sanatorium, "despite her exhaustion . . . she continued co-managing all aspects of the London office."[8]

She had chosen Dengler's through a recommendation from her acquaintance the leftist writer Louise Bryant, who had retreated to the sanatorium after her (second) husband, John Reed, died in 1920.

Bryant had returned now when her third marriage was in peril, and she had attempted suicide. Van Vechten photographed the two women at an earlier dinner party, their facial expressions suggesting the intensity of their conversation. Louise had surely repeated to Blanche much of what she told the editor of *The Liberator* (the major American Marxist newspaper) about Reed's death: that he suffered a great deal of pain and fought bravely for his life. Reed's story affected Blanche deeply, and when the writer said she was returning to Baden-Baden that summer, Blanche decided to go as well. The two had discussed the illness Louise was now suffering: Dercum's disease, which came with "painful, subcutaneous tumors" and sudden, inexplicable weight gain. Formerly a shapely woman, she was now showing signs of what she told Blanche was elephantiasis, though she wore elaborate lace mantillas to hide her swollen arms. Given that Blanche had been constantly fighting extra pounds ever since Pat's birth, Louise's previously unexplained obesity must have filled her with dread.

Even at the sanatorium, Blanche dressed stylishly. One photograph shows her wearing her beautifully printed silk robe designed by Erté, the Russian-born Art Deco designer. In 1928, Erté created costumes for endless revues, from the Folies-Bergère in Paris to George White's *Scandals* in New York, for which George Gershwin's early work was used in the 1920–24 editions. Blanche had managed to take a bit of her Manhattan sensibility even to the quiet mountain retreat.

The two women inevitably discussed a provocative book for which Blanche was negotiating American rights. *The Well of Loneliness*, Radclyffe Hall's novel about lesbian love, was of particular interest to Louise, who would be divorced in two years due to gossip about her own sexual affinity for women. Louise had heard of *The Well of Loneliness*, to be released in July, three months before Virginia Woolf's novel *Orlando*, whose protagonist undergoes a sex change. When Knopf's English office had told Blanche in April of the forthcoming Radclyffe Hall publication, she immediately wrote Sir Newman

Flower, the Knopfs' old associate (whose wife had shrugged off Blanche's suicide attempt seven years earlier), now serving as Hall's English agent. Flower let her know that their mutual friend Carl Brandt was representing U.S. rights. Blanche had moved fast after reading the manuscript, and by April 16, when she received typed and bound copies, she had already made a date to meet with Hall to finalize a contract. Blanche would publish the book soon after the U.K. edition appeared, she proudly told Louise Bryant.[9] Publisher and author both knew that the novel would create controversy, and they welcomed it.

The sex researcher Havelock Ellis, who said he had recognized the attractive, self-possessed Hall as a lesbian upon first meeting her at a party, wrote her that he would look forward to providing a critical blurb for her book, due to his intense interest in the subject. Unlike the punishing attitudes of earlier sexologists, such as Richard von Krafft-Ebing, Ellis was of the new school, well acquainted with Freud's theories of the bisexual nature of men and women. Freud's basic concept of human sexuality, though different from Ellis's, was equally humane for its time.

Blanche, who had long enjoyed thinking outside the boundaries of polite society, was as excited about publishing *The Well of Loneliness* as she'd been about any manuscript. It was likely her reading about psychoanalysis and sexuality, during an era when both were intellectually serious subjects—as well as the language of the speakeasies— that motivated her to publish Hall's novel.

That summer, after leaving Baden-Baden, Blanche met the author for a celebratory lunch at London's elegant Maison Basque. But before Blanche could get her hands on the printed and gathered sheets promised her by the English publisher, John Lane, what many consider the most important twentieth-century novel about lesbianism was derailed by the British censors on grounds of immorality. When Blanche protested, the Knopfs were warned that a legal conflict backed by the forces of the vice fighter John Sumner could literally bankrupt their company. Scoffing at the accusations of obscenity, but fearful of losing costly court battles, the couple didn't want to risk fighting and instead accepted an offer from a relatively new publisher, Covici-Friede, to pay for the available sheets and take ownership of the manuscript.

Blanche wrote John Lane that the four professionals her firm had paid to read the novel agreed its writer was gifted and could probably anticipate a "distinguished career." She commended Hall's ability to "deal with a very delicate subject and one that might be regarded by many as taboo . . . without offense." Nonetheless, a disappointing conclusion followed:

> *On August 19 the book was viciously attacked by a leading article in the (London)* Sunday Express *. . . and four days later John Lane withdrew the book. We . . . have come to the conclusion definitely not to publish [it] . . . It would be purchased by many as a pornographic work pure and simple . . . It seems a great pity that the fate of* THE WELL OF LONELINESS *had been what it has been, but we consider that . . . much harm could possibly be done by our permitting the book to appear in print.*[10]

After *The Well of Loneliness* was banned, Radclyffe Hall gave a reading to a packed audience at Natalie Barney's Paris salon at 20, rue Jacob. A year earlier, Barney had decided to feature only women writers at her newly formed Académie des Femmes, among them Colette, Gertrude Stein, Mina Loy, and Djuna Barnes. Blanche continued to go to Barney's events, accompanied by Jenny Bradley—who with her husband, William, was herself increasingly respected for their Parisian salon at 18, rue du Bac. It seems likely that Blanche was introduced to Ezra Pound, whom she would sign to Knopf, at Barney's house. The two had often been present at the pointedly feminine salon, with its red damask floors and ceiling painted with nymphs—or at the Bradleys.

A regular reader of British *Vogue*, Blanche must have swallowed hard when the magazine's fashion editor, Madge Garland, interviewed Radclyffe Hall, then "the most scandalous woman in London." *The Well of Loneliness* was "never to be seen on anyone's table or bookshelf but read by all in secret."[11] By September 1930, after it was finally cleared of John Sumner's charges of obscenity by the New York Court of Special Sessions, *The Well of Loneliness*, published by Covici-Friede, had sold a hundred thousand copies.[12]

At least Blanche would soon have a room of her own. During the fall of 1928, the house in Purchase, less than thirty miles from Manhattan, was finally finished. Blanche would maintain her own Midtown apartment of "ample size" on the third floor at 400 East Fifty-Seventh Street, giving up the Fifth Avenue apartment. She may have been emboldened to live separately by Van Vechten's wife, Fania, who insisted that she and her husband maintain two apartments, side by side, at 101 Central Park West. When Carl got drunk he would sometimes chase Fania with a knife, so the actress felt that living apart was the sensible thing to do.[13] In any event, Blanche's decision to live apart from Alfred while staying in the marriage was irregular but not unheard-of. During this postwar period various unorthodox household arrangements were played out among Natalie Barney's French contingent as well as the English Bloomsbury crowd—but they were not an everyday occurrence in Blanche's American world.[14]

Alfred's enthusiasm for the country (as Westchester County was then considered), with Blanche a born-and-bred city girl, became the most convenient way to explain their separate living arrangements. Blanche would stay in Purchase a few weekends a month when Pat was home from school. Friends found Alfred's long-awaited edifice gloomy, its hard, backless wooden benches making for uncomfortable seats at the dining table. To some, it seemed as if the new house was meant to be intimidating.

For her own apartment, Blanche was inspired by the salons she had attended in Paris. She had decided an eclectic, inviting mode was most attractive. Once again, however, her father-in-law "interfered and insisted on my living way beyond my means in a very expensive place"—which Sam subsidized, she recalled. "Mrs. Knopf," she wrote, speaking of herself in Sam's voice, "could not live in a simple place but had to look like what she never could be or wanted to be . . . I gave up," she continued, "entertained on a large scale and lived this way for years until I moved into a small apartment of my own."[15]

Until Blanche got her "small apartment," living in a style paid for by Sam was surely not as difficult as she remembered, except for her unruly staff: according to the Knopf assistant Toni Pasquale, Sam hired her two servants, a drunken cook, and a surly French maid, in a spacious home "all in white—the carpet, the bedrooms and linen, the curtains, the walls, the bathrooms and towels: she used white paint and white peonies, *nuit et jour*, everything an almost defiant shiny white, a color whose feminine form in French was her own name. Always one deep red rosebud in a white porcelain vase took pride of place, bought daily at a bodega or imported by a florist during the winter," Pasquale remembered.[16] That "defiant shiny Blanc" alongside a bold stroke of scarlet played to Blanche's love of extremes, cultivated in 1915 at the Panama-Pacific International Exposition in San Francisco, with its explosion of color in the Tower of Jewels set among neutral shades of architecture tending toward the neoclassical. Again, Blanche took her pleasure from mixing things up till she hit upon the exact note she was after.

10

HER OWN WOMAN

B LANCHE WAS SADDENED, as the end of 1928 approached, to hear that forty-three-year-old Elinor Wylie, with whom she'd had lunch the previous week, had died of a stroke. In June Knopf had published Wylie's third book of poetry, *Trivial Breath*, and in 1929 they would release posthumously her collection *Angels and Earthly Creatures*—a series of nineteen sonnets that Wylie had already distributed privately. From the start of their acquaintance, Blanche had felt a kinship with Wylie and envied her sexual freedom. Like Blanche, the poet lived in her own apartment away from her husband. Wylie's supple intelligence and the care she took to look good were akin to Blanche's own, though Wylie's vanity was neurotic. Friends knew to compliment her as the most beautiful woman in view, or she became hysterical, bursting into tears or running out of the room.[1] Even Blanche had tensed up whenever Wylie mentioned her "hallucination of being a reincarnated [Percy Bysshe] Shelley," the publisher highly skeptical of such beliefs.[2] At the private memorial in Elinor's apartment, Blanche talked with their mutual friend Edna St. Vincent Millay, along with Carl Van Doren, one of the nine or ten mourners who most admired Wylie's poetry.

Pained at Wylie's death, Blanche was, on the other hand, happy to be rid of Joseph Hergesheimer. Hergesheimer had lost his cachet by the time the New York Stock Exchange crashed, and the Knopfs' London friend Desmond Flower acquired him from Knopf, a change too late to be worthwhile for anyone. Even the zany Anita Loos warned Flower that despite Hergesheimer's real if dated talent, the short, corpulent writer was a target for jokes. The forty-eight-year-old, long-married Hergesheimer presented himself as a "Casanova" as he pursued "vacuous socialites."[3] A Philadelphia judge wrote the Knopfs that he had long realized that Hergesheimer was a "significant grotesque. Essentially a buffoon, he posed as a gentleman from Philadelphia . . . I can imagine that everyone who ever knew the man sooner or later came to hate him, personally."[4]

If Hergesheimer's fame was at an end, the author Blanche had discovered in her slush pile while in the hospital was pursuing his. Working with Dashiell Hammett, an alcoholic, had been difficult from the start. Blanche had found him "a singularly reserved man, laconic and normally undemonstrative."[5] Later the publisher would receive tributes for her efforts: "It was Blanche Knopf, Alfred's wife, who would see Hammett's promise as a writer and would act as editor for his first book," Richard Layman, one of his biographers, writes.[6] William Nolan, another Hammett biographer, asserts that Blanche was a "brilliant woman with a keen appreciation of good writing." Nolan believes that Blanche "had a cool, knowledgeable eye" that allowed her to "influence the careers of the best of the hard-boiled writers [including Raymond Chandler and James M. Cain]."[7]

Often too drunk or broke to meet publishing deadlines, Hammett proved harder to work with than any of Blanche's previous authors. Luckily, by now Blanche had learned that an editor's resolve was just what lackadaisical writers needed. She must have known that in Hammett she had discovered the real article, a writer who wrote prose as clean and spare as that of Hemingway, to whom he would most often be compared, and with a voice that, as his biographer Diane Johnson says, "spoke of a personal code of ethics in a modern world whose institutions were corrupt."[8] Like Hemingway, who was admired by Hammett, the ex-detective needed constant babysitting to keep him sober—and to put his pen to paper. When Hammett attended Blanche's parties, he inevitably misbehaved. One night he got so drunk that Blanche had to lock him in the bathroom to allow the other guests to listen to Myra Hess play the piano.[9]

At the Knopfs' fiftieth wedding anniversary, five years after Hammett's death, Blanche would recall telling Hammett that Knopf would publish *Red Harvest* only if he'd "cut out 75 murders and he agreed."[10] She believed his strength lay partly in his terseness. As the Hammett biographer Sally Cline says, Hammett's "held-in sentences . . . convey male menace: 'Babe liked Sue. Vassos liked Sue. Sue liked Babe. Vassos didn't like that.'"[11] By the end of 1930, Hammett's reviews "were brilliant," with Knopf running an advertisement claiming that Hammett was "Better than Hemingway."[12] The writer was "recognized as an innovator in the hard-boiled school."[13] Indeed, Knopf's own André Gide would say that Hammett was America's "worthiest novelist"—because he never corrupted his art with morality, in spite of the ex-detective's personal code.[14] When Knopf had first published Hammett's *Red Harvest* on February 1, 1929, *The New York Times* seemed unaware of the book or its author. Vindication came eighty years later, when *Red Harvest* appeared on the 2010 *Time* magazine list of the hundred best English-language novels published between 1923 and 2005.

Now, a mere six months after the release of *Red Harvest*, Blanche had to get *The Dain Curse* into shape. Unlike the earlier book, *The Dain Curse*, published July 19, 1929, would immediately receive a *New York Times* review, lauding Hammett's ability to "put people down as they were, and he made them talk and think in the language they customarily used for these purposes." Praised for his realism, the detective writer "allowed murder to occur on, not offstage, and the book was fast-moving if intricately and realistically plotted"— though, as Blanche realized, disjointed, like the author himself.[15] Hammett, who seemed to those who knew him to have been the model for the main character in *The Dain Curse*—tall, lean, neat dresser, mustache, and a penchant for gambling—occupied too much of Blanche's time with his need for close supervision. How, she wondered, could she convince him to keep writing and forgo the bottle?

While working on *The Maltese Falcon*, Hammett started asking for frequent advance payments against his royalties, and Blanche decided he would have to show her what he'd written before she'd give him more money. She disliked treating him like a child, but she believed the book would be a breakthrough in the genre. The author was using the third person rather than his usual first-person voice, the change allowing him more authorial distance as well as a convincing new tone.

Blanche was sidetracked from her author when she tripped over a branch that had fallen near her office and broke her collarbone. Despite her worries over Hammett, her slow-to-heal fracture, and her preoccupation with Knopf's autumn list, the publisher, like so many women writers (including Willa Cather, who recommended Virginia Woolf to friends), could have only rejoiced when, on October 24, the Hogarth Press (established by Woolf and her husband, Leonard, in 1917) released Woolf's *A Room of One's Own*. Blanche had long been interested in Woolf's work (her writing first appeared soon after Blanche had graduated from Gardner), especially now, after having been forced to forgo Radclyffe Hall's novel. Based on a series of lectures Woolf had delivered at two women's colleges at the University of Cambridge the previous year, *A Room of One's Own* spoke of the literal and figurative spaces women writers needed—and deserved— if they were ever to achieve on the scale that men did. Of particular interest to Blanche was Woolf's discussion of the critic Desmond

MacCarthy's dismissal of Rebecca West, a friend to both women. West had responded to MacCarthy's blast at her feminism calmly: "I myself have never been able to find out what feminism is; I only know that people call me a feminist whenever I express sentiments that differentiate me from a doormat or a prostitute."[16]

A desire to be her own woman was more than ever at the fore of Blanche's thinking, but, paradoxically, such an inclination demanded perpetual dieting and smoking, too. Though as the twenties ended, many American women welcomed softer angles, Blanche did not. According to Pat, she began seeing a "Viennese diet doctor" in 1929 and was "put on a diet that eventually destroyed her," along with her "thousand organic ailments."[17]

Alfred seemed preoccupied with relocating Knopf's offices to Purchase: Mencken was right; the future lay outside big cities, he decided. Traffic jams and the costs of outfitting huge populations with utilities and water meant that urban centers had reached their limit.[18] Clearly, the Knopfs should move their business to Westchester County. Van Vechten found such a measure ill-advised, especially in light of his dire prediction for the future of publishing itself. He quoted the novelist and his fellow midwesterner Booth Tarkington's belief that "the public had practically ceased to read owing to radio, talking pictures and what not . . . When television in the home [became] practical no one would ever open a book."[19]

Such worries struck Blanche as groundless, even silly, and she believed they evidenced fears stirred by the stock market crash. Knopf publishing and the profession itself still looked to be in good shape. The December holiday season, including the treasurer's report that all was well with the business, put her in a great mood for the New Year's gathering at the Heifetzes. For years a crowd would gather around 5:00 a.m. at the violinist's Park Avenue penthouse, which he and his wife were renting for $25,000 a year (equivalent in

2015 to about $333,000). There they would listen to Heifetz and several of his friends perform.

Jascha's wife, Florence Vidor Heifetz, the beautiful silent-film actress previously married to King Vidor, recalled years later how "fun and gay" their parties were: "It didn't matter if people were tired or drunk. We'd open the curtains and dawn would break. Then we'd have breakfast—and ping pong. Gershwin and Jascha loved to play ping pong." By the second or third holiday celebration at the Heifetzes, Blanche and Jascha had become lovers—while both Florence and Alfred apparently looked the other way.[20]

In spite of the crash weighing down much of New York City— along with the rest of the country and even the world—life remained sweet for Knopf during the first months of 1930, with Blanche returning from her buying trip abroad to enthusiastic reviews of *The Maltese Falcon*. An immediate success, the book was reprinted seven times that first year. At times the praise seemed unending, with everyone agreeing that "it was the best American detective story to date." *The New Republic* critic Donald Douglas claimed that Hammett's novels showed readers "the absolute distinction of real art."[21] Van Vechten chimed in, surely at Blanche's request: "Hammett is raising the detective story to that plane to which Alexandre Dumas raised the historical novel."[22]

Hammett celebrated by giving himself a makeover. He had his striking gray hair styled into a pompadour and grew a mustache that he would keep for most of his life, he got his rotten teeth fixed, and he started showing off his lean body in close-fitting clothes. His friends thought he had become a dandy.[23] *The Maltese Falcon* helped to protect Knopf from the financial disaster the rest of the country faced. In late June, Warner Bros. offered Knopf $8,500 for the film rights, signaling the strong possibility that a movie would be made. When the producer David O. Selznick, then working for Paramount, heard about the Warner proposal, he bid higher and won the rights himself.

Blanche spent a fair amount of that spring in Mencken's company, often in Baltimore. But she sensed that their collegial forays into the surrounding countryside were coming to an end; rumors were flying about several women who'd caught her friend's eye. Still, Mencken wrote Blanche to prepare for a Hoboken pilgrimage with Van Vechten in late April, when the three friends would meet first at the Algonquin at 6:00, "take a small stimulant," and then set upon their journey.[24]

Soon Henry confirmed his otherwise closely guarded secret. He and Sara Haardt were to be married at the end of the summer. Mencken had courted her sporadically for seven years, while continuing to enjoy his bachelorhood. Not the beauty that his other girlfriends had been, Sara, who had led (unsuccessful) efforts in her home state of Alabama to ratify the Nineteenth Amendment, met Mencken in 1923, when she spoke to him after his lecture at Goucher College. (An English professor at the school, she wrote newspaper reviews, articles, and essays.) Even as the couple announced their engagement, their happiness was shadowed: doctors had told them that the tubercular Sara had at most five years to live.

But there was no talk of mortality on August 27, 1930, when, a week after the couple got their license at City Hall (with Mencken blushing furiously while newspapers' cameras flashed), they married. The young woman from Mobile had gone to school with Zelda Sayre (with whom she would remain friends until the Fitzgeralds' drinking became untenable).

Mencken's choice of a southerner confused those not attuned to his contrarianism, whereby he sought to point out the hypocrisy within everyone: he was just as likely to castigate the American South for its racism as pluck its fairest flower; he was as quick to excoriate African-Americans for what he considered their laziness and Jews for their preoccupation with money. Readers were surprised that Mencken, who had frequently joked about the hopelessness of marriage, was actually taking this step.

To avoid a spectacle, only their closest relatives and two fellow journalists from Mencken's *Evening Sun* attended the wedding, though reporters were three deep on the pavement outside. Sara, carrying a spray of green orchids, wore a beige crepe ensemble and a brown felt cloche hat. Originally, Menck had asked friends to loan him a coat, but after a local minister suggested that the groom might do well to "put on plenty of dog," he sprung for a pinstriped business suit, much to Blanche's relief. A few days later, on their honeymoon in Halifax, the benedict wrote Blanche that while Sara was "out combing the beach for shells," he was writing a piece for *The Evening Sun* on the malt liquor situation in Quebec. Blanche immediately told Van Vechten that she sensed Sara and Henry were "blissfully happy."[25] From the beginning of their relationship, the two had known when to give each other space and when to create a cocoon for two. In notes to friends, Sara wrote, "I have the one perfect husband."[26]

The new couple missed a slew of parties while they were gone, including a cocktail party given in Manhattan for Blanche by the actress (and later Dame) Judith Anderson, its guests including Condé Nast, Groucho Marx, and Bennett Cerf. And in November, Sinclair Lewis won the Nobel Prize, cause for another shared dinner. The first American winner in literature, Lewis took as his subject American corporate greed and banality, as depicted in *Elmer Gantry*, *Main Street*, and *Babbitt*—though the Nobel committee circumspectly cited his "vigorous and graphic art of description and his ability to create, with wit and humor, new types of characters."[27] Before the prize was announced, Lewis had been badgering Knopf for months to take him on. Following his Nobel, Lewis still wanted to publish with Blanche, who was leery of his drinking. Besides, the author expected Knopf to include exorbitant bonuses in his contract. Alfred wrote Mencken that Lewis had "made violent love to him in London" earlier in the year, but Mencken agreed with Blanche that an advance of thirty thousand dollars was too high and would simply tempt the author to "loaf." Blanche had long observed that Lewis seemed unable to settle down to work.[28] After divorcing Grace Hegger, he had married the political newspaper columnist Dorothy Thompson, a friend of Rebecca West, to whom Thompson had confirmed Blanche's concern. Nobel or not, the publishers reluctantly decided against bringing Lewis to Knopf.

Nonetheless, the years that brought the twenties to a close could be said to belong to Lewis and Mencken, its two "most important rebels."[29] Both men wrote with broad strokes, depicting a country they loved fiercely even as they exhorted its citizens to emerge from their stupor. In the end, however different their politics, both writers wanted their fellow patriots to stop slavering and to start thinking. As the journalist Walter Lippmann had said the year before, Mencken was currently "the most powerful personal influence on this whole generation of educated people."[30] And now, with Lewis's Nobel Prize honoring his critique of an American society that ignored the little guy, the two were arguably the seminal critics of the age.

At thirty-six, Blanche was at the height of her beauty—a slender body, meant to show off her striking wardrobe, her ginger-colored bob just the right length. Equal to her appearance was her knowledge of her trade and of the world of culture that she moved in. She had many friends—both men and women. She had accepted long ago her lack of a loving husband. What she wanted now was a great love of her own.

11

LOVER

T THE BEGINNING OF 1931, when Blanche was in London, she was afflicted with what Mencken called "a dreadful flu epidemic" she'd carried overseas from the States. After chiding his friend for neglecting her health, Mencken asked, plaintively, "When are you coming home?" He was worried about beginning his new book without her advice.[1] She was in no hurry to return, however, as she was tense about juggling her lovers, whom she knew she shared with others—Koussevitzky and Heifetz especially. Perhaps Heifetz reminded Blanche too much of Alfred: the author Robert Nathan, whose novella *Portrait of Jennie* would be a bestseller for Knopf, recalled the ways in which Alfred resembled Heifetz, both men "egotistical, domineering, indifferent . . . there was a thing around [them], you couldn't get through it."[2]

At least Blanche had determined how to bring out the best in her husband: she gathered friends with whom he was comfortable—those he felt were his equal but that he could, during the meal he supervised, dominate. And she was pleased that the summer ahead would involve her son. She gave her annual birthday party at Purchase for Pat, Van Vechten, and James Weldon Johnson (the "birthday club" later to include John Hersey), all three born on the same day: June 17. A group photograph taken by Alfred shows Blanche with Ettie Stettheimer, one of a trio of sisters famous for their wealth and their talents, looking with interest at a dog whose tail alone is caught by the camera. Pat gazes straight ahead, while Van Vechten, with Fania; Johnson, with his wife, Grace; and the Knopf poet Witter Bynner, all smile broadly as they stand.[3] William Koshland remembered that "[Blanche's parties at Purchase or Manhattan] were wonderful . . . she had an instinct, she'd even know if somebody was stuck with somebody. [The salesmen] even liked it better at Blanche's; she was much easier." Blanche was so savvy, Koshland said, "she could have made it in another firm," unlike Alfred's occasional threat to the contrary. She was as bold as anyone he'd ever met: during an elevator strike, she walked up fourteen flights to her floor, expecting Koshland to follow. He didn't.[4]

Later that summer, when the Galsworthys came to visit, Blanche gathered friends for a late dinner following a Boston Symphony performance in Manhattan, with Heifetz and Koussevitzky both present. Besides possibly Van Vechten, no one knew both men were her lovers, at some level a triumph on Blanche's part. Even so, there were prickly moments. Van Vechten, dressed in white buck shoes, was taunted by the easily envious Heifetz: "Where do you play tennis?" After Van Vechten sniffed that Samuel Clemens had worn white flannels the last twenty years of his life, Heifetz, never one to concede defeat, replied, "He was, after all, Mark Twain." Galsworthy quickly changed the subject, compounding the awkwardness by innocently commenting that these days he was finding Americans "noticeably quieter and pleasanter—perhaps as a result of the Depression."[5]

The Depression, however, only exacerbated the hard drinking

that many authors depended on for their inspiration. One afternoon in late fall, finishing lunch with Bennett Cerf at '21,' Dashiell Hammett and the equally boozy William Faulkner pleaded with Cerf to get them an invitation to the Knopfs' dinner party that night, with the guests including a mixed slate from Koussevitzky to Willa Cather, whose *Shadows on the Rock* had recently sold ninety-thousand copies through the Book-of-the-Month Club.

Cerf explained that it was strictly black-tie: only half sarcastic, he asked them if they understood. Of course, Hammett assured him, wounded. When Cerf picked up the men, however, they hadn't even changed their clothes. Appearing in their well-worn tweeds, they promptly got drunk at the Knopfs and then passed out—sliding off the couch onto the floor quietly, as if in deference to Blanche, who had shot them baleful looks all evening.[6]

On November 19, to mark the first concert of the Boston Symphony Orchestra's New York series for the 1931–32 season, with Koussevitzky, naturally, at the podium, the Knopfs took a box at Carnegie Hall, where they served champagne and strawberries at intermission. It was a decidedly romantic program, consisting of Gustav Mahler's Symphony no. 9 in D Major; Claude Debussy's "Nuages" and "Fêtes," from *Nocturnes*; and Maurice Ravel's Suite no. 2 from *Daphnis et Chloé*. Blanche held her traditional dinner in the conductor's honor at her apartment, with the guest list composed mostly of thirty regulars, among them Gershwin, Henry and Sara Mencken, Willa Cather, Judge John M. Woolsey (who would soon be adjudicating the obscenity case against James Joyce's *Ulysses*) and his wife, Judith Anderson, Fanny Hurst, and Dashiell Hammett—his invitation conditional, Blanche had admonished him: Was he working regularly on his next book under contract, *The Thin Man*?

But in spite of his promises, Hammett continued to frustrate his publisher. At the end of November he again brought Hemingway to one of her parties. Drunk as usual upon his arrival, Hemingway begged to go to a speakeasy, and just before the sun rose, Blanche, a little tipsy herself, relented. With Eddie Wasserman, the "famously homosexual" party man madly in love with Blanche, she tried the neighborhood clubs, but they were still closed for Thanksgiving.[7] She and Eddie hauled Hemingway back to his hotel; he couldn't stand up but could nonetheless conduct a grueling, nonsensical monologue. Increasingly Blanche saw him through Mencken's lens, in which the writer appeared as an "excessively vain fellow—challenging, bellicose and not infrequently absurd. Anyone who refused to hail him as a towering genius was an evil doer." What Blanche noticed was what her adoring butler, John Kilar, also disdained: "the powerful odor of alcohol wherever he went."[8]

But she was undeterred from planning her annual holiday event in December. Kilar (who, late in life, would recall Blanche in her "black riding suit" as "very sexy, her figure like Goldie Hawn") had found an eggnog recipe that would take on a life of its own.[9] Asked by a friend for the formula, Blanche passed it on, until the recipe reached the food critic Craig Claiborne, who would immortalize it as "Blanche Knopf's Eggnog." The recipe called for twelve raw eggs; one and a half cups of powdered sugar; a quart of pure cream; a fifth of cognac, bourbon, or whiskey; a cup of dark rum; and orange, lemon, and nutmeg for good health, a concoction, Blanche joked, to ensure that everyone would leave her party happy. But she herself drank only bourbon, straight.[10]

As 1932 progressed, a commercial dry spell would plague publishers. It was as if the Depression had finally caught up with the Knopfs, and Joe Lesser was forced to tighten production budgets.[11] The stock market had lost almost 90 percent of its value, and Simon & Schuster developed a system that year that allowed booksellers to return unsold copies of books for credit against future purchases, an arrangement that would become the standard for the industry. Blanche and Alfred were pleased to elect Mencken to Knopf's board of directors, where Sam, too, held a seat. (After Sam died, the board would include Henry, Blanche, Alfred, Sidney Jacobs, William Koshland, and Joe Lesser.) Mencken welcomed his new role with the firm, and the additional income that came with it.

What the Knopfs couldn't yet see was the Depression's real effect on their balance sheet. It took a blizzard in February for Blanche to understand the difficulty they were in. Examining the recent financial records she had brought home from the office, she was reminded of the misfortunes of her wealthy butcher grandfather, who had gone bankrupt in an earlier financial calamity. Possibly motivated by fears of a similar disaster befalling Knopf, she started allowing the annoying Eddie Wasserman to hang around her more often: Knopf might need new sources of financing. John Kilar later recalled how Pat Knopf had been upset by Wasserman, who was "clearly in love with Mrs. Knopf." Not that Kilar blamed Wasserman: according to him, Blanche was irresistible to anyone she set her sights on. Though she could be a "demanding businesswoman," when she asked you "to do something you hated doing, you did it—with pleasure. She just asked in such a way you couldn't refuse." After her death, Kilar recalled that when she ran into him at the St. Regis hotel, where he eventually took a job, she always introduced him to her guests, saying "something very beautiful about me, even to [the Nobel Prize winner] Sigrid Undset."[12]

Though he assumed the attitude of the "three monkeys: no see, no hear, etc.," the butler observed Eddie Wasserman staying over "frequently" when Alfred was away. In contrast, he noted, Alfred was discreet, "Mr. K" inviting the occasional woman friend to Purchase for what was nothing more than "a friendly visit." Yet it was Blanche he respected: "She was a strong-willed woman but with a heart. I admired her as I admire a tiger . . . She got everything she wanted."[13]

She didn't, of course. A marriage that had apparently devolved into one we would today call "open" wasn't at all what she'd hoped for seventeen years before. Now, on June 11, 1932, Blanche's seventy-year-old father-in-law died suddenly of a heart attack, with his last action in the name of Knopf that of "winding up" the long-defunct London office.[14] Mencken, who had been friendly with Sam Knopf for ten years at least, had recently recognized that the current financial problems of *The American Mercury* largely resulted from the "extravagant and indeed almost insane management of Knopf's father . . . I came to the conclusion that the elder Knopf was hopeless."[15] In large part due to his capricious management, Knopf nearly went bankrupt after Sam died: Alfred and Blanche's combined salary for 1934 was $35,000, with $20,000 for Alfred and $15,000 for Blanche, the couple waiving $13,333.33 of their year's pay (to keep the firm solvent).

The hundred attendees at Sam's funeral somehow got translated by *The New York Times* into "more than six hundred persons" present at the Beth-El Chapel of Temple Emanu-El. Alfred gave no eulogy, but the rabbi, who hadn't known either Knopf, effused over the relationship between "Mr. Knopf and his son Alfred as 'extraordinary and beautiful.'" Sam's "friendliness, sympathy and generosity" were deserving of "especial tribute." The energetic Samuel Knopf would not retire but was at his office the day before his death, dying "like a soldier at his post." Alfred, who displayed little emotion at his father's death, immediately took George Bellows's portrait of Sam to hang in his own bedroom.[16] Like Blanche's parents, Sam was buried at Salem Fields Cemetery.[17]

By the end of September, Blanche was more than ready to get away. Setting sail for London on the SS *Bremen*, she arrived to find several dozen writers seeking a publisher. She visited favorite authors and friends, from the Galsworthys to Knopf's money-making novelist Warwick Deeping, to Rebecca West, with whom Blanche shared Fannie Hurst's friendship. Now West was preoccupied with mother-son disagreements over her boy Anthony's father, H. G. Wells. She talked to Blanche about the perils of mothering a boy alone—or with a partner with whom one was at complete odds—and about her painful decision to grant custody of Anthony to Wells.

The conversation surely reminded Blanche of her frustration over Pat's parenting. Then, in Paris, she spent days soothing André Gide's easily ruffled feathers. Gide felt ignored of late, and Blanche reassured him that the Knopfs always had him in their sights—that Alfred, too, was reading Gide and praising him, even though she knew her husband wasn't interested in such literature.[18]

With perfect timing, the reporter Anita Block, who had helped found one of the first socialist newspapers in the United States, *The New York Call*, contacted Blanche, hoping to interview Mrs. Knopf about marriage. Blanche agreed to participate in one of a four-part newspaper series published by a western syndicate. Its subject was the irrelevance of marital fidelity in the modern age.

12

BECOMING FREE

THE INTERVIEW WITH ANITA BLOCK seemed an open letter to Alfred, through Blanche's answers to Block's questions about "outgrowing" both marriage and monogamy. "Why," Blanche asked rhetorically, "do we extract a model of monogamy [from the 'social structure' of marriage] where a man and his wife . . . become Siamese twins? . . . the matter of fidelity in the relationship count[s] for far less than others think."[1] Boldly, if a bit defensively, Blanche went on the record for open marriage. If her marriage had turned out the way she'd expected—and, from all indications, wanted—Blanche's opinion wouldn't have been sought. Instead, as a result of the relationship she got, she now meant to send her husband a message: they were both free to sleep with anyone they wanted, as long as they were discreet. And Alfred, who seemed to many acquaintances sexless, had recently renewed interest in several women from his past, though it remains unclear to what ends. Pat later remembered three such "girlfriends," the son claiming his father "got so lonely living out there [in Purchase]."[2]

Blanche's April interview, titled "Holds Monogamy and Marriage Are Different Institutions," makes it clear that multiple partners were fine by her. "Marriage is a useful institution for society, especially where there are children," the publisher maintained. "But other than caring together for their offspring, marital partners should be free to go their own way." Blanche concluded the interview: "When I was very young Joseph Hergesheimer once said to me: 'The most important thing in any marriage is the ability to shut the door against the rest of the world, and have someone with you.' But that shut-in space must be a sanctuary, not a prison. Otherwise the inmates will hate it."[3]

Seven weeks later, Blanche wrote Mencken about her need to talk with him confidentially. To his response that he would visit her in a week or so, she wrote: "Thanks for your letter and I hope it is frankly all right with you regarding the tenth and eleventh [of June]. Let us have our private session and let us make sure with Eddie [Wasserman] on the thirteenth so keep that definitely. If Sara comes it will be absolutely perfect. If she does not, let me know. There are a lot of things I want to talk to you about privately and we might have a further dinner chez moi alone."[4]

Since the Knopfs were rarely speaking to each other outside work in those days, Blanche may have wanted to discuss divorce with the only friend both Knopfs trusted. She also may have sought unbiased information on the financial state of the company from a board member who owned Knopf stock. Book sales, in step with the Depression after all, seemed to be dropping everywhere and would continue to do so till the end of the thirties. Though Alfred remained steadfast in his conviction that publishing was a gentleman's business—if they "went under, they would do so with grace"—Blanche felt her life would be worth little if they lost the company. In contrast, her husband believed that money sullied the publishing world, causing people to think of it as a business instead of a blessed vocation.[5]

It must have come as a relief to them both that Pat was headed to Phillips Exeter Academy in New Hampshire. The Knopfs' friend Judge John Woolsey had advised them that Exeter was a better choice than Andover. Woolsey, a frequent dinner guest of the Knopfs, was a man both parents trusted—and, almost as important, he had connections at Phillips. That August, excited about the fine preparatory education her son would receive, Blanche took Pat shopping for clothes, at least as much as he would tolerate. When he complained of a severe stomachache, she assumed he was just tired of trying on blazers and wanted to go home. But after he vomited in Brooks Brothers, she rushed him to Mount Sinai Hospital on Manhattan's Upper East Side, where doctors removed his appendix. Blanche was terrified that she'd lose her child, not least because the crisis occurred while Pat was under her care. Alfred, who was abroad, would never forgive her.

Decades after his mother's death, Pat told the story of her sleeping both nights on the hard floor next to his hospital bed, with no implication that she'd rather be in her office.[6] Or at home, in bed, he might have added. Dieting hard again, Blanche, under a good deal of stress, was not at her diplomatic best in those days. When she got news that Ivan Bunin had just become Knopf's sixth Nobel winner, she uncharacteristically muttered, "What in the world did *he* win it for?"[7] A Russian novelist whose criticism was aimed equally at Bolshevism and at Hitler, Bunin left her cold.

She grew especially irritable about the ten pounds that arbitrarily came and went and that on her small frame were magnified. She had tried Van Vechten's solution for losing weight—"Dearest Grand Duchee," he had coached her, "Macy's has Nutra diet grapefruit juice in cases . . . [If] they get out again call Nutra diet—they have a wholesale place in Brooklyn and they will tell you where to buy."[8]

Eventually, she discovered new pills that not only obliterated her appetite but also added a kick to her day. They became her "magic" pills. Used during World War I by the French to manufacture dynamite, DNP caused those employees inadvertently dusted with the chemical to lose weight. Scientists later understood why: the nutrient energy burned off as heat, which was effective for calorie loss but capable of literally cooking people to death internally if they took too large a dose.

Very little of this was appreciated in 1933, however, when word leaked out about the paper to be published the next summer in the well-regarded *Journal of Clinical Investigation*.[9] Even as a newly inaugurated president promised he would end the massive hunger caused by the Depression, W. C. Cutting, D. A. Rytand, and M. L. Tainter—all researchers at Stanford University School of Medicine—reported on using DNP for weight control in their (now classic) paper "Relationship Between Blood Cholesterol and Increased Metabolism from Dinitrophenol and Thyroid." The story about instant weight loss, as it was soon dubbed by the media, spread virally, and anyone who had a doctor with connections could get the miracle pill. As early as December, *Popular Science* would run an ad claiming "Safe Drug Takes Off Two Pounds a Week."[10] Within two years, at least a hundred thousand Americans were taking DNP, and, never hungry, they were indeed losing two to three pounds a week. Within another three years, however, it was clear that DNP was dangerous stuff. A sizeable number of people died for no apparent reason, while hundreds more had developed severe cataracts that would leave them blind. In 1939, the FDA would ban DNP for all human use in the United States.

But for now Blanche felt she had found the answer, a pill whose only side effect was to make her a bit edgy. Even that edge had its value, as she celebrated the preholiday extravaganza sweeping the city: at last Prohibition had been officially repealed. Alfred, who claimed to be one of six publishers to attend the alcoholic Horace

Liveright's funeral in 1933, wondered aloud at the abuse the tyrannical law had provoked, while Mencken wrote eloquently of the absurd Volstead Act itself:

> Years of Prohibition have had, at least, this one benign effect: they have completely disposed of all the favorite arguments of the Prohibitionists. None of the great boons and usufructs that were to follow the passage of the Eighteenth Amendment has come to pass. There is not less drunkenness in the Republic, but more. There is not less crime, but more. There is not less insanity, but more.[11]

And on December 6, 1933, the day after Prohibition was officially pronounced dead, Judge John M. Woolsey ruled in a landmark case that *Ulysses* was not obscene. Meanwhile, Joe Lesser's end-of-year report was disheartening: for 1933, Knopf's sales totaled $500,500, with a loss of $18,800.[12] Blanche would have to fight hard to keep Alfred from moving the company to White Plains, a shift he'd long been hinting at, and a change that would leave Blanche out in the cold.

PART THREE

13

MONEY PROBLEMS

SIX MONTHS AFTER ITS RELEASE IN 1933, the novel *Anthony Adverse*, by Hervey Allen, had become a huge commercial success. Published by Farrar and Rinehart, who had begun publishing in 1929 (persuading Floyd Dell to leave Knopf for the new company's higher advances), the novel with its Byzantine intricacy seems a forerunner of *The Da Vinci Code*. *Anthony Adverse* ended the year at the top of the bestseller list, where it would remain throughout 1934, selling more than two million hardcover copies. The timing was right for the 1,224-page behemoth: the three-dollar cover price made it a bargain when a good deal on anything was hard to find, paperbacks still a few years in the future. Blanche wrote John Farrar, whom she knew and liked, a brief note of congratulations. Twelve years later, with the arrival of Roger Straus and his focus on international literature, Farrar and Rinehart had morphed into Farrar, Straus, and a third partner, Robert Giroux, was eventually added. They would quickly become, along with Knopf, one of the finest boutique firms around.[1]

Blanche trusted John Farrar from the first. Relieved at, rather than envious of, *Anthony Adverse*'s success, she was similarly pleased that Bennett Cerf and *Ulysses* had finally made it through the censors' hoops. Publishers were starting to band together, and Blanche shared a real sense of camaraderie with her competitors. Of course, she was relieved when *The Thin Man* was praised. On January 7, 1934, *The New York Times* said that "those who enjoy a good story, racily told in the sort of language that a roughneck might be expected to use will find . . . a welcome relief from the neatly patterned solutions of the miracle men of detective fiction."[2] The *New Statesman* called *The Thin Man* "an unusually brilliant read as a detective story—[one that] has every right to consideration on its literary merits."[3] Before long, *The Thin Man* had become an "overnight sensation," due in part to Knopf's deft publicity: an ad in *The New York Times* featured Alfred protesting that "the question on page 192 of Dashiell Hammett's *The Thin Man*" has "nothing to do with its popularity . . . Twenty thousand people don't buy a book within three weeks to read a five-word question." Alfred was cannily referring to Nora Charles's query to her husband, Nick: When wrestling with Mimi (a major character in the novel), didn't Charles "have an erection?"[4] The open marriage practiced by Nick and Nora and the "risqué" bordering on "immoral" treatment of sex in general caused *The Thin Man* to be banned in Canada, while the book would save Knopf from bankruptcy during what was, arguably, their worst Depression year. The novel was made into a movie shot in twelve days that summer, starring Myrna Loy and William Powell, who between them downed thirty-three drinks in the course of the film.

The Thin Man features Nick Charles, a former New York City private detective whose wealthy young wife, Nora, supports him, having enabled him to quit work and do little but drink cocktails around the clock. In real life, working with the alcoholic and melodramatic Hammett had worn out Blanche. In *The Thin Man*, Nora comes up with a plan to get her husband back into the thick of life, and Blanche must have wished that art had imitated life a bit more. In the novel, Nora motivates Nick to rejoin the real world, where he investigates the disappearance of the eccentric patriarch Clyde Wynant. The police suspect Wynant of faking a crime and absconding with others' money. Instead, Wynant is found dead, a murder victim, his thin corpse stuffed inside a "fat suit."

Just one month after *The Thin Man* was published, Knopf released James M. Cain's *The Postman Always Rings Twice*. Before the war, Cain had been managing editor of *The New Yorker* and then, upon his return, at Mencken's behest, a writer for *The Baltimore Sun*—and had squired Mencken's future wife, Sara Haardt, around town. Now, back home in Annapolis, he'd begun writing occasional pieces for *The American Mercury* and, until it folded in 1931, *The (New York) World*. The previous summer, *The World*'s editor, Walter Lippmann, a longtime friend of Blanche, had urged her to take on a "hard-boiled" mystery written by the ex-soldier Jimmy Cain. Lippmann offered Knopf right of first refusal, if she acted fast—within hours, according to the account the Knopfs later gave. Blanche read the 35,000-word novel immediately and proclaimed it top-notch. In keeping with the couple's agreement to consult each other before accepting a book, Blanche tried frantically to reach Alfred, who was playing golf at Sands Point, Long Island. When she got hold of him, the Knopfs decided to take it at once. (Cain would instead tell Drew Dudley, a friend of Blanche's, that Alfred, in a "curmudgeonly letter," had at first declined *Postman*.)[5]

Throughout the next decade, a trail of spectacular Knopf mystery writers would be signed by Blanche, including Raymond Chandler and Eric Ambler. Detective fiction, whose unreliable characters, bad luck, and exotic violence paralleled the country's struggles, was perfect for the times. That Blanche could move from the rarefied French translations she acquired at Knopf's founding, to the twentieth-century English-language poetry and fiction she secured, to the bold

African-American literature she had quickly appreciated, and now to this gritty Depression-era aesthetic, suggests an extraordinary, intuitive sensitivity and ability to anticipate the popular reading tastes of the times.

After both detective novels proved successful (though Cain's had disappointing sales, the studios fell in line to buy film rights), Blanche was secure enough about the company's survival to go abroad as usual. First, however, she came up with a press notice that got all the papers talking: "A number of book-page editors were astonished at a [recent] Knopf release announcing that Mrs. Knopf was going to Europe on the *Conte di Savoia* to meet Fafner Niederholtz, Tristan Traumweig, Serafino Umilerto, Albertine Disparue, Ga Fraaloma, Gregor Visilovitch Yakounchikov, Hacken Trom Golfstein, Pakves, Agememnon Parpadulion, and Moden Salchuvenec." This piece of news, which was faithfully reported by the major wire services, was followed the next day by a Knopf press release clarifying that Mrs. Knopf would in fact be seeing Hugh Walpole, Lion Feuchtwanger (a German-Jewish novelist who influenced Bertolt Brecht), Virginia Woolf, and other writers with recognizable names. A journalist recounted that "the joke, it appears, was Mrs. Knopf's idea."[6]

Among several manuscripts to be delivered to her while she was overseas was a small book of poems by Langston Hughes, which Blanche imagined would bring Hughes—and Knopf—further literary distinction. But when Carl Van Vechten sent her Hughes's latest work, Blanche genuinely disliked it. The polemical emphasis on the downtrodden worker might have found an audience some years ago, she told him, but its hopelessness was unsuitable now, in the heart of the Depression.

Typical of the collection were poems such as "Let America Be America Again" and "Park Bench," where the tone is set by such phrases as "America never was America to me" and "I live on a park bench. / You, Park Avenue." Some of the poems seemed sympathetic to communism, though the collection is ostensibly about the disadvantaged of all creeds and colors, with the majority of the seventeen poems highlighting the mistreatment of black Americans, including "Lynching Song," with its inflammatory "Pull at the rope!"

After communicating with Van Vechten, who shared her opinion, Blanche cabled Hughes that she agreed strongly with Carl's rejection of his political poetry: the timing was bad for this kind of protest literature, especially by a relatively new voice. Attempting to soften the blow, she wrote that he had already become "much too important than this [political] poetry" and such a publication would "tend to harm [his] name rather than help it."[7]

Hughes wasted no time reacting to his publisher's rejection, coldly addressing his response to "Mrs. Knopf" instead of the usual "Blanche." On reflection, he had decided he wanted to put out a cheap edition aimed at "the working class audience," and if Knopf wouldn't publish it, would they object if he put it out with International Publishers or a similar press? Blanche quickly agreed, and in April 1938, the twenty-page collection, *A New Song*, finally saw print when the International Workers Order printed fifteen thousand copies that sold for fifteen cents each. Meanwhile, Blanche and Hughes became close again.[8] And there were other riches Blanche approved in 1934: Knopf published Hughes's *The Ways of White Folks*, fourteen short stories that are among his best-known works.

Once she'd worked out the Langston Hughes contretemps, Blanche spent time at the Manns' comfortable old villa at Küsnacht, near Zurich. She invited "Tommy" (as Katia called him) and his wife to join her in New York in a few months, at Knopf's expense, to celebrate publication of the first volume of Mann's tetralogy, *Joseph and His Brothers*. "*Wir kommen*," the writer said. From the other side of the Atlantic, Leopold Stokowski wrote Blanche, imploring her to come to his early concert in Philadelphia, but she replied that she would still be at the Manns'. By now, Stokowski was among Blanche's least favorite lovers anyway. According to Larry Huffman, who maintains a Stokowski website, the conductor was "particularly secretive about his activities, and a person he was with one day usually would not know of his activities the day before or the day after."[9] Though Huffman ascribes such secrecy to the conductor's natural discretion, Blanche would have found it unsatisfying, since his furtiveness made her feel less than special.

Stokowski wrote that he recalled first meeting her "a long time ago"—probably referring to their liaison of 1925. She had praised his hour-long Ninth Symphony, applauding him for not insisting on dragging it out, as so many conductors did; and in return he used his notoriously overripe prose to describe the "lifetime of feeling" he experienced during those sixty minutes as he "penetrated deeply into such a colossal work"—"enter[ing] a vast temple . . . the very heart and mind of Beethoven." Remembering their first encounter, Stokowski wrote: "I was running up some steps, and you were standing at the top; and I was so struck by your beauty that I asked someone who you were, and everybody seemed either shocked or amused." After begging her to meet him again soon, after a concert in Philadelphia ("I should like so much to see you"), he concluded by thanking her for the pleasure she gave writing to him about the Ninth Symphony years ago.[10]

On her return in February, Blanche appeared at a tea for the exile Emma Goldman, allowed into the United States for a lecture tour; later that day she went to a party given for Gertrude Stein and Alice B. Toklas by Random House. But she was once again preoccupied with the future of the house she and Alfred had built together. The 1934 financials showed that, their many successes notwithstanding, their future was precarious. The Depression had finally taken its toll on the publishing industry, including on Knopf.

Publishers needed to tread more carefully than in the recent past. When the notoriously irascible Lillian Hellman accompanied her lover Dashiell Hammett to Blanche's office one afternoon, after her play *The Children's Hour* had opened on Broadway, Blanche congratulated her and offered to publish it with an advance of "$150.00." Hellman responded, "$500.00." Blanche looked her squarely in the eye and said, "Why does a girl who's sitting over there wearing a brand new mink coat need $500?" But she paid it because she wanted the play—and to ensure, as long as she could manage him, that Hammett would stay with Knopf.[11]

Unlike Blanche, Alfred seemed energized by their financial woes. He decided Knopf should have its own book club, though on a more modest level than the Book-of-the-Month, that still novel but highly successful enterprise. Blanche's opinion (she was against the idea) didn't matter: as before, Alfred's plan referred only to himself. Even when Alfred cited specific European writers Blanche had signed, he continued to speak in the first-person singular, as if Knopf consisted of him alone.[12]

Alfred wrote in *The Borzoi Quarterly* to subscribers:

During the last 20 years, I have introduced to America many writers so far ahead of their times that even competent critics found difficulty in adequately appraising their worth and the importance of my discoveries. You cannot establish a Cather, a Hudson, an Undset or a Mann with the customary publishing ballyhoo . . . My problem has been to find the comparatively few intelligent minds, ready and eager for great discoveries. In this I have had a measure of success. I have published six Nobel Prize winners.

The dominant "I" must again have infuriated Blanche. Probably due to timing—it was the depth of the Depression after all—the club failed.[13]

Meanwhile, Edwin Knopf was thriving in Hollywood. Currently a story editor at Metro-Goldwyn-Mayer, he was climbing the ladder to become a producer. (In 1935, Samuel Goldwyn would put out *The Wedding Night*, starring Gary Cooper and based on Edwin's script.) While Alfred went to see his brother that fall, Blanche would travel abroad, even allowing herself a side excursion to Jenny Bradley's vacation home at Cap d'Antibes, where she could forget her trials with Hammett and Hughes for a few days.

Her fall trip was so successful that as soon as she returned to New York, she started planning her buying trip for January. When she was reminded that Florence Heifetz was throwing a surprise birthday party for Jascha on February 2, she decided to stay in Manhattan another month instead. Fortuitously, her change of plans allowed her time to review Knopf's finances, supposedly left in top shape by Sam. Instead, as she delved more deeply, she was horrified at the mess she found: Knopf was unable, she realized, to meet their $75,000 note due the Bank of Manhattan.

On March 21, 1935, Alfred, Blanche, and Joe Lesser assessed Knopf's financial reality: they were about to default on a loan. Alfred closed up the Purchase house (later renting "the Hovel" to Harry Winston, the "diamond king") and took up temporary residence at Delmonico's, rather than stay in Blanche's extra bedroom at 400 East Fifty-Seventh. He swapped his hotel bill for free advertising in *The American Mercury*. The Knopfs immediately contacted an attorney who had gotten other publishing firms out of financial difficulty.

"We were in real trouble," Alfred later admitted. But rather than accept responsibility for the company's management, Alfred impugned the entire banking profession, referring to "men who lent you an umbrella when the sun is shining but refuse you when it rains."[14] After one of the Knopfs' Irving Trust bankers, at a branch on Madison Avenue and Forty-Sixth Street (where Sam had maintained a connection for years), was shocked to see that "you've been using the banks for capital," Alfred sniffed, later commending his self-restraint in not countering, "Any fool could see that."[15] While serving as business manager of the Knopf firm, Sam had apparently overvalued its inventory and even used his own money to buy numerous shares of the company stock at an inflated worth. The branch manager, Charles Fagg, now insisted that Alfred assign to the bank the life insurance Sam had taken out on his son years before, with a current face value of $300,000 (about $5.2 million today).

Alfred also held a personal account at Irving Trust, where his old friend Felix Warburg sat next to Fagg. Now Alfred complained to anyone who would listen that Knopf had been told that instead of using Irving Trust for both their personal and their professional accounts, the Knopfs should have a second bank with which they could always pay off loans from the first. Every year both banks set their line of credit at $200,000, so that "we could actually borrow up to $400,000." Their bankers, Alfred later lamented, "hadn't understood a book publisher's balance sheet too well or one of them might have years before discovered how greatly we over-valued our inventory."[16]

Nor was Charles Fagg, associate of Felix Warburg or not, willing to give the Knopfs a break. Alfred then turned to his lawyer friend Jim Rosenberg, who had helped him buy the Purchase house. The Knopfs borrowed $40,000—$30,000 from Jim, and $10,000 from another acquaintance. (When the Knopfs paid back the loans two years later, the men refused any interest.) As if Blanche had not begged her husband years before to keep Sam out of the business, Alfred took from the current disaster his own strange lesson: his two best friends had "proved an unique exception to the conviction that Blanche and I had . . . arrived at that the only money worthwhile in a personal business is what you supply yourself and that the price of outside capital comes too high."[17]

Belatedly, both Knopfs turned to the Cheney report on American book trade economics published in early 1932. Throughout a study declaring poor distribution of books the "tragedy of the book industry," O. H. Cheney, in a rigorous reading of the American publishing industry, talked hard facts, some of which resonate to this day.[18] The Knopfs' overdue attention to the report resulted in their developing "a set of useful statistics," recording them in what they thereafter called their "black book." When he was alive, Sam Knopf had done things his way, and now, with this new (actually conventional) method—and without Sam around—they could "project [their] sales and cash positions at least a year ahead."[19]

"It all seems so unbelievably dreadful that there is nothing to be said . . . All I wanted you to know is that I am here and will come down if you want me and if I can do anything for you . . . I am afraid I am never good at saying what is really in my mind. But perhaps you will understand."[20] Consumed with Knopf's financial woes, Blanche had been slow to register that Mencken's wife was seriously ill. She had failed to read between the lines of the insouciant letters Mencken had sent her in the past months. Though she knew that Sara was struggling with what was then called her post-tubercular lungs, she had no idea of the gravity of the situation.

In May, Henry sent Blanche a blunt note: Sara was, it seemed, sicker than anyone had realized. In April, she had returned to Johns Hopkins, where Henry, optimistic, noted that the crocuses were already in bloom. He wrote Blanche that he was "very hopeful that her rest cure will rid her of her troubles permanently."[21] Instead Sara deteriorated, and now, his wife still in the hospital, Mencken wrote Blanche in a telegram that "the poor girl has had a horrible year. She has born it bravely, but if the quacks don't turn her loose pretty soon I think she'll begin to shoot."[22]

Later that day, Blanche sent Mencken a telegram that she would be at her office that afternoon from three on. She signed the message "desperately sorry love Blanche."[23] On Wednesday, May 29, a lumbar puncture revealed tubercular meningitis (usually fatal) in Sara's spinal fluid. But before Blanche got down to Baltimore, on Friday, May 31, 1935, Mencken's wife of five years was dead. Mencken was so "dazed with grief" that he was incapable of making funeral arrangements, and, refusing to look at her lifeless body, he immediately had her cremated and placed in a plot in Baltimore's Loudon Park beside one reserved for him.[24]

The newspaperman, quietly devastated, wrote in his journal only once the rest of that year. That entry concerned his lifelong obsession with the number 13—the day of Sara's death, 31, reversed: "I came down from New York yesterday, Friday the 13th, leaving on the 11.30 train, Eastern Standard Time. There is another 13 in 11.30. The Pullman agent gave me seat No. 13 in car 231. Another 13 in 231, this time reversed. I fully expected the train to roll off the track."[25]

It took five years for Mencken to mention Sara's death directly. On May 31, 1940, he wrote: "I still think of Sara every day of my life, and almost every hour of the day . . . I am always thinking of things to tell her."[26] In the aftermath of Sara's death, Mencken busied himself preparing her collection of short stories and memoirs, *Southern Album*, to be published by Doubleday, which had put out her novel *The Making of a Lady* in 1931, to avoid any conflict of interest with Knopf.

14

HARBINGERS OF WAR

MENCKEN'S GRIEF OVER SARA'S DEATH caused Blanche to register her own loneliness more acutely. She was pleased when Pat, on holiday from Exeter, chose to live with her again at 400 East Fifty-Seventh Street, occupying the extra bedroom, as he had the previous summer. Pat would later say that he liked the ambience of life with his mother. From parties with Noël Coward playing his latest songs in their apartment to seeing her off to work in the morning, he enjoyed being with her. He noticed that even at the office she had style: a porkpie hat and a gold "BK" pin on her jacket lapel became her trademarks.[1]

Pat could be jealous of male guests who showed up too often. Eddie Wasserman, Blanche's friend from the 1920s, was still actively hoping for a chance, and Pat sensed his mother was ready to give it to him. Even Eddie realized, however, that no matter how much he idolized Blanche, for her theirs was a relationship of convenience. To show his affection, he bought Blanche a new car, a yellow Ford

Phaeton convertible (she rarely drove it and never with the top down). For once, Blanche's paramour gave her a gift, instead of the other way around.[2] She told Mencken that Eddie was her "walker,"[3] but Joe Lesser thought he was Blanche's lover.[4] In any event, Pat, who said that his mother "hung out with fairies" (Wasserman was assumed to be a closeted homosexual), recalled decades later that his father was infuriated at the gift.[5] Blanche's friend Judith Anderson recalled Eddie as being "very fond of Blanche," and "fun, very brilliant . . . with a charming apartment" where everyone "from New York and Paris went in 1935."[6] Blanche eventually gave Eddie her signature gift of a gold Dunhill lighter with his initials engraved, implying (if only for appearance's sake) that they were lovers.

When Pat went to Wyoming to spend the rest of the summer at a dude ranch, Blanche took off for Europe, returning in September to get him back to school. The Knopfs' summer trips bore no signs of downsizing: advance sales by the summer of 1935 showed the business back in strong financial shape, for now at least, chiefly through the publications of Clarence Day's memoir *Life with Father* and Willa Cather's *Lucy Gayheart*, a novel about a young woman living on the Platte River in Nebraska—whose desire for a richer life leads to her death.

At the end of the summer, Alfred took his first flight—to Los Angeles to visit his brother, Edwin—and then traveled by train to Albuquerque to meet Conrad Richter, whose manuscript he knew Blanche wanted to see. That trip opened Alfred's eyes to the beauty of the Southwest, which soon became a beloved part of the American landscape for him. Blanche, alone at her Midtown apartment throughout her son's school year, now accompanied her husband socially only when she had to. Together they appeared at the "brilliant first performance" of Gershwin's opera *Porgy and Bess* when it premiered at the Alvin Theatre on October 10, 1935. And together they attended the gala in Gershwin's honor given by Condé Nast at his Park Avenue duplex.[7]

Blanche would have preferred to be escorted by Mencken, but

she respected his wish to remain a friend to both Knopfs. She sent him her own holiday presents, and on December 22, 1935, he wrote her that "those magnificent herring came in just in time for my Sabbath supper . . . They arrived without a scratch, and looking like the Crown Jewels. My very best thanks. But in conscience I must add the corollary: Christmas be damned."[8] She also made a list of tasks he might do for her while she was abroad the next month, doubtless because she wanted to keep him occupied while he mourned Sara.

In January, Dashiell Hammett less successfully tried to elicit Blanche's sympathy. Forced to deal with Hammett's need for near-constant babysitting, Blanche was now privy to his confidence at a *Black Mask* writers' dinner in Los Angeles: he'd contracted the clap. He flew back to New York, where he checked into Lenox Hill Hospital until early February, during which time Blanche sent him books to read as well as reminding him, halfheartedly, of his promise to deliver a new novel by the end of the year.

But that January also saw Blanche meeting briefly with Elizabeth Bowen in London, the two bonding immediately, with Blanche's enthusiasm over the upcoming American publication of *The House in Paris* predisposing Bowen to like her at once. *The House in Paris* appeared to strong reviews in early 1936. When the book came out in England a year earlier, Virginia Woolf had lavished praise upon it, surprised at how much Bowen's world intersected with her own. Indeed, the story's tone felt distinctly influenced by Woolf. Bowen kept peeling back its imperturbable and aloof outer shell until a sometimes vicious core emerged, only to end at the beginning: a daylong account of two adolescents trying to get home, wherever that turned out to be.

The novel received raves in the American press as well, if less than spectacular results at the cash register: *The New York Times* said *The House in Paris* was "indisputably the best of Miss Bowen's novels. It has all the sensitive qualities of its predecessors combined with greater warmth and feeling." *The Saturday Review of Literature* said, "The author has a sentient intuition for the depths and complexities of personality and she has the imaginative intelligence to make human relationship the *raison d'etre* of an unstereotyped, interesting novel." *The Nation* dissented: the lack of a large (probably Russian-type) framework deprived the novel's readers of the grand passions implied but coolly withheld.[9] Most important, both for the number of copies sold and for generating publicity, it was a Book-of-the-Month Club selection.

For a few months, Blanche was at ease. On January 14, 1936, Jascha Heifetz played a benefit at Carnegie Hall for the New York Women's Trade Union League. Eleanor Roosevelt was the chair of the benefit committee, which included Mrs. Andrew Carnegie, Mrs. William Randolph Hearst, and others. Later in the month the Metropolitan Museum of Art mounted a grand Van Gogh exhibition that Blanche was eager to see. She also planned to attend the performances of the Ballet Russe, where she would relish the dancers' graceful and athletic movement. And in an increasingly rare instance of the Knopfs being together socially twice in one month, Blanche and Alfred were back at Carnegie Hall to honor their British friend the conductor Sir Thomas Beecham. When they checked in at the Fifty-Sixth Street entrance, the longtime house manager, John Totten, told them, to their surprise, "Your friends are here," meaning Koussevitzky and his wife, Natalya.

Beecham was sailing home the next day and had invited the Knopfs to a "supper party" at the Savoy-Plaza after the concert, the hotel where, Blanche well knew, the Koussevitzkys always stayed. After the concert, the Knopfs proceeded to Beecham's party at the hotel, and while Blanche was in the powder room, Natalya walked in. She insisted that the couple come up to their suite. Thinking they'd stay just a few minutes, the Knopfs relented. Once Serge opened the door, however, embracing them as Natalya said, "Look what I found," Lord Beecham's party was forgotten.

That summer, after Alfred learned that his wife was planning to take Pat to the Gaspé Peninsula near Quebec, he preempted her by suggesting to their son that the two of them—and Blanche, too, if she wanted—first go on a canoe trip together (for which Alfred grew a beard "rather like Joseph Conrad's").[10] Asking friends for recommendations, he settled on the Cains River in New Brunswick. The little crew, Blanche included, spent the night in Fredericton and then, taking a train with guides early the next morning, dropped off their equipment at a nearby point on the river. That's when Blanche decided to turn back. The whole experience was too primitive for her taste, and between swatting at the mosquitoes and slipping in the mud, she decided to let it be a boys-only event. Managing some good fly casting that evening, Alfred and Pat then "struck mostly shallow water and had to slosh through it on foot and pull the canoes."[11] When Blanche and Pat each arrived home separately in late summer, they immediately took off for their long-planned vacation to Gaspé, Blanche hoping to match Alfred's adventure.

Little record remains of the mother-son trip, and Pat was soon back at school, while Blanche took off for Paris and London. Through the Knopf writer Paul Gallico, who had come to Berlin for the 1936 summer Olympics, she was introduced to William Shirer. After only a few minutes of talk, Blanche, as ever trusting her instincts, told the reporter to forget about his novel and let her sign right away the diary Shirer told her he was keeping. Impressed by her perseverance, Shirer suggested they talk again in a few years. The reporter would later boast that when he first met Blanche there were rumors that "she was sort of crazy to go to bed with me, but she never made any advances."[12] Shirer didn't yet realize that Blanche could sound like a seductress when she went hunting for books. She would cable Shirer frequently after their meeting, convincing him to keep detailed notes when back in Berlin, where he was on assignment for the International News Service, followed by CBS. Later, she arranged meetings with the journalist in Paris and London as well.

The revelations in Shirer's diaries, written over the previous few

Blanche and her borzoi, the breed that inspired the Knopf colophon, 1917

Portrait of Blanche by G. Maillard Kesslere, circa 1920s

Bertha Samuels Wolf and
Julius Wolf, circa 1910

An unclothed Alfred,
in a rare photo taken
by Blanche, 1921

Blanche and Alfred with their bloodhound in Mount Kisco, N.Y., 1924. It was the only English bloodhound to exhibit that year and won a ribbon by default.

Blanche with Bertha Samuels Wolf and Alfred A. "Pat" Knopf, Jr., 1921

Sam Knopf, Blanche,
and Alfred on a midnight
sail around Manhattan,
circa 1925

Blanche at the riding stables, with her and Alfred's first Stutz, 1925.
They received the car in exchange for advertising in *The American Mercury*.

Portrait of Blanche, circa 1920s, probably taken by Alfred

Caricature of Blanche by Miguel Covarrubias, circa late 1920s (© Maria Elena Rico Covarrubias)

Willa Cather, circa 1924. "For you, with love, dear Blanche."
(© Nickolas Murray Archives)

Blanche in Baden-Baden, Germany, taking in the sun on a balcony, July 4, 1928

H. L. and Sara Mencken in Jamaica, January 1932

TOP Blanche reading a manuscript, January 1936

ABOVE Blanche with Aldous Huxley in Billings, near Rhinebeck, N.Y., April 25, 1937

Blanche with Jascha Heifetz and Florence Vidor Heifetz, May 1937

Blanche arriving in Vienna at USFA Headquarters
(occupation HQ) as the guest of General Mark Clark, July 24, 1945

Blanche (seated center) on the Rhine with the Nuremberg trials prosecutor Justice Robert H. Jackson (seated to Blanche's left) and the trial group, undated, 1946

Blanche with Alfred, Jr. ("Pat"), in his army uniform in Purchase, April 1945

RIGHT Blanche reading a
manuscript in the morning sun
with a magnifying glass, at the
Farandole Hotel, Cap d'Antibes,
France, August 1949

BELOW Blanche and Alfred with
Allen Dulles and Alice Roosevelt
Longworth at the 1952 early
autumn wedding in Washington,
D.C., of Mary Bancroft to Robert
Taft's son

ABOVE Blanche showing the diplomat Sumner Welles her Chevalier of the Order of the Southern Cross medal, Brazilian Embassy, Washington, D.C., November 2, 1950

LEFT Thomas Mann at the Dorset Hotel, April 20, 1937

H. L. Mencken in Purchase with Tapiola

Albert Camus, French Cultural Services, 1950s

Luncheon with Blanche, Alfred, Bennett Cerf, and Donald Klopfer, circa 1960, photograph by Peter Stackpole (The LIFE Picture Collection; © Getty Images)

Blanche and Alfred, circa 1965

years and given to Blanche to read in rough form, had both appalled and enlightened her. Shirer had thought it a good idea, for instance, to observe the September 1934 Nuremberg Rally to take his own measure of the country. Held since 1923 as the yearly gathering of Germany's Nazi Party, the event, following Hitler's rise to power, had evolved into an annual propaganda show. This year, before Shirer had even settled into his hotel, he'd found himself stuck in front of Hitler's hotel, among a mob of ten thousand shouting: "We want our Führer!"

Shirer detailed his 1934 experience, saying: "I was a little shocked at the faces . . . They reminded me of the crazed expressions I once saw in the back country of Louisiana on the faces of some Holy Rollers . . . they looked up at [Hitler] as if he were a Messiah, their faces transformed into something positively inhuman."[13]

When Blanche herself traveled to Berlin after her brief stop in Paris, she saw bedlam everywhere. Distressed by the obviously unstable Deutschland, she told a *New York Times* reporter on July 14, 1936: "There is not a German writer left in Germany who is worth thinking about. The gifted writers and enterprising publishers who had any independence have left Germany. [Thomas Mann had fled to Switzerland.] Only the Nazi writers and publishers remain so as to please the Nazi government."

Around this time, Mencken, who had entirely miscalculated the severity of the German political scene, advised Blanche against publishing books on the history of Jewish persecution. She needn't worry, Mencken assured her: the "*Baltimore Sun* . . . and the leading Jewish organizations of the [United States] . . . say that the slaughter of Jews in Germany is imaginary."[14] Since Blanche considered Mencken one of America's most acute political thinkers, she hoped he was right.

She was pleased to tell him that the second edition of *The American Language* had increased its sales that year to 9,274 copies, an impressive achievement for a reference book. From now on, the compendium would be issued as a two-volume set. Mencken was gratified, but he was also concerned about Blanche's health. There were rumors of her being sick, and when he confronted her, she crumbled. She was struggling with a severe nerve pain on one side of her face, a horrible sensation that seemed to last forever when it was really just a few seconds or minutes. Her friend insisted she return with him to Baltimore to see his ophthalmologist at Hopkins, where she had already met his internist, Benjamin Baker (later to become General Douglas MacArthur's consultant). There was nothing the doctors could do. Her vision continued to blur occasionally, though she admitted her disability to a select few, wearing glasses only in private. When Henry suggested that her odd request for an all-black bathroom at the Purchase house was ill-advised—due to her sight, if nothing else—she refused to listen, determined to make her feelings about the dark domicile clear, and black it was.[15] She would seldom be at the country house anyway.

That November Blanche went on a few day trips with Alfred, after the couple threw their annual party to celebrate Koussevitzky's opening of the New York concert season. They stopped at the Old Drovers Inn, a historic bed-and-breakfast in Dover Plains, near Poughkeepsie, and then started off to the Troutbeck Estate (a frequent stopover for the writer/naturalist John Burroughs) to see Joel and Amy Spingarn, old friends instrumental in the work of the NAACP. They planned to stay overnight at the Spingarns' historic home, just outside the town of Amenia in the Hudson Valley. But the night proved colder than anyone had expected, and since the Knopfs' garage had failed to put antifreeze in their Ford, the engine froze, making it impossible for them to continue their trip. When their car eventually came back to life, Blanche returned to the city to hear about a surgical procedure Mencken was undergoing in Baltimore over the December holidays; she urged him to get away while he healed from what, given his uncharacteristic discretion, was probably a prostate operation.

Early in the new year, Henry took Blanche's advice and recuperated at Daytona Beach, where Blanche sent him a note saying that she wanted to commission a fancy Florida rendition of the Knopf logo—

something Mencken could oversee while she was on her seasonal business trip abroad. Her instructions were to produce a truly original piece, and Mencken relished the assignment. Uncertain of the reason for "the first Borzoi lamp ever made on this coast," a resident sculptor took on the commission. The lamp was a monstrosity of surrealist and Biedermeier flourishes, its shade made of "oyster shells, red berries, gilt buttons, and palm nuts." Enchanted, Blanche wired Mencken, urging him to hurry back to all those who loved him.[16] What she finally made of the lamp goes unnoted, but it probably became a gift for a writer or agent abroad—or perhaps a present for her husband.

On her last overseas trip, Blanche had had a fortuitous meeting with D. H. Lawrence's friend the author Aldous Huxley, with whom she felt an immediate bond due to his kindness toward and appreciation of Lawrence, whose letters Huxley had edited after the writer's death in 1930. Only forty-four, Lawrence had died in Vence, a region in southeastern France between Nice and Antibes, of pulmonary tuberculosis, with Aldous and Maria Huxley tending him during his illness. In addition to such faithfulness, Blanche also admired Huxley's pacifist views, and she felt an added kinship due to his partial blindness. Within months of Blanche's return from Europe, the Knopfs were joining the couple for lunch in Rhinebeck, New York, a two-hour drive from Midtown Manhattan.

They met at the home of the Huxleys' improbable friends William and Marjory (Worthington) Seabrook, he a famous student of the occult, eater of human flesh, and mental patient. Harcourt, Brace had published Seabrook's *Jungle Ways* in 1931, in which the student of exotica, embedded among the friendly tribes of West Africa, had been offered a cutting from the flank of a thirty-year-old man "freshly" killed in an accident. The human meat was excellent, the "cooking odors, wholly pleasant, were like those of beefsteak and roast beef."[17] *Jungle Ways* was dedicated to Paul Morand, an anti-Semitic modernist writer who would support the Vichy government. Though Seabrook was prolific, there is no suggestion that Blanche ever asked him for a book. In 1945, eight years after her lunch with him, the anthropologist committed suicide.

In late April 1937, Henry ventured to a cocktail party given by the Knopfs to show off their new offices at 501 Madison Avenue, where, though "Blanche dragged me into it," he "escaped after a few minutes, and without drinking any of the cocktails."[18] Blanche's party was given a two-page spread in *Publishers Weekly*, complete with photographs of the couple's offices and the anteroom to the sixteenth-floor reception area. Shiny black linoleum floor, dull black walls, indirect lighting, and a "large doorway of natural walnut" led into the lobby papered with jackets of Knopf's most celebrated publications. Beyond was the blue-and-beige reception room, "accented by natural walnut, glass and polished brass." The firm's current books were displayed in a "long, narrow illumined case recessed in the north wall." Blanche's pleasure in mixing periods resulted in a comfortable library that featured modern shelving, Chippendale chairs, and a Persian rug. Alfred's office was notable for its heavy, dark wood antique desk, surrounded by "original Beerbohm drawings and old maps framed in bamboo," while Blanche's was "completely modern . . . its color scheme off-white and beige with striking [red] accents." She had two windows, the larger looking west and the other facing diagonally down over the spire of St. Patrick's Cathedral, with one of her walls "completely composed of bookshelves, the other walls covered in a neutral grass cloth." Blanche's desk was light walnut, and she had "three small round modern chairs upholstered in brilliant crimson corduroy for seating visitors."[19]

Mencken recorded in his diary his concerns: Knopf was making very little profit and would need some popular books to stay afloat. There was a price Knopf paid for remaining small, unlike such up-and-coming-firms as Doubleday, Random House, and Simon & Schuster. As the former Knopf publicity director Pete Lemay explains, "The medium-sized house of Knopf maintained a solid financial position by publishing steady selling fiction and non-fiction instead of very popular best sellers . . . [The Knopfs] turned down a number of best-selling writers because . . . they wanted to maintain the high literary standards that made [the] company notable."[20]

In 1937, concerned that a recession loomed, the Knopfs again decided to rent out their Purchase house for the summer, this time to Carol and Carl Pforzheimer. Alfred and Blanche alternated weeks at a cottage in Falmouth on Cape Cod, where Alfred sailed and played tennis and Blanche typically read outside in a deck chair. Although they were not together, somehow the couple still managed to fight over who should invite Mencken to stay at the bungalow. Unsurprisingly, he never found the time to visit either one of them.

Before the vacation got off the ground, their friend George Gershwin died of brain cancer at the age of thirty-eight. His *Porgy and Bess* (later deemed an operatic masterpiece) had been judged unsuccessful, and he had recently moved to Los Angeles to work on movie scores. Within months, however, he began suffering various neurological oddities, from perceiving the phantom smell of burning rubber to attempting to push his driver out of the car. Unable to eat without spilling food, he was taken to Cedars of Lebanon, a hospital in Hollywood, where he was diagnosed as a hysteric and released. Two weeks later, unable to speak or move normally, Gershwin was rushed back to the hospital, where he died within days.

His casket brought on a train back to New York for his funeral at Temple Emanu-El, Gershwin was honored by more than 3,500 mourners, with another thousand standing outside the building in the drizzling rain. Though Blanche and Alfred were surely there, the only Knopf listed among the guests was the movie producer Edwin Knopf. Edwin had remained among Gershwin's closest friends since their getaway to Asheville for the composer to finish *Rhapsody in Blue*.[21] And the honorary pallbearer, New York mayor Fiorello La Guardia, son of a Jewish mother and an Italian father, was the perfect symbol of the city and its music as Gershwin and his fans heard it—New York City first and foremost.

Again for less-than-gratifying reasons, the Knopfs were brought together during the summer of 1937. Pat, who'd stayed in New York City to retake a course he'd failed at Exeter, finally graduated in August—and promptly ran away from home. In a note written to his parents, he said he was depressed over being turned down by Princeton and intended not to return until he made good. Following a police search, he was found in Salt Lake City, "sleeping on a lawn," because only "truck drivers" would lend him a hand: as if mimicking his father's way of talking, he complained that "the rest of the population was a bunch of damned snobs." Pat had stayed on a park bench while "police in seven states" looked for him. Once he was found, his parents were quickly contacted, and they flew out to get him. Alfred seemed almost proud of Pat's behavior, while Blanche, who'd been frantically calling police around the country, was furious at what her son had done. Still, both parents beamed at local reporters as a picture was snapped of Pat.[22]

On August 4, Mencken wrote Blanche of his relief when the Associated Press reported that Pat had been found. "I surely hope that your troubles are now over," he wrote. "What a nuisance it has been!" Henry knew that Blanche constantly worried she was a poor mother, and for her benefit he recalled his cousin's attempt to get him, when a boy, "to run out West and fight Indians with him." Though he'd refused the offer, he recalled "six boys from his neighborhood alone doing something along those lines. Life to a boy in his teens is certainly not pleasant," he added kindly, aware that Blanche believed she'd failed her son. "He is always policed, and most of the things he is asked to do are disagreeable to him."[23]

Years later, Knopf's accountant-turned-treasurer Joe Lesser said about the highly publicized event that "I think the story was a bunch of hooey Pat cooked up to be the center of attention, as always, and to avoid the issue of not getting into a college. I imagine he made sure his parents knew where he was the whole time."[24] After the Knopfs retrieved Pat, Alfred introduced him to people in the publishing world, and he ended up working in Doubleday's stockroom for a year. It may have been at this time that Alfred started "procuring" women for both Pat and himself at Purchase, twice a week, according to Bill Koshland. Competition over Pat continued, and hiring women who "serviced" father and son (without Blanche's knowledge) guaranteed that "the boy" would choose Purchase over Blanche's New York apartment from now on. Blanche must have assumed that her son simply preferred living with his father.[25]

In September 1937, Blanche sailed to England on the *Normandie*, and returned having acquired Franz Kafka's *The Trial*. Knopf published an especially fine slate of literature that year, including Clarence Day's posthumous *Life with Mother* as well as André Gide's repudiation of communism, *Return from the U.S.S.R.*, along with the British writer Eric Ambler's first export, *Background to Danger*, a spy novel. James M. Cain's recently published *Serenade* was, Blanche and Henry believed, a masterpiece, less a mystery than a romance.[26]

As if it were a celebration of the year that had proceeded so badly with Pat's escapade, Arthur and Nela Rubinstein (he to become one of Blanche's occasional lovers, she to become one of Mildred Knopf's friends) made the publisher's voyage home on the *Queen Mary* all the more pleasurable. When she disembarked in New York on November 15, Blanche told Pat she would take him with her to Los Angeles over the Christmas holidays. This year they'd stay at the glamorous Beverly Wilshire Hotel, instead of at Edwin and Mildred Knopf's house, as Blanche had done in the past. Knopf seemed to be entering a period of financial stability, though it was hardly flourishing. Its 1937 figures, as recorded by Joe Lesser, were sales of $645,000 (about $10.8 million today), profits of $10,657, and Alfred and Blanche's combined salaries of $45,600 (Blanche's $15,000). There was reason for optimism, of a financial sort at least.

15

SIGMUND FREUD, THOMAS MANN, AND OTHERS

O N MARCH 12, 1938, Hitler annexed Austria. Blanche realized that she needed to complete any lingering business abroad quickly and visit various authors, several of whom lay in harm's way. The *Anschluss* had forced Sigmund Freud to immigrate to England before finishing his book *Moses and Monotheism*. Between his June relocation to London and his death the following year, Blanche would meet with him privately at least once and convince him to allow Knopf to translate and publish the book, his last completed work. His friend the writer Stefan Zweig, an acquaintance of Blanche's—or possibly Thomas Mann, who was also close to Freud—had likely put the two in contact.[1]

Before she could travel abroad again, Blanche had two assignments for the early summer: ensuring Pat would be attending college, and providing at least rudimentary training to her new personal assistant, nineteen-year-old Ruth Levine (later Nasoff). Though she'd never anticipated it, Ruth, just out of secretarial school and the cousin of Joe Lesser's wife, would stay for eight years, from 1938 to 1946, "loving it all." As an elderly woman, she remembered her years with Blanche as the most exciting time of her life.[2]

Pat was a more difficult matter. Apparently, Alfred, who knew the Yale dean of admissions, had thoughtlessly urged Pat to apply to the Ivy League again. At least when he was rejected this time, their son didn't overreact. After a fruitless trip to see the Woolseys, during which the judge disingenuously claimed to have no influence at Yale, Alfred finally accepted that Pat was not destined for a top university. The Knopfs then drove to Union College, a liberal-arts school in Schenectady, New York. Thanks to the president, whom Alfred knew from Columbia, and the Knopfs' friend Frank Bailey, a trustee, in late June 1938 Pat was admitted to Union.

Before Blanche went abroad, the three Knopfs escaped New York's summer heat by visiting Judith Anderson in Berkeley, as well as Edwin and Mildred in Santa Monica. They even saw the Heifetzes (Judith was said to be having an affair with Jascha) at their cottage in Balboa Island, California. Leaving Pat with his aunt and uncle (Mildred later confessed she had always found Pat a "mischiefmaker"), Blanche and Alfred then traveled to the Grand Canyon, a setting that Blanche found rigid, cold, and without appeal.[3] Blanche's eyesight must have made the landscape particularly intimidating—she was having a harder time seeing than ever, her eyes receiving medical treatments that hurt more than helped her vision. Also, leaving Pat with Alfred's brother preyed on her; she had sensed (and Mildred Knopf confirmed years later) that Edwin had a "vile temper and difficult nature." Over the past few years, the more success Edwin had achieved, the more unbearable he became. Mildred's friends told Blanche that he was pompous and "horrible" to his wife, whom most people thought "a saint."[4] Pat, however, considered him "the most wonderful Knopf in the family" (other than his father) and was pleased that his uncle so clearly emulated Alfred, down to his clothes.[5] Mildred herself recalled how "Alfred was always dominant over

Edwin." At one of the inevitable dinner parties the Hollywood Knopfs gave when Alfred was in town, Edwin, imitating his brother's lofty behavior, insisted they begin rather than wait half an hour for Marlene Dietrich, held up at the studio.[6]

Later in the month, Blanche took off for Europe. She planned to spend several days at Elizabeth Bowen's Irish country estate, Bowen's Court at Kildorrery, in County Cork, where, Bowen teased her, she would be forced to unwind. Blanche and Bowen had lots to talk about, and it was surely hard for anyone to imagine Blanche relaxing, even at Bowen's Court. Before she left port she was already busy organizing an onboard cocktail party for the evening, gathering guests that included the author and rare book collector Wilmarth Lewis; Walter Damrosch, an American conductor and composer; and Arthur Krock, a Washington journalist whom she knew slightly. She hoped to invite one of Krock's frequent sources, Joseph P. Kennedy, as well, no doubt to suggest he write a book. But the ambassador was impossible to reach. Remembering Blanche after her death, Lewis would say that she "was very hospitable and a little overwhelming." He remembered publishing his first book with her in 1922, *Tutor's Lane*. "To become a Knopf author was already like being asked to join a club," he said.[7]

Blanche fell in love with Bowen's country home, the "lush green surroundings" and its gentle hills similar to what delighted her about the Hudson Valley. She and Bowen opened themselves up to each other on this visit, causing Blanche to realize that though Bowen clearly loved her husband, the somewhat younger Alan Cameron, she was not in love with him. In fact, they had never consummated their marriage. But Bowen had had a thirty-year sexual liaison with a Canadian diplomat, who was also younger than she. Upon her return to New York, Blanche wrote Bowen, her words about the glorious landscape laden with meaning: "I never realized how beautiful living that way could possibly be."[8] She had, in fact, found mental repose in nature, though the opposite of the nature that inspired her husband.

Aware that this might be her last chance at luxury transatlantic travel for a long time, Blanche had sailed back to the States on the palatial *Île de France*.[9] The 1926 ocean liner with its four-story foyer was one of her favorite ships, primarily because of its three-decks-high swimming pools, and for the lavish Art Deco motif adorning the *salle à manger*, a design that would be re-created at Eaton's, a ninth-floor restaurant in Quebec.

Though she would happily have stayed abroad for months, she had to be home in time for negotiations with Bennett Cerf. After consulting with others, she'd decided to encourage Dashiell Hammett to move to Random House, where he'd get more money—and she'd get rid of a major headache. Decades later, Cerf would recall Alfred warning him, "Go ahead, [take him,] you'll have nothing but trouble with Hammett. He [is] a terrible man and I want nothing more to do with him."[10] Of course, it was Blanche who handled Hammett.

In October 1938, Blanche and Alfred visited the writer Dorothy Canfield Fisher, Norman Rockwell's neighbor in Arlington, Vermont. Blanche knew Canfield slightly through her long friendship with Willa Cather, the two writers frequently exchanging rough drafts of their work. Alfred wanted to publish a book about Vermont and thought Blanche could convince Canfield to write one. While traveling, the Knopfs had just missed the fall hurricane that swept the Atlantic coast, hammering Long Island—and now the source of a great deal of conversation. Manhattan had escaped the worst of the storm, Blanche told Dorothy, though with 60-mile-per-hour winds in Central Park and 120 miles per hour recorded at the top of the Empire State Building, its residents didn't get off scot-free either. Obviously, this was the time to get Canfield signed to Knopf, when she could write a timely book about her valiant state. Signs of the storm's ravage surrounded them even as the two women conversed: they chatted in damaged Adirondack chairs as they gazed at the wreckage strewn over Canfield's yard, Alfred shooting photographs of them talking.[11]

The women enjoyed each other. Dorothy, whose work as a Book-of-the-Month Club judge conferred its own cachet, talked about her efforts on behalf of Montessori, a school program whose focus on independent learning interested Blanche. Even more relevant to Blanche's personal concerns was the Braille press Dorothy had established for blind World War I veterans. When she left, Blanche had no contract for a book on Vermont, but Canfield had agreed to do a children's book, *Tell Me a Story*, published by Knopf in 1940.[12]

Home from New England in time to vote for governor of New York, Blanche went to the *Times* offices with Alfred to hear the election returns on November 8: Tom and Frances Dewey were old friends. After insensitively informing Frances that he had voted for Herbert Lehman rather than for her husband, Alfred told Blanche they'd lost a friend. Blanche was exasperated: Why would he say such a thing? But all such concerns were overshadowed by the news coming from Europe. On November 9, at the command of Adolf Hitler and Joseph Goebbels, mob violence broke out in Germany, Austria, and other Nazi-controlled areas. The police and spectators looked on as if at a carnival while synagogues and houses were broken into and some burned down, and shop windows were smashed. Thousands of Jewish men were rounded up and later sent to concentration camps. *Kristallnacht* was the most extreme state-sanctioned violence against German and Austrian Jews yet.

When Blanche traveled to Europe in late November, she went first to London to meet with the famous émigré now residing at Maresfield Gardens in Hampstead. Freud, according to his biographer Ernest Jones, had already granted Knopf the rights for an English-language translation of his recently finished *Moses and Monotheism*, written in German. Though Freud had an advanced case of throat cancer, he continued working, even after the death of his beloved dog, always at his feet while he wrote. Having realized as he reread his German text that he'd omitted important material in the original, he could now remedy his mistake in the Knopf edition. Though Blanche knew that such alterations would hold up publication, she let the great doctor have his way. His changes were considerable, and he risked repetition while further developing his thesis. The translator Blanche hired, Katherine Jones, required a good deal of back-and-forth with the writer to shape the work for an English-speaking audience, though as Ernest Jones's wife, she had a strong sense of the milieu of psychoanalysis as well as firsthand access to Freud.

Blanche feared that Freud would die before they finished. She wanted him to view the final manuscript, to know his last written work was in good hands. She wrote him gently:

> *Since all details of the translation are gone over by you with Dr. Jones I thought it most convenient that I [send] him my suggestions in order not to trouble you unduly.*
>
> *. . . You know how proud and happy I am to be privileged to publish your work; and I want it put in the hands of the public very soon. With the inevitable onrush of events your book becomes more important every day. I hope that we can achieve for you a scientific success and a popular one as well . . .*
>
> *With all kind regards and very good wishes to you in eufrichtiger Verehrung ["sincere admiration"—it should have been "aufrichtiger Verehrung"; Blanche's secretary must have mistaken Blanche's "a" for an "e"]—I am yours sincerely, Mrs. Alfred A. Knopf.*[13]

Turning from Freud, Blanche worked on Raymond Chandler's first detective novel, psychologically acute in its own right. In February 1939, Knopf's winter sales were boosted by publication of *The Big Sleep*, which sold five thousand copies. Constructed from stories Chandler had published in *The Black Cat*, the novel was a fast-paced blend of murder and madness. Reviews were positive and critics looked forward to his future. *The Nation* admired "its subtle workmanship," while *The New Yorker* liked its "story of degeneracy" that made "Dashiell Hammett look like Winnie the Pooh." *The New York Times* pronounced it excellent "as a study of depravity."

More than eighty years later, Stephen King would lament in his book *On Writing* that Chandler was still vastly underrated in the twenty-first century, critics and other writers considering him "a hack . . . a hack with pretensions! The worst kind." Those who read Chandler carefully, King said, tend to see him instead as an "important figure in twentieth-century American literature, an early voice describing the anomie of urban life in the years after World War II."[14] Blanche had counseled Chandler well, urging him to undertake the serious novels he wanted to write but to "keep the character of Marlowe—as you would anyway in all probability—but give him another name. In this way we think you would avoid leading casual readers to suspect they were getting another mystery whatever we said on the wrapper."[15]

Even as she was praising Chandler for the fine reviews of *The Big Sleep*, Blanche was impatient to see the early March press for *Moses and Monotheism*. She knew Freud had toiled to finish the book, even when respected Jewish scholars begged him not to release it at such an unstable time—fearing its radical revision of the Moses story might fuel anti-Semitism. He gently but firmly explained that he would not let the monsters triumph over his ability to write what he believed. If he did that, such forces of evil would have won.

In May, far from Freud's world, Blanche flew with Alfred to Hollywood, where they met Raymond Chandler in person for the first time and had lunch with him and his wife, Cissy. The couple was living in the mountains about two hours away, near Big Bear, where Chandler could escape the debilitating heat of Los Angeles. They all wanted to discuss the possibility of having *The Big Sleep* and its detective, Philip Marlowe, optioned for a film, but Blanche was focused on Chandler's next book as well. To be titled *Farewell, My Lovely* (Blanche had refused Chandler's half-teasing preference for *Zounds, He Dies*), the book would be made into a movie twice, first with the title *Murder, My Sweet*, with Marlowe played by Dick Powell, and later starring Robert Mitchum; in 1993, Elliott Gould did an audio recording of the book. Marlowe has proven an irresistible role for actors.

On June 1, 1939, Knopf released Elizabeth Bowen's *The Death of the Heart*, one of her strongest novels, its themes of emotional distance and submerged heartbreak infused with a Jamesian melancholy. But some critics found the writing remote, resisting emotional engagement by the reader. Generally, however, reviews were positive, and the book's original sales reached around five thousand, average for the novelist.

Finally, while Freud was still alive to see it, *Moses and Monotheism* appeared. Predictably, opinions varied dramatically. For the most part, Blanche was pleased at the reviews, which in their radical diversity proved to her Freud's courage. Some took the tack of near deification—*The Commonweal* declared it an "epoch making work" and *The New Yorker* declared that "his insights deriving from psychoanalysis are brilliant; his style, grave and scientific"—while others vilified it. *The New York Times* complained: "For one who professes such devotion to Science and Reason . . . , [Freud's] procedure is shockingly unscientific and irrational," and the *Catholic World* dismissed it entirely, calling the book "poorly written" and "spoiled by the author's atheistic bias and his flimsy psycho-analytical fancies."

Blanche surely rushed a bound copy to Freud, telling him that the book was well received. A heavy cigar smoker, Freud had endured more than thirty operations until his friend Max Schur, honoring Freud's request to help him kill himself, with Anna Freud's reluctant permission, gave him lethal doses of morphine on September 21 and 22. On September 23, 1939, without a tremor, Freud died.

At last, with Alfred in Europe, there was a lull in the office, enabling Blanche to fully train Ruth, on whom she would be depending heavily in the fall. Ruth Levine Nasoff, who never called Blanche by her first name, was "awed by her and everything she stood for." The young assistant found Blanche "an intimidating but generous" employer, who, after traveling, always brought her a gift as if "to show her a gentle side."

In an interview given in her eighties, Nasoff became animated when talking about her former boss: "She had such energy . . . That's one of the things I always admired about her. She stayed up all night dictating into a recorder. It seems to me she never slept." When Ruth told Blanche that English was her best subject in school, her employer encouraged her to practice writing letters in Blanche's "style of writing." As soon as she saw that Ruth could "formulate a sentence properly," she started dictating "distracted" letters, which she counted on Ruth to make "cohesive." Unlike Alfred, whose writing was often too ponderous for readers to finish, Blanche had a clear, direct style that Ruth thought easy "to capture."[16] Often, when Blanche had a sudden idea, Ruth would take notes on matchstick books or a menu and from one or two words compose a letter, so intuitive had their working relationship become.

Most days Blanche appeared at her office each morning around 9:00 "and [got] right to work, her desk always piled high." Having spent much of the night awake, dictating letters from bed, Blanche would hand Ruth the wax cylinder (soon a more modern disc) and immediately turn to the sales reports: "She had to have [those] out in front of her every morning." Much of Blanche's day was spent "seeing people, really working meetings." Late afternoons, she might go to her hairdresser's, to tend to not only her hair but her nails as well. She already had her "long claws, dark purple and a nail guard for when she had a broken nail."[17] (After her death, Pete Lemay would remark,

"I could find no suitable explanation for the fingernails . . . which curled at the tips like the claws of a jungle bird." Unlike those employees from Knopf's early days, Pete failed to associate the claws with the bird girl in *Green Mansions*.)[18]

Blanche gave out hundreds of books for the December holidays, which Ruth wrapped and mailed, occasionally working out of Blanche's "beautiful [white] apartment . . . The fabrics . . . Fireplace, terrace going around it, floor-to-ceiling sliding doors."[19] In contrast, at Purchase "you had to turn on [the] light on [the] second floor in broad daylight [because of all the] dark oak, doors stained dark. [Alfred] lived in darkness, she in light," Ruth said.[20] When Knopf was doing a children's book on Christmas with Eleanor Roosevelt (to be published the following year, 1940, as *Christmas: A Story*), Ruth was startled to see both Alfred and Blanche race out of their offices to greet the First Lady first, until she realized the Knopfs needed to pit themselves against each other, so deeply ingrained was their competitive urge.

For the next few months, after Alfred's return from Europe, the Knopfs spent pleasant summer weekends with Carl and Carol Brandt, major New York literary agents with a grand country house near Clinton, New Jersey, just an hour from Manhattan but allowing guests to feel they were escaping the city. There were finally opportunities to relax: Thomas Mann and his wife, Katia, having fled their home in Germany, had been depending on Blanche for everything, it seemed, from stocking their refrigerator to using the telephone. Soon, however, they became acclimated to Princeton, where Blanche had helped Mann secure a short-term faculty position. Mann stayed at Princeton until 1942, when he and his family moved to Pacific Palisades, where the author eventually settled at 1550 San Remo Drive, an address he was assured was worthy of his eminence.

She was pleased to receive a cable from William Shirer, who was now ready to write about the genesis of war he'd witnessed in Berlin—

if Blanche could help him think of a way to frame his observations. She responded immediately, suggesting that he collate his notebook observations in Germany with his broadcasts from overseas. She concluded by assuring Shirer that she would draw up a contract soon, and that, in the end, she trusted him to inform *her* about how he would tell his story: "The book is there to be written and you have the stuff, and I want to publish it, so there we are."[21]

16

A MAN OF HER OWN

THE DECEMBER HOLIDAYS OF 1939 held a new poignancy, with Blanche deeply apprehensive about Pat's eagerness to go to war. "There is not going to be any war in Europe this year," Roosevelt had insisted, only to be preempted on September 1 by the German invasion of Poland.[1] Determined to celebrate this Christmas Day as a family, Blanche asked the Van Vechtens to join her, Alfred, and Pat in Purchase, with both couples meeting again the following week at the Pforzheimers' New Year's Eve party.

Shortly after midnight Blanche and Alfred "sneaked away" to their car, parked on a side street, and drove for an hour to the Heifetzes' "Potato Farm" near Ridgefield, Connecticut.[2] As on every January 1 (though usually at the Heifetzes' Park Avenue apartment), there was an abundance of chamber music and a lavish predawn breakfast. Still in evening clothes, Alfred drove Blanche to the White Plains station, where she caught a train back to the city to prepare for her customary eggnog party later that day at her apartment.

Preoccupied with fear of another war, everyone—the Manns, Rubinsteins, and Heifetzes—dipped with unusual abandon into Blanche's heavily spiked drink, which was stronger than ever, guests noted.[3]

Four weeks into 1940, Blanche was the focus of a *Publishers Weekly* feature titled "Knopf Marks Anniversary with Big List." Explaining that though "last year [Blanche] went to the Pacific Coast" (referring to her trip to California and the Northwest), until "recently," Knopf business had required that she go to Europe. Her readers were told, "She is active in every branch of the business." While pleased by the publicity, Blanche had hoped the journalist would discuss her excitement over the long-anticipated two-volume Shelley biography by Newman Ivey White, published in 1940 and still highly regarded today.

Two earlier books by White, a southern gentleman, had further educated Blanche in the culture Van Vechten had first shown her: *An Anthology of Verse by American Negroes* in 1924, and *American Negro Folk Songs* four years later. Over the years, the Whites and the Knopfs, along with the publishers' neighbor the philanthropist and book collector Carl Pforzheimer, had become close. In his Shelley biography, White acknowledged Pforzheimer for letting him use a journal belonging to Claire Clairmont, no small favor: Clairmont, the stepsister of the writer Mary Shelley, was also Lord Byron's lover and the mother of his daughter Allegra. The collector had long amassed material on the British Romantics, storing it at his Purchase home. (By 1986, with the cooperation of Carl Pforzheimer's son, the New York Public Library would become one of the world's leading repositories for the study of English Romanticism.)[4]

That spring of 1940, White and Pforzheimer attended a small party that Blanche gave at Purchase in honor of the Chicago-born couturier Mainbocher, a recent émigré from Paris, where he had established the first American atelier in the city. He and his lover spent the weekend of May 17 with Blanche, and when they heard of the fall of France, "it was as if their closest friend had died."[5]

The party, which included Thomas Mann, Mencken, and a clutch of fashionable socialites who clearly could afford expensive clothes, was one of the very eclectic mixes that only Blanche could pull off. She intended to show the designer that even the backwaters outside New York City provided plenty of well-known, international figures to whom he could ply his craft; imagine what Manhattan itself would offer his business. Just a year earlier, Mainbocher had been immortalized by his farewell to Paris, an elaborate corset that was a highlight of his last French collection. Horst (whose full name was Horst Paul Albert Bohrmann) captured the garment in one of his most famous photographs, known today as *The Mainbocher Corset*, a shot of a highly constructed item that redefined the drab fashion of the decade. The corset, listed in *Town & Country* as one of the major events of 1939, had caused a furor in France, according to *Vanity Fair*, especially when the designer announced he was exchanging Paris for New York City.[6]

That summer, Blanche was pleased to resume her relationship with Serge Koussevitzky, who regaled her with news about the talent he had assembled at Tanglewood, which would become the Boston Symphony's summer home. Koussevitzky's friend Aaron Copland had introduced the maestro to a young man who wanted to take the master conducting class, and from the moment that Koussevitzky had seen Leonard Bernstein—even before watching him work—he was sure the musician was preternaturally gifted. The master didn't have to teach "Lenny" much technique, so he became a kind of father figure instead, encouraging Bernstein to "let it all out" on the podium. At some point Copland would introduce Van Vechten to the "boy" who was "the Maestro's favorite pupil," and Van Vechten reported to Blanche: Bernstein wore a pair of sparkling cuff links, his gift from Koussevitzky, at every concert he conducted.[7]

When the Tanglewood season was over, Blanche went to Los

Angeles. Many of her authors, she realized, found it easier to see her on the West Coast than in New York. From Raymond Chandler, to Conrad Richter, to Arthur and Nela Rubinstein, who were living in Brentwood during the war, while the Manns were settled in Pacific Palisades—many of Blanche's friends and writers had gone west. Edwin and Mildred had decided to buy in Hollywood, where they, Blanche, and her authors often lunched at the Brown Derby, opposite the Beverly Wilshire Hotel. Mildred would later recall Blanche wondering aloud, as she had with Florence Heifetz, how Mildred managed it all: to be such a great mother, superb cook, and attentive wife, while she herself had failed at all three. Mildred disagreed, reminding Blanche of all she'd achieved. But Blanche demurred, and in an oddly defeated voice told her, "No, I could never have accomplished what you have."[8]

Mildred had thrown her earlier gifts for acting into entertaining Edwin's celebrity friends in Hollywood, her success resulting in a cookbook Knopf would publish in 1950. With 650 recipes, *The Perfect Hostess Cook Book* was a look at "how the privileged class in New York City and California entertained, and what they ate." According to the four rules stated on the vividly colored book jacket— "Enthusiasm, Pride in what you serve, Confidence in yourself and Confidence once again!!"—a recipe existed to enhance the perfect host as well as her food.[9] Blanche had clearly learned much about giving parties from her sister-in-law in the early days of Mildred's marriage.

Back in New York, Blanche found herself seated next to a fascinating guest at a friend's dinner. Before long, she was chatting with the stranger about the "City of Angels" she had just visited, even as she lamented not being able to go to Paris because of the war. If visiting her talented sister-in-law made Blanche feel deficient, her trips to France were always uplifting. Surprising her by responding in French, her dinner partner said quietly: "Perhaps one day we will visit together." Whether the gentleman meant Paris or Los Angeles,

Blanche was smitten with the elegant Hubert Hohe, referred to as "Hohe" by Blanche and her associates throughout his life. According to Toni Pasquale, "He was one of those foreign charmers, average height but tan."[10] An émigré from Germany ten years earlier who was now a supposedly successful Manhattan stockbrocker, he would never seem entirely trustworthy to Blanche's friends, yet he would become the love of Blanche's life.

A large part of Hohe's attraction for Blanche was his complete separation from Alfred and the publishing world. Soon she invented a reason to return to California, this time with her beau at her side. In high spirits, she took Hohe to meet the Heifetzes, who were vacationing nearby—appalling Florence with her flagrant disregard of proprieties. Then she took Hohe to meet Alfred's brother and sister-in-law, expecting Edwin and Mildred to welcome them for an overnight visit. Shocked by Blanche's behavior, the Knopfs did not. The couple stayed at the Beverly Hills Hotel instead.

Exactly who Hubert Hohe was and what his intentions were remain uncertain, but he swiftly became a magnet for Blanche. To Florence Heifetz, the Frenchman seemed "a gigolo." Ruth Levine Nasoff remembered Hohe as a "gaunt, pallid" man, "far less attractive than Alfred." Yet, after only a few months, Blanche decided she would finally leave Alfred and marry her lover—until Hohe "realized" his own divorce wasn't final yet.[11]

Blanche confessed to Ruth, now a confidante, that at forty-five she had fallen in love for the first time. As if instinctively, the Francophile publisher was acting the part of Balzac's *A Woman of Thirty* (*La Femme de Trente Ans*), born again through romance for which she was willing to risk disaster. Florence Heifetz, among others, remembers Blanche proudly "showing Hohe off" at Rockaway Beach in Queens, and at the Heifetzes' dinner parties in Manhattan. "Frankly, I just don't understand . . . Blanche doted on him."[12]

Clearly Alfred knew of his wife's latest affair. For the Knopfs' celebration of their twenty-fifth year of publishing, he set up separate parties: for Blanche, he arranged a luncheon on December 18, 1940, at the Dorset Hotel at 30 West Fifty-Fourth Street, where the Knopfs were now living (Alfred's room upstairs and Blanche's below). He held a separate party at a club, unspecified in his records, for himself and guests. At Blanche's lunch Robert Nathan recited a poem he wrote in her honor, and Thomas Mann, in his eccentric English, gave a tribute acknowledging her importance to Knopf. Mann had always appreciated Blanche's kindnesses to him, dating from their first meeting. When Knopf signed him, he had known no English, so he and Blanche had spoken French (his second language). Formal in prose and in nature, Mann still seemed to Blanche the quintessential old-world European.

Mencken spoke in carefully chosen words that were flattering to both Knopfs, attempting to balance on a very fine wire. He, Anne O'Hare McCormick, and Fannie Hurst were the hosts, the women among Blanche's good friends by now. McCormick, whose book Blanche wanted to publish, was one of the most distinguished women in the country, the first female journalist to receive a Pulitzer Prize for foreign correspondence. Blanche prized Hurst for her ability to spin a tale, and for her moral courage as well: she used race relations as the theme for her most famous novel, *Imitation of Life*. A champion of Zora Neale Hurston, she had hired the writer briefly as her live-in secretary in 1925.

For years, Fannie and Blanche had traded news of the latest diet crazes, not to mention pills, until Fannie penned a book, *No Food with My Meals* (1935), that, through humor, condemned the cult of skinniness. Hurst candidly discussed body issues that remain current today. She decried the "ideal weights" assigned adults in their mid-thirties as "usually those of underdeveloped boys," and describes becoming "nasty in spirit" while she starved herself.[13] Forcing upon her guests platters of rich food, she prayed that they gained weight.

"I schemed for the obesity of my lean friends," she wrote.[14] Hurst's book struck Blanche as gospel truth, and for a few years she weighed ten pounds more than she had on her diet pills.

Inevitably in those months, no matter how determined the gaiety, conversation turned to the war. Blanche and Mencken were unable to meet without discussing the conflict that they, along with most Americans, felt sure their country would join. A few days before Christmas, Blanche wrote to Myra Hess, who, in an effort to boost the national morale, had organized low-cost concerts at Britain's National Gallery: "Dearest Myra, England is doing a superb job and I think we over here are now girding our loins and really getting underway ourselves . . . You see, a public has to be made conscious and you know how long it took England to realize what was going on. It is taking us not quite as long perhaps but it is taking a lot of time."[15]

As 1941 rolled along with President Roosevelt's third inauguration, Blanche was impatient to get William Shirer's book back from the printer. Its subject—anti-Semitism and Nazi tyranny in Berlin, where Shirer remained from the *Anschluss* until late 1940—was obviously time-sensitive. She wanted it out quickly.

Frustrated by the limits imposed on her going overseas, Blanche took a trip west. She trekked to Texas with Alfred, then traveled to New Orleans to meet with Henry Miller to discuss the possibility of Knopf publishing his letters (they didn't). Finally, "the Baroness," as Van Vechten wrote to Langston Hughes, using the appellation her close friends employed, went to Los Angeles to do deals, check on Thomas Mann, and talk yet again with Raymond Chandler about *Farewell, My Lovely*. Always pleased to see Mildred Knopf, even for coffee, Blanche was aware of how disapproving she was of her relationship with Hohe, who stayed behind this time. The women stuck to safe topics.

Once home, Blanche became involved with *The Mind of the South*, by W. J. Cash, an editor of the progressive *Charlotte News*, who was writing extraordinary features on the world crisis, for which he would later receive a Pulitzer Prize nomination. Published on February 10, 1941, *The Mind of the South* was praised lavishly by sources ranging from the NAACP to *The Saturday Review of Literature* and *The New York Times*. Most well-respected southern newspapers would eventually share the opinion of *Time* magazine: "Anything written about the South henceforth must start where [Cash] leaves off."[16] The book ended: "Proud, brave, courteous, personally generous . . . sometimes terrible, in its action—such was the South at its best. Violence, intolerance, aversion and suspicion toward new ideas [and] above all . . . a tendency to justify cruelty and injustice in the name of those values . . . remain its characteristic vices today."[17]

There turned out to be little time for Blanche or her writer to revel in the book's reception. Tragically, on July 1, in Mexico City, where Cash was due to speak at a university, he was found hanging from a doorknob by a tie, his death an apparent murder staged as a suicide by a North American Nazi group. Instead, long a depressive, Cash had in fact killed himself.

Another signal of the times appeared with the arrival of the publishers Kurt and Helen Wolff, who fled Germany and immigrated to Manhattan. The American journalist Varian Fry, later called the Oskar Schindler of France, arranged the couple's escape—along with at least four thousand other refugees. The following year the Wolffs founded Pantheon Books, which specialized in European literature. Regardless of her company's strength, Blanche must have been wary of the "new Knopfs" in town. Her approach was to befriend them at once, inviting them frequently to Purchase dinners, according to the Knopf editor Henry Carlisle.

Four decades later, Herbert Mitgang's *New Yorker* account of the Wolffs seems a peculiar revision of history, given that at the time of the new firm's formation in 1942, Alfred A. Knopf had already become a legendary house. Sixteen years after Blanche's death, in 1982, Mitgang would write that in the early forties, Helen Wolff, with her husband, Kurt, had "transformed the nature of publishing in this country by introducing first-rate foreign writers"—a description taking no account of the similar Knopf trajectory preceding the Wolffs' by more than twenty-five years. Also like the earlier publishers, the Wolffs put out "only what they considered worthwhile, refusing to compromise or to be diverted by commerce"—language long invoked to describe Knopf.[18]

In 1941, the year that the war relocated the Wolffs to America, Knopf brought out Paul Gallico's *The Snow Goose: A Story of Dunkirk*, an O. Henry Award–winning novella about the horrors of battle— and, finally, *Berlin Diary*. Shirer had told the Knopfs that he needed a ten-thousand-dollar advance, half up front, and he never forgot Alfred grumbling: "Only H. G. Wells ever received such an advance." After all, Shirer was "only a journalist, not a writer."[19] When Alfred balked, Blanche had to remind her husband of her meetings with Shirer in Berlin, Paris, and London, of her years of relentlessly pursuing Shirer's book. She was certain that Knopf would recover its expenses.

Her persistence paid off: although higher bids came in, Shirer wanted Blanche to publish his book, and Alfred relented. Knopf sent Shirer his check due on signing, which paid for the writer's rent and expenses at his house in Chappaqua, New York, where he sat down with "paste and scissors" and "tried to make a book out of the diaries," just as Blanche had advised. Worried that his daily writing wasn't "that interesting," with Blanche's reassurance he plowed forward, finishing the book that April and "lugging it to Knopf." Blanche handed him the second half of his advance before she even read the manuscript.[20]

Berlin Diary was optioned by the Book-of-the-Month Club within twenty-four hours of their receiving a copy, enabling the Knopfs to recoup their advance immediately, as Blanche had predicted. Shirer later joked with friends about how Alfred became an instant pal, suddenly calling *Berlin Diary* a "grand book."[21] The timing was perfect: Germany was about to sequester and devastate Russia. Soon Edward R. Murrow and James Reston, the young *New York Times* reporter, were working on books for Knopf as well.

Both *The New York Times* and the *New York Herald Tribune* gave *Berlin Diary* front-page reviews. Smaller papers throughout the country published excerpts from the book, such as Shirer's account of the German army entering Belgium on May 20, 1940:

> Here for the first time we suddenly came across real devastation. A good part of the town through which we drove was smashed to pieces. The railroad station was a shambles; obviously hit by Stukas. The railroad tracks all around torn and twisted; cars and locomotives derailed. One could—or could one?—imagine the consternation of the inhabitants. When they had gone to bed that Thursday night (May 9), Belgium had been at peace with the world, including Germany. At dawn on Friday the German bombers were levelling the station and town—the houses in which they had gone to bed so peacefully—reduced to a charred mass of ruins.[22]

Time magazine claimed that the *Diary* was "so sound and so illuminating that it should be read by every American." The Book-of-the-Month Club's Clifton Fadiman wrote in *The New Yorker*, "No matter how carefully you have followed the news . . . you will find *Berlin Diary* compelling reading."[23] Fadiman's review pointed to one reason for the book's success: though Shirer, firsthand, had "carefully . . . followed the news," even he was not prepared for its initial shock, narrated as it occurs, when more or less ordinary Third Reich days turn into days of horror. He learns, for instance, of Nazi doctors releasing to soldiers and scientists mentally ill patients to use for experiments, on the grounds that the "mentally deficient," and even those "suffering temporary derangement" or "plain nervous breakdown," weaken the German races. "If the insane are killed off . . . ," the Nazis realize, "there will be plenty of hospital space for the war wounded should the war be prolonged and large casualties occur."[24]

But the book also elicited menacing anti-Semitic phone calls to the author, and Shirer had to unlist his phone number. By summer, the book had climbed to the top of the bestseller lists. Between the Knopf and the Book-of-the-Month Club editions, *Berlin Diary* eventually sold nearly a million copies.[25]

Bill Koshland believed that *Berlin Diary* was responsible for moving the firm from the "realm of the boutique to the big time." At the beginning of the war, Knopf consisted of Blanche, Alfred, and Joe Lesser, "with maybe 39 other employees," and at the end it was twice that.[26]

During the summer that the *Diary* was published, Pat Knopf was on break from Union College and working as a bartender in Schenectady. He'd seen enough movies "to know [he] didn't want to be in the trenches." Having already registered for the draft, he was provisionally accepted into the Army Air Corps in Albany, if he was needed. Blanche tried to relax about her son, but by the fall she was so tense with worry that her neck was stiff. The brief respite from marital hostilities afforded by the success of *Berlin Diary* had already given way to the habitual rancor. Pat recalls such anger in the house when he visited Purchase that "there was no peace at home [if Blanche was there]. Alfred used to get in the car at midnight and drive off somewhere . . . [We] never discussed this."[27]

When Blanche finally gave in and called Mencken yet again to discuss her son, he managed to reassure her, before redirecting the conversation to his own concerns: How were the sales of *Newspaper Days*, his new book? At least Blanche could deliver good news on that front: 6,260 copies had sold in two weeks, with 300 on order.[28] There were other reasons for professional optimism as well: Knopf was publishing *Mildred Pierce*, another of Blanche's mystery novels by her author James M. Cain. Centered upon incest and infidelity, the noir novel would at first be deemed too risky for Hollywood. But a few years later, it was simply recast as a murder mystery told in flashback, thereby eliminating its most objectionable scenes.

Another Knopf publication that year was of a far different caliber from the company's typical fiction. A Western called *The Blood Remembers*, it was written by Helen Hedrick, a sturdy woman from Oregon, one of the wide-open states out west that Alfred increasingly found magical. Hedrick, who battled rattlesnakes with her bare hands, eventually wrote for quality magazines, including *The New Yorker*, *Harper's*, *The Atlantic Monthly*, *Liberty*, *Collier's*, and *The Saturday Evening Post*, and won an O. Henry Award for a short story, though she would never write another novel.[29] She would, however, become the second Mrs. Alfred A. Knopf, less than a year after Blanche died.

17

GOING OVERSEAS

BLANCHE HAD BEEN PLANNING A SCOUTING TRIP to England since early 1941, when it seemed that the Battle of Britain was over. One of her authors, the journalist Ben Robertson, offered to help her get permission to enter the country. Robertson's *I Saw England*, published just before William Shirer's book, had proved a timely and hopeful adjunct to the *Berlin Diary*, and Blanche—as had everyone, it seemed—had grown to love the young, ever-gracious writer from South Carolina. More reflective than Clare Boothe's *Europe in the Spring*, released by Knopf in 1940 (and a book Dorothy Parker would call "All Clare on the Western Front"),[1] *I Saw England* was praised for Robertson's "facility for picking up what the men and women are feeling, thinking, saying, in all classes," conveying a "real vitality" and a sense of true life.[2]

Recounting the stories of Dunkirk he heard from ordinary citizens, Robertson had a down-home style that elevated the common citizen to a sage, quietly reinforcing the drama of war stories: "At the cigarette store a gnome-like man, who looked as if a rabbit would scare him, told us about going out in a boat to bring the men home from France. Like Lady Astor, he believed it was God who had stilled the English Channel. 'It was a miracle.'"[3]

Pleased at the chance to help Blanche get to Europe, Robertson, reporting on the war from Australia at the time, cabled Brendan Bracken, the British minister for information, urging him to allow the publisher into England. But by the time plans were made, the Blitz had begun, a nine-month period of air attacks on sixteen British cities, with London the chief objective. On September 23 Blanche wrote Robertson to thank him for his efforts. "Confidentially," she said, "[the trip] is for me, of course, [not for war-related projects,] but I don't want anyone here to know about it at all until I am gone, if I do get there."[4] While Robertson worked with Murrow covering the war, Blanche ended up "calling off England," disappointed to bypass what her comrades were now routinely enduring.[5] She would try again the following year, she assured Robertson.

On December 7, Blanche was in New York City when she, along with millions of other Americans, heard that Pearl Harbor had been attacked at 1:55 p.m. EST. Three weeks later, Pat Knopf would be inducted into the Air Corps (then part of the U.S. Army) and deployed to Alabama.[6] His mother was terrified that she'd never see him again (Mencken wondered the same in his diary). When the Knopfs next dined with their neighbors Peggy and Howard Cullman, he variously chairman of the Port of New York Authority and owner of Benson & Hedges tobacco, Blanche kept returning to the topic of her son. Preoccupied with Pat, she failed to be the gracious guest she usually was, and instead tried to joke about her boy flying into battle before long. Peggy, always jealous of Blanche, assumed she was being callous.[7]

On December 10, Blanche would write Ben Robertson, briefly home in South Carolina: "Despite the fact that we are at war, I think you should go right ahead with your book on the South just as you are doing. I agree with you that we should tell the country what the South could contribute to its future and I certainly wouldn't let anything deflect me now. I am delighted that you are nearly [done] and do please keep right on your way." She added a P.S.: he should send her his cable bill to pay.[8]

In January 1942, Pat's military training in Alabama was finished. Blanche had visited her son frequently at Maxwell Field, a training facility for pilots. At some point during this period she broached the subject of her and Alfred divorcing. As usual, there are various versions of the story. In the early nineties, when his father was dead, Pat shared a letter that he wrote his parents the day after Christmas, 1941: "I hope you two won't do anything rash. I know that at this stage of the game, such a move would hardly be rash. I think you're both too swell to have anything like such a move spoil a lifetime of happiness and success."[9] Other accounts have Pat, outraged, shouting, *No, you can't do that!* In yet another rendering, Pat remembered: "[Alfred] was willing to say yes—but then she'd be out of the publishing world for good and he'd ensure she never got a job elsewhere." Fiercely loyal to his father, Pat believed Alfred "loved [Blanche] and never would have given her a divorce anyway."[10] Upon hearing this version, Bill Koshland told Susan Sheehan that Pat's account of his father's determination to hold on to Blanche was surely the most accurate: "Alfred was always in love with her," Koshland stressed, "[and] he loved her much more than she loved him."[11]

The crisis passed, and when Pat earned his wings, both his parents attended the graduation ceremony together at the Southeast Air Corps Training Center in Montgomery, the "only time" Pat remembered Alfred being visibly proud of him.[12] Getting his wings allowed Pat to stop fearing his father; he would say, "I never grew up until I got my wings."[13] Over the next two to three years, Pat performed bravely with Britain's 446th Bomb Group, Eighth Air Force. Stationed in Bungay, a market town on the Suffolk Coast of England, he was deployed to a strategic site: the seaboard had few cliffs and was an ideal location from which the enemy could invade. He was ultimately awarded the Distinguished Flying Cross, rising to the rank of captain and flying tactical bombing missions over Munich, Koblenz, and Hamburg—all places his parents had visited in what must have seemed a different world. In 1942, the year he should have graduated, Pat won Union College's Frank Bailey Cup, donated by his family's friend for that member of the senior class "who has rendered the greatest service to the College in any field." He received his diploma in 1945. (As a courtesy he is listed with the Class of '42.)[14] Pat "went to war knowing I'd never come back [and so] I gave away my things." He would later say that his stint in the army was the best time of his life.[15]

Blanche focused her attention on organizing her first trip to South America, where she had decided to go in place of Europe that year. Though she had been appointed to U.S. Director of Civil Defense Fiorello La Guardia's Women in Literature Committee (with Lillian Hellman and Fannie Hurst), she was eager to do something more active, since the committee seemed moribund from its inception.[16] From the stories Mildred recounted to her sister-in-law, she was far more engaged in war work than Blanche's group. Mildred's organization of women was spearheaded by Mrs. Louis B. Mayer to tend to the social needs of returning servicemen. The Santa Monica project created a canteen where more than a thousand volunteers served drinks and provided entertainment—movies, books, and appearances by actors and comedians—for the soldiers. The assemblage voted Mildred their president.

FDR's undersecretary of state, Sumner Welles, then proposed Blanche as an unofficial envoy to South America on behalf of the State Department. (Welles knew Blanche through her acquaintance with his wife, Mathilde, and from Knopf's attempt to sign Welles's book, *The*

Time for Decision.) For years the United States had been sponsoring a "good neighbors" program. Aware of rumors that some South American countries might befriend the Axis powers, President Roosevelt wanted to reinvigorate the program, and Welles was carrying out his mandate. Now, with Blanche soon to visit a continent entirely foreign to her, she'd been trying to learn rudimentary Portuguese and Spanish, though she'd be accompanied by interpreters throughout her travels.

The amount of red tape it took even for highly placed officials to arrange such a trip was daunting. Meanwhile, Blanche remembered it was time for her yearly eye exam in Baltimore, so she slipped in a short stay at the Belvedere, where she dined with Mencken. The ophthalmologist who treated them both said her eyes were, as expected, somewhat worse than last year, but not in need of further surgery. Interested in discussing her son more than her deteriorating sight (though Mencken always enjoyed talking about illness), Blanche fretted that Pat, still in the army, showed little interest in joining the firm after he was discharged and finished college. Mencken was unclear whether Blanche was actually disappointed or relieved.[17]

On the train back to Manhattan, she decided to throw a dinner party for two of her current favorite authors, William Shirer and Paul Gallico. The menu was different from the heavy fare Alfred served when he alone was responsible:

4th April 1942

BROILED SHRIMPS

STEINBERGER

AUSLESE 1921

KABINETT WEIN

ROAST TURKEY

PEAS AND CARROTS

LEOVILLE POYFERRE 1870

SALAD

PINEAPPLE ICE AND CAKE

CHATEAU D'YQUEM 1921

RESERVE PERSONNELLE DE

M LE MARQUIS DE LUR SALUCES

COFFEE.[18]

In June, the impatient publisher finally received notice that her trip had been approved by the necessary channels. Blanche's flight on the Douglas C-54 depended, like all aviation of the day, upon the navigator reading land cues as well as using "dead reckoning." This method, essentially a means of calculating one's current position by using a previously determined point, or "fix," and advancing based upon known or estimated speeds, is prone to cumulative errors and rarely in use today. Blanche was flying much as Charles Lindbergh had in 1927, his single-engine *Spirit of St. Louis* equipped with crude instruments and its pilot dependent on dead reckoning most of the trip.

The earplugs handed out to passengers helped to blunt the engine noise. And having her lover at her side surely eased Blanche's journey: inexplicably, Hubert Hohe was given clearance to take the trip as well. Over the next six weeks (June to August 1942), Blanche would travel more than sixteen thousand miles, almost entirely by air (including the occasional seaplane), flying to Colombia, Peru, Chile, Argentina, Uruguay, and Brazil—scouring the continent for authors in search of a publisher.

"The chief impression" she gained was "one of newness, of aliveness . . . people who found joy and excitement . . . and a great hope for the future." In an account she later wrote, Blanche also remarked on the "stratification of classes and the impact on the writers" who therefore "turn to Europe rather than their own countries."[19] She was particularly enamored of a local friend of Virginia Woolf, Victoria Ocampo, an Argentinian woman "of very great charm and ability, and a brilliant writer." Blanche signed at least five new writers on this trip (for whom she immediately sought first-rate translators), including authors still read today.[20] She didn't care about the genre as much as overall literary quality. Yet the trip was motivated by wartime politics more than she would divulge to anyone but Mencken. Sumner Welles had asked her to be his eyes and ears, and, as always, she was thorough.

Met in Lima by "a Peruvian Indian, who stuck by [her] during the stay," she found the silent "ghost" a bit shady. She had little time to worry: Peru had no publishers, and whenever Blanche opened her door "there was a line of writers, of varying kinds, essayists, poets, etc. waiting the whole length of the corridor; no knowledge of what language we publish in, merely the fact that we publish important to them." The "Indian," leaving Blanche unsure which side he was on, warned her that it was dangerous to be in the region because local Germans "had records of all the anti-Nazi publicity." Blanche learned that "the embassy was aware of my danger [and the Indian asked] was I aware of it? I was, I told him, but if he or anyone liquidated me then, the books would go on anyway."[21]

She continued on to Santiago, where her hotel was German "and full of spies," so she packed up and went to another. After a large luncheon—"senators, govt officials, about 50"—she flew nine hours over the Andes, finally arriving in Buenos Aires. "Here, too, I was met by writers with manuscripts—people I had never heard of. Met old friend, Arnaldo Cortesi of *Times*, stayed at Plaza one of the really charming hotels in the world." That night, Blanche dined at one of the best steak houses in Argentina. Eager to be a gracious guest, she answered that yes, the hors d'oeuvres looked delicious. "I was unaware until the course came that [everything] consisted of all the horrible insides of the animal. I refused to eat and almost had to leave the table. This was the great *pièce de résistance* of the Argentines; I was so embarrassed."

When she discovered that the country's major newspaper, *La Prensa*, was allowed only a small paper ration because of its pro-

North American and anti-Nazi views, she arranged to see the mayor of Buenos Aires: "I had to go and listen to a diatribe against North America losing the war and the Argentines going along with the Germans because of this. 'You win a battle and we might think of coming along with you' the man said." (Blessedly, she was assured at her next stop, in Montevideo, that there were no Nazis in Uruguay.) She was given the "usual ambassador's lunch" but planned not to eat anything raw, since she'd been told before she left home to stick to the cooked food. Eating some watercress soup, she "suddenly remembered and couldn't decide between manners and typhoid." She spit it out, "sitting at the right of the ambassador." Thankfully, after dinner she shone, as she was urged to speak French, rather than use a translator for Spanish. "Without any other Americans around [the Argentinians] spoke very freely of their country, of the war, of culture, and I got a great deal of information," she said in her report home.

In addition to acting as a cultural attaché, she was asked by Sumner Welles to "do favors" for United States consulates, including sending updates to the American government. German sympathizers in Brazil were about to launch a coup. "This was being put down gently," Blanche wrote to Washington, "which I was enabled to see at close quarters by official Brazilians and the Secret Service officers." Pro-Nazis were all around, one of whom, like the Indian in Peru, was clearly assigned as her "tail" the entire time she was abroad. She finally confronted the Brazilian ambassador, who, as the Indian had, essentially told her she was on the wrong side of the war. At lunch in São Paulo, she was introduced to American Secret Service agents sitting to her left, who were there to monitor the uprising, with an officer on her right explaining that he rode in an armored car with a wrestler sitting beside him. Apparently, Germany had put a price on his head, and several Brazilian Germans were eager to collect the reward.

Local Brazilian officials asked Blanche to take back some "politically explosive" papers to the States, and, reluctantly, she agreed. "They were planning [their own] political coup in the autumn, had no leader, wanted help from us. It certainly had to be then or later so I took the documents . . . in my briefcase." En route to Miami from Trinidad, she received more attention than she had expected. Two months earlier Clare Boothe had visited the country, the only female to precede Blanche on a Good Neighbor trip, and once Boothe's importance was recognized, Brazilian Customs had been told to "give the works to any woman coming through." They held Blanche's briefcase till midnight, as they would with any potential spy.

In Miami, Blanche turned over the satchel to U.S. Customs, with instructions to deliver it to Undersecretary of State Welles in Washington. Then she herself stopped in D.C. to be debriefed by Welles. The war would prove a turning point in Blanche's life, a time when she realized she could make it on her own. Her strength, apparent to others for decades, finally felt real to her. And as always, she was most excited about the literature she was bringing to her country: she'd gotten a novel by the Brazilian Jorge Amado, his work eventually translated into nearly fifty languages. She was further gratified when she signed the controversial cultural anthropologist Gilberto Freyre, whose three-volume critique of twentieth-century "multiculturalism" by means of his social history of Brazil's racial and economic development remains a bible for American graduate students.

Both men would be published by Knopf in 1946. Blanche teased Mencken upon her return, ribbing him for saying she'd find no masterpieces in South America.[22]

Back in New York with Hubert Hohe, Blanche inspected an apartment renovation at 24 West Fifty-Fifth Street that she'd had Ruth supervise while she was away. She'd hired a contractor to break through her walk-in closet, enabling her to access the apartment next door, which they had bought, linking the two condos through a secret passage undetectable from the outside. Her assistant used the connection "all the time . . . No one who went into Blanche's apartment would ever know [about his]."[23] Until now, Blanche's lover had rented an apartment in the East Sixties, which he probably still shared with his wife—from whom he would be divorced in Reno six months later, in January 1943.

Ruth believed her boss to be a liberated woman with a queenly freedom to have others scurry at her every word: "I used to get her paycheck each week and deposit it in her checking account. I took care of all her bills. When she went out, her purse had nothing in it. Her money—I would take a certain amount of cash from her paycheck each week—she had a money clip. Each had to be folded individually; she had nice new bills. I put them in her purse when she went out. She never counted them; she had to trust me completely. Nothing else, maybe a lipstick in her purse." And always, the ubiquitous cigarette lighter; she was an incessant smoker. Daily, "when Blanche went out to lunch, I'd have to go into her office and stop the fire that was in her wastebasket. She couldn't see and she was a chain smoker," Ruth recalled. "Demanding, that's the word"—seeming to need no sleep.[24]

Meanwhile, Alfred was starting to feel isolated in Purchase, complaining to Mencken that he had few visitors because dinner guests required a car to get to his "deserted home."[25] There were exceptions: from an account that Thomas Mann gave of Thanksgiving 1942, it seems that Blanche invited several South American diplomats to a traditional turkey dinner at Purchase. A few of the guests asked Mann to read, so he spent an hour reciting "relatively 'surefire' passages from the work [he was currently] struggling with," the last of the "Joseph story" tetralogy.[26] *Joseph and His Brothers* was a four-part novel retelling the story of Genesis from Jacob to Joseph, written over the course of sixteen years.

In early January, to Blanche's great relief, Hubert Hohe showed her the divorce decree that had finally arrived from Reno, Nevada, for him and his wife, Sonja S. Hohe.[27] Blanche and her beau celebrated by going to the Stork Club on East Fifty-Third Street, just east of Fifth Avenue, where the rich and famous who inhabited the nightclub showed little awareness of the war. At the end of the month, the Knopfs showed up together to give a luncheon at the St. Regis in honor of their production head, Sidney Jacobs, for his fifteen years of service to the firm. The publishers used the occasion to announce a pension fund they were setting up for their forty-five employees: their finances were beginning to reflect those of an established house.

Walter Benton's *This Is My Beloved* was another surprise success, almost at the level of *The Prophet*. Timed for Valentine's Day 1943, the collection of fairly explicit love poems was written by a returning veteran. The poetry, centered on a mystery girl, Lillian, proved especially popular with soldiers still far from home.[28] Too bold for other firms, the manuscript was sent to Knopf by a poetry editor at Scribner's, who thought Blanche and Alfred should take a look. Blanche believed the book might be commercially popular, but first she had several well-respected poets and critics, including Louis Untermeyer, Van Wyck Brooks, and John Crowe Ransom, read it and agree to write blurbs. After its Valentine's Day launch, *This Is My Beloved* was never advertised again. According to Joe Lesser, "it sold by word of mouth. Sold because sweethearts read it; we launched it very quietly, with great dignity, never tried to appeal to those looking for a thrill." The slim two-dollar book averaged more than two thousand copies a month.[29] Over the next twenty-five years it reached the six hundred thousand mark, remarkable sales for any book of poems. Privately, Blanche told Mencken that she found *This Is My Beloved* more provocative than the much-lauded sensual poetry she had read in South America.

Benton's poetry eventually became the backbone of much of the singer/songwriter/poet Rod McKuen's music. Various recorded versions kept appearing, including one in 1962 that was Blanche's favorite, the jazz flautist Herbie Mann accompanying the actor Laurence Harvey.

Book sales in general were soaring in those days. Scarce goods might not be found on the shelves, but the market for books was robust. In 1943, there were more than 250 million books published, versus roughly 111 million in 1933. When the book clubs were started in 1926, they had sold an average of a half million books a year; by 1946, the Book-of-the-Month Club alone, not including the Armed Services Editions, would sell three million.[30]

That spring, since the focus of the enemy seemed to have shifted from England to the Continent, Blanche was again maneuvering for a ticket to London. Sadly, this time she had less assistance. On February 22, 1943, Ben Robertson, who had been assigned to head the *Herald Tribune*'s British bureau, boarded the *Yankee Clipper*, a seaplane. On its approach to Lisbon's airport, as the pilot was descending, the plane's left wingtip hit the water and crashed into the Tagus River. The failed landing killed twenty-four of the thirty-nine passengers, including Robertson.

Through other contacts, Blanche had wrangled an army transport ticket to London. Now there was the military's interminable "hurry up and wait." Mencken took her mind off the delays—and Robertson's death—when he came to town to discuss marketing strategies for sales of *Happy Days*, which looked strong at 10,953 orders. The third segment of three autobiographical accounts of his life, *Happy Days* was selling better than the earlier two in part due to the war, with the navy purchasing books for their ships and stations.

In July, while she was waiting to be processed, Blanche and Hohe went out to East Hampton, which was not too far from Montauk, on the tip of Long Island, where Knopf's Bill Koshland had a few days' leave before going overseas. Koshland remembered how "Blanche had a cocktail party for me at the Sea Spray hotel and restaurant [the area's most elegant accommodation]. Hohe was with her then and I met him for the first time. [He wasn't] particularly handsome and he had a receding hairline and was younger than Blanche," but, added Koshland, "you would know that this was a European gentleman."[31]

Blanche returned from the beach the following month to have lunch with Mencken on August 8 at '21.' That night, which was unbearably hot, Alfred served his friend his usual heavy dinner, pork and sauerkraut.[32] The two men practiced Schubert's *Rosamunde* ballet as a piano duet, the music causing Alfred to retract his earlier statement about being lonely, having decided that he "really liked" his solitary life at Purchase. These days he even found the tremendous upkeep it required gratifying and good for his health.[33]

This was a time of particular tension between the Knopfs, Hubert Hohe clearly the elephant in the room. The publicist Frances Lindley remembered how she had never seen such fraught office meetings. "I wanted to die," Lindley remembered. "[The Knopfs would] be shouting or Alfred would turn to Joe Lesser and say something absolutely . . . I couldn't believe that a human being would speak to another human being like that."[34]

The Knopf staff sat around the table like poltroons, unwilling to risk a word in Blanche's defense, while Lesser developed ulcers and began walking out of the meetings. "Alfred and Blanche would go at each other and at subordinates about the design of a [book] jacket. Alfred was worse than Blanche; her sense of her own image kept her from starting it. Alfred would lash and lash and lash until she'd finally take the bait. You wanted to escape that moment."[35]

Unlike at his office, where Alfred seemed determined to prove himself the sovereign, at Purchase, with or without Mencken, he was on his best behavior, feeling no challenge to his authority. Purchase, in contrast, was where Blanche tended to retaliate against Alfred's untoward behavior at work. While guests waited to see if Alfred deemed them worthy of his finest wine, Blanche often came late to the table. Though never an alcoholic, she would make a show of walking down the stairs with "the biggest glass of bourbon" anyone had seen, "no apologies, no nothing," Bill Koshland remembered. Free to release the temperament she usually contained at Knopf meetings, Blanche would act as "an absolute hellcat" at the dreaded Sunday brunches where top staff or close friends were the usual guests.[36]

After getting clearance from Washington—with the stipulation that she wear an official army uniform in case of enemy capture—finally, on October 3, 1943, Blanche took a car service to the gorgeous Art Deco clipper terminal near what is today's LaGuardia Airport and flew to London via a C-47 military transport. Her companion was a hearty Texan, J. Frank Dobie, on his way to Cambridge as visiting professor of American literature. Blanche would take precise notes during the trip: "Dobie, Stetson hat, weather-beaten, insisted on fishing when the plane was forced to land in Gander, Newfoundland, because of the dark. We caught smelts. We had to walk back with the smelts. Walked down a long corridor at the inn where we had to stay. You travel with your handbag, a little zipper case, for all but your big things: me, a pair of moles [fur slippers] and a pajama top."[37]

The temporarily appointed Lieutenant Colonel Blanche Knopf had flown to England via Newfoundland and Ireland, and at one of those stops, when told she couldn't take a bath—"H_2O restricted for drinking"—she traded her food rations for water. She didn't eat much anyway, she assured the soldiers. Her bags were "chiefly full of concentrated foods, nylons and lipsticks to give [to friends], very few clothes except to give away."[38] Mencken wrote her that he hoped she was "comfortable" and "finding a lot of good books. If you encounter any of my old friends, please tell them that I pray for them regularly. If you feel like it, send me a picture postcard showing Westminster Abbey, the Cheshire Cheese, or some other such point of interest."[39]

On October 17, the *Syracuse Herald-Journal* announced Blanche's travel, declaring that "there have been few other American publishers [daring] to make the journey."

In London, she settled into the Ritz as usual. (She would later comment how reassured she'd been to learn that de Gaulle, Churchill, and finally Eisenhower held summit meetings there.) She gave a small party to toast James "Scotty" Reston, back in London after time at home on sick leave, and his book *Prelude to Victory*, published in 1942 by Knopf. Viking had offered Reston a thousand dollars, but Knopf bid more—surely at Blanche's insistence. As the Washington correspondent for *The New York Times*, Scotty was known for his integrity. According to his biographer John Stacks, Blanche had personally edited every page of *Prelude to Victory*, a favor Reston requested and Blanche was happy to oblige.[40] Ed Murrow, whom Blanche was pursuing for Knopf, had provided a quote— whether out of fondness for Blanche or for the author's work is unclear: "I know of no newspaper man who has more intelligence and integrity than James Reston and everything he writes shows these qualities."[41]

Blanche was deeply impressed by Scotty's loyalty to others, constancy being one of the virtues she most valued. The reporter had recently refused to share "dirt" on Undersecretary Welles, who was now being hounded by Secretary of State Cordell Hull, jealous of Welles's friendship with FDR. In response to Reston's coldness, Hull brought to (the Pulitzer Prize–winning reporter) Arthur Krock his own files detailing Welles's homosexual relationships, but Krock also scuttled the gossip, even with the hard evidence and photographs that Hull showed him.[42] Blanche was proud to call both newspapermen her friends.[43] Her only disappointment during her 1943 London trip was that she "lost Mr. Sumner Welles' book because nobody in New York did anything about it. I would have done better staying here [in New York] and getting it." Even so, she admitted, "I did get a lot of other books."[44]

As always, Blanche went to the source to get those books. While dining with the reporters at the hotel, she started asking Murrow to let her publish his radio reports, which he was currently sending regularly to the United States through CBS feeds. She would work on Murrow, according to his wife, Janet, for the next twenty-two years, until his death in 1965, just as he was finally compiling his collection for Knopf. It was Janet who finished the project, turning over the classic broadcasts to Blanche. They became Knopf's *In Search of Light*, which Murrow's widow dedicated to "Blanche with love and appreciation."[45]

18

THE WAR'S END

AT AN AFTERNOON BUFFET LUNCH at Manhattan's Dorset Hotel in early November 1943, Blanche shared stories with Mencken of her brief trip overseas. The newspaperman, rarely jealous, turned up his nose at what he considered the flashy tactics of the war journalists, writing about their own exploits instead of focusing on the soldiers. Sensing his envy, Blanche quickly turned to the reason for the day's event: guests were celebrating the twentieth anniversary of Joe Lesser as a Knopf employee. Lesser, by now the company's treasurer and a board member, was feted by forty-two well-wishers, mostly fellow employees, and with Blanche and Alfred seated at the same table. Though the Knopfs had agreed with their board on the unusually generous gift of a five-week winter trip to the destination of their choice for Lesser and his wife, no one gave a speech or even offered a toast. Alfred asked Mencken to announce the gift, and Menck's brief tribute focused on Mrs. Lesser appearing "so proud" of her husband—possibly a jab at Blanche for the neglect with which she'd been treating her spouse of late in favor of Hohe.

Having come to the firm as a clerk, Lesser was now one of its key officers. Though the Knopfs still brought in two-thirds of the books, Lesser was the only employee who could sign contracts. At least the company had developed a practical if demanding method to track their publications. After an author delivered the finished manuscript, whoever had been conducting the negotiations conferred with those in sales, advertising, and production, after which a five-by-seven-inch pink slip of paper was clipped to a card for estimates of advance sales, "sales during the first six months, sales after six months, college sales, advertising appropriations, and print orders." There was also a space for comments on "General" as well as "Special" markets, meant for media, publicity, and advertising-copy suggestions. Months before publication, and after the card had been circulated for comments, it was "batted around at weekly business meetings." One year after a particular book was published, the original estimated sales were compared with the results. According to Alfred, the cards "enabled Mr. Lesser to make a reasonably accurate forecast of the firm's profits a year in advance."[1]

Blanche especially wished Joe well: despite his typically fair-minded approach to both Knopfs, when the going got really rough, she felt she could trust him to take her side. She had urged Alfred to approve the gift, especially in light of the company's recently released financial report for the second half of the fiscal year—and in light of her expectations for the forthcoming fiction *A Bell for Adano*. Knopf was doing well these days, the budget analysis "very satisfactory," according to Mencken. The net profit for six months was $40,000, after federal taxes of $63,000, with the current assets of the company $501,000 and its liabilities $245,000.[2]

Now Blanche fixed her attention upon the journalist John Hersey's first novel: she considered *A Bell for Adano* an important book, and she was right. When it appeared in February 1944, it was immediately popular, the following year winning the Pulitzer Prize and soon becoming the basis for Paul Osborn's play by the same name starring Fredric March and then a movie with Gene Tierney. The novel takes place during World War II in a Sicilian coastal town; Fascists have melted down the church bell in the center of Adano to make munitions to be used against the Allies. A sympathetic Italian-American officer, Major Victor Joppolo (based on the real-life Major Frank E. Toscani), becomes the village's military governor, and when he learns that the townspeople's dearest wish is for the bell's return, he somehow obtains a substitute from a navy destroyer.

Though *A Bell for Adano* sold 170,500 copies, Hersey would take to heart Diana Trilling's criticism of what she found sentimental in an otherwise impressive novel.[3] The author's direct style alongside his eye for detail impressed Trilling and most other readers, though critics suggested that his fiction bore too many marks of his life as a journalist rather than the novelist he was trying to become.

In spite of Knopf's current financial health, its revenues steadily increasing, whenever Mencken was around Blanche these days he seemed unusually grouchy, even negative. It must have been difficult for him to ignore the obvious subject of her lover; he had always appreciated Blanche's keeping her love life private, and her current carelessness surely rankled him. Yet Mencken never mentioned Hubert Hohe's name or presence in his diary or journals. Hohe is rendered invisible.

It wasn't until April 1944 that Mencken even made it to Blanche's "new" apartment at 24 West Fifty-Fifth Street, which had been renovated a year and a half earlier. Pat's memory suggested a better-looking venue than Mencken recorded: "There was a coat closet on the left and a very small kitchen door to the right, no windows. As you went out the kitchen door you went into a circular area with windows over a street where she had a circular dining room, attached to the living room. Open, no door. You walk into the apartment past the kitchen and on the right is a very large living room with a big Dubuffet [added later] hanging on the wall" (a defiant nod at the 1913 Armory Show she had admired, against Alfred's instruction).[4] Blanche had an affinity for the aesthetics of so-called low art, abandoning traditional beauty in favor of what she believed a more humanistic approach to making images.

Mencken had become increasingly irritated as he and Blanche waited an hour on a Sunday night for a table at Voisin before getting to Blanche's apartment. Back at his hotel at the end of the evening, he wrote in his diary that "the house is a new building in the ultra-modernist manner . . . The apartment is done in white and pale shades of gray, with here and there a touch of metallic copper. The effect is appalling, and [Blanche] says that it is almost impossible to keep the place clean. It is smaller than her last apartment on 54th street, but costs $2500 a year [more]. Its only attraction is a roof-garden about as big as a dining-room table." Continuing to find fault with the "new" place, he called the modernist prints on the wall "ghastly" and said the furniture was "fit only for a boudoir."[5]

After his tour of the apartment, Mencken had settled down with Blanche for some "gabble," which went in an unpleasant direction. He was "offended," he told her, "by the little book of prayers" for soldiers that Knopf had just released. He thought the company had "disgraced its list and damaged its trade-mark" by publishing prayers written by Generals Eisenhower and Patton—the latter a hero who was lately in the newspapers for "cuffing a wounded soldier." Mencken railed on, declaring such trash to have "undone the work of years, and left the house imprint ridiculous."

Just as bad, he continued, were the "preposterous books by war correspondents and other fakers." Blanche had defended Scotty Reston's *Prelude to Victory* and other Knopf books about the war on the grounds that they sold well while serving the country, promoting dialogue among its citizens. Mencken insisted, however, that such books "sold the firm down the river." Blanche avoided stating the obvious: her friend no longer knew the leading war correspondents. In spite of his populism, Mencken was losing touch with the culture; even the GI Bill enacted that year didn't entirely please him.

Early that summer, Blanche and Hohe would go to Whiteface Mountain Inn at Lake Placid, New York. She thought it would be good for them to get away from Knopf for a while, even if she had to take work with her. Ruth made all the arrangements, but their vacation was cut short.[6] Blanche's eyesight was deteriorating rapidly, now causing not only loss of vision but sharp pain as well. In Baltimore, her ophthalmologist prescribed a newly released eyedrop for glaucoma, which was her current diagnosis. She was back home in time for the liberation of Paris on August 25, which she celebrated in her apartment with the writer MacKinlay Kantor, his sister, and a friend. The women fell asleep early on the couch while Blanche and her notoriously womanizing guest drank champagne late into the night.[7] There was no sign of Hohe.

Alfred and Mencken were at Purchase, which seemed gloomier each time the journalist visited. He increasingly disliked going to the country, where he sat "swathed in darkness," and where Alfred felt obliged to discuss his prostate problems. In his diary, Mencken assaulted Alfred's "incompetent doctors," one of whom "massaged him violently and as a result he became very uncomfortable." Upon seeing a urologist, who could find "no sign whatsoever of infection," Alfred started feeling better—as if what he had really needed was attention.[8]

The next evening the two men returned to Purchase, planning to relax after a tiring day. Instead, they were greeted by the butler, who "rushed out with the news that the Swedish cook had fallen down the steps." Alfred recalled, "When we got to the kitchen we found her propped up with one ankle swollen and still swelling. The poor woman was somewhat shaken up and so she was put to bed in the hospital." The house seemed to confer a curse upon Knopf's servants, Mencken decided. A year or so earlier the gardener had somehow "blown up the heating plant in the garage and was so badly injured that he was in the hospital for eight or nine months. Soon afterward the butler, a sad Alsatian, had an accident and was disabled for weeks."[9]

When it was time for the December meeting, Mencken was too busy putting the finishing touches on the latest version of his dictionary to make it to New York. "I surely hope [it all] passes off without any approach to bloodshed or mutilation," he wrote to Blanche. "If anyone is actually killed, please send a wreath in my name." He was jovial because his work was going well: "I am making pretty good progress with my two indexes, and hope to be able to finish the job by Christmas." Since Knopf's first edition of *The American Language*, the company had published three more editions, each updated. This time, Mencken concluded that it was American, not British, English that was in the ascendancy. He was currently working on two more supplemental indexes to the book, one to be published in 1945, the other not until 1948, the year he would see his writing end for good.[10]

As the new year began, Blanche's eye troubles escalated, her eyes sometimes so dry she had to blink incessantly, squinting to keep them open. And surely they were not improved by her spending the next few months on still more trips out west to toil over the latest ideas of Raymond Chandler, who was living in the Santa Monica hills and whose needs—his writerly insecurities and his fears—seemed endless. She pushed herself hard, anticipating celebrating the end of the European war. But just before May 8, when Blanche was back at the office and victory bells rang out over Manhattan, such plans were squelched. Pat, surprising her with his early army discharge, was stunned to walk in on his mother and Hubert Hohe, kissing passionately in Blanche's office. Furious, he went to live with his father in Purchase, at least as Pat told the story after his mother's death.

According to an interview that the biographer Peter Prescott had with Mildred Knopf near the end of her life, however, she and Edwin had warned Pat about the affair during his discharge visit with them before he went on to New York.

Whether or not Blanche and Hohe met Pat with the amorous scene he recalled, he was outraged that his mother was willing to have an affair right under his father's nose. Blanche seems to have assumed Pat would come to terms with Hohe's presence, and she turned to the planning of her first trip to the Continent since the war had begun. She wrote Jenny Bradley, "There must be many new writers who are doing work that will be invaluable for us . . . I hear that Jean-Paul Sartre is doing good work."[11] Early in 1945 she had written Bradley that "I am naturally eager to get whatever good books there are in France today and perhaps there are a good many I do not know about."[12] Three weeks and a few days after Germany's surrender, in June, Blanche was able to get a job as a War Department employee, whose files list her as a consultant earning twenty-five dollars per diem. Starting in France, she then traveled to nine German cities, probably, in light of her army ID card stamped "valid only if captured by the enemy," officially on behalf of the United States government (similar to her earlier efforts in South America). "I knew the war [in Europe] was over when Blanche turned up in Paris," one journalist said.[13] As if to pick up where she and her writers had left off, she took a suite at the Ritz, as always facing the Place Vendôme with its magnificent garden.

Here she met with authors who were eager to have an audience. Among her immediate acquisitions in 1945 was Jean-Paul Sartre's existential drama No Exit, with a few more pieces promised, all beautifully translated by Stuart Gilbert and published by Knopf in 1947 as No Exit (Huis Clos): A Play in One Act along with The Flies (Les Mouches): A Play in Three Acts.

Still performed today, No Exit focuses on three characters—two women and one man—who are confined together in a locked space in hell. The play posits mental torture as being worse than its physical counterpart. Though Blanche believed the work intellectually provocative, the recent book for which she felt the deepest emotional attachment was Albert Camus's *The Stranger*, to be released by Knopf in April 1946. She was eager to meet Camus, who, like Blanche (and most in her world), was adamantly antitotalitarian. His writing had fascinated her from the moment Jenny Bradley convinced her to read *The Stranger* in French several years earlier. The novel told the story of Meursault, a solitary Algerian who lived with little sense of communal connection. Neither living nor dying seemed of consequence. Its title alone (the French original closer to meaning "The Foreigner") evoked isolation and alienation, the narrative opening with its main character delivering the flat line "Mother died today." As does everything, her death leaves Meursault cold, a fact that others around him add to the list of his shortcomings. As a white Frenchman born in the North American colony of Algeria, Meursault is both local and alien—the human condition, the novel suggests. A thriller leeched of power, the book's plot of a killing and the resultant punishment is perceived by the murderer as if in a dream. Its protagonist neither accepting nor railing against his punishment—his own death—*The Stranger* emphasizes that what we hold to be normal will be denied its hero. When Meursault is sentenced to death by guillotine, he finally experiences fear, though still no remorse.[14]

During their first meeting in 1945, Blanche was immediately dazzled by the writer. She and Camus met several more times during this visit, and spoke "about his writing, his future, his past, his plans, young writers in France, Pasternak, English writers, American writers, ourselves, everything, in these curious sessions we had together."[15] Blanche also convinced him to talk about his work in the Resistance as a French-Alsatian journalist, as well as his writing motivated by Vichy France. Just twenty-seven when the Germans occupied Paris, Camus evoked strong maternal, even romantic feelings in Blanche; throughout the next decade she lavished him with gifts and infused her letters with just a hint of intimacy. Bill Koshland would dismiss an interviewer's suggestion that she and Camus had an affair, saying instead that she obviously had a "crush" on him.[16] From her initial reading of *The Stranger*—with its focus on individual freedom, and on choosing how to feel even when we have no control over actual events—Blanche had known she would sign the author.

She hadn't realized, however, before that lunch at the Paris Ritz, that she would encounter a man whose worldview matched her own more closely than that of anyone she had ever met. "Who would have guessed you would be the one I've been seeking all my life?" she wrote to Camus.[17] From their first meeting in 1945, at least twice a year thereafter she and Camus would meet, usually at the Ritz for tea or coffee, always in the mid-afternoon, when they could be assured of privacy. Conversing for hours, the author granted Blanche's opinions a kind of respect and interest she rarely experienced. At their cafe table, topics ranged from existentialism to "absurdism," lending an intellectual charge to their discourse.

Blanche soon knew all about Camus's unhappy wife and his various love affairs. World War II and the long marital separations it caused had hit the Camus marriage hard, leading Albert to consider divorce. Simon Lea, president of the Camus Society UK, believes that Camus treated his wife, Francine, "like a sister" while wanting to marry his lover, the actress María Casares. Francine, suffering a severe depression that caused her to be hospitalized, leapt from her window in a failed suicide attempt. According to Lea, Camus was horrified and felt powerless to intercede, a scenario he replayed in *The Fall*, with its plummeting woman whom the hero fails to rescue. Blanche was aware that her friend believed his infidelities had brought on his wife's depression—at an early stage in Francine's breakdown she had repeatedly mumbled "María Casares"—an assumption that led to immense guilt on his part. Blanche was too devoted to Camus to allow him to accept such responsibility, and she assured him that when people were depressed, only time, with luck, could heal them.

Not everyone was impressed by Blanche's dedication to her writers. In Purchase, neighbor Peggy Cullman, a volunteer with Army Air Forces intelligence and public relations, was "surprised and frozen with horror"—as was Pat, she claimed—that Blanche was "one of the first civilians to go [to Europe]." Not abroad to assist the military, Blanche showed herself "entirely inappropriate; she was over there selfishly to sign up authors. No one was going to be benefited except Knopf publishing or Blanche herself." This was the kind of thing, Peggy suggested, that Alfred would "never do," though she grudgingly admitted that "in an odd way" he clearly respected his wife for doing it.[18] Peggy, a striking young woman who in more than one photograph laughs admiringly as Alfred flourishes his cigar, at times sounds as if she's jealous of Blanche—who missed too many of her dinner parties in Purchase and had gained unseemly renown during the war. She failed to understand how often Blanche served as a nursemaid to displaced authors in those days, and how taking care of writers was the publisher's self-appointed mission.

That summer of 1945, Blanche was busy tending to Thomas Mann, who was celebrating his seventieth birthday in New York City, where he delivered a lecture at Hunter College. While New Yorkers were sweltering from a heat wave, he arrived to rooms at the St. Regis festooned with flowers, many of which Blanche had sent. Mann, his wife, Katia, and their daughter Monika went on to spend June 13–24 at Mohonk Mountain House at the edge of the Catskills. They occupied rooms 468 and 470, as a concierge will tell the curious even today. Mann was working on *Doctor Faustus* and would use the Mohonk setting for his novel. "The stately hotel . . . built in the Swiss style and run by Quakers, is situated in a park-like landscape of rugged hills, a kind of nature sanctuary in the Victorian taste," he wrote. "It was just the place for a rest, and at this time of year the air was a good deal cooler than sweltering, stuffy New York."[19]

On some evenings Alfred and Blanche joined the Manns for the chamber music played in the lounge, but Blanche was eager to get to the Alps, not the Catskills. After she was sure the Manns were well acclimated, she turned to Elizabeth Bowen, who had written that she was without shoes that fit. Blanche knew that her long feet were hard to accommodate, so she went to Saks and bought three pairs that "delighted her." Elizabeth's pleasant but platonic marriage alongside a long-lived, sexually rewarding love affair was just what Blanche sought at this point in her life. Now Bowen thanked Blanche by joking that "Alan [her spouse] loved the shoes too; he [is] just short of being a fetishist."[20] Blanche had no difficulty incorporating the purchase of footwear into her routine, if it meant making a writer—or dear friend—happy. Wartime shortages had allowed her to minister usefully to her authors, such service a source of pleasure for her and the basis of further fealty from others.

Late that summer, Blanche returned to Purchase, where she continued to retaliate for Alfred's mistreatment of her in the office. On a hot September afternoon at the wedding of the Cullmans' son, the cleric was taken aback by Blanche's black lace camisole—when she removed her matching silk jacket to dance with him. "Mrs. Knopf is wearing an interesting outfit. For a horrible moment I had the feeling she was in her underwear," the minister said to Peggy. At first, the groom's mother tried to cover for Blanche. "That is the latest thing in Paris suits," she responded. But when the minister persisted, saying, "Doesn't it look like underwear?" Peggy replied, "I can understand your thinking it was."[21] Others who were present remember how on "the very warm wedding day Blanche shocked and amused guests by taking off her dress and dancing in her shift with the clergyman."[22] Apparently the minister didn't object to Blanche entirely.

The Cullmans saw much more of Alfred in Purchase than of his wife, "who was never there." When Blanche did in fact show up for dinner from time to time, Peggy disliked the "phony" way she acted, not realizing that her neighbor was responding to the host's obvious disdain. "She'd take three pieces of asparagus on her plate and say, 'This is undoubtedly the most marvelous asparagus I've ever tasted; you must tell me what your cook does to it.'" Or "Alfred, dear, what is the wine? Write it down."[23] Reluctantly, Cullman admitted that Alfred was also difficult, mercurial at the least. Even when Blanche tried to meet him halfway, he'd have none of it. "Blanche would say, 'It's a nice day' and Alfred would respond, 'If you like this kind of day, I suppose it is; you always like peculiar days, Blanche.' They quarreled 99 times out of 100."[24]

On New Year's Eve, 1945, crowds cheered: there were at least 750,000 people gathered in Times Square when, at the top of the *New York Times* building, the famous ball appeared. This was the first time after a two-year blackout that the globe would make its slow but certain descent to welcome a new year. There was no mistake: the war was truly over. Blanche was probably looking out her apartment's plate-glass window, watching crowds of New Yorkers walking toward Midtown, many with tear-streaked cheeks like her own. She had been deeply worried about her son, and now, even though there were tensions, he was home, one of the lucky ones.

On January 1, 1946, Knopf released James M. Cain's *Past All Dishonor*, which Blanche had encouraged Cain to write. The historical murder mystery was a complicated book whose theme of mixed loyalties seems at times another variation on *Romeo and Juliet*. Within weeks of its successful launch, with sales solid, Blanche, in strong spirits, took another brief trip to visit friends in England. In London, she was dismayed to see how the country continued to struggle; at Brown's Hotel, for instance, even tea was half a crown. Having assessed the British reality, back in Manhattan she immediately sent off generous boxes to her London friends: silk stockings for the women along with sumptuous food for everyone, including butter and filet mignon—accompanied by instructions from her cook on preparing the beef.

Working in her office, Blanche prepared the first of several invitation lists for the lavish parties she was throwing in honor of Albert Camus, who was traveling to New York City for the April 11 American release of *The Stranger*, translated into English by the British scholar (and friend of James Joyce, as the publishers often said) Stuart Gilbert. Sailing on the *Oregon* from Le Havre, the writer arrived in Manhattan on March 25. Within three days, Camus had embarked on a jam-packed speaking tour, starting with a talk he gave at Columbia University's McMillin Theatre. In early April Blanche gave the fanciest of her dinners in his honor, her guest list including M. and Mme René Julliard, M. and Mme Raymond Gallimard, Ambassador and Mrs. David Bruce, Elizabeth Bowen, and others. But the connection Camus treasured most occurred at the French Institute on April 16, where the thirty-two-year-old writer met a nineteen-year-old student, Patricia Blake, with whom he was "instantly" infatuated and who became one of his many lovers. (She was still with him more than ten years later, in France.)

Camus, handled brilliantly by Blanche, was a smash in New York. *Partisan Review*'s editor, William Phillips, called him "the most attractive man I have ever met."[25] The journalist Adam Gopnik noted, more than half a century later, that Camus enjoyed his American reception enough to write home to his French publisher: "You know, I can get a film contract whenever I want." As Gopnik reminds us, "Looking at the famous portrait of Camus by Henri Cartier-Bresson from the forties—trenchcoat collar up, hair swept back, and cigarette in mouth; long, appealing lined face and active, warm eyes—you see why people thought of him as a star and not just as a sage; you also see that he knew the effect he was having."[26]

The *New Yorker* writers who met Camus during his 1946 visit were less starstruck. In a comment published after Camus's death, A. J. Liebling sympathetically recalled the author's only visit to the States: "He was thirty-two but looked barely twenty, and he was pale and thin from tuberculosis and from erratic feeding during the occupation. His clothes were at once immature and archaic, since he had bought them when he was much younger."[27] And Lewis Thompson, who wrote a 1946 "Talk of the Town" piece about the visit, took note of Camus's "type" of look, "slicked hair, patterned sweater and baggy trousers."[28]

The Stranger initially sold more than twelve thousand copies, a good number for most novels and excellent for a book in translation (now regarded as a classic of modern literature). During Camus's visit, Blanche convinced him that Knopf should publish his second novel, *The Plague* (released in France in 1947), before putting out any of his earlier plays or philosophical works. She pushed Knopf's board to allot a larger-than-usual advertising budget, creating such strong sales (larger even than those of *The Stranger*) that Camus soon bought himself the motorcycle he had long dreamed of owning.[29]

∾ PART FOUR ∾

19

MORE BATTLES AFTER ALL

BEFORE CAMUS LEFT NEW YORK, Blanche shared with him her plans for the first war-free summer in years: in July 1946, after stopping with Alfred in London, she would continue to Germany, just months before the initial phase of the Nuremberg trials of Nazi war criminals would be concluded in October. Early that year, Knopf had published Robert H. Jackson's *The Case Against the Nazi War Criminals*, the book leading to an invitation from Jackson, chief justice and United States prosecutor, for Blanche and Alfred to be his guests at the trials. They had begun the previous November, soon after the war's end, and this continuing phase dealt with the major war criminals. Tasked with trying twenty-three of the most important political and military leaders of the Third Reich, the tribunal was frequently a wrenching experience, its testimony filled with accounts of inhumanity so brutal that Blanche would never speak about what she heard.[1] Alfred had opted to return home from London, claiming his wife had a stronger constitution. "I had no stomach for what, I admit, must have been a fascinating experience."[2]

Soon Blanche would publish John Hersey's *Hiroshima*, a seminal account of the atomic bomb's impact on the Japanese after the attack on August 6, 1945. The Knopfs had agreed that Hersey's book would first appear in the August 31, 1946, *New Yorker*, an issue devoted entirely to his work. Never before had the magazine turned over a complete issue to a single piece of reportage, and it sold out instantly. Albert Einstein alone ordered a thousand copies and Bernard Baruch five hundred. Knopf followed with its October book release, which eventually sold 3.5 million copies. The Book-of-the-Month Club distributed *Hiroshima* as a "special gift book."[3]

Considered a precursor of the New Journalism of the sixties and seventies, *Hiroshima* is an account of six people who lived through the world's first atomic attack. Hersey's meticulous prose details the bombing of the city and its aftermath, allowing the tragedy to unfold intimately and in deeply human terms. About a young clerk whose body was mangled in the explosion and had bookcases fall on top of her, Hersey writes, "In the first moment of the atomic age, a human being was crushed by books."[4] Decades after their original talk, one of the victims Hersey had interviewed told him that among his most bitter regrets was being unable to bury the dead or keep track of the corpses dragged to mass cremations. In March 1999, New York University's journalism department announced the winner of its contest (judged by a thirty-five-member panel) to determine the hundred best pieces of twentieth-century American journalism; Hersey's book was number one.[5]

Blanche was thrilled at *Hiroshima*'s success: she believed nothing could be more gratifying than publishing a book that changed how we look at the world, and Hersey's unblinking accounts forced readers to engage with philosophical questions about war. From the beginning of Knopf, Blanche had sensed that her profession enabled such discourse. And the reading public these days offered new opportunities. Before the war, higher education had been for the privileged, but in 1947, nearly 500,000 Americans graduated from college, compared with 160,000 in 1939. Among those graduates were readers eager to find books that spoke to them of what they'd experienced, or at least heard about, overseas.

But by the end of the year, Blanche was forced to deal with a personal crisis. Without warning, Hubert Hohe had left her.

One night Bill Koshland escorted Blanche to the opera, where they spotted Hohe in the guest box of the singer Elisabeth Schwarzkopf—Hohe obviously making no attempt to keep his new romance secret. According to Ruth, Blanche was shattered, sobbing for days. The worst of it was Hohe's insistence upon having deliberately loud, "violent" sex with new lovers in his next-door apartment, whose thin walls had been engineered for the easy "visits" between Hohe and Blanche.[6]

Maybe Hohe was tired of being at Blanche's beck and call, in essence, her kept lover. Ruth would recall that for whatever reason, he became cruel, remaining in the duplex and, as Koshland had said, "deliberately torturing Blanche . . . in his passion slamming against their shared door just so she would hear." Eventually Blanche recovered enough from the trauma to worry about the prosaic: Hohe had borrowed "a lot of her gold flatware—Dirilyte, very expensive—and dishes and things were in his apartment and she was worried about how she was going to get them back. Now that he had another girlfriend." Added to the years of dedicated but nonetheless demanding work for Blanche, the drama and intrigue with Hohe were more than Ruth could take, and as soon as her employer seemed sturdy enough, she quit.[7]

Whether this was one of the times when Blanche tried to kill herself, obliquely referred to by Knopf board members and family during interviews after her death, is unknown. What little we do know about the aftermath of Blanche's affair with Hohe comes from vague references to her unhappiness that she makes in letters to friends, including the agents Jenny Bradley in Paris and Carol Brandt in New York. Carol, in a long-term relationship with the Little, Brown author John Marquand (her husband, Carl Brandt, was perfectly fine with the arrangement; the threesome often dined together), had counseled her friend to live as she did, finding a new lover with whom Alfred was comfortable, making their meetings more comfortable for everyone. Blanche's husband wasn't as pliant as Carol's, and though Blanche had tried to pull off her own kind of triangular relationship, keeping her husband and her lover apart, at moments she must have felt she had lost both men.

Within six months, however, Blanche had not only recovered but had rededicated herself to putting her marriage back on track, establishing a tolerable equilibrium. On July 18, as if overcome by nepenthe, she wrote to Alfred, smiley face included:

Very late

Darling—today I got a wonderful long hand letter from you which I appreciate and love and will cherish; you object to my letters from England—Darling I saw about 200 people in three weeks—it is worth going there and seeing them but anything personal is 1. Not to be dictated and 2. Long hand letters at this hour are the best one can do . . .

I doubt that I will go to Milan—it is all too complicated—I have a plane out of Guyana to London 3 August which I will postpone a couple of days if I can: I fly to Zurich on the 26th and if I don't go to Milan I'll go to Geneva on the 30 where I will be at the Hotel Beau Rivage—going to Lancôme, etc. until I leave on the 3rd. Doubt the plane on the 6th for New York—more likely 8th or

10th—that all depends on Milan and how many days London takes—the 4th is a bank holiday and no one will be back until Tuesday lunch the 5th.

    Now, if this letter sounds mad pay no attention to it—it is 2 am . . . I haven't seen Camus, Sartre, Labmiet or Gaston G. everyone is away but I'll pray! I saw Gide however for two hours yesterday and he is really a very great man—wonderful.

    Take care of yourself—France is funny but all right I guess: it reminds me of us! They spend more than they have and like their comforts and luxuries too—wine—food, lunch at Larve just as always.

    That the publishing business is bad does honestly not surprise me—it had to go this way: certainly you have talked about its happening for months.

    Take care—it's fun to know you and be part of you etc etc
    Devotedly ☺[8]

It was a difficult spring and Blanche missed Koussevitzky's concerts for the first time ever. To Natalya she wrote of sinus problems "plus something they call Tic Delarosa [*sic*] was too much for me."[9] Tic douloureux, a syndrome whose episodes of excruciating pain on the sides of the face last up to several minutes, runs along the trigeminal nerve, responsible for facial sensation and for biting and chewing. Blanche had reported several such episodes throughout her life, the cause unexplained until recently, and the pain possibly another reason she typically ate so little.

On April 24, 1947, the seventy-three-year-old Willa Cather died of a cerebral hemorrhage in her home at 570 Park Avenue. She had completed her last book, *Sapphira and the Slave Girl*, in 1940, confessing to the Knopfs her dark conviction that the world was self-destructing. She was interred in the Old Burying Ground in Jaffrey, New Hampshire.

On July 17, Blanche lost another author when MacKinlay Kantor chose Random House (which paid much better than Knopf) to publish his next book. The midwestern writer and London war correspondent who had celebrated the liberation of Paris at Blanche's New York apartment wrote her that while he was certain he and Bennett Cerf would get along, he believed that he and Alfred would be at odds constantly.

That winter there was a rapprochement in the Knopfs' seesaw marriage, and Alfred holed up in Blanche's apartment after work during a treacherous storm. Holding the record at the time for the worst snowstorm in New York City history, the blizzard of 1947 dropped 26.4 inches of snow in Central Park over the last few days of December. As the storm barreled its way through Manhattan, stranding cars and buses and halting subway service, it claimed seventy-seven lives. The next day, determined to catch a train at Grand Central for a meeting in Cleveland, Alfred set out from the apartment. Finding that nothing was running, he checked into a hotel; his having spent one night on his wife's turf was enough for them both. Pat believed his father was "afraid of whom he might find there." But in telling the story himself decades later, Alfred, emphasizing Blanche's "hospitality" to him, said Blanche was "giving a party but that she'd been right about the weather and he was embarrassed to return."[10]

On the first day of 1948, Knopf officially released *The Collected Tales of E. M. Forster* (sent to reviewers earlier), along with *The Blood of Others*, Simone de Beauvoir's novel. Forster's stories were a combination of his 1911 and 1928 collections, while *The Blood of Others* was written during the war. Beauvoir herself would, in 1960, criticize her book, about the paradoxical nature of freedom, for being tendentious.

Soon after these launches, Blanche headed to La Jolla, a suburb of San Diego, where Raymond Chandler now lived and where Blanche still tended to his frequent attacks of "nerves." She then took a short spring trip to London, Paris, and Rome, where, alert to opportune book topics, she began a dialogue with various officials about the worrisome situation of the Russians in Berlin. When she got home, she sent to Europe still more boxes of supplies that her authors and various friends and acquaintances had requested.

As usual upon Blanche's arrival in New York, Alfred greeted her enthusiastically, though anger eddied in the air minutes after the Knopfs said hello. Blanche wrote Jenny Bradley that "it was all back to normal within hours."[11] But another mood swing soon occurred when she and Alfred were honored as the premier publishers and participants at Dallas's national book exhibition. In an optimistic state of mind, Blanche agreed to take a cross-country road trip with her husband in June. Neither could have foreseen its enormous impact on Alfred's future, though his enthusiasm proved yet another hindrance to the marriage. Where Alfred saw the rugged beauty of the West, Blanche was unnerved by it, her vision and her physical stamina unequal to the rigorous hikes Alfred gloried in taking. When they entered Yellowstone, Alfred stood in awe of the sublime landscape, while Blanche was filled with dread.

"The West has gotten in my blood something awful," Alfred would later tell Wallace Stegner when the two worked together on a collection of essays about Yellowstone's Dinosaur park. More than he realized, Alfred, who these days had become much less emotionally invested in Knopf than Blanche was, had found something of his own. "I have just got to go out there again to make sure it's real."[12] Dating from his 1948 trip, Alfred thereafter planned a long working vacation in the West every summer, with shorter trips in between. Surprisingly, his most substantial contribution to conservation would not be through publishing so much as his efforts with conservation groups of the 1950s and 1960s—a passion that put even more responsibility on Blanche back in New York.

On August 11, Mencken, in Manhattan for the first time since covering the presidential conventions in Philadelphia, took Blanche to lunch at '21.' Dropping by the office to pick her up, he recorded in his journal his shock at seeing her read a letter with an oversized magnifying glass. When she still couldn't make out what she saw, thinking no one was looking, she handed the page to her secretary to read aloud.[13] By October, in part because of her weakened physical state and her worsening ocular problems, Blanche reversed her habit of sending supplies to her friends in war-ravaged Europe. She wrote Jenny Bradley several times to ask her help. Dresses, coats, jewelry, bags, glassware, napkins, bed linen—Jenny boxed it all, many of the requests executed to Blanche's specifications.

Only once was the agent exasperated: the Knopf mailing labels said "book," and she and Blanche could be charged with fraud if anyone opened the packages. Knowing how tedious going through customs could be of late, and eager to conform to legal standards, Blanche told Jenny to mark the labels correctly. But mail was not yet back to normal, certainly not overseas mail, and it took several back-and-forths, with the boxes delayed, while the two women figured out the new regulations.[14] Both were taken aback by how much work such a previously simple task had become.

Things Italian rather than French were on Blanche's mind of late, her energies directed toward Bernard Berenson, the great connoisseur of Renaissance art, at I Tatti, his home outside Florence. Having met him while abroad through their mutual acquaintance Natalie Barney, Blanche wanted to persuade Berenson to write a book for Knopf, and her shrewd letters to him sound like a quattrocento maiden flattering a would-be lover: "I have just seen your article in *Harper's Bazaar*," she wrote, "together with a quite magnificent photograph of you that I would like to have if you can spare one. It was a very high point in my visit, I assure you, to meet you, and I shall not forget the few moments we had together."[15] The fulsome Berenson responded with the Latin phrase Catholics spoke before receiving communion, "Domine non sum dignus" ("Lord, I am not worthy"), before continuing to write, "No other publisher has ever been so generous to me. How can I put myself even with you!"[16]

Blanche was eager for the first of Geoffrey Hellman's three-part *New Yorker* series on the Knopfs to hit the stands, which would be as always a week earlier than its official publication date of November 20, 1948. But the title, "Publisher," with its singular noun, was an indication of what was to come. Blanche had been rendered largely invisible. According to Hellman, Alfred was a "more durable topic of conversation" than any other publisher in the past thirty years.[17] With a list of around four thousand published titles, Knopf issued about a hundred titles a year. The man is "at once both Olympian and dressy; few literary men can stare him down. His aspect is bold and piratical. He has bushy black eyebrows; a bristling moustache, once jet and now gray."[18] Hellman quotes the writer Robert Nathan, fiercely loyal to Blanche, who bought *Portrait of Jennie*, his strong-selling 1940 novel about a Depression-era, hallucinatory romance: "He and Blanche are like Jupiter and Juno. He is the ultimate, she the penultimate, but in her own right just as ultimate."[19] The journalist explained that the Knopfs themselves brought in about two-thirds of the books they published, and their editors the rest.

Once again, Blanche felt blindsided: Hellman had interviewed both Knopfs, leading her to believe that the long article would be about the couple, with the focus divided equally between them. Certainly Hellman managed to suggest Blanche's importance, even naming several of her authors—but the pieces made it clear that Knopf was really Alfred, and his wife his assistant. Blanche complained to Mencken, who mentioned in a letter to his old fellow writer from *The Smart Set* and *The American Mercury* George Jean Nathan that she was furious. Allowing Blanche to vent her anger, Mencken advised her to let the article pass, though he agreed that Hellman was indiscreet to write that Knopf did a $2 million annual business.

It would be the last time she would turn to her shrewd companion for advice. That November, the Knopfs lost their best friend. Just a few weeks after they went to Philadelphia to hear him lecture, Henry Mencken had a massive stroke. They had lauded his eloquence at dinner after the talk, when they finally got the chance to discuss his coverage of Philly's Republican and Democratic conventions. The stroke permanently damaged several brain areas, leaving the journalist unable to read or write. Though he lived another seven years, the Knopfs hardly recognized the man they both adored.

Blanche was distraught. The idea of Henry reduced to this state was impossible for her to grasp until she went down to Baltimore to see him. After all, Henry had been the only reliable connection between her and Alfred, and a driving force behind their company. She was glad he still had his brother, August, to care for him at his family home at 1524 Hollins Street. Geoffrey Hellman's next two *New Yorker* articles suddenly mattered little, with her dear Menck clearly so diminished.

In part to take her mind off her friend, Blanche made her carefully planned diplomatic journey to Germany a priority. She would recount that "last July, in 1948, I thought that General Clay was doing so important a job with the Berlin airlift that it should be put into permanent record. I wrote him and suggested his doing a book. We corresponded for several months and he asked that when I came to Europe next I come down to his theatre . . . I was [there again] in the early autumn, and I let him know, and he invited me to see him."[20]

She applauded the Berlin Airlift, with America and its allies working through the Marshall Plan to keep the Germans from starving, transporting food and water to the millions in need. General Lucius Clay didn't think Americans understood what their military was doing, and Clay told Blanche he wanted her to help him spread the word back home. He also wanted to discuss a potential contract for a book he might write for Knopf once he resigned. Flying on an army transport from Springfield, Massachusetts, in early 1949, Blanche recorded in a small notebook every detail of the trip, called "Operation Vittles" by Americans but Operation Airlift by others. Ultimately an eleven-month effort, it had been ongoing for six and a half months by the time Blanche arrived in Frankfurt, where in a few days she would board a C-57 to fly into Berlin's Tempelhof Airport again.

The plane circled Frankfurt for an hour in the fog before landing, in what Blanche would consider "the coldest most miserable post I have ever been in. Worse than Dakar. Two small coal fires, no lights, all of us freezing, Parachutes, top coats, hats on." Three hours later they landed, and, "to my surprise, both Clay's and Air Force officers met me, and cleared me in five minutes."

Now she just had to fly to Berlin, some three hundred miles away. She boarded a C-54, with parachutes distributed after everyone was seated. Meanwhile, the small crew was struggling to load onto the plane the huge sacks of flour that hungry Germans awaited. At the last minute, Major General William Tunner, chief of the airlift, arrived (his parachute already in place) to serve as copilot. The winter storms out of Frankfurt meant he had to fly low, about 6,500 feet, with a tonnage of ten thousand pounds, well above the regulation six thousand. Planes took off or landed at Tempelhof every five minutes from two runways—the second one recently built to accommodate the allies' endeavor.

From four thousand feet, Tunner descended on target, via directions from the tower that he listened to through earphones. He dropped fast, roughly a thousand feet per minute, almost missing the Berlin airstrip. Blanche would remember how a "mere boy" from the Midwest told everyone to prepare for a crash landing. "We were all plenty tense," she recalled. "But we made it in."

Blanche was given guest quarters at General Clay's Harnock House. Deutsche marks were three to a dollar legally; on the black market, they were up to twenty-one. The night she arrived, she invited eight newspapermen and -women to a late dinner, then "went back to CBS's broadcast journalist Bill Downs' house—no lights, candles, all of us with flashlights." The next morning in General Clay's office, previously the secondary Luftwaffe headquarters with "black and white marble floors, marble walls, gardens, etc," the two had a long session, "nine to almost twelve." They liked each other, and Blanche wrote in her own Berlin diary that she was "very impressed with Clay, good personality; certainly no sympathy for the Germans but understanding that unless we work with them and put them on their feet ultimately the Russians will take over . . . The general dictated and signed a letter agreeing to give me his book as soon as he resigned, which he trusted would be a matter of months."

Blanche lunched with Time-Life's bureau chief, Emmett Hughes, who had "done several articles on Hitler before his election, on Berlin, and on the occupation of Germany," and who wanted Knopf to publish his next book. Then she "saw two more German publishers. Paper difficulties are still great . . . About three o'clock by then, had coffee and went to find various publishers. Berlin dark at four, no electricity until six, inside and outside black except in military government buildings." Still, she became uncharacteristically impatient with the complaints of German publishers: "I finally lost my temper with one and explained that England and France did not have too much and had very little electricity as well."

Dropping her bags at the Press Club for her departure the next day, Blanche was surprised to find the atmosphere "that of war . . . there were no lights and news had just come in that a C-54 had crashed in England and all six boys aboard all dead. No news of who they were—everyone waiting for the names and details. What kind of music did I want?—schmaltz. [Everyone] sang and danced [until] news came in about the plane which had burned and all the boys had been burned. There was a feeling of disaster, of being dead by morning, of living only for that moment, exactly as one felt during the war and the bombings in England."

Her flight back to Frankfurt was nominally better than the earlier one to Berlin: "I took off next morning after finding a plane with parachutes. The plane had dumped coal dust, the most combustible and the worst kind of empty plane to fly, so they swept it out the best they could." Bad visibility, with ice on the wings and windshield, added to their problems. "Co-pilot brought us in by opening his port and hanging out. We were the last plane into Frankfurt that day."

In the end, despite his preliminary agreement with Blanche, Clay published with Greenwood, an independent press whose offer was four times that of Knopf. Greenwood also approved taking Clay's story "as is," no editing required—something, the soldier knew, that would never fly with Blanche.

20

THE SECOND SEX

BACK IN NEW YORK, eager to give credit to the rank-and-file American soldiers she had found unfailingly helpful, Blanche sent several politicians her observations of the ongoing airlift. Then she turned to the January launch of Elizabeth Bowen's *The Heat of the Day*. Set in the years after the London Blitz, its story revolves around the relationship of two lovers, Stella and Robert. A British intelligence agent, convinced that Robert is a spy, worries that Stella is as well. The novel emphasized the "inextricable knitting together of the individual and the national, the personal and the political." It had been the hardest of Bowen's novels for her to finish, and she worried that it might be a "point-blank failure."[1] Released in England with Jonathan Cape a year earlier, in 1948, selling well at forty-five thousand copies, it moved the British novelist Rosamond Lehmann to call it a great tragedy. In the United States, Bowen's novel, replete with espionage and free love, proved harder for some readers to accept, and *The Heat of the Day* received respectful if cautious reviews. In *The New York Times*, Orville Prescott (father of the writer Peter Prescott) lamented that Bowen's prose was simply too steely for American tastes. To Blanche's relief, the book was a selection of the Literary Guild.[2]

Blanche had grown to love Elizabeth, and she felt protective of *The Heat of the Day* as Bowen's American publisher. Its heroine, who sleeps indiscriminately with men and women—though rarely doubting that she loves her husband—could almost have been based on Blanche, who did find both sexes attractive. Even the novel's subplot, with its protagonist secretly working as an intelligence agent, seemed to echo Blanche's wartime accounts of her trip to South America.

In a subsequent interview for *House Beautiful*, Blanche claimed that her satisfaction in life came from her involvement in the world of books. "I would not change it for any other, but to pretend that publishing is anything but a constant round of overcoming obstacles and frustrating difficulties would be untrue."[3] Knopf was releasing Kenneth Millar's first book under the pseudonym Ross Macdonald (except for the first edition, which would read "John Macdonald"). *The Moving Target* features Lew Archer, who would become a seminal character in the gumshoe world. In *The Moving Target*, Archer is hired by the wife of a missing eccentric oil baron, who is the focus of the detective's long list of Los Angeles criminals as he tries to solve the mystery. Critics immediately placed Macdonald among the front ranks of his genre, where he was considered the heir apparent of Raymond Chandler and Dashiell Hammett. To Blanche's relief, Macdonald was easier and rewarding to work with, his prose more psychologically nuanced than her other mystery writers. (Macdonald would tell the philanthropist and Knopf friend W. H. "Ping" Ferry that he thought "Alfred never read" one of his books, all of which, from now until the writer's death, were published by Knopf.)[4]

But the detective genre was still second to readers' fascination with books about sex, and Blanche kept waiting to be the target of the day's aggressive vice squad, which would have been costly for the firm. The Knopfs were particularly nervous about the chance of being prosecuted over Harold Robbins's *Never Love a Stranger* (which even Blanche and Alfred thought sleazy). They were right: in Pennsylvania on March 18, an obscenity court case was filed against various publishers for producing nine obscene works, including Faulkner's *Sanctuary* and James T. Farrell's *Studs Lonigan* trilogy, as well as Robbins's novel. The Knopfs' friend Judge Curtis Bok ended the trial by citing earlier rulings on *Ulysses* (and other books), in which another friend, U.S. Federal Judge John Woolsey, had ruled in favor of Joyce. At that time, at the appeals level, New York's Judge Learned Hand had affirmed that *Ulysses* was not obscene, on grounds that Joyce was "loyal to his technique." In time, Woolsey's earlier decision would be considered the keystone of American law on obscenity, clearly maintaining that "indictable obscenity must be 'dirt for dirt's sake.'"[5]

Alfred would send out to friends, other publishers, and Knopf writers the fifty-seven-page ruling as a Christmas present. Its cover sheet said: "Five hundred copies have been printed by the Grabhorn Press for Blanche and Alfred Knopf, Christmas 1949"—for once, Blanche's name first.[6]

In late April, Alfred wrote to the Knopfs' friend Mary Bancroft, whose Boston family had inherited *The Wall Street Journal*. During the war, Mary had worked in Switzerland for U.S. Intelligence, and Alfred informed her that he had become a "full-blooded" American.

> I used to alternate trips to Europe with Mrs. Knopf but since 1939, I have only gone over once and then spent but three weeks in London and came home. Somehow or other I have lost all interest in Europe since the war. I just do not, as an American, like the look of things. And I have meanwhile faced West and begun really to discover the vast riches of our own land. So, I usually make my friends laugh when I say "You can have Paris, but I'll take Montana."[7]

Apprehensively, Blanche joined Alfred on a vacation to Jackson Hole, Wyoming, where they stayed at a dude ranch for two weeks. The trip was yet another challenge for the increasingly frail woman, her eyes degenerating from the diet drug DNP, just as Mencken's eye specialists at Johns Hopkins had warned her they would. In the office she wore dramatic, oversized glasses whose flair hid their utilitarian purpose, but at home her lenses were so thick they looked like the bottoms of Coke bottles. For the next trip west in June, Alfred would travel alone.

At the office, Blanche found herself phoning frequent encouragement to Camus, who was about to leave for South America, where Blanche's own trip had given her such a lift. But Camus seemed very anxious and on the verge of a nervous collapse. He was possessed, he said, by a feeling that death was imminent. Upon arrival in South America, he felt "evil in the air"—perhaps because his play *Cross Purpose* had been banned in Argentina. As a result, he had refused to lecture on any topic other than censorship. Just two weeks later, after he gave a few lectures in Chile (while suffering from undiagnosed tuberculosis), he was ready to go home.[8]

Blanche was already regretting that she'd not gone to South America with Camus when she was informed that she'd been awarded Brazil's National Order of the Southern Cross. A result of her 1942 trip, the award was meant to honor foreigners or local citizens who had contributed in significant ways to Brazil's culture. A library was being named in recognition of the publisher. Surely Blanche's author Gilberto Freyre, who had conceived of the cultural center several years earlier, was behind the dedication: Blanche had arranged to have the great Latin American scholar's magisterial *The Masters and the Slaves* translated into English. A three-part study of race and culture considered seminal to an understanding of black heritage in

Brazil, *The Masters and the Slaves* came out in 1933, followed by *The Mansions and the Shanties* in 1938 and *Order and Progress* in 1957.

By late August 1949, Blanche had resumed her regular fall scouting trips. Over tea at Claridge's in London, she met with authors whose current books might be right for Knopf. She rejected Vita Sackville-West's *Nursery Rhymes* but accepted Ivy Compton-Burnett's *Darkness and Day*, which would prove one of the author's weakest novels. Probably Blanche found fascinating the obvious influence of Oscar Wilde on Compton-Burnett's book, which was written almost entirely in (arch) dialogue. After Blanche had finished her scouting, she invited writers who were already signed to Knopf for American publication to dine: the obligatory, such as V. S. Pritchett, to lunch, and her favorites, such as Eric Ambler and Elizabeth Taylor (the novelist), to dinner.

Blanche was taken aback by the rationing still in effect overseas, and she immediately wrote an office assistant back at Knopf to send over packages of bacon, rice, and cheese, in addition to underclothes and soap for her English chauffeur's wife. To her London agent, Grace Dadd, she directed "marvelous parcels [of] olive oil by the gallon, a seven pound tin of ham," and for Grace's children "tins of powdered milk, canned fruit, and Hawaiian pineapples—through Bloomingdales and CARE." She brought still more nylons and beef from Paris, again with strict instruction on how to cook the meat. To other publishers in England and France and also Denmark and Norway, she sent cartons of cigarettes mailed from the States. Nor did she overlook Jenny Bradley, to whom she gave Kleenex, coffee, and soap. Blanche continued helping her European friends until 1953, when most items were no longer rationed, except in London, where butter, meat, and nylons were still coveted.[9]

While in Paris she stayed at Jenny's apartment at 18 Quai de Béthune (a building once owned by Cardinal Richelieu)—where the agent told her the talk of the city was of Simone de Beauvoir's revolutionary book *The Second Sex*. The women stayed up late into the night debating whether it was right for Knopf: How would Americans regard the French philosopher's arguments? Blanche was still unsure by the time she left Paris.

Back in New York, she was delighted at the news already awaiting her from her French agent. "Jenny Darling," she wrote back at once. "Yesterday morning I looked at my mail casually and there, thanks entirely to you, was the letter announcing that I was being given the Legion [award]; well, it will be fun and I well know that you are entirely responsible." She'd been named a *chevalier* (knight) of the Légion d'Honneur, for developing and promoting French literature. She turned back at once to her recent trip: "You have been fabulous to me and the joy of being with you is something very special—as you describe it—and I think maybe you are right—on se comprends."[10]

Jenny, a lesbian, a stodgy, maternal woman and French agent for American literary stars, including Truman Capote, was unfailingly generous in sharing her most interesting friends with Blanche, and the two had developed an intense sororal friendship. "Jenny, a tough cookie, loved Blanche, she really did," Pete Lemay said.[11]

Still mulling over *The Second Sex*, Blanche was caught off guard by Alfred's renewed determination to move the company to Purchase. Even as she wrote Jenny about a book she had bought while in France, leaving it to her to execute the deal, she made it clear that her domestic life was once again on the skids: Blanche had ordered French napkins for Alfred's eight-foot dining table, but she now did a volte-face, telling Jenny to wait on these: "At the moment I am not very eager to [do anything] for Alfred . . . Things could not be more horrible than they are and I can only wish that I had stayed away longer . . . The trip home was all right—you know what they are like—Alfred was charming when I got in but now it is all over— the moment I assert myself there is a row.[12] With Pat, Alfred,

Koshland, and Lesser all promoting their views on taking the office to Purchase, there was inevitable jousting for position; all Blanche wanted was to ensure that Knopf stayed in Manhattan.

Jenny answered in early November, focused on Beauvoir: "Darling, I seem to have responded very badly to all your sweet letters, but I am busier than ever, in spite of my honest efforts to keep some time for minor human feelings! But let us be serious."[13] Jenny thought it was time for Blanche to make her move on *The Second Sex*, which, mocked and reviled upon its release, was suddenly selling six to seven hundred copies a day. Especially in light of the Kinsey report on American women she'd heard was about to be published (it would in fact not come out until 1953), Blanche had taken a wait-and-see attitude. She knew that Beauvior's book would take an unusually long time to translate for an American edition, in light of its more than eight hundred pages.

Just as Blanche decided, however, that she wanted the two-volume work after all, Beauvoir's agent decided to go elsewhere—unless Blanche offered $750 for each volume. With Jenny's help, by November 9, 1949, Blanche had secured American rights. She proceeded at once to hire a friend of Mencken's, Howard M. Parshley, to read volume one.[14] Bradley agreed with Blanche that they would have to make some cuts, a specification the publisher shared with Beauvoir: *The Second Sex* was just too long and dense for an American audience. Indeed, sometimes the text proved too much even for the French.[15]

After Thanksgiving, Blanche took another fall. For the remainder of 1949, all talk of moving to the country was delayed indefinitely, with Blanche's increasing blindness and her brittle bones arguing against the move. Perhaps her habitual dislike of Christmas—Jenny invited her to her Antibes home for the holidays, but Blanche said the trip would be too short—gave her an excuse to stay put, especially in light of the forthcoming ceremony for her French award, to be held in Manhattan. Her subsequent buying spree, which Jenny coordinated from afar, included bills from Violette Cornille Sacs, 32, Rue de la Bois: three purses for 360 French francs (around $100 at the time) and a Dior dress billed at 500 francs, or about $140 (equivalent to $3,800 in 2015). She sent Jenny back to Balenciaga to see which way the stripes went on a dress she was interested in.[16]

Ordering porcelain cups and plates from the fine tableware store Jean Luce near the Ritz, Blanche found the postwar prices amazingly low. But she waited too long for a coat she wanted and, to her irritation, it was bought by Mrs. David Bruce.

In December, at the French award ceremony, Blanche was pinned with an elaborate brooch and ribbon honoring her as a *chevalier* of the Legion of Honor. She beamed with pride, as did Alfred, more than one guest observed. In an interview about Blanche after her death, the former Knopf editor and Blanche's friend Frances Lindley said: "When she got [the honor], a dozen of us were invited to go up and see her that day. She looked absolutely terrific. She had on a sort of medium-brown Balenciaga gabardine. She stood there like a very well-brought up young girl while [the presentation was made]. I remember going up to Alfred after it was over when we were clustering around and drinking champagne. Alfred said, 'All I need to do is bask in Blanche's reflected glory.' Not nasty; it was a very tender and proud statement."[17] Though husband and wife often engaged in rows even at public celebrations, now Alfred announced, "If anyone could do this, Blanche is that one."[18]

In an article in *The American Scholar* twenty years after her death, the film critic Stanley Kauffmann recalled Blanche during this period "as much a grand lady as her frame would permit. She was short and very thin. Her thinness was incongruous with her chic . . . her dyed and carefully arranged hair. Her modish dress, her bangled arms made her look like an expensively attired starveling."[19] *The New Yorker*'s Janet Flanner would remember that during these years she got to know Blanche better (Jenny Bradley claimed Flanner and the publisher had an affair) and said, "I liked Blanche. I thought she had a vital intelligence. She always had a toplofty attitude to herself and the House of Knopf, as indeed she should have had. She was quite elegant and at the very top of the profession in her estimation and the opinion of other people. Not modest."[20] At one point, the writer asked the publisher for a long list of books she had published, all of which Blanche was happy to provide. Flanner was especially impressed by Blanche's acquisition of the postwar journal of André Gide, he who "never wasted a moment being wrong."[21]

Before she went abroad for her January buying trip, Blanche resolved to take dance lessons with Pat; she'd decided to take an active role in his finding a spouse. Frances Lindley recalled that Blanche ended up treating him like her beau, not the "best relationship to have with your son."[22] Blanche was able to spend even more time with Pat when she had to cancel, suddenly, her first trip of 1950. She had already seen one of her Baltimore doctors, who prescribed exercises for her newly stiff neck, and she'd bought her Air France ticket, with Jenny arranging the room at the Ritz and the car and driver to meet her at Le Bourget Airport. She was ready to go, when everything was put on hold.

Alfred, unbeknown to Blanche, had scheduled a board meeting about moving the company to Purchase. Quickly, her secretary ensured she made it, with Alfred pretending he'd forgotten she'd be gone. Blanche dived in: she agreed that they were pressed for office space at 501 Madison, and that "New York is getting almost impossible." Still, she had "not made up my mind that it is wise and in fact, I think it unwise for a small business like ours to move out of the center."[23] A vote was taken within a week and the company stayed in Manhattan, where they continued publishing an average of a hundred books a year (versus, for instance, Doubleday's four hundred).

Much of 1950 would be spent developing Blanche's publishing

plan for *The Second Sex*. Excited about buying what she knew would be an important book, especially for women, Blanche wasted no time coming up with ways to promote it far in advance of publication. In the early part of the year, she suggested to Beauvoir that the author and the anthropologist Margaret Mead exchange thoughts at an interview, in Paris or New York. Having gotten no response, Blanche went to Beauvoir's French publisher, Gallimard, when she knew Mead was abroad. An arrangement was made, but Beauvoir felt corralled, and she did everything possible to make Blanche regret the maneuver. Planning all along to cancel at the last minute, Beauvoir agreed to a luncheon with Mead, both French and English translators at the ready.

Blanche had assumed the event would benefit both pioneers. They would conduct a dialogue, perhaps even inspiring a series of conversations to be published later. Beauvoir, however, behaved rudely to Mead, possibly out of insecurity around the celebrated anthropologist. During their preliminary prelunch discussion, in front of the increasingly befuddled Mead, Beauvoir had flirted relentlessly with the "prettier women" assistants instead of speaking to the famous American. Blanche was furious, finding such behavior unforgiveable, and from that point on she and Beauvoir loathed each other. Apparently, however, Beauvoir didn't object to "Blanche's personality"; she disapproved of Blanche's "violently anti-communist" beliefs. The following year, in 1951, after meeting with the publisher in Paris, Beauvoir wrote to her Chicago lover, the writer Nelson Algren, that "perhaps [Blanche's plane] will crash" on her way home.[24]

In April 1950, after visiting Elizabeth Bowen in Ireland (Bowen reciprocated that August, staying at Blanche's West Fifty-Fifth Street apartment), Blanche sought the novelist's help convincing Carson McCullers to leave Houghton Mifflin. McCullers was clearly displeased with her publisher. Unlike poaching, following up on news of an unhappy author was entirely ethical, Blanche decided. Upon returning to the States, she wrote to Bowen, whom she knew

McCullers admired: "Once she is completely clear of them, we want very much to publish her . . . If you could give me a hand with her, I would be grateful. I think she is a beautiful writer and I honestly think she wants to come with us, and she should be on our list. Anyway, I leave it all to you." Whether or not Bowen intervened, McCullers stayed with Houghton Mifflin in the end.

Similarly, though eager to approach Colette, whose writing Blanche enjoyed and with whom she'd become friends in Paris, she waited to court the Frenchwoman until Farrar, Straus seemed uninterested in renewing Colette's contract. But then Alfred stepped in, telling Blanche that since the other secretive publisher (whose identity Alfred withheld) set to compete for Colette was a friend of his, he insisted Knopf not pursue her. The fuss was for naught: the writer returned to Farrar, Straus after all—a great disappointment to Blanche—and Alfred conceded that he'd been wrong to interfere. (He would do so again in 1954, when he refused Norman Mailer's *The Deer Park*, despite Blanche's ardent wooing of the author.)

In June Knopf released John Hersey's six-hundred-page novel *The Wall*, selling 97,860 copies with an additional Book-of-the-Month Club distribution of 230,000. *The Wall* concerned the fate of Jews living in the Warsaw Ghetto. Like *Hiroshima*, the book was infused with a powerful sense of humanity and was a major bestseller.

By September, Blanche was back at Claridge's. She had missed seeing Ed Murrow in London, and now wrote pleading letters to the reporter to give her a book on his coverage of the Korean War. Finally home, Murrow, who was tired, wanted to recycle a cache of old essays instead. While Blanche was still abroad, Murrow and the Knopf editor Harold Strauss corresponded, Blanche hoping Strauss, who was one of their best, could make it all work. Strauss wrote:

> *Dear Mr. Murrow,*
> *As you know, Blanche is still in Europe, but I have hastened to read your seven Korean broadcasts which you sent over at her request.*

I had heard three of them on the air, and I am glad to say that they read as well as they listen.

Nevertheless, he reluctantly explained:

[I can't quite sanction] reprinting the old broadcasts, wonderful though they were, just to make a bulky enough book. I know you sent these transcripts over because Blanche asked for them, and this does not necessarily imply that you yourself think there is a book here. As to that, I am sure that Blanche still feels and will continue to feel, as she wrote you on July 24th, that "If you write a book I want to publish it and have always wanted to . . ." Blanche will see all this material when she comes back, but meanwhile, if there is anything more you want me to do, or if you have tangible plans for a book about which I don't know, please let me know.[25]

Blanche's actually being able to see the material was unlikely, given the rapidly diminishing state of her vision. According to one assistant, "We used to dread watching her go across Madison Avenue for lunch. God was with her half the time. She walked right out into the middle of the street, never looked up or down [or left or right]—always straight-ahead."[26] Various treatments for her "burnt" eyeballs and her cataracts were tried, but her eyes only worsened. Defiantly, she pretended she could still see as well as always, remembering her mother's lesson that presentation was an important part of success.

21

A WEDDING AND OTHER RIBBONS

OR HER SUCCESS in fostering intercultural relations between the Americas, Blanche was awarded the Order of the Southern Cross on Thursday, November 2, 1950. She was cited for her "outstanding work in the editorial field in promoting a better knowledge of Brazilian culture in the United States" by publishing English translations of "outstanding Brazilian literary works." The publisher was one of a distinguished list of recipients that would over the years include Dwight Eisenhower, Librarian of Congress James Billington, Marshal Tito, Václav Havel, and Che Guevara—august company for the bookish girl from the Upper West Side. After the ceremony in Washington, Ambassador Mauricio Nabuco held a reception for Blanche at the Brazilian Embassy. Oddly, though the *New York Herald Tribune* covered the occasion, the title of their article was "Brazil Honors Mrs. Knopf: Makes Publisher's Wife a Chevalier in Order of the Southern Cross."

Back in New York, Blanche was trying to decide whether to

bring out Beauvoir's book as one volume or two. The question had been bounced back and forth between sales and publicity, with the concern eating into Blanche's time. She was thrilled to relax with Elizabeth Bowen when the writer stopped in Manhattan to see her publisher and friend and praised the appearance of Blanche's apartment, where Bowen stayed. After the novelist returned home, Blanche wrote her that "I can't tell you the blank there was at 24 West after you left. I really felt completely bereft."[1]

The decor might have impressed Bowen, but it was certainly not to the British writer's taste, her own home seeming to envelop Blanche and other guests in its warmth. Blanche's apartment at 24 West Fifty-Fifth Street was designed for entertaining, most often drinks and dinner with "French publishers and certain other industry figures, among her favorites *The New Yorker*'s fiction editor William Maxwell and his wife, Emily," remembers Pete Lemay, hired a few years later. "It was a very pleasant, tastefully decorated rather large room, most comfortable for conversation and book talk." The publicist and his wife also had many lunches in Purchase, where "it was not as easy an environment as Blanche's apartment," due perhaps to the tension Alfred usually contributed to the conversation. No matter who the guests were, "Alfred, . . . at home as in the office, seldom permitted conversation to stray from himself . . . I did see his upstairs study occasionally and it was no more cheerful than the rest of the rather intimidating mansion. I must add that we never really enjoyed the meals at Alfred's but always appreciated Blanche's graciousness and skill with her authors and colleagues, and looked forward to her invitations."[2]

Midway through June in 1951, seventy-six-year-old Serge Koussevitzky died in Boston, leaving his legacy, the Tanglewood Music Festival, in Lenox, Massachusetts. Blanche wasn't surprised—she had said her goodbyes the previous season, when it was clear he was ill—but she must have been nostalgic for their shared past. Robert Nathan remembered that "she wore Koussevitzky like a little corsage on her shoulder."[3] But Blanche had never been one to dwell in sorrow; she was wont to feel great pain at her losses and then determinedly resume her life.

In July a cordial letter arrived at 501 Madison Avenue from Dwight Eisenhower, who was supreme commander of the Allied Forces in Europe, thanking Blanche for the cartons of books she had recently donated to the military commanders. She had carefully chosen what she thought might complement their interests. Probably she had included advance copies of August releases, their reissue of Ford Madox Ford's World War I novel *The Good Soldier* as well as Nicholas Monsarrat's World War II novel *The Cruel Sea*, which would sell 169,000 copies and be made into a movie within a few years. *The Cruel Sea* followed the lives of a group of Royal Navy sailors fighting the Battle of the Atlantic, each of its seven chapters describing one year during the war.

The two books proved the market for war stories hadn't been saturated yet. General Eisenhower wrote to Blanche:

Colonel Lawrence has told me of your generous gift to the SHAPE Library. Your selection includes books which will be invaluable to our staff, drawn from ten nations. It is my hope that this headquarters will be a model for international understanding, and I look upon good books as a very important avenue toward this goal.

On behalf of SHAPE, I wish to thank you for your fine contribution to our effort.[4]

That fall, her energies returned to the Beauvoir text, which she was determined to publish while the French version was still selling. After talking over Beauvoir's expectations with Jenny, Blanche accompanied her friend to the Cote d'Azur, the two making their way to the agent's house in Antibes, where they relaxed for several weeks. When Blanche returned to New York, Alfred was still touring out west. She wrote Jenny, "I do not see why I came back, and would much prefer being in apartment 71 at the Ritz; you remember that was my reaction when I left . . . I miss you more than I can say and it is ridiculous, but what I want to do if I can manage is to come to Nice as we agreed." After her "dreamlike" visit to Antibes, where she "was surrounded by thought and kindness and affection," she registered the paradox of being lonely at home though always busy, adding that she "somehow" felt much more lost in Manhattan "than I do at the Place Vendome."[5]

Surely Blanche's eyesight problems were depressing her, as she found herself almost totally dependent upon her assistants, whether for travel or at the office or even working at home. When she didn't use a magnifying glass, she asked her assistant to be her eyes. "She trusted me and depended on me," her secretary (and later copy editor) Shirley Chidney recalled.

I kept her files, did her errands, called up 10,000 people . . . I had to read all the letters—to me and then to her. I read each letter out loud to her. She kept different colored folders so she'd know without having to read anything what it was. I could speak French. Once she told someone she knew there was an apartment empty in her building because she saw them taking the coffin out that A.M. Said it in French, surprised I understood. She thought that was even funnier.

When she had a secretary who could do the job that she liked, they stayed 10 years; there were only two of us over a period of 20 years. [But] some stayed only a few days or weeks—they couldn't take the demands of the job.[6]

Shirley felt that Blanche treated her as an equal, leaving her in charge when she was away—as she had with Ruth. The secretary found Blanche interesting and generous, though often unaware that her quirks made work more difficult for others: Blanche "kept a rubber stamp of Tapiola's paw print in her desk," for instance, often requiring Shirley to apply it to friends' correspondence. Blanche's beloved pet had been killed by one of Alfred's dogs, grieving her doubly because she hadn't been around to intervene. From this point on, she began bringing her well-trained terriers or poodles to the office.

Blanche allowed herself to be vulnerable around Shirley—again, as she had with Ruth, occasionally openly crying at home, especially when she felt she'd been disregarded at the office. After the war, Pat had joined Knopf as secretary and trade books manager; he often aggressively sided with Alfred during office disagreements—causing Blanche to reveal her emotions to the trustworthy Shirley. At times the assistant even found her employer amusing, as when she sent Shirley "to Abercrombie to buy a lot of dog candy. She sent it out as Xmas presents, showing off that she knew some people called her a bitch."

Shirley accepted gratefully the slightly used Dior and Balmain suits Blanche gave her, which the assistant still had twenty years later. She especially appreciated the delicacy with which Blanche offered them, careful not to offend through largesse. The British agent Grace Dadd would appreciate such bounteousness as well: "[Blanche] was very, very generous. Clothes were part of her life. She had to keep changing. I know she sold some [of the designer fashions], she told me. I was a book agent wearing nothing [normally] in Piguet and Balenciaga . . . I'd have ten Paris suits in my wardrobe, beautiful evening dresses. I didn't let anyone know where I obtained them."[7]

Though preoccupied with the continuing difficulties of translating the Beauvoir book, Blanche was determined to spend more time with her son, hoping to grow close again, as they'd been before the war—and before Hohe. It seemed clear to her that Pat was imitating the other men in the office, siding with Alfred against her, because it was obviously safer to do so. By the end of December 1951, she had decided to reactivate her dance lessons with Pat: she wanted to see her son married, and she knew she'd have to work hard to convince him to listen to her advice. Before the new year began, however, Pat assured her that marriage was, as a matter of fact, part of his plan as well. Then, at the start of 1952, Pat proposed to Alice Laine, his secretary at Knopf, and she accepted. Astounded at his decision, Blanche eventually learned from Frances Lindley that when Pat lunched with her some months before, he had launched into a tirade, telling Frances that "one reason I'm going to marry [Alice] is that she's not one goddamn bit like my mother." Frances could never figure out what "changed him" into a young man with "a long list of indictments of his mother."[8] (It seems unlikely that she knew that Pat had walked in on Blanche with Hohe.)

Though Alfred didn't think the choice of a wife so important, Blanche must have been devastated that Pat was marrying a retired police officer's daughter who didn't even seem particularly genial. She elected to skip her January trip to Europe after all, deciding instead to accompany Alfred out west. The director of the National Park Service personally made all of the Knopfs' arrangements at Yellowstone. Smiling wanly in photos at Carlsbad Caverns, Blanche is swaddled in layers of wool, while Alfred is dressed in the winter as if for a perfect spring day.

Aware of Pat's desire to keep his wife and his mother completely separate in his life, Blanche assumed that with time relations would be better between her and the young couple. When Pat insisted that the parents not meet one another until the wedding, Blanche and Alfred demurred, finding such behavior rude. Alfred demanded that the three of them take the three Laines to dinner. The event proved at best listless, since Mr. Laine's profession encouraged little interaction, Alfred would later say, and "there wasn't much common ground on which Blanche and Mrs. Laine could meet," either.[9] While Alfred lacked a talent for small talk, Blanche had taught herself to socialize with anyone, and she probably rose to the occasion. Alfred would recall the dinner somewhat condescendingly: "As a matter of fact, the young people proved extremely discreet about this [the class difference], and I don't believe either of us laid eyes on the Laines again except, perhaps, at the wedding. They turned out to be perfectly good people and served Alice and Pat well for a long time as baby-sitters" for the three children who would be born within a few years—Alison, Susan, and David.[10] Bill Koshland would remember Alice as "a little on the dull side" but felt that she "made something of herself," and she "wasn't snowed under by Pat."[11]

On July 27, 1952, the wedding took place in a small Catholic church in Carmel, New York, roughly an hour and a half north of Manhattan. In the catty mode that some women adopted when discussing Blanche, Betsy Johnson, a family friend, interviewed in 1990, claimed that "Blanche wore a black dress to the wedding and as the vows were taken she turned around to wiggle her finger [hello] at friends, undercutting its solemnity."[12] The socialite Georgia Glin confirmed the story that Blanche wore "a black Balenciaga dress to Pat's wedding—the epitome of spite. A wedding in the country in the kind of dress you'd wear to an ambassador's tea party in Paris. To show Alice, who has many qualities, but not chic." Alice, however, was adamant: Blanche's mother-of-the-groom dress was turquoise, and she wore a "large green hat." Pat concurred. He told Peter Prescott that his mother was in green or turquoise. "And Betsy Johnson wasn't even at the wedding!"[13]

If mothers of sons tend to have fraught relationships with their sons' wives, Blanche clearly tried to get along with Alice. But Pat's ambivalence about his mother made Alice wary of her mother-in-law. Undeterred, Blanche suggested books for Alice to read and offered to buy her designer clothes or to pass on her own, which until now she'd given to others. But Alice refused such gifts, preferring to read her own books and to shop at middlebrow Peck & Peck. When the young couple's children were born, Blanche gave them fancy Parisian outfits in which Alice never dressed them, even to show Blanche how adorable they looked. Once she brought back from France a beautiful embroidered smock for their firstborn, Alison, but it was tossed aside with an excuse. When Alison was two, with Blanche hoping to choose a gift everyone would like, she brought her a "terribly expensive doll" from Paris, appropriate, Pat later recalled, for a six-year-old. "Alison didn't know what to do with this and screamed in terror when she saw it."[14]

Pat would admit, after Blanche's death, that Alice never felt badly treated by her mother-in-law, though she didn't appreciate Blanche's ill-conceived attempts to teach her how to dress. What "destroyed any hope of a decent relationship between me, Alice and Blanche," Pat later said, was a trip the couple had made to Purchase. Supposedly, Blanche took Alice aside to ask what Pat had said about her and added, "They're a pack of lies." When Alice told Pat, he was "furious. It was a hell of a way to greet your new daughter."[15] Alice and Pat rented an apartment in Manhattan for the first four years of their marriage, until, in 1956, without asking his parents for help, Pat unaccountably borrowed five thousand dollars from Bennett Cerf and Donald Klopfer, acquaintances of some years at Random House, to build a house in Westport, Connecticut, embarrassing Blanche and enraging Alfred.[16]

On September 8, 1952, the Knopfs attended a slightly less fraught event than other recent unions they'd witnessed. Mary Jane Badger, daughter of the World War II spy and Knopf friend Mary Bancroft, was marrying former president William Taft's grandson, Robert Taft's son Horace. Irene Jackson and her husband, Supreme Court Justice Robert H. Jackson, invited the Knopfs to a celebratory dinner at the Jacksons' hotel suite in Washington. Other guests included Deputy Director of Central Intelligence Allen Dulles (former lover of the bride's mother), who gave the bride away, and the French ambassador, Henri Bonnet, both with their wives, as usual noted but not named.

Blanche was in her element. As Frances Lindley said years later, "she was one of the world's great listeners. Watching her listen to people from whom she wanted information was extraordinary. She would listen to men talking about business affairs. You could see her mind going . . . She was a hard woman to snow intellectually or conversationally."[17] From Blanche's habit of close observation, Lindley believed that the publisher had become someone worth listening to: "She didn't often volunteer advice, but when she did it was of a singularly wise and realistic nature."[18]

Back at the office, everyone was eagerly awaiting proofs of *The Second Sex*. The previous year, several Knopf editors had argued for a two-volume edition because it would bring in more revenue. But the publishers ended up charging ten dollars (equivalent to eighty dollars six decades later) for one large book, which would be less costly to produce. Now Blanche wrote Beauvoir, genially mentioning the author's continued lack of contact, and suggesting that Beauvoir come over for the American publication, when a "big campaign" was planned. She received no response, as usual.

Though in January 1953 Knopf brought out a mini biography of Willa Cather written by her longtime companion, Edith Lewis, *The Second Sex* commanded all the attention. Striving to stress the scholarly nature of the book while allowing ads and brochures to suggest the sexual content as well, weeks of a Knopf publicity blitz preceded its appearance. Finally, on February 24, 1953, the English version of *The Second Sex* arrived in stores, the bulky ten-dollar volume proving an immediate academic and commercial success.

Still, the book was criticized for its difficulty, which was generally blamed on the translation, though the original prose had been considered hard going in French as well. At least Blanche had had confidence in the translator, Howard Parshley, a highly respected anthropology professor at Smith College, who repeatedly asked Beauvoir for her preferences and clarifications. (She often failed to answer, at times seeming deliberately, even maliciously uncooperative, just to impede the American publication. Parshley had a heart attack in 1950, but quickly resumed work on *The Second Sex*.) Emeritus before he finished the project, the scholar would eventually be fingered as the culprit in what later scholars consider a flawed translation. The faults, however, resulted at least in part from working with an erratic writer, as well as with the various Knopf editors and advisers who further muddled an already complicated text.[19]

As Blanche predicted, the book's significance far outlasted that of the Kinsey Report on women, whose forthcoming publication on the heels of the Beauvoir volume had worried Blanche, who feared it would capture the women's market. *The Second Sex*, however, was more than a thesis on women's sexuality: it drew on sociology, culture, physiology, psychoanalysis, anthropology, and more.

Whether translated as "One is not born, but rather becomes, a woman" or "One is not born, but rather becomes, woman"—dropping the "a" to make "woman" universal—Beauvoir's message was incendiary, her book igniting a fresh wave of feminism. The Vatican banned it. The anthropologist Ashley Montagu would declare in a prepublication blurb that "*The Second Sex* is the healthiest, wealthiest, and wisest book that has ever been written on women and, therefore, also on men. It will be read, I predict, for generations as one of the great expressions of the human spirit of our culture." He continued: "It is a great book . . . [ranking next to] John Stuart Mill's 'The Subjection of Women.'"[20] But in his contribution to a collection of opinions in the February 21, 1953, issue of the *Saturday Review*, he would admit to being disappointed with Beauvoir's acceptance of the stereotype sometimes made of the American woman. Karl Menninger believed *The Second Sex* to be repetitive and to overlook the place of men in sexual relations. Philip Wylie, best known for his *A Generation of Vipers*, which excoriates just about the entire American culture of the 1940s, especially middle-aged American women, said, "*The Second Sex* is one of the few great books of our era"— flowing from "a quality men often deny to women: genius."[21]

Finally, Margaret Mead, forthright but respectful, had her say:

Beauvoir's treatise deserved more knowledge than its author possessed. Too, the writer failed to confront the great difference between American and French attitudes toward women, France still denying them birth control although its abortion rate was the same as its birthrate. It was a culture in which women had traditionally hidden their power behind men's. Nonetheless, *The Second Sex* was a "rare, exasperating, but unfailingly interesting experience . . . torrential, brilliant, wonderfully angry."[22] Decades later, in the feminist 1980s, the literary critic Jane Gallop would say that "she learned how to masturbate by reading Beauvoir."[23]

Howard Parshley's name as translator and editor of *The Second Sex* was inadvertently omitted from the volume's dust jacket, deeply disappointing the man. At least he finally allowed himself to buy a new Buick with his hard-won royalties: it had been a trial to complete the translation with so little help from Beauvoir. Sadly, the retired professor would enjoy the car a mere four months before dying on May 19, 1953. Assuming Beauvoir hadn't heard the distressing news, Blanche sent her the *Times* obituary saying, "I thought you might want to know about Howard Parshley's death." Apparently the writer didn't respond; she found Blanche trivial.

While such animated book reviews were producing a largely positive audience, Blanche worried about several of her other authors, closer to home and threatened with testifying before the House Un-American Activities Committee (HUAC). Langston Hughes and Dashiell Hammett were to appear before the group on March 24. Eloquent and respectful, Hughes managed to outmaneuver Roy Cohn and the rest of Joseph McCarthy's lieutenants.[24] Explaining why several years ago he had repudiated his earlier sympathy for Soviet ideals and goals, Hughes gracefully explained that he no longer trusted the USSR—though, as one biographer has noted, "not once had he unequivocally attacked" its form of government.[25]

At the end of his hearing, Hughes would tell a friend he was bewildered by the wink Joseph McCarthy gave him. If McCarthy really believed that he and Hughes were now equal, he was missing completely what the biographer Arnold Rampersad would call the writer's "tour de force," where he had disarmed the committee's "hostility and preserved something of his dignity."[26] After Hughes testified that day, Hammett, who had served five months in prison in 1951, was recalled before HUAC, where he once again refused to answer even benign questions (such as his current address), making Blanche still happier that he was no longer her problem. Edward R. Murrow, yet another Knopf connection, would be the force that led "the counterattack on McCarthy."[27] Earlier that year, after *The New York Times* implied that Thomas Mann, through his association with Paul Robeson, was linked to communism, Mann wrote the *Times* an angry letter that Alfred dissuaded him from sending. Mann's disappointment and disgust at what he saw as America's present "hysteria" led him to move, in 1952, to Zurich.[28]

Given the climate, Alfred and Blanche probably assumed (correctly) that they, too, were on some low-level anticommunist watch. FBI files show a halfhearted attempt to keep track of Alfred, overlooking entirely the hundreds of letters he wrote to congressmen denouncing McCarthy. After all, Alfred was considered the publisher of Dashiell Hammett, with Blanche assessed as the "Vice President" who "takes no active part in the business affairs." Especially after Knopf published a 1957 book by the accused communist spy Alger Hiss, *In the Court of Public Opinion*, the FBI kept an eye on the publishers. Years later, in a 1964 report, Blanche was said to have "supported various front organizations"—the most important being the ACLU—that were "heavily infiltrated with Communists" at the time.[29]

In April, just as tensions over the HUAC hearings subsided, Blanche read about a recent concert of Jascha Heifetz's that had gone awry in the state of Israel, officially formed in May 1948. During his third visit to the still emotionally raw Jewish country, Heifetz had included in his program the Violin Sonata in E-flat by Richard Strauss, considered by many Israelis to be a Nazi composer, whose works were unofficially banned along with Richard Wagner's. The Holocaust had taken place a little more than ten years before, but Heifetz stood his ground: in its purity, music had nothing to do with politics. Even though the Israeli minister of education implored Heifetz to respect local sentiment, he refused, declaring that "the music is above these factors . . . I will not change my program. I have the right to decide on my repertoire." He played in six cities, where his performance of the Strauss sonata was met with silence, until, at the second concert in Tel Aviv, a heckler threw something that managed to injure Heifetz's hand, the wound causing the violinist to cancel the following night's performance. The news appeared in all the major American newspapers, and Blanche immediately wrote to him of her shock and concern.[30]

In what was surely a reprieve from recent politics, including the publication of *The Second Sex*, Knopf soon released a different kind of book about a modern woman, *The Fabulous Fanny: The Story of Fanny Brice*, by Norman Katkov. (The biography of the recently deceased entertainer would become the basis of the 1960s Broadway musical and Hollywood movie *Funny Girl*.) In addition, Knopf published Ross Macdonald's *Meet Me at the Morgue*. Blanche knew that Macdonald, even with his ups and downs, was a first-rate writer. Though most reviews were tepid, *The New York Times* commended the novel as a complex study of a kidnapping with "all the pace and excitement of earlier Macdonald" and a "hard-headed and humane detective." *The Saturday Review* was less enthusiastic, calling the writing "capable" but with "chatter [that] occasionally retards action."[31] Blanche remained confident that Macdonald was destined for great appreciation.

She was deeply distressed, however, by Raymond Chandler's decision to decamp to Houghton Mifflin. The nervous writer needed higher sales, he told her, apologetically. She'd believed in *The Long Goodbye*, which had taken him an extended period to finish, and which was soon to be published by Hamish Hamilton in London to all the praise Blanche had anticipated. At least she could now focus on James Baldwin, who was unyielding about rough language he thought appropriate for his new book. Blanche, along with several Knopf editors, had argued against the provocative words and phrases that Baldwin insisted on using in his novel *Go Tell It on the Mountain*. The writer, who stood his ground, convinced Blanche that he was right, whereupon she turned the manuscript over to the house editor Philip Vaudrin. She and Baldwin approved Vaudrin's editorial suggestions, the three of them working well together. After Baldwin had written a new opening for the book, created stronger characters, and revised the ending, Vaudrin recommended offering $250 for the changes against a $750 advance, but when Blanche wrote Baldwin, she increased the advance to $1,000 instead.[32]

Still, the months leading up to publication of *Go Tell It on the Mountain* had been difficult, and Vaudrin explained to Baldwin that he and Blanche had needed to make more small changes:

Nothing serious, as you will see, but all advisable from the point of view of censorship . . . The phrase "and rubbing his hand, before the eyes of Jesus, over his cock" now reads "and making obscene gestures before the eyes of Jesus" . . . In the scene describing Gabriel's baptism by immersion, we must drop the last five words of the sentence: "He was drenched, and his thin, white clothes clung like another skin to his black body, and his sex stood up." I hope you will agree that these last five words don't alter the force of the whole thing . . .

But there was a bit more: where a white cop told an African-American woman, "Well, it ain't black, honey, but it's mighty long and hard," Vaudrin said they were advised to omit the sentence.[33]

Baldwin replied from Paris that there was nothing obscene about the book. As for the word "cock," no one objected to Shakespeare using it—to which Vaudrin, surely with Blanche's encouragement, politely pointed out that Shakespeare couldn't be dragged into court. In the end, Baldwin agreed to drop "it ain't black" but not "and his sex stood up," explaining at length the crucial relevance of the phrase to the meaning of the story. Vaudrin then cited a House committee currently investigating the morality of paperback novels—"our self-appointed wards of public morality . . . Why give them any chance at all?"—and insisted on the changes.[34]

When it was released to the public in May 1953, *Go Tell It on the Mountain* had an advance sale of only three thousand copies, but it received strong reviews. It was a coming-of-age novel that reflected upon the King James Bible as well as Baldwin's own life under a severe Pentecostal stepfather. *The New York Times* called it a "beautiful, furious first novel," while *Kirkus* called *Go Tell It on the Mountain* "a first novel of considerable distinction as well as feeling." Baldwin's next submission to Knopf was *Giovanni's Room*, one of the earliest books with overt homosexual scenes. The board didn't think the writing strong enough to justify the publishing risk. Baldwin had refused to amend passages about "cocksucking," and to Blanche's reminder that Gide and Van Vechten had both dealt with homosexuality, Alfred said, "But they somehow made it right. Jimmy didn't."[35] After the board (the term variously used for monthly meetings of stockholders such as Mencken and Alfred's siblings, or of the editors) voted down the acquisition, with Alfred and Blanche having final say, Baldwin left Knopf for the Dial Press.

Blanche was deeply disappointed. Baldwin belonged to the literary world she'd envisioned from the start of her career in 1915. She had wanted to challenge convention, to push the boundaries, often building on her political instincts, as she had told *The New Yorker* in 1948. Books on subjects such as those dealt with by African-American writers or war reporters or audacious political philosophers such as Beauvoir seemed important to her, even necessary, and she was determined to keep pushing.

While the country was abuzz with *The Second Sex*, Knopf released what would prove to be the Polish writer and Nobel Prize winner

Czesław Miłosz's strongest, bravest nonfiction. *The Captive Mind* explored the intellectual conflicts faced by people living under any type of totalitarianism, left or right, communism or Nazism. A critical success, the book drew commentators from the top ranks: Stephen Spender called it "a masterpiece . . . that in a hundred years" will be read as a "passionate apologia" for peace. Years after its publication, Jerzy Kosiński called it "a faultlessly perceptive analysis of the moral and historical dilemma we all face . . . as timely today as when it was first written."[36] Buoyed by the attention that *The Captive Mind* received, Blanche, when she returned to Paris in July, wrote Alfred on Ritz stationery, "Darling: I miss you much more than ever before and can't wait until the 11th Aout when you arrive: It is better with you than without you anywhere!"[37] The Knopfs, in the middle of one of their innumerable swings in the marriage, could even consider returning to the beginning of their relationship: four days later Blanche wrote Alfred again, discussing the chance to establish a "single home and social life."[38] Unfortunately, they would never create the marital household Blanche now decided that, for a few hours, she wanted.

At the end of 1953, they did spend several weeks together in Los Angeles. Blanche saw several of her authors before joining Alfred to visit Edwin and Mildred, at whose home they met many of the couple's movie friends. Edwin was "sitting pretty," as he put it, having produced the award-winning musical *Lili* that year, and Blanche, glad for the change of pace, happily watched the film, starring Leslie Caron, Mel Ferrer, and Zsa Zsa Gabor, in Edwin and Mildred's screening room. When Mildred gave a dinner party for Alfred and Blanche along with "lots of Hollywood stars," she asked her brother-in-law whom he would like to sit next to. Alfred answered, "You know there is only one woman in the world for me." As Mildred had surmised years before, "It's the old story: he couldn't live with her, he couldn't live without her."[39]

But Blanche found Alfred's love too capricious. When she was at Purchase, she would often beseech him to throw more logs onto the fire in the paneled family room. He'd refuse, saying the temperature was fine, although he realized that she had no body fat. This would go on until Alfred relented and turned up the heat, before putting on a bathing suit.[40] In general, Alfred mocked Blanche more mercilessly than ever, often in front of others at the office, to the point of critiquing the way she folded the bills in her wallet or the style in which she had one of the dogs clipped. Nothing seemed beyond reproach.

Nonetheless, that spring the Knopfs did manage to pay their respects to Dorothy Hergesheimer, whose husband, Joseph, the popular Knopf writer of the twenties and early thirties, had died in April in Cape May County, New Jersey. A few months later, Blanche and Alfred agreed to fly to France together but to go their own ways once abroad, Blanche to southern France with Jenny, and Alfred with the wine connoisseur Alexis Lichine to Châteauneuf-du-Pape, six miles from Avignon and close to Provence. Alfred had engaged Lichine to tour the French vineyards with him and teach him "all about red Rhone vines." From a room next to Alfred's, through what Lichine would later tactfully call the thin walls of their five-star hotel, the wine expert could hear Alfred shouting on the phone at Blanche, "forcing her to join them though she didn't want to."[41]

On October 1, Blanche threw a party for Wallace Stevens at the Harmonie Club, the second-oldest private club in New York City, which had been created by German Jews not allowed membership in such clubs as the Union and the Metropolitan. (The Harmonie Club had been opened to non-Jews at the end of World War II.) Stevens's *Collected Poems* was scheduled for release by Knopf the following day, on the poet's seventy-fifth birthday.[42] *The New York Times* reported that the "biggest group of major poets you ever saw got together at a recent New York lunch to pay tribute to one of their number. The guest of honor (a quiet man) had already won the Bollingen Prize for 1949 and the National Book Award for 1950: wouldn't this be a fine year for him to receive the Pulitzer?" Which he did, in April, before dying in August of stomach cancer. Blanche had mixed feelings about Stevens; she admired his work and surely felt a sympathy for him. Stevens had married a woman whom his parents considered beneath him. As a result, he severed relations with them until after his wife's death. Stevens's racism, however, never failed to shock and dismay Blanche, as when he referred to Gwendolyn Brooks as "a coon" while judging the National Book Awards.[43]

By the end of 1954, Pat Knopf had become an official part of the family business, and (though Alfred would take the credit) he had enabled the launch of Knopf's new paperback imprint, Vintage Books, which published high-quality paperbacks of Knopf's earlier hardback issues. Alfred would later state, "There isn't very much to say about the Vintage experiment. There we were frank imitators. The true and only begetter of this kind of paperback is Jason Epstein, the young man who developed Anchor Books for Doubleday [the year before]. And the only credit we can take for it is that we were at least smart enough and not too proud to follow and not too long thereafter." Pat worked out in detail the general scheme for Vintage, with Alfred maintaining that it was a somewhat mysterious publishing operation "in the sense that I have never been able to discover what it is that makes one title right" to print in paperback versus another.[44]

Meanwhile, Blanche was working hard to convince the board, and especially Alfred, to buy Norman Mailer's *The Deer Park* away from Rinehart & Company, who'd published *The Naked and the Dead*. According to Joe Lesser, "when Alfred did sometimes interfere with Blanche's choices, [it was] almost always to the firm's detriment. She had excellent judgment."[45] But Alfred had been snubbed years before by Mailer, or thought he had, and the publisher disliked him as a result. Now declaring that the novel's excessive sex was reason enough to reject it, Alfred joked that the only part of the book not about sex was its title. Exercising the right of either partner to refuse an acquisition, he declined Blanche's request to bid on *The Deer Park*, citing other editorial opinions, which, for fear of offending their (primary) boss, always lined up with Alfred's when matters were put to a vote.

Arguably, Norman Mailer had led the postwar literary revolution with *The Naked and the Dead* in 1948. Tom Wolfe would soon experiment with the mixed genre of truth and fiction, just as Willa Cather had by inserting historical figures into *Death Comes for the Archbishop*. Blanche saw that the mid-fifties evinced a new age, just as the 1920s had. In 1955 she worked tirelessly to get Mailer's *The Deer Park*, but Pat and Alfred kept erecting roadblocks. Finally, after being rejected by half a dozen publishers, *The Deer Park* went to Putnam (which paid the highest advance in its history).[46]

Pat remembers the decision to pass on *The Deer Park* as being all his fault. Someone in the business "came up to me before a sales conference and said, 'I hear you've got a Norman Mailer manuscript called *Deer Park* and if your father doesn't know about it you have to tell him: It's an absolutely dreadful book and it cannot be published.' Well, I didn't know anything about it, so I sent a note to my father"—a decision that infuriated Blanche, who usually dealt with fiction. At least Alfred wrote Pat back, saying, "If someone has anything to say about this, tell him to say it to your mother." So Pat "got hell from her for getting involved."[47]

Similarly, Joe Lesser would later reveal that it was Alfred who had refused to acquire Sinclair Lewis when he left Harcourt Brace, because the books were being auctioned and "AAK refused to compete whether it's Lewis or anyone else." Decades earlier, Knopf had also lost their chance at Thomas Wolfe, whom Blanche had wanted to publish. Wolfe had told her he didn't like Scribner, a patrician firm, and was ready to leave them. But Alfred thought that was a poor reason to move to Knopf. He wanted writers who considered

Knopf superior to other houses, pure and simple. He told Blanche that if she acquired Wolfe he, Alfred, would leave the firm. "Blanche was much more intuitive in her judgments," Alfred would eventually decide. "I was intuitive part of the time. Can't trust it all the time, to publish with your fingertips, so to speak."[48]

22

NEW TERRITORIES

I N EARLY 1955, Blanche and Alfred were photographed for an
Associated Press news release as they "greet[ed] their new
poodles at New York International Airport [Idlewild] after the
show dogs arrived on a Pan American World Airways clipper from
Paris." Four months old, the dogs had been bred in "the kennels of
Princess Amedee de Broglie in Chantilly."[1] A new secretary, Eleanor
French, had arranged the publicity. Towering over her employer by a
good foot, French would remain with Blanche for the rest of her life.
John Hersey recalled that the "two poodles . . . looked exactly like
[the Knopfs]. After a few months, Alfred's dog, Engel, had long
mustaches and swaggered and was very grumpy. And Blanche's
dog, ZZ, was a tiny little starving creature curled up on a pillow on
a chair."[2] Louis Kronenberger, drama critic for *Time*, remembered
that the dogs got "Abercrombie and Fitch . . . cases of grooming
equipment for Christmas."[3]

Blanche had robust plans for her European trip that summer of 1955. According to *Publishers Weekly*:

She will be visiting publishers as well as many European writers . . . In France, she will see, among others, Albert Camus, Pierre Daninos, author of *The Notebooks of Major Thompson*; and Jules Roy, author of *The Navigator*. In Switzerland, she will see Thomas Mann, whose *Confessions of Felix Krull* comes out September 19 and Arthur Meeker, whose *Chicago, with Love* was a valentine to the [city. She will] visit Jose Maria Gironella, author of *The Cypresses Believe in God*. In Italy, she will see, among others, Count Valentina Bompiani, the famous Italian publisher who recently was in the United States. She will also visit Rome and Milan, Bonn and Frankfurt, and will spend several weeks in England, including a side trip to Ireland to see Elizabeth Bowen.[4]

Most of the appointments went well, especially her excursion to Bowen's estate, where she found she could relax. Katia Mann, however, ended up taking Blanche not to her home for lunch, as she'd suggested in a letter months earlier, but to her husband's grave, where Blanche laid flowers. Thomas Mann had died of an embolism on August 12—a month before Knopf released the first part of *Felix Krull*. A novel that expanded on Mann's earlier story of a charming confidence man, *Felix Krull* was possibly a reflection on the ease with which Mann had lived a double life himself, his family on one side and his homosexual yearnings on the other.

Blanche was still aggrieved over losing *The Deer Park*, especially after learning that Knopf's third-quarter sales were the largest in the firm's history. Mailer would only have added to the luster. In October 1955, soon after the novel's release, she gave a large cocktail party, audaciously inviting Mailer. "I think Mrs. Mailer was a Mexican," Alfred said, apropos of nothing. "Toward the end of the party,

I felt that I had been a rude host so at the door I shook hands with the Mailers and talked to him." Mailer told Alfred he would regret his decision not to take *The Deer Park*: he bet his book would sell more than one hundred thousand copies. Alfred responded that he didn't bet. He later received a nasty letter from Mailer, who was helping launch *The Village Voice*, inviting Alfred to "suck his cock."[5] Pat Knopf remembered his mother's party differently. "There were 50 or 75 people there, Norman Mailer walked in. My father came in about 20 minutes later, took one look [at Mailer], and put his hat and coat back on and left."[6]

The year 1955 proved to be Knopf's most profitable yet, and a near record for American publishers in general. Knopf had released Camus's *The Myth of Sisyphus*; Randall Jarrell's *Selected Poems*; Thomas Mann's (unfinished) *Confessions of Felix Krull*; Elizabeth Bowen's *A World of Love*; and their friend Richard Hofstadter's Pulitzer Prize–winning *The Age of Reform*, a subtle view of America's Populist movement in the 1890s and Progressive movement of the early twentieth century. By now, however, Blanche could see that Alfred was as interested in the West as in their book business. A few days before Christmas, he wrote to the National Park Service about what seemed the "substandard housing which [was all that was] available to many employees in the National Park Service."[7] He ended by saying how grateful he was to them, as they were always generous with their park planes when he visited. As difficult as he could be in the office, Alfred could be equally gracious when his beloved landscape was involved.

On January 29, 1956, H. L. Mencken, the man who, since 1915, had advised the Knopfs on the development of their company and been the one man loved equally by Blanche and Alfred, passed to what he would have joked had to be a better life. Newspapers remarked upon the quick, small service held that Tuesday at Witzke Funeral Home at the corner of Hollins and Gilmore in Baltimore, a half block from Mencken's home. The guests included Alfred Knopf (Blanche was abroad) and James M. Cain representing the world of letters, along with Johns Hopkins's pathologist Dr. Arnold Rich, the father of the poet Adrienne Rich. Mencken's ashes were interred in Baltimore's Loudon Park Cemetery next to his beloved Sara's. A few months later Alfred would note in *The Borzoi Quarterly* (the irregularly published, handsomely designed chapbook about Knopf's forthcoming books) that Mencken "was a very dear and intimate friend and had a greater influence on the Knopfs who publish books than anyone else who ever entered their lives."[8]

In February, Alfred and Blanche created for Columbia University's oral history project an account of Knopf's early days. Though Blanche enjoyed recording anecdotal information about their beginnings, she was very focused on the present moment, in which Eleanor French would prove literally a lifesaver. By now Blanche's vision was so impaired that her assistant made up reasons to accompany her as she crossed the street: French would suddenly remember something she needed to do and link arms with Blanche, both women leaving the office together.

As her own vulnerabilities mounted, Blanche grew increasingly aware of her employees' needs. Pete Lemay remembers Blanche as "very courteous." Her kind treatment of his wife included ensuring ahead of time that "Dorothy had a shawl when they went to dinner parties in Purchase . . . She wanted to be sure you were comfortable; she didn't ignore you. That's really all Blanche had to do for a colleague's wife: to make her feel she was . . . not unwanted. Alfred could make anyone feel unwanted . . . [With Alfred] you never knew when you were going to get swatted. With Blanche, you knew you'd not be insulted."[9] When Pete was out for a week with chicken pox, she sent him fresh Italian grapes, and when his daughter was sick, she insisted he return home to tend to her. "Blanche was interested in what you were feeling; Alfred never was. That's why writers liked her."[10]

Just as Blanche learned that John Hersey was having marriage problems, *Reader's Digest* published a heartfelt article by her old friend and author Paul Gallico about his. Gallico's divorce perhaps caused Blanche to rethink how much effort she had put into her own marriage. Gallico (with whom she'd had an affair years before) assumed he'd been more or less happily wed for the past fourteen years, but his wife had suddenly left him. In *Reader's Digest* he recounted the loss of sharing life with someone "who understood your every move."[11] Her regrets notwithstanding, after reflecting upon Gallico's article Blanche must have wondered what life without Alfred would mean.

That fall, feeling stronger than she had for months, Blanche once again tried to participate in her husband's love of the West. (Years later, Alfred's early girlfriend Elsie Alsberg, still unable to resist a jab at Blanche, said that "Blanche went to parks with Alfred because she'd reached the point where she needed him badly.")[12] Eager for something to improve their relationship, she and Alfred took a trip with John and Frances Ann Hersey to Monument Valley and the Grand Canyon, on the Arizona-Utah state line, much of it within the Navajo Nation.

The trip was extremely pleasant, though Blanche was made nervous by some of the jagged landscapes they encountered. Alfred and Hersey kept copious notes, as did a government official who joined them at times, Dr. A. M. Mortensen. After eating a family-style dinner at Harry Goulding's lodge (where the award-winning *Stagecoach*, with John Wayne, had been filmed in 1939), the Knopfs and Herseys were provided an official park plane. At first Mortensen had a bad impression of Blanche, who "had on heavy eye makeup, and she was talking in French to a scientist at the lunch table, and I thought that was rude . . . She took forever to eat her fish, and I didn't like her till 1½ hours later, when I [suddenly] did." Blanche, it seemed, was actually down-to-earth and self-deprecating, with "all the big and little fears and weaknesses everyone had." She wasn't afraid to laugh at herself. When Mortensen and "Mrs. Hersey were sauntering to the powder room, [we] encountered Blanche with a pack of Chesterfields in one hand and a book of matches in the other, and she had a cigarette in her mouth already lit . . . Three were lit and she was trying to light another one with both hands occupied; 'I better quit this habit' she said."[13]

Alfred's account was more focused on the wonders of nature.

We flew to Albuquerque then drove to Gallup, [three of us] stopping on the way to climb the steep and sandy road to the Acoma Pueblo of Willa Cather's *Death* [*Comes for the Archbishop*]—a fine view, to be sure, but a rather shabby and shoddy place, with the Indians charging whatever they thought the traffic would bear for photographing them. They were neither attractive nor friendly. When we got down again, Blanche was sitting comfortably in the shade of a small building smoking a Chesterfield and chatting with an elderly Indian woman. She said that two or three men had stopped to offer to carry her up to the top if she wanted to go.[14]

Between Gallup and Canyon de Chelly, the foursome came upon Indian women with a flat tire, which Hersey helped them fix while the others went on ahead. Finally they all arrived at Chelly, where they obtained "crude accommodations" at Thunderbird Lodge. "A hired guide drove a Park Service 4-wheel drive wagon over a treacherous floor of canyon. Anything less than 4-wheel drive would sink into the sand and never be seen again," Alfred recorded.[15] Packing a picnic lunch, the four friends spent the next morning meandering through the Canyon del Muerto, lunching at the Mummy Cave. In the afternoon, they were taken to Rim Drive by a Forest Service guide, who ensured that their "view of the canyons and, later, the setting sun were absolutely superb," Alfred observed. Finally, according to her husband, Blanche managed to relax. "The group spent one more day in the canyon" before moving on to Monument Valley. "Took pick, shovel & heavy rope for towing."[16]

On their bus tour at Monument Valley the men became uncomfortable when Frances Ann, eventually joined by Blanche, made snide remarks about the tourists and their cameras—though, Alfred noted, "nobody took offense." As the Knopfs set out for the top of Hoskininni Mesa, everything halted when Blanche lost one of her earrings. "Quite characteristically," Alfred recalled, "she had chosen to wear in this wild and out-of-the-way place some [jewelry] made for her by Manhattan designer Seaman Schepps. [We] had to turn back and rake the ground around the [Indians'] fire. One earring found."[17]

Then, using the park's single-engine plane, they were flown to the South Rim of the Grand Canyon. Staying at Oak Creek Canyon in a small cabin, Hersey availed himself of the bountiful fishing while Blanche and Frances Ann complained about the primitive lodgings. When they all drove farther up the canyon, visiting Sunset Crater and Montezuma Castle, Alfred, at the wheel, got distracted by a sign pointing to a golf club and hit a large rock, "leaving the handbrake broken for rest of trip."[18]

In the following days, the foursome visited the Painted Desert and Petrified Forest, sections of Arizona and New Mexico, and crossed the border from El Paso to Juárez for dinner. A few handwritten notes Blanche sent friends suggest that she had been bearing up over the long three weeks—sort of. Alfred recalled only that "we had three very interesting weeks in the Southwest though Blanche came back in poor shape because she couldn't stomach the food and literally starved herself."[19] But both Alfred and Blanche agreed that the Herseys were great company.[20] John Hersey would fondly recall the trip as well, remembering how Blanche and Alfred kept "whistling and humming themes" from Schubert's *The Trout Quintet* and from late Beethoven quartets, alternating stanzas to rescue each other from boredom while they were all trapped on a bus tour across the desert.[21]

Back home, in early 1957, Blanche launched a campaign for Albert Camus to win the Nobel Prize in Literature. Calling in all her chips with foreign publishers, she sought their letters of endorsement for her adored European author. In October Blanche got word that he had won, in large part due to her lobbying, as everyone, including the writer, knew. Camus, with his American girlfriend, Patricia Blake, got the news while drinking coffee on the second floor of Chez Marius in Paris.[22] The hard work done, Blanche immediately set about having a dress made for the Nobel ceremony in Stockholm. Though she had cut back a bit on her trips abroad, she had kept up her relationships with French couturiers, and for Camus's ceremonies in December she engaged Christian Dior and Balenciaga to create several outfits for her. She cabled Dior, "You have my measurements, can't spend too much but it must be elegant," and Dior offered her a silk dress in a "ravishing green faille" that was, "conveniently," he assured her, on sale.

Even as she tended to all things concerning Knopf's latest Nobel laureate, Blanche battled with Farrar, Straus and Cudahy over Carlo Levi's *Words Are Stones*. To the last minute, the outcome was uncertain, negotiations "going by fast carrier pigeon to Rome at high noon," according to accounts at FSG. The transaction "might mean that . . . dear Blanche Knopf will end up publishing C. Levi, but I am afraid that is in the lap of the gods, and will depend on the current condition of Carlo's tummy." Farrar, Straus assumed that Knopf was outbidding them; instead, the opposite was true and they, not Knopf, got the book.[23] Jenny Bradley scolded Blanche for "taking too long to read books . . . taking too many months to consider them . . . Thus [you] occasionally lose one you want."[24] Nonetheless, that June Knopf published the three-volume *Byron: A Biography* by Leslie

Marchand. The book had taken a decade to research and write. Like Newman Ivey White's magnum opus on Shelley, Marchand's *Byron* would be a long-lived presence on the Knopf backlist.

For two and a half weeks that summer, Alfred and Blanche traveled together again, though not with friends. The trip to Washington, Oregon, and northern Colorado was, Blanche wrote Jenny when they returned, "hot but interesting."[25] Alfred, in an interview with Susan Sheehan decades later, said it wasn't true that Blanche rarely ate: "In the national parks, [we took] the fish we caught back to the hotel to be cooked for dinner, she ate those trout all right. I think she drank more bourbon than wine." Pondering, he then decided that "she could have eaten much more than she ate . . . I think she had lost her appetite for food."[26]

While they were out west, they turned over their Purchase home to their production manager, Sidney Jacobs, and his wife, knowing that the childless couple would act as caretakers while they got a break from the city. The Knopfs' failure to offer Purchase to Pat and Alice and their now three children seemed a final blow to Pat, who would write his father a long letter about the grievances he had amassed over the years—from a failure to receive thank-you notes to not being invited to Purchase often enough.

But in 1957 Blanche was so excited about Camus's triumph that she barely registered Pat's complaints, which had persisted at least since he discovered her in the office with Hohe thirteen years earlier. She had always preferred to deal with matters she might influence—such as Bernard Berenson's next book, which she was trying to acquire. When Blanche informed Berenson that she was going to Stockholm for Camus's Nobel ceremony, the art connoisseur said, "You doubtless will meet his majesty, the King, and I hope the Queen as well. If you do, do not be ashamed of telling them you're a dear friend of mine."[27]

On December 3 Blanche flew to Paris, from where, with Camus

(who was unable to fly due to lungs damaged by TB), his wife, Francine, and some of their friends, she took the Nord Express train to Stockholm. According to the Camus Society UK's Simon Lea, Camus was living those days in a state of "partial asphyxiation" and had to "stop off at his doctor's frequently to inhale oxygen."[28] Without it, he had severe panic attacks. He had spent the last months of 1957 in a state of near-constant anxiety.

When they met at the Gare de Vénissieux, Camus was wearing the Brooks Brothers coat Blanche had bought him, while she shocked more than one traveler with her green nail polish. Alfred arrived in Stockholm on December 9 on a direct flight from New York. The following day, at the City Hall in Stockholm, Blanche was called onto the dais when Camus was awarded the Nobel Prize in Literature. Photographs show her in a simple white wool Balenciaga coat dress, magnificently tailored, yet seeming to cling slightly when she walked, as if it were made of chiffon.

In his acceptance speech, Camus sought to align himself with the common citizen, first referring to the privileged position of the writer—while speaking of the responsibilities such privilege entails: "It obliges the artist not to keep himself apart; it subjects him to the most humble and the most universal truth. And often he who has chosen the fate of the artist because he felt himself to be different soon realizes that he can maintain neither his art nor his difference unless he admits that he is like the others."[29]

Early in 1958, Camus wrote to Blanche to tell her that he was already hard at work on his autobiographical novel *The First Man*, which both he and his publisher believed would be his masterpiece, more personally inspired than any of his previous works. (It would be edited by his daughter, long after its publisher's and author's deaths.)

Around this time Knopf added to its small, select editorial staff their second full-time female editor, an attractive young talent in her twenties, Judith Jones.[30] (By the early 1960s the roster of editors would also include Angus Cameron, Ash Green, Herbert Weinstock, Harold Strauss, and Patrick Gregory.)[31] To this day, Jones is considered one of the great editors in the company's history, having nurtured the talent of the young John Updike and Anne Tyler, among others. Hired in part for her perspicacity in pulling out of a slush pile *Anne Frank: The Diary of a Young Girl* (for Doubleday, where she then worked), Jones, through Bill Koshland and Herbert Weinstock, was now acquiring for Knopf Julia Child's landmark cookbook *Mastering the Art of French Cooking*. According to Pete Lemay, who had been hired as publicity director shortly before Judith arrived, Blanche was a bit envious of Jones's youth and undoubtedly aware that Jones would inherit some of her dearest writers, such as John Hersey, Elizabeth Bowen, and Langston Hughes.[32]

Blanche, as usual, acted out her emotional neediness through her relationship with her dogs. Her poodle, ZZ, proved far less sturdy than Alfred's. On September 14, 1959, four and a half years after she'd picked him up at the airport, Blanche wrote to Jenny Bradley:

> *ZZ succumb[ed] to convulsions in June, which Dr. Kinney, the vet, said would continue all his life. It is pretty difficult to see a little dog you love suffering with his legs going and frothing, biting his tongue in pain. I could not take it any longer, nor could Virgie [Blanche's new maid], therefore I gave him very fast to Cecile [the previous maid] in Stroudsburg, Pennsylvania who knows all about him. Knew him when he was a puppy. At the moment we are all in tears and it is curious that a small object like that should make such a deep impression on us . . . Virgie is in tears and I am, but we will probably get over it. As Virgie said, this is much worse than letting a [puppy] go, and I think she is right. Anyway, there it is and I have done it. As far as ZZ goes, I think he will be infinitely better off, though we will not.[33]*

Blanche soon transferred her near obsession with ZZ to a new Yorkshire terrier, whom she would name Monsieur.

Soon afterward, she headed for Los Angeles to tend to book business and to see her sister-in-law, Mildred. She was picked up at the airport by a handsome, charming part-time driver who frequently transported Alfred when he came to town. Scotty Bowers—a gas station attendant, driver, bartender, and, as he now admits cheerfully, "pimp for the Hollywood crowd"—was immediately smitten with the "sweet little thing" who got into his limousine at Los Angeles International Airport. "It was a mutual attraction," the ninety-two-year-old Scotty remembers, his striking good looks—thick white hair, cerulean eyes, and surprisingly buff body—still turning heads today as he signs copies of his memoir, *Full Service*.[34] After he made a few carefully suggestive comments, Blanche invited him to her hotel room for a drink. They quickly became lovers, with Scotty recalling "how natural everything seemed from the start." Blanche was "a pleasant enough looking woman and the chemistry between us was good."[35]

Unlike Alfred, Scotty stresses, Blanche was never one of his "professional" customers, except for her use of his private limousine business. They simply reveled in each other's company. To this day, Bowers is unsure if Blanche realized he also made arrangements for her husband. He assumes the Knopfs didn't know about each other, although, as he pauses to reflect, he says, "Maybe they did. I had no proof of that, and whenever they were in town at the same time, they stayed at different hotels—the Beverly Hills or Beverly Wilshire." Once again, as with her musicians, Blanche took a lover who was connected to Alfred but whose affair with Blanche would be hers alone. "Mr. and Mrs. Knopf complemented each other," Bowers remembers. "Different as night and day."[36]

According to Bowers, Blanche seems to have had a real, if limited, romance with him. She "occasionally made trips out here from New York under the pretext that she was seeing friends, but it was really only to spend time with me," he recalls proudly. When Blanche returned home, without fail she mailed Scotty a box of books "picked out specially" for him.[37]

23

A SON'S DEFECTION

A FEW DAYS BEFORE Pat Knopf left for his summer vacation in 1958 he asked Pete Lemay to read the galleys of a book his mother had bought in Paris, advising the head of sales, without Blanche's knowledge, not to "waste" too much time promoting it. The history of a young Spaniard who had grown to manhood in a concentration camp, *Child of Our Time* by Michel del Castillo was instead endorsed, through Pete's efforts, by readers ranging from Adlai Stevenson and Karl Menninger to Eleanor Roosevelt, and continued to sell well—though it was never a bestseller—year after year.[1]

"Knopf had fewer mediocrities on its list than most publishing houses," Lemay points out. "What their imprint represented . . . was quality in literature," he says. "They weren't a huge commercial success," since, as Lemay had discovered, "books with a skein of literary prizes didn't necessarily sell lots of copies," a reality the Knopfs accepted. "While Doubleday and Simon and Schuster issued several titles a year that sold over a hundred thousand copies, forty years of Borzoi books included no more than twelve books that sold at those levels by the mid-fifties." Among these books, however, were hundreds of solid repeat sellers, creating Knopf's economic stability through its backlist. From the start the couple had been determined to earn their keep by selling "good books" that would endure rather than "making a quick buck on the transitory success of a bad one."[2]

Blanche was abroad on Easter weekend in 1959, when she opened the *International Herald Tribune* to read the startling news that her son was leaving Knopf and forming a new publishing house, Atheneum Publishers, with two partners. (On Sunday morning, March 15, *The New York Times* carried the story on its front page—unusual in the world of book publishing.) Despite Pat's promise to his father not to release the news before his mother returned from Europe, Blanche hadn't finished her winter buying trip when the story broke. She read how her son had joined the family business after the war, becoming company secretary and trade books manager, and subsequently vice president of sales, having been rewarded for helping create Knopf's paperback division, Vintage—and now was ready to exit the publishing house. Later, Pat would blame the split on his mother, telling Peter Prescott that from the beginning of Vintage, there was fighting among the editors about which books to put into paperback, and Blanche especially argued hard for hers. According to Pat, the turmoil over running the imprint and fighting with his mother was what made him leave the firm that bore his last name.

The reality was a bit different: a few years earlier, Alfred and Blanche had, with disappointment on both sides, carefully admitted to each other and to their son that their long-expressed hope to turn Knopf over to him one day no longer seemed viable; they had changed their minds when they realized he did not possess the necessary skills (unlike the progeny of Charles Scribner) to run the company. Feeling betrayed by his parents, Pat began hatching plans for his own publishing house without their knowledge. Furious that his parents had reneged on what he considered his birthright, Pat started talking to industry friends who commuted with him from Westport to the city.

Just before Christmas in 1958, Pat authorized the veteran book men Simon Michael Bessie and Hiram Haydn to discuss with several investors the funding of a new publishing firm. Haydn, who had a secure job at Random House, had been slow to come on board and said no at first, while Bessie, having been passed over for top editor at Harper & Row, was eager to start anew. When Haydn suddenly surfaced with two wealthy friends ready to supply financial support, the millionaire William M. Roth and Marc Friedlaender, a Princeton professor with family money, everything jelled.[3]

By early March 1959, Pat, Bessie, and Haydn had secretly established Atheneum Publishers. Its first three lists would produce a trio of bestsellers: *The Last of the Just* (1960), a groundbreaking novel about the Holocaust by André Schwarz-Bart translated from the French; *The Making of the President, 1960* (1961), the first in Theodore H. White's iconic series on presidential campaigns; and *The Rothschilds: A Family Portrait* (1962), by Frederic Morton. Other books, if not bestsellers, also did well for the house in its early days, including Edward Albee's play *Who's Afraid of Virginia Woolf?* (1962), which sold more than seventy thousand copies in hard- and softcover editions.

According to several people who knew him in his new role of cofounder and chairman, Pat modeled his leadership after his father's, down to the smoking of a pipe. But at social events, he was his mother's son: better-looking than Alfred, he assumed the role of gracious host. His partner Hiram Haydn remembered that Pat was never still; social occasions at his home "kept him in perpetual motion." He once "point[ed] at himself [in mock dismay,] saying 'I've got Saint Vitus's dance, for God's sake.'" He worked at charming his guests every chance he had, cooing "from one to another, crying 'Mary! Yum! How wonderful you look! . . . Barbara, you look beautiful, yum, yum . . . Helen, how great!'"[4]

Pat's "desertion" wounded Blanche deeply, according to Frances Lindley, who remembered her talking incessantly about how betrayed she felt when she picked up the newspaper in London.[5] Fortunately, at the time, Mildred Knopf was staying with Blanche at the Ritz, and her sister-in-law's presence encouraged Blanche to handle the event gracefully. Still, Mildred recalled, "she was horribly offended—it was horribly hard—she was [most] upset because it made a fool of her" around people she knew in the business.[6]

Grace Dadd recalled that "it hit her below the belt . . . My feeling was that her face was smacked in public."[7] The last one to know, Blanche was humiliated.[8]

Furious at her son's "abandonment" and her public mortification, Blanche had Pat locked out of his office. Until she cooled off, she wouldn't even let him retrieve his personal items. (After she died, Alfred would tell an interviewer that it was the furtive way Pat made the break, not his decision itself, that had caused the schism.) Though at a superficial level, Blanche and Pat eventually reconciled, they remained suspicious of each other until the end of her life, and the feelings were passed down to the next generation. When Pat and Alice's daughter Susan was five or six years old, and the family was staying overnight at "the Hovel," Susan got up in the night and then ran back to bed when she saw Blanche standing in the dark, smoking a cigarette. She thought she was a witch, not her grandmother.

The day after the Sunday *Times* announced Pat Knopf's new publishing venture, everyone on Knopf's staff waited nervously for Alfred to return from Texas and Blanche from overseas. On Monday morning Pat arrived to find Bill Koshland, Joe Lesser, and Sidney Jacobs in a state. "Did Alfred know?" they yelled at him. As if, Pat said calmly, he would have done it without informing his father.[9] When Alfred got home, he told Pat to vacate the office before his mother came back at the end of the week.

The Knopf editor Avis DeVoto (an early editor of *Mastering the Art of French Cooking*) wrote to Julia Child that they'd had "a positive earthquake of a turnover recently" when "Pat Knopf left his parents' company and formed his own."[10] For years, according to Frances Lindley, Blanche would badmouth her son "as only someone deeply wounded could."[11] And yet, as Harding Lemay recalls, "once Atheneum was successful, Blanche was very proud of Pat."[12]

Knopf's publication on March 23 of Langston Hughes's *Selected Poems* temporarily grounded Blanche, especially since Hughes agreed to exclude his radical socialist verse.[13] Most reviewers lauded his gifts as a lyric poet with "the voice of pain and isolation, of a deeply felt contemporary anguish," though they often regretted "Hughes' lapses of quality."[14] James Baldwin was vicious, however, his "nonchalant dismissal" payback for grievances and jealousies of the past. Wounded deeply, Hughes seemed the victim of an "Oedipal need: to slay the paternal figure in the field of black poetry." Years later, Baldwin would regret his review, admitting he hadn't even read the book.[15]

By midsummer, to celebrate paying off the thirty-year mortgage on the Purchase house, Alfred planned another trip out west. Hoping that shifting the attention to his conservation projects would help distract both him and Blanche from Pat's defection, he suggested she accompany him. But Raymond Chandler had died that spring, his death removing the primary motivation for Blanche to endure the hardships of Alfred's journeys. On July 17, she wrote Jenny that "I have vaguely promised to go to Wyoming until the 4th of September. You know I always try to get out of this."[16] Surely this time it was easy to beg off: she needed to tend to Elizabeth Bowen, widowed in 1952, who had recently lost Bowen's Court due to bankruptcy. For the next five years, Bowen would have to take occasional academic jobs in Europe and America, even as she continued writing her novels.

These days, when Blanche gave editorial feedback to her writers, she was forced to share with them her secret: by 1959, using a magnifying glass to see the text was no longer optional. To respond to readers' reports, which arrived on her desk single-spaced, Blanche's assistant retyped their reactions, double-spaced at least.[17] Her near-blindness was increasingly defining her life—she now consistently ate lunch nearby, and even so, she often asked someone to walk her. Five years earlier, Amy Loveman, a founding editor at *The Saturday Review* and an editor at the Book-of-the-Month Club, had actually talked Blanche into having lunch at the Algonquin. "There was all hell," someone in the office remembered. Blanche claimed never to have been below Forty-Second Street in her life. Amy told her the Algonquin wasn't below Forty-Second Street. "It's still too far downtown," Blanche said, before giving in.[18] Now such a stroll would be impossible.

The cultural energies then infusing Manhattan, a reminder of the twenties, were too much for Blanche to take on this time around. From Robert Rauschenberg's new abstract painting and sculpture made from street objects (the mix of high and low always to Blanche's taste) to Miles Davis's jazz album *Kind of Blue*, arguably as important as Gershwin's *Rhapsody in Blue*, that same excitement about change filled the air.[19] (Unlike Gershwin, however, Davis would be beaten in the head by police when he played certain Manhattan jazz clubs.) Even the silliness of the Roaring Twenties had returned: Manhattan's new, fashionable "Happenings," for instance, were for a time street theater, eventually staged in more conventional venues. During the "play" called *The Burning Bridge*, people dressed in firemen's costumes ran around the audience, wielding cardboard axes as they screamed before diving out of fake windows.[20]

After receiving what Alfred considered a lukewarm response from Yale regarding donating the Knopf archives, he and Blanche decided to give them instead to the newly formed Harry Ransom Center at the University of Texas at Austin.[21] Dr. Harry Huntt Ransom, the university's chancellor, had a vision of creating "a premiere center for research and study in the humanities," an enormously fertile collection enabled by an extraordinary endowment.[22] Alfred, taking another long trip out west while Blanche went to Europe, seemed to be thinking a lot about the future. He'd been home two months when a hurricane destroyed the thirty-to-forty-foot Norway spruce he had grown from a sapling, causing him to ruminate about changing weather patterns and his own mortality. Meanwhile, Blanche remained fixated on the loss of her son and the need to win him back. Then, less than a week into 1960, the phone rang in Blanche's office. A secretary answered on the first ring, as Blanche preferred, and then, after a long pause, turned to her boss and gently suggested she get this call. Sighing, Blanche took the phone, impatient to catch up on work postponed by the holiday break. "What is it?" she asked.

The speaker on the other end came through with unusual clarity compared with the transatlantic phone calls with which the office often struggled. "Camus is dead," a Frenchman with Gallimard told her bluntly. "He was in a car accident in Le Grand Fossard in Villeblevin [a small town sixty-five miles from Paris] on his way back from his winter vacation in Burgundy." The Gallimards—Michel, his wife, and their eighteen-year-old daughter—had arrived in the country on January 2, in time for lunch and an overnight with Camus and his family. The writer planned to return to Paris by train the next day, and had even bought his tickets. But Michel persuaded Camus to return with the Gallimards in their car.

Reluctantly, the writer saw Francine and the kids off at the station. He didn't like fast cars, and he liked even less how fast Michel drove them, but he must have assumed that since Gallimard's wife and child were with them, the publisher would drive more carefully. He couldn't have known about the repair shop records urging Gallimard to replace his worn tires, with the publisher promising to do so when he got home. According to a detailed account written by the journalist Stephen Bayley, the journey toward Sens on January 4 continued with a drizzle that coated the straight roads, quiet and lined with beautiful, but intimidating, old forests. Janine, Michel's wife, later said that before the accident she could recall no explosion or screech, but that Michel Gallimard might have exclaimed *"Merde!"* After a violent wobble, the car left the road. The next thing she remembered was sitting in the mud and shouting for the dog, which was never seen again.[23]

As Bayley recounts, Gallimard's Facel Vega hit one tree with great force and then another, "wrapping itself horribly, around the latter. Newspaper photographs showed that the out-of-control car had ripped-up the damp tarmac road surface for about one hundred and fifty feet . . . the debris scattered over a five hundred foot radius . . . The only witness . . . had a little earlier been passed by the distinctive car . . . traveling at about 150km/h, evidently—despite the Nobel Laureate's preferences—in a hurry."

Michel's wife and daughter were unhurt, but Camus was thrown from the car and died instantly of a broken neck. It took the *pompiers* two hours to free Michel's body from the wreckage. Initially conscious enough to ask, "Was I driving?" Gallimard died of a brain hemorrhage five days later. In Camus's bag was the unused train ticket he had intended for his trip home to Paris with Francine.

"The crash was world news. André Malraux, the French cultural minister, sent his chief *adjoint de cabinet* to represent the Republique at the crash scene. He was told to respect Camus's world view and not allow any inappropriate religious interference or associations in the proceedings," Bayley continues. "Camus's corpse was at rest in the local town hall, where an Algerian journalist who paid homage at Villeblevin said that 'under the light of a naked bulb, he had the expression of a very tired sleeper.'" The Gallimard heir became a detested figure, with people blaming him for Camus's death.

Stunned by the news, Blanche said nothing, then suddenly let out a scream that pierced the entire hall. Rushing to her office,

Knopf employees found her distraught and incoherent, trembling. Alfred actually put his arms around her as she "burst into tears, the first time anyone had ever seen him touch her," said Pete Lemay.[24]

Though the sixty-eight-year-old Alfred had wanted to retire for years—even discussing over lighthearted lunches with Bennett Cerf possible future mergers, Blanche, only two years younger, had resisted. Her talks with Elizabeth Bowen had left the writer sure that her publisher had no intention of cutting back on her work, though she was currently "so slight she could almost blow through a keyhole" while somehow emanating the "aura" of an aristocrat. Had she been an idle, aimless soul, Bowen wrote, Blanche "could have been a destructive woman."[25] Surely Blanche realized the impossible was becoming real, though not in time to benefit her. As the editor and publisher Al Silverman has written about women in publishing, heads of firms had always assumed women weren't up to playing their game hard enough to win. In the sixties, Blanche would see her efforts rewarded as barriers yielded to at least fourteen highly successful women, including Nan Talese and Judith Jones, who around 1960 took over Langston Hughes from Blanche.

Just a few weeks after Camus died, Alfred's business lunches with Bennett Cerf turned serious. Cerf offered the full $3 million asking price to Knopf, and Alfred and Blanche decided to accept and become part of the Random House board. Though Phyllis Cerf opposed the merger, her husband longed to share the Knopfs' reputation for literary distinction.[26] *Publishers Weekly* would detail "the Knopf success," achieved without the help of huge bestsellers. After all, Knopf had published only twelve books that sold more than a hundred thousand copies, among them *The Prophet, Death Comes for the Archbishop, A Bell for Adano, The Snow Goose, Berlin Diary, Life with Father, The Wall,* and *Markings,* Dag Hammarskjöld's spiritual journey. But the company had published many books that sold more than fifty thousand copies—and what Random House was after, "the Knopf backlist," currently accounted for 57 percent of the company's total sales.[27]

It was a good time for Blanche and Alfred to sell Knopf. Similar to when they founded the company in 1915, now, as they wound down, publishing was changing. The age of the gentleman publisher was essentially over—except to ensure a strong balance sheet. Alfred rewarded himself by buying a Rolls-Royce, which he picked up in England that fall after the merger was completed.

In 1960, Knopf, along with Vintage, eventually merged with Random House. The acquisition story would be told differently over the years, but the ease with which everything was decided, a benefit of doing business with lifelong friends, was undisputed. Alfred would recall that "one day" in 1959, "at lunch, in the Cub Room of the Stork Club [at its original site, East Fifty-Third Street,] I finally said to Bennett: 'Why don't you make a proposal?'" Bennett asked to look over Knopf's books and a few weeks later met in Alfred's office with Blanche and Cerf's partner, Donald Klopfer, and they reached an agreement. In the merger, Knopf preserved everything from its editorial sovereignty to its advertising, a kind of perfect union, Alfred would always maintain. The poet Witter Bynner, to whom Alfred had once confided that he himself was "constitutionally unable to appreciate good poetry," and who believed himself the "longest-lived" of Knopf's writers, would publish his last book with Knopf on January 1, before the merger.[28]

However well the merger worked for everyone business-wise, it took some getting used to on the part of Random House personnel. Donald Klopfer and Bennett Cerf were appalled at how the Knopfs behaved at the first joint board meeting, when Blanche clearly meant to control the conversation and Alfred to frustrate her. The Knopf staff was accustomed to the partners' vicious back and forth and their harsh public criticism of each other, with editors expected to take sides (Alfred's), but at Random House, jaws dropped: Cerf and Klopfer were used to chairing board meetings with "laughter, [where] nobody shouted," where there was no collateral damage. Klopfer would remember years later how taken aback he was, "Jesus, the way he talked to her." The Random House publisher thought Alfred callous, "the most selfish man in the world."[29] As for Blanche, he was horrified that she didn't stand up to him.

By now, the Knopfs had been married forty-four years. In public, especially in their offices and at parties attended mostly by Knopf staff, the two still snarled at and tangled with each other as if in a boxing ring, with Alfred almost always the victor. But as the British journalist and publisher Sir Robert Lusty wrote in his memoir, *Bound to Be Read*, "they battled with a verbal intensity which misled some. There existed between them a most touching devotion."[30] Those who saw them up close maintained that Alfred actually adored Blanche—an observation Mildred Knopf had first made soon after she married Edwin. No one ever seemed to suggest that the adoration was mutual. Blanche's erratic eruptions of hope that the two could be proper marital spouses again either never went beyond Alfred's mail—the two seemed unable to talk—or were too ephemeral to count. Alfred kept her occasional entreaties in his archives, their presence perhaps reminding him of the possibilities.

At the end of March, Alfred told Blanche she "looked like hell," and in fact she was not feeling well. Physicians found a bowel obstruction, caused by adhesions from the hysterectomy she'd had more than thirty years before. She underwent emergency surgery, even though her doctor, according to Alfred, thought her a poor risk. She pulled through the operation, and Alfred eventually went all the way home to Purchase, but the surgeon called at 4:00 a.m. "She was sinking—no blood pressure and kidneys not functioning. I'd better come up and see her," Alfred wrote in his journal.

Well, by the time I got there she was almost chipper, though they'd been working all night with her—plasma, glucose & something intravenous to help blood pressure. At 8 a.m. she phoned me . . . Went up to see her at 11 am. She looks much better and was very aware of everything. Talked about London and Paris and some dates she has here. I went back at 4. She's wearing down as the day advances and they work over her almost all the time and blood pressure every 30 minutes—but her condition miraculous, considering. I drove home: am absolutely pooped. That hour between 4 and 5 this morning was something.[31]

Eventually Alfred realized how much Blanche's lack of appetite, by now part of her reputation, was caused by her inability to eat much at one time without feeling pain from her abdominal condition.

She was soon to be made an *officier* of the Légion d'Honneur, the honor above *chevalier*. On April 13, looking as magnificent as her emaciated form would allow and barely able to stand, she received the award, which was pinned to her chest like the earlier one. As usual, Blanche charmed everyone at the ceremony—whose focus she managed to turn around to honoring the guests.[32]

Against doctors' advice, she spent much of the fall in England and Europe, where at the Paris Ritz she slipped on the bathroom floor, knocking herself out. A long visit with Elizabeth Bowen soothed both women. By early 1961, however, colleagues and friends at home had to wonder if Blanche was becoming suicidal. Though crossing Madison Avenue was dangerous before, she now began wearing a white ermine coat that the staff thought sure to get her killed, especially in the snow, which she walked through almost daily "when she went to lunch at a French restaurant in the Lombardy hotel." Her longtime friend Carol Brandt often arrived at her office just in time to accompany her, Blanche offering her hand as if to help Carol.[33]

Soon Blanche fell yet again, this time in the elevator. "She was very brave . . . [on the floor of] the elevator, obviously in agony. It was taking her a long time to get up, and she said to a Knopf clerk whom Bill Koshland later quoted: 'Don't look . . . and don't help me.'"³⁴ At Lenox Hill Hospital she was told that her hip was broken, but the orthopedist had her out of bed the day after the operation, getting around with a walker, and at the end of the week sent her home with a three-pronged rubber-tipped cane. Back in the office, she pampered Monsieur, letting the dog run—or limp—free. Her maid had accidentally crippled Monsieur by falling on him during a blackout, and he had remained in a coma for three weeks. Now at least she and he could share their recoveries.

As soon as she was able, Blanche went on her spring scouting trip, but she had barely arrived in Paris when she decided to return home. The disastrous American-backed invasion of Cuba's Bay of Pigs began on April 17, 1961, its objective to oust the communist Fidel Castro. Blanche wasted no time contacting Allen Dulles, assuming her friend would finally give her a book, but his response disappointed her: "Dear Blanche, it is always good to hear from you and I have not forgotten—and have been deeply flattered by your suggestion about a book I might write . . . All this is postponed until I have a little more freedom and I have not really been giving any thought to when I might do it if the time for writing really returned. I only hope we can get together and trust you will let me know if you should be in Washington."³⁵ Indeed, Dulles had more urgent issues at hand: as a result of the Bay of Pigs, he would be forced out of office on November 29, a day after President Kennedy presented him with the National Security Medal at CIA headquarters in Langley, Virginia.

Blanche replied that she might see him in the summer when she was in Washington for the city's book fair. Her prescient response to change still intact, she could sense the dramatic cultural transitions under way. In the late summer, G. & C. Merriam issued the third edition of *Webster's New International Dictionary*, which contained one hundred thousand new words and definitions not in the 1934 second edition. "A-Bomb, astronaut and beatnik to loyalty oath, sit-in and Zen" suggested more of the ways that society was evolving.[36]

A conference of editors and publishers took place in June 1961 at the Statler Hilton in Washington, D.C. (A year later, the number of books published in the United States reached an all-time high, with paperbacks accounting for 31 percent of the total.)[37] The occasion appeared more animated to many than the annual Frankfurt fair, and the agent Desmond Flower and his wife, Margaret, Cass Canfield, and the Knopfs gathered at the event, which, it seemed, everyone who was anyone attended. Canfield, longtime president of Harper & Brothers, was in the process of merging his firm with Row, Peterson & Company to become Harper & Row. For a short while, the literary crowd felt it was part of a brave new world.[38] Blanche even briefly allowed herself to celebrate Judith Jones's achievement: she had made Julia Child's *Mastering the Art of French Cooking* a reality in America. Its autumn release a broadly anticipated event in American culinary circles, the book became a national bestseller.[39]

Blanche's renewed optimism proved short-lived: in November, while getting up from the table, she broke her "good" hip and had to be hospitalized to have pins inserted, further incapacitating her. Tensions escalated between the Knopfs, because Alfred was forced to supervise editors ordinarily under Blanche's purview in order to meet deadlines. The editorial pressure apparently provoked Alfred's cruel remark "Do you recognize yourself now, Mrs. Knopf?" when he caught his haggard wife looking in a mirror. Pete Lemay (recently made a vice president) overheard the comment and believed Blanche had too much "grace" to acknowledge it.[40]

At the end of the year, the Knopfs went to South America, where Alfred had been eager to go since Blanche's trip in 1942. One of

Blanche's acquaintances, the translator Harriet de Onís, urged her to follow the same itinerary as Alfred because "he enjoyed himself so much more when she was with him." Blanche responded that she would connect with her husband midway through the trip, as she was still too weak to endure his vigorous agenda.[41] The couple met in Brazil, where in Recife they visited the library named in honor of Blanche before spending a week with their author Gilberto Freyre. Even in her frail condition, Blanche charmed her authors, their love of their publisher spilling over onto Alfred so that he, too, felt welcomed. When Alfred went on to Chile to explore the Andes, Blanche stayed in Buenos Aires, where she was tended by friends she'd made decades earlier.

For the now-dreaded December holidays, without Pat or Camus or even Heifetz, Blanche flew to France to be with Jenny, both women remaining on the French Riviera late into January. There would be no eggnog party this year: illness, cigarettes, and decades of diet pills were taking their toll. By 1962, the sixty-eight-year-old Blanche's appearance shocked visitors who hadn't seen her recently: she looked more like a woman of eighty. Increasingly her days were spent in doctors' offices. But though most women her age hadn't worked outside the home at all, she refused to think about retiring—even if Alfred was eager to stop working.

In early February, Alfred went fishing in Chile, with people he'd met on the trip to South America a few months earlier. Blanche wrote him, "I cannot tell you how much I look forward to the 19th of February," when he would be home. The office was "humming along," she assured him. She described how "elegant" "the Monsieur" looked, and how vain, having been "clipped yesterday." She added, "I still do not mention your name or he goes quite mad."[42] Blanche was clearly in one of the spousal romantic moments she'd invoked from the beginning of their marriage, whenever she was anticipating rather than actually being with Alfred.

While Alfred was away, Blanche's driver, a necessity these days, was squiring her around town in Alfred's Rolls-Royce. "It has been heaven to have it here," she told her husband. She closed with news of Julia Child's cookbook: twelve thousand copies had been sold since its October release, and it was now "being displayed at the Brasserie along with *Larousse's GASTRONOMIQUE.*"[43]

"You may get this letter and you may not but it goes with my love, with Monsieur's licks, and with the whole office's missing you. Please take care of yourself on this last lap and arrive safely and well. Devotedly ☺."[44] She closed her note with a revivified smiley face; Van Vechten had used them in the twenties and Blanche had occasionally resurrected them in the forties.

That May, Blanche was strong enough to attend a publishers' conference in Barcelona, arriving home in time to receive an honorary doctor of letters from Franklin & Marshall College in Lancaster, Pennsylvania—along with the drama critic Brooks Atkinson. Unlike in previous years when she worked hard to conceal her physical condition, Blanche was now forthright about her infirmities, especially the slow-to-heal broken hip from months earlier. After the celebration was over, she wrote the officials who had handled her trip that she had enjoyed not only the event itself but also the generous and delicate treatment the college staff had extended to her. As usual, she incorporated the larger field of books into her closing, recalling her discussion with the vice president of Sartre's *Search for a Method* (*Questions de Méthode*) that she would be publishing, then adding that she was sending to the college president, with whom she'd discussed the importance of reading, selections she thought he would enjoy: *Training Your Own Dog, Mastering the Art of French Cooking,* John Updike's *Rabbit, Run* and his book of short stories *Pigeon Feathers.* Though only thirty, Updike was, in Blanche's opinion, brilliant.[45]

In late summer, before Blanche left for Europe, she and Alfred drove to Weston, Connecticut, to have lunch with John Hersey and his second wife, Barbara, whom Hersey had married in 1958, months after divorcing Frances Ann. Barbara, the ex-wife of the cartoonist

Charles Addams and allegedly the model for Morticia Addams, was even more fun than Frances Ann. Both Knopfs were nonetheless taken aback by the antics of the Herseys' young toddler, who, in Barbara's bra and panties, sashayed with her nanny down the stairs to the dining room. Hersey recalled the incident later for the shock he saw on his guests' faces, though he himself was laughing. But unlike Alfred, who became a mossback whenever sexual jokes were made, Blanche was simply taken aback.[46]

Abroad in September, Blanche once again revealed the occasional affection that still underpinned her difficult marriage to Alfred. Writing from London, she marked her letter "Personal" and sent it to Purchase, rather than to the office as she typically did: "Ridiculous that at our ages we (or I?) should have discovered how much we care—perhaps we were too proud, or whatever we were before and then perhaps it is better so but I do care and deeply and seldom enjoyed anything as much as our being together much as I think I dislike packing and unpacking! You were, are, wonderful to me! . . . I miss you terribly . . . All my love and thanks for us."[47]

24

NO MORE DEALS

I N WASHINGTON, just before Langston Hughes took part in the first national poetry festival in the United States, with a reception at the White House hosted by Mrs. Kennedy, the Cuban Missile Crisis erupted.[1] On October 15, 1962, the United States, using spy planes, had discovered that the Soviets were building medium-range missile sites in Cuba. ExComm, an executive committee formed by President Kennedy, decided on a naval quarantine until the complete removal of the missiles was ensured. For the next nine days, the two superpowers seemed to be on the brink of nuclear war, with the United States military on the highest alert since World War II.

When the United States appeared serious about invading Cuba, the Soviets presented a proposal that seemed acceptable—but the following day Khrushchev decided it should include additional concessions from the Americans, including eliminating U.S. missile bases in Turkey. More tension ensued, until Kennedy and his advisers agreed to dismantle the missile sites, though Turkey was an important NATO member—but at a later date, in order to prevent the United States ally from feeling shabbily treated. Kennedy called off the blockade after all the weapons were removed, and in April 1963 the remaining American missiles in Turkey were eradicated.

The crisis was hardly resolved before Blanche was trying to commission a book about the near catastrophe, though with little success. Journalists, including Scotty Reston, were ruminating about the Kennedy administration and its tense political scene but weren't ready to commit to print ironclad conclusions. John Hersey, whom she'd counted on, was writing about civil rights these days and declared himself done with the subject of war, which nonetheless remained a major concern of mid-century literature. Even the novel Blanche wanted from Muriel Spark, *The Girls of Slender Means*, used V-E and V-J Days in London as one of its themes. Blanche wrote to Alfred: "I am reading probably the best book I have read in a great many years, Richard Hughes' *The Fox in the Attic* and am halfway through and cannot wait to get back to it. There is not a word wasted so that it is slow-going and brilliant and probably the best picture of post–first war Germany that has been written."[2] Harper & Row published it after its British appearance, implying Knopf's London scouts had been slow on the uptake—or that Harper & Row was willing to spend more money to acquire it. Blanche still disliked being beaten by other publishers a step ahead of Knopf in signing a book, but even now her house was known not only for its quality but for its frugality as well.

In November 1962, having healed enough physically and secure that war had been averted, Blanche boarded her usual flight, TWA 830, to Paris. Though Knopf now employed at least six editors who acquired books from home and abroad, Blanche remained Knopf's primary scout overseas, even with her diminished stamina. Back in New York in time to welcome 1963 with her famous eggnog, Blanche saw her marital life take another downturn, the reason unclear. The couple's peace was always frangible, exhausted before it even registered. Predictably, Blanche turned to her work for solace: at last the third and final volume of her South American acquisition from twenty years ago was coming to market.

On January 1, 1963, Harriet de Onís's beautifully subtle translation of Gilberto Freyre's *Sobrados e Mucambos* (*The Mansions and the Shanties: The Making of Modern Brazil*) was published. But Blanche continued to be acquisitive. She wrote to Scotty Reston that his newspaper radio program on WQXR was "always better" than the others. "No one is saying what needs to be said more clearly and simply than you." Please write us a book, she implored him. Reston replied that after Washington stopped getting itself into trouble he would consider such a project.[3]

The immediate publishing coup was Muriel Spark's decision to move to Knopf. On January 9 Blanche found out that Knopf had outbid Lippincott for *The Girls of Slender Means*, as well as a future novel, *The Mandelbaum Gate*. Through Elizabeth Bowen, Blanche had been working to get the novelist since 1961, when Spark published *The Prime of Miss Jean Brodie* in *The New Yorker*. Though the Knopf staff came to despise working with the prickly woman—Bill Koshland remembered how "terribly bitchy" Muriel was—Blanche drew close to her, the two strong women closing ranks. They became so comfortable with each other that Blanche cajoled Muriel to lose weight and pay more attention to her appearance, insisting that it was important for a writer to look "put together" for her public. Eventually, Muriel took her counsel and "transformed" her looks, to the surprise of Knopf's staff.[4]

Meanwhile, Spark herself was shocked at her friend's deterioration. At brunch, Blanche would sometimes pour coffee onto the table, her inability to make out shapes progressing monthly.[5] Pat recalled his mother holding letters upside down in the office even before he left Knopf, "but nobody said a word. [Often] she'd start to pour the coffee and I'd grab the pot, because it wasn't going into the cup, [and] she didn't interfere."[6] Now Blanche would pick up her dog, Monsieur, thinking it was her fashionable cabbage-shaped purse, and after realizing her mistake, quickly murmur, *"Mon petit chou."*[7] Her voice compensated somewhat for her lack of sight. More than twenty years after her death, the Knopf editor Stanley Kauffmann would remember Blanche's voice: "Oh, a pleasure to experience, low and warm, so much more attractive than his [Alfred's]."[8]

Because of Alfred's interest in amateur photography (another mark of a gentleman of leisure, he told Pete Lemay, along with a "wine cellar, honorary degrees, and self-education in music and conservation"), the last years of Blanche's life are well documented visually.[9] Alfred was so proud of his photography that he "ordered" Pete to get his pictures into a national magazine. But the two-page spread that ran in *Life* allowed an "error" to slip through. According to *Life*, all Knopf writers were under Alfred's wing. In an "icy rage," Blanche called Pete into her office. Half the writers were not "his" but "hers," she made clear, after throwing the magazine across the room. From now on, she informed him, there was a moratorium on her husband's turning his camera on her or her authors without her permission.[10]

Pete had become a good friend to both Knopfs, a substitute in part for the impartial voice they lost when Mencken died and Van Vechten began his precipitous decline. (Around this time, the photographer Richard Avedon shot a portrait of Carl and Langston Hughes, with Carl's arms around his friend, and though both men had aged, Carl looked battered.) In spite of Alfred's fondness, he was often hard for Pete to take, and he understood why Dorothy Lemay said that Alfred was the rudest man she'd ever met.

In contrast, Pete never forgot how when he introduced his wife, Blanche showed genuine pleasure at meeting her. The Lemays were out shopping and ran into Blanche, looking into a store window. Smiling and repeating Dorothy's name, Blanche told her that "Elizabeth Bowen, who ordinarily detests children, tells me you have the most enchanting boy and girl she's ever seen."[11] Pete grew to love

Blanche, even though he was acutely aware of "the quixotic and sometimes ridiculous defenses she erected against humiliation and the pain that constantly assailed her."[12]

In March 1963, Blanche wrote Muriel Spark that she'd just been in a "period piece place" in Arizona for several weeks, a trip she had hated but she made for Alfred, and which she'd tell her new author about when she saw her in September.[13] She sent separately a letter from Monsieur, thanking "Miss Spark" lavishly for the silver pillbox from Birmingham, England, that the dog used daily. After speculating on the world a hundred years hence, Blanche suggested, half seriously, that dogs might even read by then. For now, Monsieur especially appreciated the gift because his "mama" had been going out too often at night to suit him, and Muriel's present reminded him that he was loved. Monsieur closed with "Miss Spark, I hope you will come to see us very soon. My mameing [*sic*] I know loves you dearly and thinks you very grand and I do, too, and would like to give you a lick for his surprise." Then, over a stamped paw print, the signature read, "Your small friend."[14]

Blanche worked closely with Spark to ensure *The Girls of Slender Means* was ready for early-fall publication. In May, she wrote that she was thrilled the author was coming to the States, where Knopf would "[create] some fun" for her on publication day. In a few weeks the staff would be holding their "big Sales meeting . . . talking about *The Girls of Slender Means* with joy."[15] Whatever her own travels, Blanche stressed, Muriel must stay in New York until the publisher returned from abroad in September. But the early-autumn trip was canceled when Blanche was hospitalized, doubled over once again with abdominal pain.

Alfred brought his brother, Edwin, up to date on September 20 about her progress at Lenox Hill, where she was "doing well"— though more surgery was probably ahead to deal with the adhesions from prior operations. "Blanche is going to require a lot of attention, and I still have to play the thing by ear. Up to now her morale has been surprisingly good, but as you say, 'There are limits.'"[16] She would be home soon, her rapid recovery allowing Alfred to take his trip to California and see Edwin as planned. Still, he cautioned, one never knew. In the meantime, Blanche was focused on Muriel's novel.

Book Week published the first American review of *The Girls of Slender Means*, lauding its "freedom from cant" and lamenting the novel's brevity, the reviewer wanting more pages from "such a talent." In the character-driven story set in the period between the end of the war in Europe and the one in the Pacific, forty girls are forced to live away from home in a lowly institution. "Ominous" to some critics, the author tortured her characters as a "cat playing with a bird," allowing them "moments of hope only to pounce on them." The journalist Virgilia Peterson (who had told Pete Lemay, "At least I didn't have a nervous breakdown after my affair with Stokowski the way Blanche did") claimed that "admirers of Miss Spark's last and brilliant little tale, *The Prime of Miss Jean Brodie*, may find *The Girls of Slender Means* more oblique and ambiguous" but more impressive as a result.[17] Peterson applauded the sharp edge of Spark's fiction, quoting her: "'Few people alive at the time were more delightful, more ingenuous, more movingly lovely, and as it might happen, more savage than the girls of slender means.'"[18]

Back at Lenox Hill, Blanche discovered that her pain wasn't from adhesions after all: she had cancer in her abdomen and liver. Told she had two years to live, she forbade Alfred to tell anyone but a few confidants. Although she didn't believe that a stricken individual was responsible for her disease, as some did, she still belonged to a generation that thought there was something shameful about cancer. Alfred agreed to do as she wished.

Dr. Herman Tarnower, later of Scarsdale Diet fame, claimed to have ordered the biopsy that first identified Blanche's abdominal tumor. Tarnower, who lived in the house next to the Knopfs' in Purchase, had initially refused to give the results to Blanche; he assumed in such instances the patient should be told nothing. Alfred had persuaded his friend otherwise, however, telling him he'd shatter Blanche's confidence in him if he withheld the truth. In a late-life interview, Alfred would recall that "she knew anyway. They [the doctors] just had her all wrong."[19] Ultimately, it was Alfred, not Tarnower, who gave her the news, which she said she'd already guessed.

Tarnower surgically removed as much of the tumors as he could, and he and Blanche devised a schedule for heavy radiation that she would receive many months later. He remembered her as fatalistic but uncomplaining. She told Alfred she planned to continue working to the end. Office stalwarts such as Eleanor French had to be told the truth, she agreed, so they could take her to medical appointments.

Receiving an explanation for her recent years of chronic pain allowed Blanche an odd sense of peace. In addition to her publishing work, she drew up seventeen pages of end-of-life documents, including a will and instructions for her funeral. Telling Joe Lesser the news after pledging him to secrecy, she asked for his help in "making the next two years the best of Alfred's life."[20] She decided to buy a co-op at the Sherry-Netherland, where she and Alfred could live together (she didn't sell her apartment), and she set about hiring architects to make the necessary renovations.

That her work proceeded unabated was the result of a determined effort to make her life seem like "business as usual"—to herself as well as to those around her. She would have assistants with her at every turn, packing her bags, getting her to airports and hotels, ordering her food, or sitting beside her, taking notes during interviews with authors.

After Blanche left the hospital, Alfred wrote their daughter-in-law, Alice, that though Blanche would miss Thanksgiving this year, late November would be a good time for the Knopfs to celebrate Christmas in Westport, with Pat and his family. Alfred couldn't be sure Blanche would be back from France by then, but they could hope. Clearly, Alfred was laying the groundwork for Blanche to miss a dreaded family gathering.

Pat's invitations to Westport were rare, and family interactions remained stiff. Blanche was still a proud woman, and, feeling unwelcome in her son's life, she must have refused to yield at all in their fraught relationship. Soon after President Kennedy was shot in Dallas on November 22, she left for Paris, where she would process the tragedy with friends rather than family.

Upon her return, she was thrilled when Alfred appeared at the airport with Monsieur to greet her. Blanche wrote Jenny Bradley not about seeing her grandchildren, but about her dog, as if he were her child: "Alfred brought him to Idlewild which was a surprise and a wonderful one. He [Monsieur] was enchanting . . . really very gay and great fun." Just as the Knopfs had bonded over their impossible but lovable bloodhounds, so again they had come together through their affection for the seven-pound terrier. From abroad she had written elaborate instructions for his care, the letters signed with the same paw print she'd used on Muriel Spark's thank-you letter. In Paris, worried about Monsieur's health, Blanche had cabled Eleanor French, suggesting she confer with another assistant about the shape his "cigars" were now taking.

Blanche wasn't sure that Alfred would see her through the difficult days ahead. He had rarely been sick himself, and he might not be up to dealing with physical suffering. Remembering how, as a boy, he had hid under his sheets when he heard his mother writhing in pain, Blanche understood his possible reticence.

If Blanche was becoming a little more forgiving of herself as well as of others, she was particularly pleased that Random's Bennett Cerf and his associates clearly respected her. And surely, regardless of how sparing she was with her praise, Blanche must have been proud of her son's success: in less than a year, in January 1965, he would publish Theodore White's *The Making of the President, 1964*, which covered the Kennedy assassination.

After recovering from several rounds of radiation, Blanche flew to France for a month's stay with Jenny. Just before she left New York, she sent Muriel Spark a telegram to have a happy Easter: "Joyeux Paques Love Blanche."[21] Then, in July 1964, she and Alfred returned to South America for three weeks, having a "fascinating time," according to a letter Blanche wrote to Scotty Reston in September. Reston and his wife, Sally, were by now Blanche's good friends, and she wanted to congratulate him on his new job as associate editor of *The New York Times*. Blanche had bet well on him during the war with his book *Prelude to Victory*: Scotty had gone on to win two Pulitzers. Teasing while at the same time prodding him, she reminded Reston that this new position at the *Times*—a safe desk job for a change—would give him a chance to finish the manuscript he had long been working on.[22]

That fall, Knopf released a first novel by Anne Tyler to high praise. Orville Prescott wrote in *The New York Times* that *If Morning Ever Comes* was "a brilliant first novel . . . so mature, so gently wise and so brightly amusing . . . If it weren't printed right there on the jacket, few readers would suspect that Mrs. Tyler was only 22. Some industrious novelists never learn how to write good fiction. Others seem to be born knowing how. Mrs. Tyler is one of these . . . Her people are triumphantly alive."[23] Tyler would always remember the oddity of her first lunch with Blanche, who had "spent the entire meal discussing her little lap dog. She said she was thinking about getting her dog 'married.' She kept pondering what sort of 'husband' would be most satisfactory."[24]

Somehow, at the end of September, Blanche squeezed in another trip to Paris. According to a letter to Muriel Spark, who had remained in New York, she "caught her heel in one of those holes on a mat at the top of three steps" at the Paris Ritz and injured her hip yet again. As soon as she was "seeable and not in too much agony" she looked forward to visiting her friend. By November, at least Blanche was strong enough to attend a ceremony in her honor at the

Brazilian embassy in Washington, D.C., where she received a second decoration on behalf of the Brazilian government.

She healed in time to take a trip with Alfred to Puerto Rico in early December, where they met Pablo Casals (from whom they hoped to pry a book). Blanche managed to stay away from home until the last days of the month, writing Spark again of her sense of sadness at the Christmas holidays, which was worse than ever this year. According to Grace Dadd in London, in spite of her brave front, Blanche was terrified of cancer, which she believed the publisher "never admitted she had to anyone or to Eleanor French back home." Joe Lesser thought she was in denial. Even after her death, Alfred, like most people of that era, refused to utter the "C" word. Instead, he told people "the machine just broke down."[25] If she needed any further memento mori, she got home from their trip in time to mourn Carl Van Vechten's death on December 21, 1964. Carl had arranged for his eighty-four-year-old body to be "cremated and his ashes scattered in the Shakespeare Garden in Central Park," the memorial service two days before Christmas.[26]

In early January 1965, Blanche finally managed to have dinner with Muriel Spark at La Grenouille, a restaurant frequented by the publishing crowd at 3 East Fifty-Second Street. It had been open "about a year [it was closer to three] and [was] quite good. I have been there once and everyone speaks well of it," she assured her picky friend, seeming to be in fine fettle even as she secretly suffered.[27] The following month *Publishers Weekly* published an interview with Blanche in which, like others before her, the journalist could hardly contain her enthusiasm: "The word 'chic,' appropriately a French word, could have been coined to describe Blanche Wolf Knopf. [Her] apartment study's walls and flat surfaces are uncluttered . . . [with the owner's] fondness for clean fabric and polished wood."[28]

By the end of March, with Spark back in London, Blanche wrote her that colleagues had been reading the proofs of *The Mandelbaum Gate* and were "wildly enthusiastic."[29] Admittedly, Blanche said, the readers knew how much the book meant to its publisher, but she correctly believed the staff thought it a "beautiful and important book."[30] A love story centered upon the dangerous division of Jerusalem between Palestinians and Jews, Spark's political fiction displayed "muscular writing" and boldness, according to most reviewers, though the novelist Doris Grumbach found it muddy and boring.[31] Sales didn't reach the numbers the author had wanted, and Blanche found herself reassuring her friend, as other publishers had before her, that Muriel just had to give Knopf more time.

Determined to squelch any rumors of bad health, at the end of May, on the arms of Alfred and Bill Koshland, Blanche attended the opening session of the International Publishers Congress in Washington. But within weeks, to everyone's shock, Alfred was the one who needed propping up. He suffered a severe heart attack, which would keep him in the hospital for an entire month, including seven days in intensive care. There had been no warning except for an ominous quotation embedded in a *Newsweek* interview, commemorating Knopf's fiftieth anniversary several weeks before, in which Alfred spoke as if he were ancient and the Arcadia of publishing he once inhabited long gone: "a Golden Age before the decline of just about everything." Only once in the long article did Alfred allude to Blanche, who was still acquiring books for Knopf and who had come up with the borzoi as their colophon: "We wanted something that would set us off from other publishers." By "we," the reporter explained, Alfred meant him and his wife, Blanche, "who has worked closely with him throughout their joint career."[32]

As he recovered from his heart attack, Alfred talked to anyone who'd listen about Blanche's devoted care. She traveled to White Plains Hospital virtually every day—as she had done when her exigent son was hospitalized for his appendix. As she did with herself, she disclosed as little medical information about Alfred as possible, assuring their authors that Alfred was fine: "It was just a little angina."[33] Initially, Blanche didn't even tell Pat about his father—which angered their son more than ever. Instead, from the hospital, Alfred wrote to friends about the wine trip he and the cardiologist Hy Tarnower planned to take soon. Confident that Alfred was on the mend, Blanche went to France for a week in July, unhappy about getting professionally sideswiped again by what was her husband's carelessness at best. In the July 23, 1965, issue of *Life*, the authors whose photographs appeared in an article on Knopf were Conrad, Mann, Camus, Sartre, Stevens, Mencken, Bowen, Hersey, Updike, and Richter, all said to be Alfred's, though they were in fact Blanche's authors, with the single exception of Judith Jones's Updike.[34]

In early August, Blanche spoke on the phone with Jascha Heifetz, who was now living in Beverly Hills, and she told her friend of Alfred's heart attack. She wrote him afterward, to say that their phone conversation had brought her "so much joy." Jascha had provided her with a litany of his recent successes and his plans for new recordings. Though she praised him for his upcoming teaching assignment in Los Angeles, her deepest interest was in the tapes he'd be making: "This is very important and there is much still missing that needs to be heard again and again." Turning to her own life, she explained that Alfred was due home from the hospital shortly. She herself would be confined to New York through September caring for him, and Jascha must let her know if he'd be in Manhattan during that period or later, at the end of October: "I long to see you again," she wrote.[35]

She regretted having few books to send him, except for *The Mandelbaum Gate*, set in the Middle East, "and you know . . . that part of the world well. To me it is a great book." She signed it, "Much love et a bientot, Blanche." In London at the end of September, she told Grace Dadd that she had "kept a record of every book she'd considered on her trips to England," and she'd asked Dadd to read the list aloud to her. The agent got the feeling that "this would be Blanche's last visit."[36]

Grace was shocked to see the frail woman at work in her hotel room in the early morning and not in bed before 2:30 a.m.[37] Caught off guard in London, Blanche told Grace that she was "scared of dying," Grace gently assuring her that such fear was normal.[38] Recalling her employer during an interview conducted after Blanche's death, Dadd remembered "walking into the room at Claridge's one time when Alfred was there—saw him looking down at her—thought went through my mind 'My God that man still loves her!'"[39]

Before Blanche had left for Europe, the overbearing Herman Tarnower announced to Alfred that "we're going on that vineyard trip—this [heart attack] isn't going to spoil it."[40] After all, the cardiologist would be there as his personal attendant. Indeed, with Blanche already overseas, Alfred, Tarnower, and the doctor's current "lady" friend, Lise Dolfi, would go to Strasbourg, France, where they would meet up with Blanche. In the end, with the help of a French maid, she stayed in Europe for a month and a half more, often using a wheelchair against her will.

Back in New York City, when the Knopfs celebrated their half century of publishing, Blanche was at last treated, virtually, as an equal. The couple held a reception and dinner at the Hotel Astor on October 29, 1965. On the dais with them were seventeen colleagues and dear friends, including the Bennett Cerfs, the John Herseys, Elizabeth Bowen, Langston Hughes, and Fania Marinoff, or Mrs. Carl Van Vechten—Carlo dead now ten months. Among those seated at the tables were the Pforzheimers, Muriel Spark, the Updikes, and Paul and Julia Child.

A reporter from the *San Francisco Chronicle* remembered that Blanche "under that harsh light, looked like a decaying movie actress, Gloria Swanson—she was grotesque."[41] As if to assure herself that she had plenty of time left despite her diagnosis, Blanche went forward with the massive redesign of her new apartment. (She would still be at West Fifty-Fifth Street when she died.) In December, Alfred reported to Edwin that relations among him and Pat and Blanche had warmed "considerably." Even though Blanche's bad hip kept her in bed much of the time, Alice and Pat and the two girls "came to lunch at Purchase with Blanche and me, and everything went off very well."[42]

Ensuring such good will was also Alfred's knowledge that RCA was buying Random House/Knopf for $40 million in stock (no cash), the sale in January 1966 signaling a new age of corporate mergers and acquisitions in publishing. In Alfred's personal files at the Ransom Center is a booklet sent to Random House shareholders asking for their input on the RCA merger, in which it was stated that "shareholders of Random House will receive .62 of a share of RCA Common Stock for each of their Random House Common Shares. The Directors believe the rate of exchange is fair and equitable."[43]

A more dramatic contrast to Knopf's beginnings some fifty years earlier would be hard to imagine, but Blanche, who had always been one to welcome change (though she had still never watched television, according to Pete Lemay), was too sick to care about figuring out this new publishing world.[44] Alfred released a press statement reassuring the reading public that Knopf's integrity would not be diminished: "I'm quite satisfied that the merging of RH into the Radio Corporation of America . . . will not in foreseeable future affect in any way whatever the day to day operations of AAK Inc." Random House and Knopf would continue as separate entities, Knopf "with complete editorial autonomy . . . and no changes in its present personnel and management."[45] Somehow, Alfred had also managed to intimidate the historian Charles A. Madison into making major revisions to his book published by McGraw-Hill, *Book Publishing in America*. The naïve Madison had sent Alfred a draft, which the publisher immediately pronounced inaccurate, especially the accounts Pat gave Madison about founding Atheneum.

Happy to get away, in mid-February, Alfred, his recovery already complete the previous fall, convinced Blanche to take a month's trip with him to South America, on a cruise ship that would naturally provide her with a bed. Alfred recorded in his diary, "Blanche in stateroom all day [lying down]. Blanche unable to eat."[46] She stayed in Brazil for much of the time he spent touring the continent. Blanche's needs for rest and comfort were kindly tended to by writers who revered her, and now, seeing her deeply valued, just as he had when she received the French citation, her husband behaved graciously in their presence. Nonetheless, it must have seemed odd to some observers that two people either ill or recently so were traveling far from home.

Back in Manhattan, walking on the street—always with a companion—Blanche wore wigs, due to the increasing side effects of radiation therapy. Though she had long gone to Elizabeth Arden, at this stage, Clark "Lyonel" Nelson, one of Manhattan's best hairdressers, came to Blanche to do her hair daily. "She and I were friends by then," Lyonel recalls, "through a wild coincidence. On a cold nasty day in February, maybe 1961, on my way to the salon on 54th and 5th, I couldn't get a taxi; they were all going super slow due to snow and ice, so I decided to walk the eight blocks to work." Halfway there, he saw "a frail woman walking through three inches of slush and I helped her up some stairs. She said, 'Aha, so you're a gentleman,'" and they both entered the Waldorf and went their separate ways. A few weeks later, Lyonel was asked to do a customer's hair, and "the lady turned out to be Mrs. Knopf." Her hair had been damaged by a permanent, and the "extremely meticulous" Blanche was thrilled that Lyonel could fix it. From then on, he was her hairdresser. "I worked up a medium blond shade with highlights, nice soft look, and she was very happy."[47] He remembers her fondly and in detail, even today. "She wore beautiful fabrics, with her French Legion of Merit award always present on the lapel of her suit jacket. [And] two large-linked gold chain bracelets with precious stones from Seaman Schepps." And of course, her nails were "long, almost talon-like, always perfectly painted with a fire red lacquer."[48] Blanche had to see the manicurist several times a week because her nails, which broke easily, needed constant repair. Her poor diet had created distinctive claws, surely reminding her and Alfred of the bird girl in *Green Mansions*.

To Lyonel, who was a hairdresser to the stars, including the Rockefellers, Kennedys, and many more, his association with Blanche was "one of the great privileges of my career," with Mrs. Knopf taking a genuine interest in his background and work.[49] Before long Blanche had remarked on his fascinating story of becoming a success right off of a midwestern farm, and she began urging him to write a book. In the meantime, they soon developed a routine to deal with her cancer treatments: Lyonel waited at her apartment door every morning at 9:00 a.m. to brush her wig upon her return.

Though she looked like a scarecrow, she refused help getting out of the cab, taking stuttering steps from the taxi to Lyonel's strong grip. "She never said a word about her disease or treatment, she just encouraged me to tell tales about my experiences as a hairdresser to the rich and famous. And every so often she'd surprise me with a box of books Knopf had published that she thought I'd like. She was always suggesting that I write about the delicious stories of the society ladies" (which he eventually did; *From Farm to Fifth Avenue* was self-published in 2014).[50]

Determined to continue her mother's long-ago lessons about the importance of self-presentation, Blanche, mercifully, didn't realize (or acknowledge to herself) what the ravages of her illness had wrought. A Knopf assistant noticed that the publisher's legs were so thin that her stockings wrinkled into rivulets on her legs, eventually sagging into bags at her ankles. Bill Koshland remembered how "you could practically see through her ankles. You could see there were bones and some skin covering the bones and there was nothing inside. How could those things hold what little there was to hold?"[51] Stanley Kauffmann less kindly recalled her "almost opaque eyes (due to glaucoma), [which] with her wrinkled skin gave her a hint of the reptile."[52] Another office assistant saw her on Fifth Avenue with a giant blob of powder on her face. "Let me wipe your cheek for you, Blanche," she said gently. "I *know* it's there," Blanche said proudly. "I want it that way."[53]

Improbably, a few days into June, Blanche gave a dinner for Pete Lemay and his wife. "I remember fondly her asking me, several weeks earlier, who Dorothy and I would most like to spend an evening with, and we told her William and Emily Maxwell, two dear friends of ours and Blanche's as well." They had convened years earlier and enjoyed themselves immensely. This time, however, Blanche ended up lying on the living-room sofa, moaning softly, struggling to survive her body's last rites. The Maxwells and Pete "knew she was at the end." Pete realized they'd never see her again, noting her "waxy pallor, her knees drawn to her sunken chest." It was a "sweet evening nonetheless." The guests hoped for a pentimento, a reminder of the old Blanche, and they got it with the only story she told that night: the fantasy that her father had taken her to France. "She went on and on about it, but she was in agony," Pete says. As he told her goodbye for the last time, he thought again of a secret conviction he had long held: "The accomplishment at Knopf was Blanche's—to have made a mark of that dimension—London '39—Freud. All of it."[54]

Nine days before she died, she still had her secretary take dictation for her, sending a letter to Cornelius Ryan congratulating him on *The Last Battle*, which he'd published with Simon & Schuster. After referring to her own trip to the area in 1945, she said only that she'd been flat with a bad back of late. Eleanor set up appointments with the architects to finish the work on the apartment that was, remarkably, meant to be shared with Alfred, but she kept having to cancel them. Blanche wrote her old friend the designer Mainbocher that life was "getting more complicated and more difficult for less reason than I have ever understood—my feeling is that I have been around much too long."[55] Certainly she had served her cause well: by now, twenty-seven Knopf writers had won the Pulitzer Prize, and sixteen the Nobel.

For weeks, along with Blanche's live-in maid, Cecile, who had returned from an early retirement to take care of Blanche, Alfred had been staying at the Fifty-Fifth Street apartment, reading to his wife for hours at a time. As if reliving his childhood family car trips, he chose an old favorite, Sherlock Holmes, and went through as many tales as necessary until she fell asleep. At some point he even wrote poetry for her, though Pete Lemay remembers her responding with the cryptic utterance that "it's much too late."[56] When Alfred had to go to Boston for a day or so, Joe Lesser came to her apartment in his stead. "There was no question that she expected to recover from this bout of illness," he would tell Susan Sheehan. "We went over architectural and design blueprints for the new apartment she was planning. That Friday night we just sat and talked over the plans and its costs," Lesser assuring her there was plenty of money to do whatever she wanted. Cecile, hinting that it was time to go, excused herself and went to her basement bedroom, taking the latest Yorkie with her. Reluctantly, Joe departed, leaving Blanche alone.[57]

Just then Muriel Spark called from East Hampton. She had noticed a "celestial light" and realized that her "hotel room was right overhanging the sea and you could hear the roar of the waves . . . I said to her, 'Blanche, can you hear the sea?' She said, 'No, but I'd like to,' so I put the telephone receiver out of the window for her to hear the waves and then she said, 'Yes, now I catch the sound of the sea.'"[58]

The next morning, June 4, when Blanche didn't respond to Cecile's typically soft tap on the door, the maid became alarmed. Knocking louder and still getting no response, she called Eleanor French rather than enter the room herself. When Eleanor arrived, she found her longtime employer unresponsive and knew that Blanche was dead. She had been in "terrible pain" the day before, causing her to swear that she was going to give her doctor an ultimatum: he had to do something or she was going to take matters into her own hands. But the doctor had replied that he could do nothing more. Eleanor assumed Blanche had committed suicide—when she and perhaps Alfred knew he would not be there to suffer as he had at his mother's death.[59]

Muriel Spark always said the sounds of the waves were the last thing her friend heard.[60]

Alfred and Herman Tarnower arrived together later that morning, Pat and Joseph Lesser before them. When Pat got there, Lesser made sure he could be alone with his mother. For two hours Pat sat by her side, sobbing. What Blanche had long wanted, evidence that her son loved her, had come, but too late. When Alfred walked in, he ignored Pat and immediately began making the funeral arrangements. Tarnower didn't want to be a witness for the death certificate, since the empty bottle of pain pills by her bed suggested Blanche might have hastened her end. Alfred begged him: otherwise, Blanche would be sent to the morgue. Reluctantly, Tarnower signed the document and the body was taken to Frank E. Campbell, the funeral home on the Upper East Side of Manhattan where Blanche had gone to pay her respects to George Gershwin almost thirty years before.

The following Tuesday, June 7, on the way to the funeral, with Pete Lemay serving as Alfred's companion, their limousine ran out of gas, and Alfred "went crazy" while the driver refueled.[61] Otherwise, the publisher tended to business papers during the short trip to Campbell's, with Pat and his family in the following car. For his mother's burial clothes, her son had selected the Balenciaga evening gown she'd worn to the Knopfs' fiftieth-anniversary celebration two months earlier. Though Blanche had specified that "my body shall be cremated and the ashes dispersed and that there shall be no religious or other funeral services of any kind," she had failed to indicate her final dress.[62]

Ignoring her directive, Alfred held an 11:30 ceremony where he alone spoke, briefly, about his wife's valor and strength. He had arranged for a Juilliard ensemble, dressed in black and white, to play a twenty-minute Haydn string quartet. Jason Epstein would remember the "stage banked with camellias."[63] Pat insisted they were white carnations, and that his father whispered to him: "They cost me $500.00."[64]

Pete Lemay still gets upset remembering how Bennett and Phyllis Cerf chattered throughout the half-hour service at Campbell's— "and not quietly"—while Peggy Cullman complained of the dead woman's nerve in forcing them to sit for thirty minutes in the summer heat (though the day's newspapers report pleasant weather).[65] The family (and Pete) then drove to the crematorium. Talking to Lemay twenty years later, Pat said, "Terrible thing to be cremated in [that dress]. It was a beautiful thing: taffeta in red and black."

Pat would tell Peter Prescott that he resented, even protested, his father's publication of encomia upon Blanche's death: Alfred had "never given her recognition in her time."[66]

Hundreds of tributes poured in, from all over the world, with Elizabeth Bowen's quiet observation summing them up: "I can't grasp that Blanche is not in this world anymore." At another occasion a few years earlier, Bowen had praised her friend as the "most extraordinary person in that she never asks a single question which is hurtful or improper to the person of creative imagination." She had gone on to speak of Blanche's ability to further a novelist's faith in herself, while never "intruding." She had "always given one that feeling of an absolute and reticent understanding."[67]

Even the staff at the Paris Ritz sent personal condolences, in the form of a letter. John Hersey wrote:

Barbara and I talk about Blanche every day—remembering small things but always remembering the great thing, her remarkable courage. I guess I had known for a long time that she must be having pain, but I never heard a word on the subject, never a sigh from her lips. She always wanted to talk about the latest thing, whatever it might be, and about my concerns. I was moved by it each time I saw her, and I am moved by it now.[68]

Knopf's Sidney Jacobs, head of production and an employee since 1928, stressed her kindness: "I shall never forget how Blanche appeared suddenly in Munich one grim day in June 1945—long before American civilians were allowed into the city. She had charmed two young Army Air Force colonels into flying her from Paris so that she could say 'Hello, Jake' and dispel my loneliness and make me believe that home really existed." "She brought so much elegance and style into publishing and into life, and we are all impoverished by her death," wrote Arthur M. Schlesinger, Jr. Eric Sevareid telegraphed, "This is very sad news for a lot of us [stop] It makes me realize again how much Blanche did for me and so many writing friends of mine." William Shirer said that "it was Blanche who took *Berlin Diary*, with an advance which shook the House of Knopf and began to shake me out of journalism and into writing books. I shall never forget the confidence she had in me from the very beginning. It gave me a start in a new life." Jason Epstein concluded that "in one way especially her loss seems to me catastrophic . . . Blanche stood for a kind of publishing which we shall never see again."[69]

EPILOGUE

NINE MONTHS AFTER BLANCHE'S DEATH Alfred would marry Helen Hedrick, whose novel *The Blood Remembers* had been published by Knopf in 1941. The friendly northwestern woman was, everybody said, as different from Blanche as anyone could be. "Helen knows how to manage me," Alfred explained to others. "Blanche never did."[1] But Alfred's friend, the philanthropist W. H. "Ping" Ferry (who delighted in wearing even gaudier pink shirts and polka-dot ties than the publisher), was shocked at how Alfred spoke to Helen. Though Ping considered himself an "intellectual provocateur in the Swiftian tradition," he found Alfred's manner to his wife intolerable: "He was rude and dismissive . . . and told her to go away when we were talking in the living room. He would verbally abuse Helen," he recalled.[2]

Letters from Helen to Pat and his children are warm. Yet the Knopfs' son would, years later, complain bitterly to Pete Lemay that just like his mother, his stepmother had "ignored his children throughout her marriage to Alfred," and that after Alfred's funeral, his second wife had "left to go back West immediately, Alfred's entire estate hers. She didn't even stop to say goodbye," apparently in a hurry to return to her four grown children and eleven grandchildren. *"Qu'est-ce que tu veux? C'est la vie,"* Blanche would have said in the language she loved. Life wasn't fair, everybody knew that. On October 1, 2015, Knopf celebrated its one hundredth anniversary, at the New York Public Library.

NOTES

ABBREVIATIONS

AAK   Alfred A. Knopf.

AAK notes   Notes of Alfred A. Knopf. Numbered by later (erratic) documentation as well as Alfred Knopf's original pagination.

AP   Private collection of Anne Prescott, including the private collection of papers and recordings of Peter Prescott. Many of the files in the Anne Prescott archives have been listed here by their original cataloging titles.

BWK   Blanche Wolf Knopf.

BWK notes   Notes of Blanche Wolf Knopf.

HRC   Harry Ransom Center, the University of Texas at Austin, Alfred A. Knopf, Inc. Records.

POP   Alfred A. Knopf, ed. *Portrait of a Publisher 1915–1965*, vol. 1, *Reminiscences and Reflections by Alfred A. Knopf*; vol. 2, *Alfred A. Knopf and the Borzoi Imprint: Recollections and Appreciations* (New York: Typophiles, 1965).

SS   Private collection of Susan Sheehan.

INTRODUCTION

1. Gregory R. Suriano, ed., *Gershwin in His Time: A Biographical Scrapbook, 1919–1937* (New York: Gramercy Books, 1998), 30; and Paul Boyer, "Knopf, Blanche Wolf," in *Notable American Women: The Modern Period*, ed. Barbara Sicherman and Carol Hurd Green. (Cambridge, MA: Belknap Press, 1986), 401.

2. John Tebbel, *A History of Book Publishing in the United States*, vol. 2, *The Expansion of an Industry, 1865–1919* (New York: R. R. Bowker, 1975), 3.

3. Stacy Schiff, *Cleopatra: A Life* (New York: Little, Brown, 2010), 4 (speaking of Rome, centuries earlier); and Susan Hertog, *Dangerous Ambition: Rebecca West and Dorothy Thompson, New Women in Search of Love and Power* (New York: Ballantine Books, 2011), book jacket.
4. AAK notes, chap. 6, 150, HRC.
5. Richard Hofstadter, in *POP*, vol. 2, 215.
6. Arnold Rampersad, e-mail to the author, April 7, 2014.
7. AAK, interviewed by Susan Sheehan, July 27, 1973, AP.
8. AAK, interviewed by Susan Sheehan, July 8, 1974, AP.
9. Drew Dudley Landmark Decisions, AP.
10. Joseph Epstein, e-mail to the author, October 10, 2012.
11. Harding Lemay, e-mail to the author, April 5, 2012.

I. HUNGRY FOR ADVENTURE

1. BWK's account of her trip to London, 1943, AP.
2. "Blanche's European Trips: 1943, 1948," AP.
3. Special thanks to David Smith, retired reference librarian at the New York Public Library, for this information.
4. Robert Josephy, interviewed by Peter Prescott, n.d., AP.
5. Lecture given by Peter Prescott, AP.
6. Rita Goodman Bodenheimer, interviewed by Susan Sheehan, in "Blanche Before Marriage," 1970s, AP.
7. "Failure of Cattle Exporters," *The New York Times*, September 25, 1877.
8. Ibid.
9. Samuels made his fortune back at a tragic cost: in early 1902 he took out insurance on a mortgage of $31,000 (equal to $900,000 today), before dying a few months later. "Assignments of Mortgages," *The New York Times*, June 28, 1902.
10. "Blanche-2, 'Three Alice,'" n.d., SS, AP.
11. Helene Fraenkel, interviewed by Susan Sheehan, n.d., AP. Alfred remembered Blanche as being close to her mother.
12. "Blanche-2, 'Three Alice,'" n.d., SS, AP.
13. Amy Root Clements, "Inventing the Borzoi: Alfred and Blanche Knopf and the Rhetoric of Prestige in Modern American Book Publishing" (doctoral dissertation, University of Texas at Austin, 2010), 31.
14. Elsie Alsberg, interviewed by Susan Sheehan, in "Blanche Before Marriage," 1970s, AP.
15. "Courting Blanche," Mem. T4—122: April 4 or 16, SS, AP.
16. Peter Prescott, "Blanche-2, 'Three Alfred,'" n.d., AP.
17. Ibid.
18. Ibid.
19. Geoffrey Hellman, in *POP*, vol. 2, 53.
20. BWK notes, n.p., AP.
21. Ibid.
22. Norma Loeb Mark, interviewed by Peter Prescott, n.d., AP.
23. Peter Prescott, "Biography of Alfred Knopf" (working paper), chap. 1, AP.

24. Ibid., 14; and Wendy Knopf, letter to Peter Prescott, April 15, 1993, recalling what Helen Knopf told her.
25. AAK notes, 33, HRC; also H. L. Mencken letter to BWK, April 24, 1915, Enoch Pratt Free Library, Baltimore, H. L. Mencken Collection.
26. AAK notes, n.p., HRC.
27. AAK notes, 17, HRC.
28. Lecture given by Peter Prescott, AP.
29. AAK notes, 17, HRC.
30. "Infidelity," *The Cincinnati Enquirer*, February 9, 1897; *The Commercial Tribune*, February 9, 1897; "Atoned," *The Cincinnati Enquirer*, February 17, 1897.
31. "Atoned."
32. "Infidelity."
33. *The Commercial Tribune*, February 9, 1897.
34. "Atoned."
35. *Brooklyn Sunday Eagle*, February 14, 1897. Quotations in the following two paragraphs are from this source.

2. THE BOOK LOVERS

1. AAK notes, chap. 3; "Mildred MK," SS, HRC: "Blanche stipulated Alfred had to use her in the firm."
2. Charles Emmerson, *1913: In Search of the World Before the Great War* (New York: Public Affairs, 2013), 171.
3. AAK notes, "Boyhood," n.p., HRC.
4. Ibid.
5. BWK, letter to AAK, December 22, 1913, AP.
6. AAK notes, n.p., AP.
7. AAK notes, March 6, 1915, 109, HRC.
8. BWK, letter to AAK, June 3, 1914, AP.
9. BWK, letters to AAK, December 22, 1913, and November 15, 1914, AP.
10. BWK notes, n.p., AP.
11. BWK notes, n.p., AP.
12. "Know Your Type: Cheltenham," *idsgn* (blog), February 3, 2010, idsgn.org/posts /know-your-type-cheltenham.
13. These included Elmer Adler, W. A. Dwiggins, and, a short while later, Bruce Rogers, George Salter, Carl Hertzog, and Vincent Torre.
14. BWK notes, n.p., AP.
15. *The Borzoi Quarterly* 15, no. 3 (1966), HRC.
16. John J. Mullen, interviewed by Susan Sheehan, April 23, 1975, AP.
17. Amy Root Clements, *The Art of Prestige: The Formative Years at Knopf, 1915–1929* (Amherst: University of Massachusetts Press, 2014), 69.
18. Wilmarth Lewis, interviewed by Peter Prescott, n.d., AP.
19. BWK notes, n.p., AP.
20. BWK notes, n.p., AP.
21. *The New York Times*, April 5, 1916, AP.
22. AAK notes, chap. 6, 143, HRC.
23. BWK notes, n.p., AP.

24. AAK notes, 145, AP.
25. Ibid., 144.
26. Ibid., 143.
27. Jeff Kennedy, "A History of the Provincetown Playhouse," provincetownplay house.com/history.html.
28. In 1959, Hudson's novel was turned into a movie with Audrey Hepburn, Anthony Perkins, and Lee J. Cobb.
29. Marian Skedgell letter to Peter Prescott, July 14, 1987, AP; and Geoffrey Hellman, in *POP*, vol. 1, 53.
30. AAK notes, n.p., HRC.
31. The offerings included James Morier, *The Adventures of Hajji Baba of Ispahan*; *Memoirs of Carlo Goldoni*; Théophile Gautier, *A Romantic in Spain*; Martin A. S. Holme, *Sir Walter Raleigh*; Francisco de Quevedo, *Pablo de Segovia*; Auguste Villiers de L'Isle-Adam, *Sardonic Tales*; Frederick Rolfe, *Hadrian the Seventh*; Multatuli (Eduard Douwes Dekker), *Max Havelaar*; *The Letters of Abelard and Heloise*; Haldane Macfall, *Wooings of Jezebel Pettyfer*; Stendhal, *The Life of Henri Brulard*; Andrew Kippis, *Captain Cook's Voyages*; Morley Roberts, *Rachel Marr*; Marmaduke Pickthall, *Said the Fisherman*; Jules Barbey d'Aurevilly, *The Diaboliques*; Richard Garnett, *The Twilight of the Gods*; and James Weldon Johnson, *The Autobiography of an Ex-Colored Man*.
32. Tape 19, "Publicity—Early Days," SS, AP.
33. Charles Dellheim, "A Fragment of a Heart in the Knopf Archives," *The Chronicle of Higher Education* 45, no. 45 (July 16, 1999): B4.
34. Bruce Kellner, ed., *Letters of Carl Van Vechten* (New Haven, CT: Yale University Press, 1987), 3–11.
35. H. L. Mencken, letter to BWK, December 10, 1921, Enoch Pratt Free Library, Baltimore, H. L. Mencken Collection.
36. Alfred A. Knopf, Inc., records, Manuscripts and Archives Division, New York Public Library, 4.11, dated August 28, 1917, HRC.
37. BWK, telegram to AAK, February 5, 1917, AP.
38. Death certificate for W. Julius Wolf, January 6, 1917, file no. 938, Manhattan W410.
39. Elsie Alsberg, interviewed by Susan Sheehan, in "BWK Child/Colin interview," n.d., AP.
40. Ibid.
41. AAK notes, 15, AP.
42. BWK, letter to AAK, May 19, 1918, AP.
43. The influenza pandemic by the end of 1918 had a death toll in New York City alone of 12,500.
44. Jill Lepore, *The Mansion of Happiness: A History of Life and Death* (New York: Alfred A. Knopf, 2012), 118–23.
45. BWK notes, n.p., HRC.
46. Ibid.
47. AAK notes, n.p., AP. Jewish childen, typically, are not named after the immediate previous generation, unless that person is deceased, but someone, either Alfred or Blanche, had insisted the baby be named after his father regardless. Hence the boy went by Blanche's chosen nickname, although her reason for de-

ciding on "Pat" is unclear. There was also an earlier intrigue over a possibly illegimate son of Sam Knopf's, named Sam.

48. AAK notes, n.p., AP.
49. Angeles "Toni" Pasquale, interviewed by Susan Sheehan, October 6, 1974, AP.

3. A THIRD KNOPF

1. Amy Root Clements, *The Art of Prestige: The Formative Years at Knopf, 1915–1929* (Amherst: University of Massachusetts Press, 2014), 99.
2. Edwin Knopf, interviewed by Susan Sheehan, circa late 1970s, AP.
3. Clifton Fadiman, interviewed by Susan Sheehan, circa late 1970s, AP.
4. Robert Josephy, *Taking Part: A Twentieth-Century Life* (Iowa City: University of Iowa Press, 1993), 36.
5. BWK notes, n.p., HRC.
6. Pat Knopf, interviewed by Susan Sheehan, February 3, 1975, AP.
7. AAK notes, n.p., HRC.
8. Beatrice Leval, interviewed by Susan Sheehan, February 6, 1975, AP.
9. "Dearest Reuben," May 11, 1919, AP.
10. BWK notes, n.p., AP.
11. BWK notes, n.p., HRC.
12. Ibid.
13. Ibid.
14. A & B menage—4, AP.
15. Quote attributed to Edmund Wilson by Coyote Canyon Press, www .coyotecanyonpress.com/h-l-mencken-the-american-language/.
16. BWK, letter to AAK in Chicago, November 2, 1918, AP.
17. Ibid.
18. Ibid.
19. Bruce Kellner, *Carl Van Vechten and the Irreverent Decades* (Norman: University of Oklahoma Press, 1968), 117; and Burton Rascoe, *Before I Forget* (Garden City, NY: Doubleday, Doran, 1937), 423.
20. Rascoe, *Before I Forget*, 422.
21. BWK notes, n.p., HRC.
22. "1918," from notebook, AP.
23. National Parks–5, AP.
24. Peter Prescott, "Biography of AAK" (working paper), 15, AP.
25. Geoffrey Hellman, in *POP*, vol. 2, 53; and B. W. Huebsch, in *POP*, vol. 2., 125.

4. A NEW WORLD OUTSIDE HER DOOR

1. AAK, "Recollections of Some Booksellers," *Publishers Weekly*, May 19, 1975.
2. Robert Josephy, interviewed by Susan Sheehan, n.d., AP.
3. Mark Schorer, *Sinclair Lewis: An American Life* (New York: McGraw-Hill, 1961), 309.
4. Cather–5, SS, AP.

5. Catherine Turner, *Marketing Modernism Between the Two World Wars* (Amherst: University of Massachusetts Press, 2003), 87.

6. Amy Root Clements, *The Art of Prestige: The Formative Years at Knopf, 1915–1929* (Amherst: University of Massachusetts Press, 2014), 85–86.

7. Edith Lewis, *Willa Cather Living: A Personal Record* (New York: Alfred A. Knopf, 1953), 108.

8. Ibid., 115–17.

9. Ibid., 116; Peter Prescott's file, about Cather's *One of Ours*; and notes from Geoffrey Hellman, in *POP*, vol. 2, 53.

10. Joseph Lesser, interviewed by Peter Prescott, n.d., AP. Clearly Cather didn't care about the money as much as the praise: she once left a twenty-thousand-dollar royalty check in a bureau drawer for six months until Blanche called her about it.

11. Geoffrey Hellman, in *POP*, vol. 2, 101.

12. Andrea Barnet, *All-Night Party: The Women of Bohemian Greenwich Village and Harlem, 1913–1930* (Chapel Hill, NC: Algonquin Books, 2004), 148.

13. Hermione Lee, *Willa Cather: Double Lives* (New York: Pantheon Books, 1989), 73.

14. G. Thomas Tanselle, "Sinclair Lewis and Floyd Dell: Two Views of the Midwest," *Twentieth-Century Literature* 9, no. 4 (January 1964).

15. Mary Alden Hopkins, "A Boy Who Dreamed," *Publishers Weekly*, December 18, 1920.

16. Ibid.

17. John Tebbel, *A History of Book Publishing in the United States*, vol. 3, *The Golden Age Between Two Wars, 1920–1940* (New York: R. R. Bowker, 1978), 332.

18. Alfred A. Knopf, ed., *The Borzoi 1920: Being a Sort of Record of Five Years' Publishing* (New York: Alfred A. Knopf, 1920), foreword.

19. Ibid.

20. Ibid., postscript.

21. AAK, interviewed by Susan Sheehan, July 5, 1974, AP.

22. Pat Knopf, letter to Peter Prescott, July 18, 1988, AP.

23. Pat Knopf, interviewed by Susan Sheehan, February 21, 1975, AP.

24. AAK notes, n.p., HRC.

25. Schorer, *Sinclair Lewis*, 309.

26. Ibid.

27. Desmond Flower, *Fellows in Foolscap: Memoirs of a Publisher* (London: Robert Hale, 1991), 23.

28. Ronald Hayman, *Thomas Mann: A Biography* (New York: Scribner, 1995), 620.

29. See John C. Thirlwall, *In Another Language: A Record of the Thirty-Year Relationship Between Thomas Mann and His American Translator, Helen Tracy Lowe-Porter* (New York: Alfred A. Knopf, 1966).

30. Ross Wetzsteon, *Republic of Dreams: Greenwich Village: The American Bohemia, 1910–1960* (New York: Simon & Schuster, 2002), 238.

31. Lloyd Morris, *Incredible New York* (New York: Random House, 1951), 337.

32. Ibid.

33. Emily Bernard, *Carl Van Vechten and the Harlem Renaissance: A Portrait in Black and White* (New Haven, CT: Yale University Press, 2012), 12–13.

34. *Along This Way: The Autobiography of James Weldon Johnson* (New York: Viking, 1933), 383.

35. BWK, telegram to AAK at Hotel Blackstone, Chicago, November 30, 1921, AP.
36. Bruce Kellner, *Carl Van Vechten and the Irreverent Decades* (Norman: University of Oklahoma Press, 1968), 136.
37. AAK notes, n.p., HRC.
38. John J. Mullen, interviewed by Susan Sheehan, April 23, 1975, AP.
39. Edwin-2, AP.
40. Pat Knopf, interviewed by Peter Prescott, November 20, 1995, AP.
41. Ibid.
42. William Koshland, interviewed by Susan Sheehan, February 2, 1975, AP.
43. Frances Lindley, interviewed by Susan Sheehan, February 18, 1975, AP.
44. Pat Knopf, interviewed by Peter Prescott, November 20, 1995, AP.
45. Stephanie Coontz, e-mail, November 10, 2012. In response to the author's inquiry about spousal abuse in the twentieth century's early decades, Coontz says, "I am not sure it would be considered normal, but it was embarrassing, especially in respectable circles. And that's a very telling word, right? It was a bad thing, but not normally so outrageous that one would risk confronting it, far less encouraging the woman to leave or sullying the name of an otherwise beloved or simply 'good enough' father."
46. Decades after Blanche's death, her sister-in-law, Mildred Knopf, remarked that "Blanche would only loosen up a show of affection to the dogs, and was never comfortable with demonstrative affection from others . . . as though she didn't think she deserved it." (Mildred Knopf, interviewed by Peter Prescott, n.d., AP.) Her close friends deny such stiffness, and probably Mildred wasn't allowing for Blanche's caution around the Knopfs, where she dared not be herself.
47. Thomas Wentworth Higginson, "Emily Dickinson's Letters," *The Atlantic*, October 1891.

5. WILD SUCCESS

1. BWK letter to H. L. Mencken, March 16, 1923, AP.
2. AAK notes, HRC.
3. Ibid.
4. Ross Wetzsteon, *Republic of Dreams: Greenwich Village; The American Bohemia, 1910–1960* (New York: Simon & Schuster, 2002), xiii.
5. Kahlil Gibran, *The Prophet* (New York: Alfred A. Knopf, 1923), page 11.
6. *The Prophet* consistently ranks in the one hundred overall "Best Sellers" on Amazon.
7. Irving Kolodin, *In Quest of Music: A Journey in Time* (Garden City, NY: Doubleday, 1980), 231.
8. Sylvia Lovegren, *Fashionable Food: Seven Decades of Food Fads* (New York: Macmillan, 1995), 29.
9. Carl Van Vechten, *The Splendid Drunken Twenties: Selections from the Daybooks, 1922–1930*, ed. Bruce Kellner (Urbana: University of Illinois Press, 2003), 97.
10. Undated photographs, #996.0016.0059, HRC.
11. Phyllis C. Robinson, *Willa: The Life of Willa Cather* (Garden City, NY: Doubleday, 1983), 235.

12. John Tebbel, *A History of Book Publishing in the United States*, vol. 3, *The Golden Age Between Two Wars, 1920–1940* (New York: R. R. Bowker, 1978), 29, table 8.

13. Bruce Kellner, *Carl Van Vechten and the Irreverent Decades* (Norman: University of Oklahoma Press, 1968), 149.

14. Ibid.

15. Dorothy Herrmann, *With Malice Toward All: The Quips, Lives and Loves of Some Celebrated 20th-Century American Wits* (New York: Putnam, 1982), 17–18 and 23. Parker probably made the remark to Franklin P. Adams, known for his column "The Conning Tower," syndicated in the *New York Tribune*, *The (New York) World*, the *New York Herald Tribune*, and the *New York Post*.

16. Kellner, *Carl Van Vechten and the Irreverent Decades*, 150.

17. PT6 1923 diary, August and September, AP.

18. Carl Van Vechten, *The Blind Bow-Boy* (New York: Alfred A. Knopf, 1923), 143 and 253.

19. AAK notes, chap. 6, 154; and PT6 1923 diary, August and September, AP.

20. Hess would teach the piano to the jazz player Dave Brubeck's mother, AP.

21. PT6 1923 diary, August and September, AP.

22. Recounted in several places, including Malcolm Gladwell, *The Tipping Point: How Little Things Can Make a Big Difference* (New York: Little, Brown, 2000), 44–45; and Edward Jablonski and Lawrence D. Stewart, *The Gershwin Years: George and Ira* (Garden City, NY: Doubleday, 1958), 247. Leann Swims at Grove Park Inn, Asheville, NC, implies the men kept the visit a secret; e-mail to the author, January 6, 2013.

23. Jablonski and Stewart, *The Gershwin Years*, 247.

24. "Entertaining," mem. 185, quoting AAK, notebook A–K, SS, AP.

25. BWK notes, n.p., HRC.

26. Kellner, *Carl Van Vechten and the Irreverent Decades*, 156–57.

27. Ibid., 156.

28. Ibid., 160–62.

29. Van Vechten, *The Splendid Drunken Twenties*, 220.

30. Beatrice Leval, interviewed by Susan Sheehan, February 6, 1975, AP.

31. Harding Lemay, interviewed by the author (telephone), July 1, 2013.

32. Pat Knopf, letter to Peter Prescott, July 18, 1988, AP. "They had different bedrooms at 1148 Fifth. I was living with my father. I was in his bedroom, with him. I shouldn't tell you."

33. BWK notes, n.p., HRC.

34. Ibid.

35. BWK notes, n.p., AP.

36. BWK notes, n.p., HRC.

37. Ibid.

38. Harry Ellis Dickson, *"Gentlemen, More Dolce, Please!": An Irreverent Memoir of Thirty Years in the Boston Symphony Orchestra* (Boston: Beacon Press, 1969), 40.

39. Abram Chasins, *Leopold Stokowski: A Profile* (New York: Hawthorn, 1979), 70.

40. Gloria Vanderbilt, *It Seemed Important at the Time: A Romance Memoir* (New York: Simon & Schuster, 2004), 51.

41. Chasins, *Leopold Stokowski*, 70.

42. Van Vechten, *The Blind Bow-Boy*, 143.

43. Pat Knopf, interviewed by Susan Sheehan, February 3, 1975, AP.
44. Joseph Lesser, interviewed by Susan Sheehan, May 22, 1976, AP.
45. Irving Kolodin, *In Quest of Music: A Journey in Time* (Garden City, NY: Double-day, 1980), 215–36. Irving Kolodin in his memoir remarked that among Alfred's closest friends were performers, with or without a baton.
46. Scotty Bowers, interviewed by the author, Los Angeles, January 31, 2013.
47. Ruth Levine Nasoff, interviewed by Susan Sheehan, February 3, 1975, AP.
48. Florence Vidor Heifetz, interviewed by Peter Prescott, n.d., AP.
49. Ibid.
50. Kellner, *Carl Van Vechten and the Irreverent Decades*, 194.
51. Ibid., 196.

6. BOOKS OF THE TWENTIES

1. Jeffrey Meyers, *D. H. Lawrence: A Biography* (New York: Knopf, 1990) 296.
2. W. Charles Pilley in *John Bull*, September 17, 1921.
3. BWK, letter to D. H. Lawrence, May 2, 1925, AP.
4. D. H. Lawrence letter to BWK, May 23, 1925, AP.
5. Meyers, *D. H. Lawrence*, 296.
6. John Worthen, *D. H. Lawrence: The Life of an Outsider* (New York: Counterpoint Press, 2007), 379.
7. Clarence Darrow, letter to the Knopfs, January 9, 1925, AP.
8. H. L. Mencken and Sara Haardt Mencken, *Mencken and Sara: A Life in Letters*, ed. Marion Elizabeth Rodgers (New York: McGraw-Hill, 1987), 38.
9. F. Scott Fitzgerald, "Echoes of the Jazz Age," *Scribner's Magazine*, November 1931, 459; and Mencken and Mencken, *Mencken and Sara*, 38.
10. *Letters of Carl Van Vechten*, ed. Bruce Kellner (New Haven, CT: Yale University Press, 1987), 75.
11. Ibid.
12. AAK, interviewed by Susan Sheehan, n.d., AP.
13. File "Koussie to friends—film," SS, AP.
14. Based on Peter Prescott's interviews of AAK's friends, all of whom supported Pat's accounts of going with him to hookers; and on author's interview of Scotty Bowers, who procured women and men for AAK, January 31, 2013, AP.
15. Mary Ellis, *Those Dancing Years: An Autobiography* (London: J. Murray, 1982), 48; and Edwin-2, AP.
16. Bennett Cerf, *At Random: The Reminiscences of Bennett Cerf* (New York: Random House, 1977), 55–56.
17. Marion Elizabeth Rodgers, *Mencken: The American Iconoclast; The Life and Times of the Bad Boy of Baltimore* (Oxford; New York: Oxford University Press, 2005), 215, 288.
18. Terry Teachout, *The Skeptic: A Life of H. L. Mencken* (New York: Harper, 2002); and H. L. Mencken, *A Religious Orgy in Tennessee: A Reporter's Account of the Scopes Monkey Trial*, introduction by Art Winslow (Hoboken, NJ: Melville House, 2006), xvi.
19. Death certificate for Bertha Wolf, June 3, 1925, file no. 15043, State of New York, Department of Health of the City of New York.

20. Ralph Colin, interviewed by Peter Prescott, September 25, 1992, AP.
21. Last Will and Testament of Bertha Wolf, by the legal firm Arnstein and Levy.
22. Ralph Colin, interviewed by Peter Prescott, September 25, 1992, AP.
23. Ibid.
24. Harding Lemay, *Inside, Looking Out: A Personal Memoir by Harding Lemay* (New York: Harper's Magazine Press, 1971), 241.
25. Julia Child, interviewed by Susan Sheehan, n.d., AP.
26. File "A & B," 6, AP.
27. William Koshland, interviewed by Susan Sheehan, February 2, 1975, AP. "[Blanche] had moments of insecurity—professional—she could get very shaky when she got scared. Didn't want Alfred to see [Koshland] was B's man, so Alfred and Pat always cold to him."
28. Francis Brown, interviewed by Susan Sheehan, April 26, 1975, AP.

7. HARLEM

1. Cecelia Garrard, "Man and His Wife Chief Officers in Publishing Firm," *Brooklyn Daily Eagle*, October 18, 1925, 11.
2. Ibid.
3. Ibid.
4. John Tebbell, *A History of Book Publishing in the United States*, vol. 3, *The Golden Age Between Two Wars, 1920–1940* (New York: R. R. Bowker, 1978), 129.
5. Arnold Rampersad, e-mail to the author, January 22, 2015.
6. Langston Hughes, *The Big Sea: An Autobiography* (New York: Alfred A. Knopf, 1940), 272; and Langston Hughes, *The Weary Blues* (New York: Alfred A. Knopf, 1926).
7. Ibid., xxvi, 26.
8. Untitled, 74, AP.
9. Amy Root Clements, *The Art of Prestige: The Formative Years at Knopf, 1915–1929* (Amherst: University of Massachusetts Press, 2014), 76.
10. AAK notes, 198, AP; "Folie de grandeur," AP.
11. "London Office" (working notes), SS, AP.
12. Alice Payne Hackett, *70 Years of Best Sellers, 1895–1965* (New York: R. R. Bowker, 1967), 7.
13. *The New York Times*, February 28, 1926; and *Literary Review*, July 3, 1926.
14. AAK notes, 206, HRC.
15. Notes of Ralph Barton 1, A–G, March 13, 1926, AP.
16. Geoffrey Hellman, *Mrs. de Peyster's Parties, and Other Lively Studies from "The New Yorker"* (New York: Macmillan, 1963), 312.
17. Published in 1927.
18. Clements, *The Art of Prestige*, 76.
19. Nathan Irvin Huggins, *Harlem Renaissance* (New York: Oxford University Press, 1971), 100.
20. AAK notes, 28, AP.
21. Knopf–Mencken correspondence, May 25, 1926, Enoch Pratt Free Library, Baltimore, H. L. Mencken Collection.

22. Edwin Clark, "Carl Van Vechten's Novel of Harlem Negro Life," *The New York Times*, August 22, 1926.
23. Van Vechten file 102ff, 111–12, HRC.
24. Emily Bernard, *Carl Van Vechten and the Harlem Renaissance: A Portrait in Black and White* (New Haven, CT: Yale University Press, 2012), 189, and quoting Czesław Miłosz.
25. Carl Van Vechten, *Nigger Heaven* (New York: Alfred A. Knopf, 1926), book jacket.
26. Ibid., 46–47.
27. Bruce Kellner, *Carl Van Vechten and the Irreverent Decades* (Norman: University of Oklahoma Press, 1968), 139; and Susan Hertog, *Dangerous Ambition: Rebecca West and Dorothy Thompson; New Women in Search of Love and Power* (New York: Ballantine Books, 2011), 13.
28. F. Scott Fitzgerald, *This Side of Paradise* (New York: Charles Scribner's Sons, 1920), 304.

8. MENCKEN

1. H. L. Mencken and Sara Haardt Mencken, *Mencken and Sara: A Life in Letters*, ed. Marion Elizabeth Rodgers (New York: McGraw-Hill, 1987), 276.
2. Michael Boriskin, artistic and executive director, Copland House, Peekskill, N.Y., e-mail to the author, March 13, 2013. Copland would begin lecturing at the New School for Social Research in New York City, continuing for ten years and publishing some of the lectures in his book *What to Listen for in Music* (New York: McGraw-Hill, 1957).
3. Emily Bernard, *Carl Van Vechten and the Harlem Renaissance: A Portrait in Black and White* (New Haven, CT: Yale University Press, 2012), 155.
4. Ibid., 156.
5. Ibid., 155.
6. Ibid., 156.
7. AAK notes, 29, AP.
8. *Dial*, June 1927; Edwin Muir, *The Nation*, July 2, 1927; *Boston Evening Transcript*, May 14, 1927; *The Times Literary Supplement*, July 7, 1927; *Saturday Review of Literature*, July 16, 1927.
9. *Boston Evening Transcript*, September 10, 1927, 2; *The Nation*, October 12, 1927; *The Spectator*, November 19, 1927.
10. Dr. Benjamin Baker, interviewed by Peter Prescott (telephone), July 30, 1991, AP.
11. Warren Sloat, *1929: America Before the Crash* (New York: Macmillan, 1979), 258.
12. H. L. Mencken, letter to BWK, December 30, 1927, Enoch Pratt Free Library, Baltimore, H. L. Mencken Collection.

9. A WELL OF LONELINESS

1. Cathy Henderson and Dave Oliphant, *The Company They Kept: Alfred A. and Blanche W. Knopf, Publishers; An Exhibition Catalog* (Austin: Harry Ransom Humanities Research Center, University of Texas at Austin, 1995), 36.
2. Andrew Klavan, "Review—Books of the Year: Raymond Chandler's Noble Noir," *The Wall Street Journal*, December 14–15, 2013.

3. Maurice Moiseiwitsch, *Moiseiwitsch: Biography of a Concert Pianist* (London: Frederick Muller, 1965), 174.

4. Stephen Parker, "Mary Bancroft: Patient and Spy," *Jungcurrents* (blog), jungcurrents.com/bancroft-sp, February 19, 2011, most of which is taken from Robert Thomas, Jr., "Mary Bancroft Dead at 93; U.S. Spy in World War II," *The New York Times*, January 19, 1997.

5. Carl Van Vechten, *The Splendid Drunken Twenties: Selections from the Daybooks, 1922–1930*, ed. Bruce Kellner (Urbana: University of Illinois Press, 2003), 195, 196–97. After Carl ordered flowers for her, Hergesheimer called him and asked him to get flowers in his name as well. "He is beginning to grate on me," Carl wrote Fania, February 15, 1928.

6. Photograph, February 28, 1928, AP.

7. "BWK as publisher," AP.

8. Amy Root Clements, *The Art of Prestige: The Formative Years at Knopf, 1915–1929* (Amherst: University of Massachusetts Press, 2014), 76.

9. Lovat Dickson, *Radclyffe Hall at the Well of Loneliness: A Sapphic Chronicle* (New York: Scribner, 1975), 146–49.

10. Ransom 9, 2012, Radclyff Hall, HRC.

11. Lisa Cohen, *All We Know: Three Lives* (New York: Farrar, Straus and Giroux, 2012), 400.

12. Charles A. Madison, *Irving to Irving: Author-Publisher Relations, 1800–1974* (New York: R. R. Bowker, 1974), 206.

13. H. L. Mencken, *My Life as Author and Editor*, ed. Jonathan Yardley (New York: Alfred A. Knopf, 1993), 312.

14. BWK notes, 49 Alfred Knopf II, AP.

15. BWK notes, n.p., AP.

16. Angeles "Toni" Pasquale, interviewed by Susan Sheehan, September 24, 1975, AP.

10. HER OWN WOMAN

1. Thomas Alexander Gray, *Elinor Wylie* (New York: Twayne, 1960), 149.

2. Julia Cluck, *Eleanor Wylie's Shelley Obsession* (New York: Modern Language Association of America, 1941), 841–60.

3. Desmond Flower, *Fellows in Foolscap: Memoirs of a Publisher* (London: Robert Hale, 1991), 69.

4. Morris Dallet, letter to AAK, September 23, 1963, AP.

5. Hammett-3, AP.

6. Richard Layman, *Shadow Man: The Life of Dashiell Hammett* (New York: Harcourt Brace Jovanovich, 1981), 91.

7. William F. Nolan, *Hammett: A Life at the Edge* (New York: Congdon & Weed, 1983), 79.

8. Diane Johnson, *Dashiell Hammett: A Life* (New York: Random House, 1983), 73.

9. AAK notes, chap. 12, 186, AP.

10. Peter Prescott's notes on Dashiell Hammett, AP.

11. Sally Cline, *Dashiell Hammett: Man of Mystery* (New York: Arcade, 2014), 45.

12. Ibid., 80.

13. Ibid., 49.

14. Michael Fanning, "André Gide, 'Roman Policier,' Structures of the Crook," *Modern Language Studies* 14, no. 1 (Winter 1984): 47–55.

15. In his book *On Writing*, the novelist Stephen King would laud Hammett's realism; see also "Dashiell Hammett, *The Dain Curse*," *The New York Times*, August 18, 1929.

16. Rebecca West, "Mr. Chesterton in Hysterics," in *The Young Rebecca: Writings of Rebecca West, 1911–17*, ed. Jane Marcus (New York: Viking, 1982), 219.

17. Pat Knopf, letter to Peter Prescott, July 18, 1988, AP.

18. Warren Sloat, *1929: America Before the Crash* (New York: Macmillan, 1979), 258.

19. Carl Van Vechten, *The Letters of Carl Van Vechten*, ed. Bruce Kellner (New Haven, CT: Yale University Press, 1987).

20. Florence Vidor Heifetz, interviewed by Peter Prescott, n.d., AP.

21. Cline, *Dashiell Hammett*, 81.

22. Nolan, *Hammett*, 107.

23. Layman, *Shadow Man*, 97.

24. H. L. Mencken, letter to BWK, April 14, 1927, HRC.

25. H. L. Mencken and Sara Haardt Mencken, *Mencken and Sara: A Life in Letters*, ed. Marion Elizabeth Rodgers (New York: McGraw-Hill, 1987), 56.

26. Ibid.

27. Carl Bode, *Mencken* (Carbondale: Southern Illinois University Press, 1969), 166.

28. Richard R. Lingeman, *Sinclair Lewis: Rebel from Main Street* (New York: Random House, 2002), 364.

29. Sloat, *1929*, 6.

30. Ibid.

II. LOVER

1. H. L. Mencken, *The New Mencken Letters*, ed. Carl Bode (New York: Dial Press, 1977), 248.

2. Robert Nathan, interviewed by Susan Sheehan, circa 1970s, AP.

3. Emily Bernard, *Carl Van Vechten and the Harlem Renaissance: A Portrait in Black and White* (New Haven, CT: Yale University Press, 2012), 213.

4. Blanche-22, AP.

5. A musical evening with Galsworthy, Mem 252 Alfred Music 3, AP.

6. Joseph Blotner, *Faulkner: A Biography* (New York: Random House, 1974), 294.

7. John Kilar, interviewed by Susan Sheehan, n.d., AP.

8. Ibid.

9. Ibid.

10. Craig Claiborne, *An Herb and Spice Cook Book* (New York: Harper & Row, 1963), 175.

11. Amy Root Clements, *The Art of Prestige: The Formative Years at Knopf, 1915–1929* (Amherst: University of Massachusetts Press, 2014), 118.

12. John Kilar, interviewed by Susan Sheehan, n.d., AP.

13. Ibid.

14. Clements, *The Art of Prestige*, 76.

15. Pat Knopf, interviewed by Susan Sheehan, February 21, 1975, AP.

16. Geoffrey Hellman, in *POP*, vol. 2, 91.

17. *The New York Times*, June 14, 1932.
18. Even as late as a *Life* magazine pictorial in 1965, Alfred publicly presented Blanche's authors as his own.

12. BECOMING FREE

1. Anita Block, "Holds Monogamy and Marriage Are Different Institutions," *El Paso Herald-Post*, April 12, 1933.
2. Pat Knopf, interviewed by Susan Sheehan, February 21, 1975, AP. Pat talked to Susan Sheehan about his father's possible amours: "Did you hear about Joan Carr, an English actress? Or Elsa Schiffert? Charlie Denhart is dead, but he was a close confidant of Alfred's. [My father] used to tell me what a marvelous man Charlie was, able to have his own private life, very, very privately. I never questioned it. I never asked what he was talking about. But in those early days in the '30s when he was still living in Purchase, Joan Carr was around all the time, Margery Henley was around all the time, Elsa Schiffert was around all the time."
3. Block, "Holds Monogamy and Marriage Are Different Institutions."
4. BWK, letter to H. L. Mencken, May 31, 1933, AP.
5. Geoffrey Hellman, in *POP*, vol. 2, 91.
6. Pat Knopf, interviewed by Susan Sheehan, February 3, 1975, and February 21, 1975, AP.
7. Hellman, in *POP*, vol. 2, 72.
8. Carl Van Vechten, letter to BWK, October 25, 1933, AP.
9. W. C. Cutting, D. A. Rytand, and M. L. Tainter, "Relationship Between Blood Cholesterol and Increased Metabolism from Dinitrophenol and Thyroid," *Journal of Clinical Investigation* 13, no. 4 (July 1934): 547–52.
10. *Popular Science*, December 1933, n.p.
11. H. L. Mencken, *The American Mercury*, December 1924.
12. "1933" notebook, AP.

13. MONEY PROBLEMS

1. Desmond Flower, *Fellows in Foolscap: Memoirs of a Publisher* (London: Robert Hale, 1991), 264–65. They were joined in 1955 by Robert Giroux, a man of means who "used his consequent freedom of movement for good purpose." Until now, Knopf and Viking, due to Ben Huebsch's European background, had made their lists the top two international ones, but Roger Straus's penchant for international literature quickly made his list a contender.
2. Isaac Anderson, *The New York Times*, January 7, 1934.
3. Peter Quennell, *New Statesman*, May 26, 1934.
4. Diane Johnson, *Dashiell Hammett: A Life* (New York: Random House, 1983), 109–10.
5. Drew Dudley, interviewed by Susan Sheehan, n.d., AP.
6. Geoffrey T. Hellman, *Mrs. de Peyster's Parties and Other Lively Studies from "The New Yorker"* (New York: Macmillan, 1963), 298.
7. BWK, letter to Langston Hughes, n.d., AP.

8. *Letters of Carl Van Vechten*, ed. Bruce Kellner (New Haven, CT: Yale University Press, 1987), 123.
9. Larry Huffman, e-mail to the author, September 8, 2014.
10. Leopold Stokowski, letter to BWK, n.d., AP.
11. Geoffrey T. Hellman, "Publisher: I—A Very Dignified Pavane," *The New Yorker*, November 20, 1948, 105.
12. Book Clubs, 2, A–G, SS, AP.
13. "'Friends of Borzoi Books' to Aid Cause of New Author," *Publishers Weekly*, February 24, 1934.
14. AAK notes, 36, AP.
15. Ibid., financial notes from 1935.
16. Ibid., 55.
17. Ibid., financial notes from 1935.
18. O. H. Cheney, *Economic Survey of the Book Industry, 1930–1931* (New York: R. R. Bowker, 1960), 224. The distribution problems that Cheney identified remain in spite of the radical changes in the industry.
19. AAK notes, financial notes from 1935, AP.
20. BWK, telegram to H. L. Mencken, May 28, 1935, AP.
21. Marion Elizabeth Rogers, *Mencken: The American Iconoclast* (Oxford; New York: Oxford University Press, 2005) 413.
22. H. L. Mencken, telegraph to BWK, May 28, 1935.
23. Ibid., May 29, 1935.
24. Sara Mayfield, *The Constant Circle: H. L. Mencken and His Friends* (New York: Delacorte Press, 1968), 212.
25. *The Diary of H. L. Mencken*, ed. Charles A. Fecher (New York: Alfred A. Knopf, 1989), 93.
26. Ibid., 139.

14. HARBINGERS OF WAR

1. Pat Knopf, interviewed by Peter Prescott, September 11, 1991, AP.
2. Ibid.
3. BWK, letter to H. L. Mencken, October 20, 1931, AP.
4. Joseph Lesser, interviewed by Peter Prescott, September 9, 1995, AP.
5. Pat Knopf, interviewed by Peter Prescott, September 19, 1991, AP.
6. Judith Anderson, interviewed by Peter Prescott, n.d., AP.
7. AAK notes, dated two years earlier, 1937, AP. Gershwin's opera was written with the collaboration of DuBose Heyward, Dorothy Heyward, and Ira Gershwin.
8. H. L. Mencken, *The New Mencken Letters*, ed. Carl Bode (New York: Dial Press, 1977), 367.
9. *The New York Times*, March 1, 1936; *The Saturday Review of Literature*, March 7, 1936; *The Nation*, April 1, 1936.
10. AAK notes, 386, AP.
11. Ibid.
12. William Shirer, interviewed by Peter Prescott, n.d., AP.
13. Quoted in Joseph Nyomarkay, *Charisma and Factionalism in the Nazi Party* (Minneapolis: University of Minnesota Press, 1967), 14.

14. Marion E. Rogers, *Mencken: The American Iconoclast* (Oxford; New York: Oxford University Press, 2005), 394.
15. Pat Knopf, letter to Peter Prescott, July 18, 1988, AP.
16. *The New Mencken Letters*, 401.
17. William Seabrook, *Jungle Ways* (New York: Harcourt, Brace, 1931), 186.
18. *The Diary of H. L. Mencken*, ed. Charles A. Fecher (New York: Alfred A. Knopf, 1989).
19. *Publishers Weekly*, May 8, 1933.
20. Harding Lemay, interviewed by Susan Sheehan, n.d., AP.
21. Malcolm Gladwell, *The Tipping Point: How Little Things Can Make a Big Difference* (New York: Little, Brown, 2000), 44–45.
22. "Books," *Time*, March 23, 1959.
23. *The New Mencken Letters*, 411.
24. Joseph Lesser, interviewed by Susan Sheehan, n.d., AP.
25. William Koshland, interviewed by Peter Prescott, n.d., AP. "Bernie Smith [one of Knopf's earliest and most trusted publicity directors, whom Blanche used for the Dashiell Hammett manuscripts] used to tell me [Koshland] when Alfred and Pat were in the country—women—would service them twice a week."
26. *The New Mencken Letters*, 412.

15. SIGMUND FREUD, THOMAS MANN, AND OTHERS

1. Ronald Hayman, *Thomas Mann: A Biography* (New York: Scribner, 1995), 63–77.
2. Ruth Levine Nasoff, interviewed by Susan Sheehan, September 24, 1975, AP.
3. Mildred Knopf, interviewed by Peter Prescott, n.d., AP.
4. Edwin H. Knopf file, AP.
5. Pat Knopf, interviewed by Susan Sheehan, n.d., AP.
6. Edwin H. Knopf file, AP.
7. Wilmarth Lewis, interviewed by Susan Sheehan, n.d., AP.
8. BWK, letter to Elizabeth Bowen, n.d., AP.
9. Blanche wouldn't be taking another trip on the *Île de France*: on September 1, 1939, Nazi Germany invaded Poland, ending civilian transatlantic traffic. Many luxury liners were converted to transport ships or warships.
10. Bennett Cerf, *At Random: The Reminiscences of Bennett Cerf* (New York: Random House, 1977), 206.
11. Arguably, 2011's Hurricane Irene, which also hit New York, damaged Vermont as badly as the storm of 1938.
12. Blanche would ultimately convince Canfield to write a book for Knopf about the great state of Vermont, published two years later, AP.
13. BWK, letter to Sigmund Freud in London, November 15, 1938, AP.
14. Stephen King, *On Writing: A Memoir of the Craft* (New York: Scribner, 2000).
15. Blanche—larger file, AP.
16. Ruth Levine Nasoff, interviewed by Susan Sheehan, September 24, 1975, AP.
17. Ruth Levine Nasoff, interviewed by Susan Sheehan, July 5, 1974, AP.
18. Harding Lemay, *Inside, Looking Out: A Personal Memoir by Harding Lemay* (New York: Harper's Magazine Press, 1971), 234.
19. Pat Knopf, letter to Peter Prescott, July 18, 1988.

20. Ruth Levine Nasoff, interviewed by Susan Sheehan, September 24, 1975, AP.
21. BWK, telegram to William Shirer, September 29, 1939, HRC.

16. A MAN OF HER OWN

1. Quoted by Jacob Heilbrun, *The New York Times Book Review*, July 28, 2013.
2. AAK notes, 479, HRC; and 1939/22, HRC.
3. Ibid; ibid.
4. Pforzheimer Collection, New York Public Library, www.nypl.org/locations /schwarzman/pforzheimer-collection.
5. Notebook titled "Blanche 10," SS, AP.
6. Laura Jacobs, "The Mark of Mainbocher," *Vanity Fair*, October 2001, 87–90.
7. Notebook titled "Entertaining," A–G, SS, AP.
8. Mildred Knopf, interviewed by Peter Prescott, n.d., AP.
9. June Platt, introduction to Mildred O. Knopf, *The Perfect Hostess Cook Book* (New York: Alfred A. Knopf, 1950).
10. Angeles "Toni" Pasquale, interviewed by Peter Prescott, n.d., AP.
11. Combining what friends and assistants told interviewers after Blanche's death with Blanche's late-life account of her first and memorable affair with a Frenchman at least allows for a bit more resonance. Blanche's anger at Alfred and Sam in the early twenties was said to have inspired an affair, her first, lasting "over several years in Paris," according to Blanche's notes, but the young publisher wasn't yet traveling to Paris by herself. Her story about her Paris devotee in the twenties must have been an amalgam of fantasy and her later years with Hohe, her German amour.
12. Florence Vidor Heifetz, interviewed by Peter Prescott, n.d., AP.
13. Fannie Hurst, *No Food with My Meals* (New York: Harper & Brothers, 1935), 49.
14. Ibid., 31.
15. BWK, letter to Myra Hess, December 23, 1940, AP.
16. Review of W. J. Cash, *The Mind of the South*, *Time*, February 24, 1941, 98.
17. W. J. Cash, *The Mind of the South* (New York: Alfred A. Knopf, 1941), 428.
18. Herbert Mitgang, "Profiles: Helen Wolff," *The New Yorker*, August 2, 1982.
19. AAK notes, 68, Shirer-2, AP.
20. Ibid.
21. AAK notes, 69–70, Shirer-2, AP.
22. William L. Shirer, *Berlin Diary: The Journal of a Foreign Correspondent, 1934–1941* (New York: Alfred A. Knopf, 1941), 350.
23. Carl Becker, *Berlin Diary* book review, *Time*, October 27, 1941; and Clifton Fadiman, "Seven Years," *The New Yorker*, June 21, 1941.
24. William L. Shirer, *Berlin Diary*, 569–74.
25. Notebook titled "Berlin Diary," private collection of Peter Prescott, AP.
26. William Koshland, interviewed by Susan Sheehan, February 2, 1975, AP.
27. Pat Knopf, interviewed by Susan Sheehan, January 3, 1975, AP.
28. H. L. Mencken, *The New Mencken Letters*, ed. Carl Bode (New York: Dial Press, 1977), 490.
29. "Helen Hedrick Knopf, Writer, 92," *The New York Times*, January 17, 1995.

17. GOING OVERSEAS

1. "Clare Boothe Luce Dies at 84: Playwright, Politician, Envoy," *The New York Times*, October 10, 1987.
2. *Kirkus Reviews*, March 31, 1941.
3. Ben Robertson, *I Saw England* (New York: Alfred A. Knopf, 1941), 52.
4. BWK, letter to Ben Robertson, September 25, 1941, HRC.
5. BWK, letter to Ben Robertson, October 20, 1941, HRC.
6. According to U.S. Army World War II enlistment records, 1938–46.
7. Pat Knopf, interviewed by Peter Prescott, September 19, 1989, AP.
8. BWK, letter to Ben Robertson, December 10, 1941, AP.
9. A & B menage—4, AP.
10. Pat Knopf, interviewed by Susan Sheehan, February 3, 1975, and February 21, 1975, AP.
11. William Koshland, interviewed by Susan Sheehan, February 2, 1975, AP.
12. File "Pat 4," 45, AP.
13. Peter Prescott, "Handwritten notes at lunch, Zhang," n.d., AP.
14. Patti Solosky, College Relations, Union College, e-mails to and from the author, August 23, 2013, AP.
15. Pat Knopf, interviewed by Peter Prescott, September 19, 1989, AP.
16. Brooke Kroeger, *Fannie: The Talent for Success of Writer Fannie Hurst* (New York: Times Books, 1999), 297.
17. *The Diary of H. L. Mencken*, ed. Charles A. Fecher (New York: Alfred A. Knopf, 1989), 246.
18. "Dinner at the Hovel," Peter Prescott papers, September 2012, 58, HRC.
19. Blanche Knopf, "An American Publisher Tours South America," *The Saturday Review of Literature*, April 10, 1943.
20. *The Literature of Latin America: A Distinguished List of Books by Latin Americans and About Latin America* (New York: Alfred A. Knopf, 1946).
21. Typed transcript dictated by BWK for her own records, AP. Quotations in the following paragraphs also come from this source.
22. Untitled typed notes of Susan Sheehan, 2, AP.
23. Ruth Levine Nasoff, interviewed by Susan Sheehan, September 24, 1975, AP.
24. Ibid.
25. *The Diary of H. L. Mencken*, 238.
26. Thomas Mann, *The Story of a Novel: The Genesis of "Doctor Faustus"* (New York: Alfred A. Knopf, 1961), 13.
27. Divorce certificate, State of Nevada, January 1943.
28. Walter Benton, *This Is My Beloved* (New York: Alfred A. Knopf, 1943).
29. Joseph Lesser, interviewed by Susan Sheehan, n.d., AP.
30. James D. Hart, *The Popular Book: A History of America's Literary Taste* (Berkeley: University of California Press, 1950), 273.
31. William Koshland, interviewed by Susan Sheehan, February 2, 1975, AP.
32. *The Diary of H. L. Mencken*, 269.
33. Ibid.
34. Frances Lindley, interviewed by Susan Sheehan, February 18, 1975, AP.
35. Ibid.

36. William Koshland, interviewed by Susan Sheehan, February 2, 1975, AP.
37. BWK, notes on 1943 London trip, HRC.
38. Ibid.
39. H. L. Mencken, letter to BWK, October 10, 1943, AP.
40. John F. Stacks, *Scotty: James B. Reston and the Rise and Fall of American Journalism* (Omaha: University of Nebraska Press, 2003), 72.
41. Edward R. Murrow, telegram to BWK and James B. Reston, New York, n.d., HRC.
42. Stacks, *Scotty*, 70.
43. Roosevelt soon dismissed Welles from his post, presumably on the basis of the FBI's dossier on him.
44. BWK, notes on 1943 London trip, HRC.
45. Janet Murrow, interviewed by Susan Sheehan, April 17, 1975, AP.

18. THE WAR'S END

1. Geoffrey T. Hellman, *Mrs. de Peyster's Parties, and Other Lively Studies from "The New Yorker"* (New York: Macmillan, 1963), 278–79.
2. *The Diary of H. L. Mencken*, ed. Charles A. Fecher (New York: Alfred A. Knopf, 1989), 296.
3. "John Hersey," 3, Peter Prescott notes, AP.
4. Pat Knopf, interviewed by Peter Prescott, July 18, 1988, AP.
5. *The Diary of H. L. Mencken*, 316–17. Quotations in the following two paragraphs are from this source.
6. BWK, letter to Jenny Bradley, June 44, 1944, AP.
7. BWK, Peter Prescott collection, AP. Some accounts cite the intimate party occurring when Germany surrendered instead.
8. "Baltimore, September 23, 1944," Peter Prescott notes, AP.
9. Ibid.
10. Vincent Fitzpatrick, interviewed by the author (telephone), August 30, 2013.
11. Bradley, Jenny 2, SS, AP.
12. Ibid.
13. Blanche-16, AP. The anecdote, the speaker anonymous, was repeated by William Shirer.
14. Thanks to Professor Bruce Fleming, U.S. Naval Academy, for his incisive plot summary.
15. BWK, quoted in Richard Oram, "'Publishing Isn't Just About Contacts; It's Equally a Matter of Human Relationships,'" *Cultural Compass* (blog), January 14, 2010, HRC.
16. See Elizabeth Hawes, *Camus: A Romance* (New York: Grove, 2010).
17. N.d., but probably second half of the fifties.
18. Peggy Cullman, interviewed by Susan Sheehan, n.d., AP.
19. See Mann's description of the visit to Mohonk Moutain House on pages 124–31 of Thomas Mann, *The Story of a Novel: The Genesis of "Doctor Faustus"* (New York: Alfred A. Knopf, 1961).
20. Victoria Glendinning, *Elizabeth Bowen: A Biography* (New York: Alfred A. Knopf, 1978), 58.

21. Peggy Cullman, interviewed by Susan Sheehan, early 1980s, AP.
22. Blanche 8, AP.
23. Peggy Cullman, interviewed by Susan Sheehan, early 1980s, AP.
24. Ibid.
25. Quoted in Adam Gopnik, "Facing History: Why We Love Camus," *The New Yorker*, April 9, 2012, 70–76.
26. Gopnik, "Facing History," 71.
27. Ibid.
28. Ibid.
29. Oram, "'Publishing Isn't Just About Contacts; It's Equally a Matter of Human Relationships.'"

19. MORE BATTLES AFTER ALL

1. Pat Knopf 8.12, HRC; Blanche-6, AP.
2. Susan Sheehan interview notes, 1946, Europe, AP.
3. David Sanders, *John Hersey* (New York: Twayne, 1967), 49.
4. John Hersey, *Hiroshima* (New York: Alfred A. Knopf, 1946), 23.
5. Felicity Barringer, "Journalism's Greatest Hits," *The New York Times*, March 1, 1999.
6. William Koshland, interviewed by Susan Sheehan, February 2, 1975, AP.
7. Ruth Levine Nasoff, interviewed by Susan Sheehan, February 3, 1975, AP.
8. BWK, letter to AAK, July 18, 1947, AP.
9. Blanche—physical, AP.
10. A & B merge—4, AP.
11. BWK, letter to Jenny Bradley, circa June 10, 1948, AP.
12. Jackson J. Benson, *Wallace Stegner: His Life and Work* (New York: Viking, 1996). The Knopf book that Alfred and Stegner helped write was *This Is Dinosaur: Echo Park Country and Its Magic Rivers* (New York: Alfred A. Knopf, 1955).
13. Blanche-22, AP.
14. BWK, letter to Jenny Bradley, October 25, 1948, AP.
15. BWK, letter to Bernard Berenson, November 18, 1948, HRC.
16. Bernard Berenson, letter to BWK, November 25, 1948, HRC.
17. Geoffrey T. Hellman, reprinted in *Mrs. de Peyster's Parties, and Other Lively Studies from "The New Yorker"* (New York: Macmillan, 1963), 268.
18. Ibid., 269.
19. Ibid., 271.
20. BWK's seven-page report on her trip to see General Lucius Clay, AP. All further quotations regarding Blanche's diplomatic trip come from this source.

20. THE SECOND SEX

1. Victoria Glendinning, *Elizabeth Bowen: A Biography* (New York: Alfred A. Knopf, 1978), 187.
2. Ibid., 190.
3. BWK, "I Dislike Clutter," *House Beautiful*, January 1949, 88–89.
4. "Ross Macdonald," AP.

5. From trial without jury, Judge Bok, March 18, 1949, Philadelphia County.
6. *Commonwealth v. Gordon et al., the Opinion of Judge Bok, March 18, 1949* (San Francisco: Grabhorn, 1949).
7. AAK, letter to Mary Bancroft, April 25, 1949, AP; Geoffrey T. Hellman, in *POP*, vol. 2, 136.
8. Simon Lea, president of the Camus Society UK, e-mail to the author, October 2, 2013.
9. Notes titled "Blanche 8," AP.
10. BWK letters to Jenny Bradley, October 5, 1949, and October 19, 1949, AP.
11. Bradley, Jenny-bi 5, SS, AP.
12. BWK, letter to Jenny Bradley, October 19, 1949, AP.
13. Jenny Bradley, letter to BWK, November 1949, AP.
14. Notes titled "Beauvoir 1, *The Second Sex*," AP.
15. Beauvoir 2, Susan, A–G, AP.
16. BWK Brad 1/Jenny and Blanche, AP.
17. Frances Lindley, interviewed by Susan Sheehan, February 18, 1975, AP.
18. Ibid.
19. Stanley Kauffmann, "Publishing: Album of the Knopfs," *The American Scholar* 56, no. 3 (Summer 1987): 371–81.
20. A note in Peter Prescott's files (Bradley, Jenny—3, AP) about an interview with Jenny Bradley, confirming that Flanner and Blanche "had an affair."
21. Janet Flanner, interviewed by Susan Sheehan, August 3, 1979, AP; and Peter Prescott's files, 152, AP.
22. Frances Lindley, interviewed by Susan Sheehan, February 18, 1975, AP.
23. BWK, confidential letter to Jenny Bradley, January 27, 1950, AP.
24. Deirdre Bair, *Simone de Beauvoir: A Biography* (New York: Summit Books, 1990), 419; and Elaine Showalter, *Inventing Herself: Claiming a Feminist Intellectual Heritage* (New York: Scribner, 2001), 217.
25. Harold Strauss, letter to Edward R. Murrow, September 18, 1950, AP.
26. Ann Merwin, interviewed by Peter Prescott, in folder "BWK as publisher," n.d., AP.

21. A WEDDING AND OTHER RIBBONS

1. BWK, letter to Elizabeth Bowen, June 18, 1951, AP.
2. Harding Lemay, e-mail to the author, October 12, 2013; and Harding Lemay, *Inside, Looking Out: A Personal Memoir by Harding Lemay* (New York: Harper's Magazine Press, 1971), 245.
3. File "'Koussie' to friends—film" (Serge Koussevitsky), SS, AP.
4. Dwight Eisenhower, letter to BWK from SHAPE, July 1951, AP.
5. Blanche-8, AP.
6. Shirley Chidney, interviewed by Peter Prescott, n.d., AP. Quotations in the following two paragraphs are also from this source.
7. Grace Dadd, interviewed by Peter Prescott, n.d., AP.
8. Frances Lindley, interviewed by Susan Sheehan, February 18, 1975, AP.
9. Mem 946, AP.
10. Ibid.

11. William Koshland, interviewed by Susan Sheehan, February 2, 1975, AP.
12. Betsy Johnson, interviewed by Peter Prescott, October 27, 1990, AP.
13. Pat Knopf, interviewed by Peter Prescott, September 11, 1991; November 18, 1991; and November 21, 1991, AP; also by Susan Sheehan, February 3, 1975, AP.
14. Pat Knopf, interviewed by Susan Sheehan, February 21, 1975, AP.
15. Peter Prescott, "Handwritten notes at lunch, Zhang," n.d., AP.
16. Ibid.
17. Harding Lemay, interviewed by Susan Sheehan regarding Frances Lindley and Blanche, n.d., AP.
18. Ibid.
19. Beauvoir's biographer Deirdre Bair generously responded concerning Beauvoir's book and its translation.
20. Ashley Montagu, letter to the Knopf publicist William Cole, used on the first-edition book jacket, December 11, 1952.
21. Philip Wylie, "A SR Panel Takes Aim at 'The Second Sex,'" *The Saturday Review*, February 21, 1953.
22. Ibid.
23. Elaine Showalter, *Inventing Herself: Claiming a Feminist Intellectual Heritage* (New York: Scribner, 2001), 216.
24. Arnold Rampersad, *The Life of Langston Hughes*, vol. 2, *1941–1967: I Dream a World* (New York: Oxford University Press, 1988), 215–18.
25. Ibid., 219.
26. Ibid.
27. Ibid.
28. John C. Thirlwall, *In Another Language: A Record of the Thirty-Year Relationship Between Thomas Mann and His American Translator, Helen Tracy Lowe-Porter* (New York: Alfred A. Knopf, 1966), 139.
29. "FBI: See also Civil Service Commission," SS, AP.
30. "Jascha Heifetz Leaves Israel; Cancels Concerts in Tel Aviv," Jewish Telegraphic Agency, April 20, 1953, www.jta.org/1953/04/20/archive/jascha-heifetz-leaves-israel-cancels-concert-in-tel-aviv#ixzz31dVKbAI8n.
31. *The New York Times*, May 31, 1953; and *The Saturday Review*, June 27, 1953.
32. Philip Vaudrin, memo to BWK, April 22, 1952, AP; and BWK, letter to James Baldwin, April 28, 1952, AP.
33. Philip Vaudrin, letter to James Baldwin, November 26, 1952, AP.
34. Philip Vaudrin, letter to James Baldwin, December 12, 1952, AP.
35. Peter Prescott file "James Baldwin," AP.
36. *The New Republic*, June 22, 1953; and *The New Yorker*, November 7, 1953.
37. File "A & B," 6, AP.
38. Ibid.
39. Mildred Knopf, interviewed by Susan Sheehan, n.d., AP.
40. Pat Knopf, letter to Peter Prescott, top of untitled page "Robert Lusty," AP.
41. Story told by Alex Lichine to Pat Knopf, repeated to Susan Sheehan, AP; and Blanche-15, AP.
42. Wallace Stevens and Holly Stevens, *Letters of Wallace Stevens* (New York: Alfred A. Knopf, 1966), 846; Joan Richardson, *Wallace Stevens, a Biography: The Later Years, 1923–1955* (New York: Beech Tree Books, 1988), 4; and Peter

Brazeau, *Parts of a World: Wallace Stevens Remembered* (New York: Random House, 1983). Holly Stevens explains that while the *Collected Poems* were supposed to have been published on Stevens's seventy-fifth birthday, October 2, 1954, they were officially published one day earlier, on October 1, because the second was a Saturday. The note doesn't say whether the party Knopf threw for Stevens's birthday was also on that Friday or on Saturday. In her biography, Joan Richardson claims that it was on Friday, too. In his letters, Stevens doesn't seem to distinguish between the date of publication and that of the party, so they were probably both on October 1. Peter Brazeau, in *Parts of a World*, 416, says the luncheon to celebrate the publication of *Collected Poems* was held on October 1, 1954.

43. Brazeau, *Parts of a World*, 195–96.
44. 167, AP.
45. Joseph Lesser, interviewed by Susan Sheehan, March 22–25, 1976, AP.
46. John Tebbel, *Between Covers: The Rise and Transformation of Book Publishing in America* (New York: Oxford University Press, 1987), 398.
47. Pat Knopf, interviewed by Susan Sheehan, February 21, 1975, AP.
48. AAK, interviewed by Susan Sheehan, July 27, 1973, AP.

22. NEW TERRITORIES

1. Dogs—Jon Godden, May 19, 1961, AP.
2. Ibid.
3. Ibid.
4. *Publishers Weekly*, April 2, 1955.
5. Norman Mailer, letter to AAK and BWK, n.d., AP.
6. Pat Knopf, interviewed by Susan Sheehan, February 2, 1975, AP.
7. AAK notes, National Parks, 5, AP.
8. March 11, 1956, Mencken, Peter Prescott collection, AP.
9. Blanche-3, AP.
10. Ibid.
11. Paul Gallico, "You Don't Know How Lucky You Are to Be Married," *Reader's Digest*, July 1956.
12. National Parks, AP.
13. Dr. A. M. Mortensen, interviewed by Susan Sheehan, May 17, 1974, AP.
14. AAK notes, account of trip with the Herseys, 1956—Blanche 1, AP.
15. Ibid.
16. Ibid.
17. Ibid.
18. Ibid.
19. AAK, letter to F. P. Griffiths, November 9, 1956, AP.
20. AAK, interviewed by Peter Prescott, November 9, 1956; "mem 1956/16f," AP.
21. *The Borzoi Quarterly* 15, no. 3 (1966): 9.
22. Simon Lea, president of the Camus Society UK, e-mail to the author, November 19, 2013.
23. Farrar, Straus & Giroux, Inc., Manuscripts and Archives Division, New York Public Library, folder 10, box 203.

24. Jenny Bradley, letter to BWK, Bradley-4, n.d., AP.
25. BWK, letter to Jenny Bradley, Bradley-4, n.d., AP.
26. AAK, interviewed by Susan Sheehan, July 25, 1974, AP.
27. Albert Camus, AP.
28. Simon Lea, e-mail to the author, November 19, 2013.
29. Albert Camus's Nobel Prize acceptance speech, City Hall, Stockholm, December 10, 1957.
30. Judith Jones, e-mail to the author, October 6, 2013.
31. Howard Kaminsky, interviewed by the author, May 5, 2014; and Daniel Okrent, e-mail to the author, May 18, 2014.
32. Harding Lemay, interviewed by the author, August 28, 2012.
33. BWK, letter to Jenny Bradley, September 14, 1959, AP.
34. Scotty Bowers, *Full Service: My Adventures in Hollywood and the Secret Sex Lives of the Stars* (New York: Grove Press, 2012).
35. Scotty Bowers, interviewed by the author (telephone), May 5, 2012.
36. Scotty Bowers, interviewed by the author (telephone), May 6, 2012.
37. Scotty Bowers, interviewed by the author (telephone), January 31, 2013.

23. A SON'S DEFECTION

1. Harding Lemay, interviewed by the author, New York, August 28, 2012.
2. Harding Lemay, *Inside, Looking Out: A Personal Memoir by Harding Lemay* (New York: Harper's Magazine Press, 1971), 237.
3. Al Silverman, *The Time of Their Lives: The Golden Age of Great American Publishers, Their Editors and Authors* (New York: Truman Talley Books, 2008), 94.
4. Hiram Haydn, *Words & Faces: An Intimate Chronicle of Book and Magazine Publishing* (New York: Harcourt Brace Jovanovich, 1974), 110–11.
5. Frances Lindley, interviewed by Susan Sheehan, February 18, 1975, AP.
6. Pat & Atheneum—2, 57, AP.
7. Ibid.
8. Robert Nathan, 3, AP.
9. Pat Knopf, interviewed by Peter Prescott, September 25, 1992, AP.
10. *As Always, Julia: The Letters of Julia Child and Avis DeVoto: Food, Friendship and the Making of a Masterpiece*, ed. Joan Reardon (Boston: Houghton Mifflin, 2010), 325.
11. Frances Lindley, interviewed by Susan Sheehan, February 18, 1975, AP.
12. 53, AP.
13. Arnold Rampersad, *The Life of Langston Hughes*, vol. 2, *1941–1967: I Dream a World* (New York: Oxford University Press, 1988), 295.
14. Ibid.
15. Ibid., 296, 299.
16. BWK, letter to Jenny Bradley, July 17, 1959, National Parks—2, AP.
17. Wayne S. Kerwood, interviewed by Peter Prescott, n.d., AP.
18. Blanche-22, Peter Prescott collection, AP.
19. Alice Y. Kaplan, *Dreaming in French: The Paris Years of Jacqueline Bouvier Kennedy, Susan Sontag, and Angela Davis* (Chicago: University of Chicago Press, 2012), 133–34.
20. Ibid., 178–79.

21. The Beinecke Rare Book & Manuscript Library at Yale can find no record of Alfred's offer.
22. Michael Winship, graduate students' publications, 27, HRC.
23. Stephen Bayley, unpublished essay, June 2011, courtesy of the author.
24. Harding Lemay, interviewed by Susan Sheehan, February 1, 1975, AP.
25. Elizabeth Bowen, draft in Bowen file, BWK, HRC.
26. Bennett Cerf/Klopfer, AP.
27. *Publishers Weekly*, 1966, AP.
28. Witter Bynner 6, 1981.
29. Donald Klopfer, interviewed by Susan Sheehan, February 3, 1975, AP. The following three paragraphs also rely on this source.
30. Robert Lusty, *Bound to Be Read* (Garden City, NY: Doubleday, 1976), 137.
31. AAK notes, March 25, 1963, AP.
32. Thanks to Professor Bruce Fleming of the United States Naval Academy, Annapolis, for confirming these details.
33. Blanche-5, AP.
34. Blanche-10, AP.
35. Allen Dulles, letter to BWK, spring 1961, Princeton University education archives.
36. James Kelly, "You Say Prescriptive, I Say Proper," *The Wall Street Journal*, October 5, 2012.
37. Alice Payne Hackett, *70 Years of Best Sellers, 1895–1965* (New York: R. R. Bowker, 1967), 21.
38. Desmond Flower, *Fellows in Foolscap: Memoirs of a Publisher* (London: Robert Hale, 1991), 360.
39. William Koshland, interviewed by Susan Sheehan, February 2, 1975, AP.
40. Harding Lemay, interviewed by Susan Sheehan, February 1, 1975, AP.
41. Harriet de Onís, letter to BWK, November 4, 1961, AP.
42. BWK, letter to AAK, February 8, 1962, AP.
43. Ibid.
44. Ibid.
45. Blanche—physical, AP.
46. John Hersey, interviewed by Susan Sheehan, n.d., AP.
47. BWK, letter to AAK, September 21, 1962, AP.

24. NO MORE DEALS

1. Arnold Rampersad, *The Life of Langston Hughes*, vol. 2, *1941–1967: I Dream a World* (New York: Oxford University Press, 1988), 356.
2. BWK, letter to AAK, February 8, 1962, AP.
3. BWK, letter to Scotty Reston, December 20, 1962, AP; and Scotty Reston letter to BWK, n.d., AP.
4. Lyonel Nelson, letter to the author, December 5, 2013, AP.
5. Muriel Spark, letter to BWK, May 2, 1963, AP.
6. Pat Knopf, interviewed by Susan Sheehan, February 21, 1975, AP.
7. Stanley Kauffmann, "Publishing: Album of the Knopfs," *The American Scholar* 56, no. 3 (Summer 1987): 371–81.

8. Ibid.
9. Harding Lemay, *Inside, Looking Out: A Personal Memoir by Harding Lemay* (New York: Harper's Magazine Press, 1971), 243–44.
10. Ibid.
11. Ibid., 245.
12. Ibid., 247.
13. BWK, letter to Muriel Spark, March 1963, AP.
14. BWK, letter to Muriel Spark, March 17, 1963, AP.
15. BWK, letter to Muriel Spark, May 1963, AP.
16. AAK, letter to Edwin Knopf, September 20, 1963, AP.
17. Harding Lemay, interviewed by the author, New York, n.d., discussing Virgilia Peterson.
18. Virgilia Peterson, "Few Were More Delightful, Lovely or Savage: *The Girls of Slender Means* by Muriel Spark," *The New York Times*, September 15, 1963.
19. AAK, interviewed by Susan Sheehan, 1975, AP.
20. Joseph Lesser, interviewed by Peter Prescott, n.d., AP.
21. BWK, telegram to Muriel Spark, March 27, 1964, AP.
22. BWK, letter to Scotty Reston, September 2, 1964, AP.
23. Orville Prescott, "Return of the Hawkes Family," *The New York Times*, November 11, 1964.
24. Dogs—Jon Godden, May 19, 1961, AP; and Blanche larger file, AP.
25. Joseph Lesser, interviewed by Susan Sheehan, March 22–25, 1976, AP; quoted Grace Dadd, Eleanor French, and AAK.
26. Rampersad, *The Life of Langston Hughes*, vol. 2, 382.
27. BWK, letter to Muriel Spark, December 31, 1964, AP.
28. *Publishers Weekly*, February 1, 1965.
29. BWK, letter to Muriel Spark, March 30, 1965, AP.
30. Ibid.
31. Doris Grumbach, "*The Mandelbaum Gate*," *America* 113, no. 17 (October 23, 1965): 474.
32. *Newsweek*, May 17, 1965.
33. David R. Johnson, *Conrad Richter: A Writer's Life* (University Park: Pennsylvania State University Press, 2001), 346.
34. "Some Reminiscences About Their Illustrious Roster of Authors," *Life*, July 23, 1965.
35. BWK, letter to Jascha Heifetz, August 2, 1965, AP.
36. Blanche—physical, AP.
37. Ibid.
38. Ibid.
39. A & B menage—4, AP.
40. Coronary 1965 Ref 74T8:8, AP.
41. Blanche—physical, AP.
42. Pat Knopf, interviewed by Susan Sheehan, February 21, 1975, AP.
43. AAK notes, HRC.
44. Harding Lemay, e-mail to the author, June 4, 2014.
45. Knopf press release, January 11, 1966. Currently Random House is the corporate umbrella for more than one hundred publishing imprints. After RCA sold it

to the Newhouse group in 1980, it was traded to the German media company Bertelsmann for $1.4 billion in 1998. Most recently, in 2013, the conglomerate Penguin Random House became a reality.

46. AAK notes, AP.

47. Lyonel Nelson, e-mail correspondence with the author, July 27, 2013.

48. Lyonel Nelson, *From Farm to Fifth Avenue: How I Became a Stylist to the Rich and Famous at the World's Most Exclusive Salon* (CreateSpace, 2014).

49. Ibid.

50. Lyonel Nelson, e-mail to the author, August 25, 2013.

51. William Koshland, interviewed by Peter Prescott, n.d., AP.

52. Stanley Kauffman, "Publishing: Album of the Knopfs," *The American Scholar*, vol. 56, no. 3 (Summer 1987): 371–81.

53. Angeles "Toni" Pasquale, interviewed by Peter Prescott, n.d., AP.

54. Harding Lemay, interviewed by Susan Sheehan, February 1, 1975, AP; and e-mail to the author, August 28, 2012.

55. BWK, letter to Mainbocher, April 29, 1966, AP.

56. Harding Lemay, interviewed by Susan Sheehan, February 1, 1975, AP; and file "A & B," 6, AP.

57. Joseph Lesser, interviewed by Susan Sheehan, March 22–25, 1976, AP.

58. Muriel Spark, interviewed by Susan Sheehan, November 23, 1974, AP.

59. Joseph Lesser, interviewed by Susan Sheehan, March 22–25, 1976, AP.

60. Muriel Spark, interviewed by Susan Sheehan, November 23, 1974, AP, copied here from Martin Stannard, *Muriel Spark: The Biography* (New York: W. W. Norton, 2010), 281–82.

61. Harding Lemay, e-mail to the author, August 26, 2012.

62. BWK's will, 10, AP.

63. Joseph Epstein, e-mail to the author, July 15, 2014.

64. Pat Knopf, interviewed by Peter Prescott, July 18, 1988, AP.

65. Harding Lemay, interviewed by the author, April 5, 2012.

66. Pat Knopf, interviewed by Peter Prescott, September 19, 1989, AP.

67. "Anniversary," AP.

68. *The Borzoi Quarterly* 15, no. 3 (1966).

69. Ibid.

EPILOGUE

1. Helen Knopf—2, AP.

2. W. H. Ferry, interviewed by Susan Sheehan, February 21, 1975, AP.

SELECTED BIBLIOGRAPHY

Allen, Frederick Lewis. *The Big Change: America Transforms Itself, 1900–1950*. New York: Harper, 1952.

Ballou, Ellen B. *The Building of the House: Houghton Mifflin's Formative Years*. Boston: Houghton Mifflin, 1970.

Barnet, Andrea. *All-Night Party: The Women of Bohemian Greenwich Village and Harlem, 1913–1930*. Chapel Hill, NC: Algonquin Books, 2004.

Beauvoir, Simone de. *The Blood of Others*. Translated by Roger Senhouse and Yvonne Moyse. New York: Pantheon Books, 1983.

———. *The Second Sex*. Translated and edited by H. M. Parshley. New York: Alfred A. Knopf, 1993.

Bell, Millicent. *Marquand: An American Life*. Boston: Little, Brown, 1979.

Berg, A. Scott. *Max Perkins: Editor of Genius*. New York: E. P. Dutton, 1978.

Bernard, Emily. *Carl Van Vechten and the Harlem Renaissance: A Portrait in Black and White*. New Haven, CT: Yale University Press, 2012.

Birkett, Jennifer. *Margaret Storm Jameson: A Life*. Oxford: Oxford University Press, 2009.

Birmingham, Stephen. *The Late John Marquand: A Biography*. Philadelphia: Lippincott, 1972.

Blotner, Joseph. *Faulkner: A Biography*. New York: Random House, 1974.

Boyer, Paul S. *Purity in Print: The Vice-Society Movement and Book Censorship in America*. New York: Scribner, 1968.

Bruccoli, Matthew J. *The Fortunes of Mitchell Kennerley, Bookman*. San Diego: Harcourt Brace Jovanovich, 1986.

————, ed. *A Life in Letters: F. Scott Fitzgerald*. New York: Simon & Schuster, 1994.

Bruccoli, Matthew J., and Richard Layman. *Hardboiled Mystery Writers: Raymond Chandler, Dashiell Hammett, Ross Macdonald; A Literary Reference*. New York: Carroll & Graf, 2002.

Butcher, Fanny. *Many Lives—One Love*. New York: Harper & Row, 1972.

Cain, James M. *The Butterfly*. New York: Alfred A. Knopf, 1947.

————. *The Embezzler*. New York: Alfred A. Knopf, 1943.

————. *Galatea*. New York: Alfred A. Knopf, 1953.

————. *Love's Lovely Counterfeit*. New York: Alfred A. Knopf, 1942.

————. *Mildred Pierce*. New York: Alfred A. Knopf, 1941.

————. *The Moth*. New York: Alfred A. Knopf, 1948.

————. *Our Government*. New York: Alfred A. Knopf, 1930.

————. *Past All Dishonor*. New York: Alfred A. Knopf, 1946.

————. *The Postman Always Rings Twice*. New York: Alfred A. Knopf, 1934.

————. *Three of a Kind*. New York: Alfred A. Knopf, 1943.

Camus, Albert. Translated by Stuart Gilbert. *Caligula & Three Other Plays*. New York: Alfred A. Knopf, 1958.

————. *Exile and the Kingdom*. Translated by Justin O'Brien. New York: Alfred A. Knopf, 1958.

————. *The Fall*. Translated by Justin O'Brien. New York: Alfred A. Knopf, 1957.

————. *The First Man*. Translated by David Hapgood. New York: Alfred A. Knopf, 1995.

————. *A Happy Death*. Translated by Richard Howard. New York: Alfred A. Knopf, 1972.

————. *Lyrical and Critical Essays*. Edited by Philip M. W. Thody, translated by Ellen Conroy Kennedy. New York: Alfred A. Knopf, 1968.

————. *The Myth of Sisyphus, and Other Essays*. Translated by Justin O'Brien. New York: Alfred A. Knopf, 1955.

————. *Notebooks*. Translated by Philip M. W. Thody and Justin O'Brien. New York: Alfred A. Knopf, 1963.

————. *The Plague*. Translated by Stuart Gilbert. New York: Alfred A. Knopf, 1948.

————. *The Possessed: A Play in Three Parts*. Translated by Justin O'Brien. New York: Alfred A. Knopf, 1960.

————. *The Rebel: An Essay on Man in Revolt*. Translated by Anthony Bower. New York: Alfred A. Knopf, 1956.

————. *Resistance, Rebellion, and Death*. Translated by Justin O'Brien. New York: Alfred A. Knopf, 1961.

————. *The Stranger*. Translated by Justin O'Brien. New York: Alfred A. Knopf, 1946.

————. *Youthful Writings*. Translated by Ellen Conroy Kennedy. New York: Alfred A. Knopf, 1976.

Caro, Robert A. *The Power Broker: Robert Moses and the Fall of New York*. New York: Alfred A. Knopf, 1974.

Cather, Willa. *April Twilights, and Other Poems*. New York: Alfred A. Knopf, 1923.

————. *Death Comes for the Archbishop*. New York: Alfred A. Knopf, 1927.

————. *A Lost Lady*. New York: Alfred A. Knopf, 1973.

————. *Lucy Gayheart*. New York: Alfred A. Knopf, 1935.

————. *My Ántonia*. New York: Houghton Mifflin, 1918.

———. *My Mortal Enemy*. New York: Alfred A. Knopf, 1926.

———. *Not Under Forty*. New York: Alfred A. Knopf, 1936.

———. "The Novel Démeublé." *The New Republic*, April 1922, suppl.: 5–6. Reprinted in *Not Under Forty*. New York: Alfred A. Knopf, 1936.

———. *Obscure Destinies*. New York: Alfred A. Knopf, 1932.

———. *The Old Beauty, and Others*. New York: Alfred A. Knopf, 1948.

———. *One of Ours*. New York: Alfred A. Knopf, 1922.

———. "On the Art of Fiction." In Knopf, *The Borzoi 1920*. Reprinted in *Willa Cather, On Writing*. New York: Alfred A. Knopf, 1949.

———. *On Writing: Critical Studies on Writing as an Art*. New York: Alfred A. Knopf, 1949.

———. *O Pioneers!* New York: Houghton Mifflin, 1913.

———. "Portrait of the Publisher as a Young Man." In Rogers. *Alfred A. Knopf*.

———. *The Professor's House*. New York: Alfred A. Knopf, 1925.

———. *Sapphira and the Slave Girl*. New York: Alfred A. Knopf, 1940.

———. *Shadows on the Rock*. New York: Alfred A. Knopf, 1931.

———. *Youth and the Bright Medusa*. New York: Alfred A. Knopf, 1920.

Cather, Willa, Andrew Jewell, and Janis P. Stout. *The Selected Letters of Willa Cather*. New York: Alfred A. Knopf, 2013.

Cerf, Bennett. *At Random: The Reminiscences of Bennett Cerf*. New York: Random House, 2002.

Cerf, Bennett, and Donald Klopfer. *Dear Donald, Dear Bennett: The Wartime Correspondence of Bennett Cerf and Donald Klopfer*. New York: Random House, 2002.

Chandler, Raymond. *The Big Sleep*. New York: Alfred A. Knopf, 1966.

———. *Collected Stories*. New York: Alfred A. Knopf, 2002.

———. *Farewell, My Lovely*. New York: Alfred A. Knopf, 1945.

———. *The High Window*. New York: Vintage Books, 1976.

———. *The Lady in the Lake*. New York: Garland, 1976.

———. *Trouble Is My Business*. New York: Vintage, 1988.

Chasins, Abram. *Leopold Stokowski: A Profile*. New York: Hawthorn Books, 1979.

Cheney, O. H. *Economic Survey of the Book Industry, 1930–1931*. New York: R. R. Bowker, 1960.

Claiborne, Craig. *An Herb and Spice Cook Book*. New York: Harper & Row, 1963.

Clements, Amy Root. *The Art of Prestige: The Formative Years at Knopf, 1915–1929*. Amherst: University of Massachusetts Press, 2014.

Cohen, Lisa. *All We Know: Three Lives*. New York: Farrar, Straus and Giroux, 2012.

Daniel, Oliver. *Stokowski: A Counterpoint of View*. New York: Dodd, Mead, 1982.

Dell, Floyd. *The Briary-Bush*. New York: Alfred A. Knopf, 1921.

———. *Janet March*. New York: Alfred A. Knopf, 1923.

———. *King Arthur's Socks and Other Village Plays*. New York: Alfred A. Knopf, 1922.

———. *Looking at Life*. New York: Alfred A. Knopf, 1924.

———. *Moon-Calf*. New York: Alfred A. Knopf, 1920.

———. *Runaway*. New York: Alfred A. Knopf, 1925.

———. *This Mad Ideal*. New York: Alfred A. Knopf, 1925.

———. *Were You Ever a Child*. New York: Alfred A. Knopf, 1919.

Dellheim, Charles. "A Fragment of a Heart in the Knopf Archives." *Chronicle of Higher Education* 45, no. 45 (July 16, 1999): B4.

Dickson, Harry Ellis. *"Gentlemen, More Dolce, Please!": An Irreverent Memoir of Thirty Years in the Boston Symphony Orchestra*. Boston: Beacon Press, 1969.

Dickson, Lovat. *Radclyffe Hall at the Well of Loneliness: A Sapphic Chronicle*. New York: Scribner, 1975.

Eliot, Simon, and Jonathan Rose, eds. *A Companion to the History of the Book*. Malden, MA: Blackwell, 2007.

Eliot, T. S. *Ezra Pound: His Metric and Poetry*. New York: Alfred A. Knopf, 1917.

——. *The Sacred Wood: Essays on Poetry and Criticism*. New York: Alfred A. Knopf, 1930.

Ellis, Edward Robb. *The Epic of New York City*. New York: Carroll & Graf, 2005.

Ellis, Mary. *Those Dancing Years: An Autobiography*. London: J. Murray, 1982.

Fitzgerald, F. Scott. *A Life in Letters*. Edited by Matthew J. Bruccoli. New York: Scribner, 1994.

Flower, Desmond. *Fellows in Foolscap: Memoirs of a Publisher*. London: Robert Hale, 1991.

Freud, Sigmund. *Moses and Monotheism*. New York: Alfred A. Knopf, 1939.

Gallico, Paul. *The Abandoned*. New York: Alfred A. Knopf, 1950.

——. *Adventures of Hiram Holliday*. New York: Alfred A. Knopf, 1939.

——. *Confessions of a Story Writer*. New York: Alfred A. Knopf, 1946.

——. *Farewell to Sport*. New York: Alfred A. Knopf, 1938.

——. *The Lonely*. New York: Alfred A. Knopf, 1949.

——. *The Secret Front*. New York: Alfred A. Knopf, 1940.

——. *The Snow Goose*. New York: Alfred A. Knopf, 1941.

——. *Trial by Terror*. New York: Alfred A. Knopf, 1952.

Gardner, Virginia. *"Friend and Lover": The Life of Louise Bryant*. New York: Horizon, 1982.

Gibran, Kahlil. *The Earth Gods*. New York: Alfred A. Knopf, 1931.

——. *The Forerunner, His Parables and Poems*. New York: Alfred A. Knopf, 1920.

——. *The Garden of the Prophet*. New York: Alfred A. Knopf, 1933.

——. *Jesus the Son of Man*. New York: Alfred A. Knopf, 1928.

——. *The Madman, His Parables and Poems*. New York: Alfred A. Knopf, 1918.

——. *Nymphs of the Valley*. Translated by H. M. Nahmad. New York: Alfred A. Knopf, 1948.

——. *The Prophet*. New York: Alfred A. Knopf, 1923.

——. *Sand and Foam: A Book of Aphorisms*. New York: Alfred A. Knopf, 1926.

——. *Spirits Rebellious*. New York: Alfred A. Knopf, 1948.

——. *A Tear and a Smile*. New York: Alfred A. Knopf, 1950.

——. *The Wanderer, His Parables and His Sayings*. New York: Alfred A. Knopf, 1932.

Glasgow, Ellen A. G. *Perfect Companionship: Ellen Glasgow's Selected Correspondence with Women*. Edited by Pamela R. Matthews. Charlottesville: University of Virginia Press, 2005.

Glendinning, Victoria. *Rebecca West: A Life*. New York: Alfred A. Knopf, 1987.

——. *Elizabeth Bowen: A Biography*. New York: Alfred A. Knopf, 1978.

Greenblatt, Stephen. *The Swerve: How the World Became Modern*. New York: W. W. Norton, 2011.

Hackett, Alice Payne. *70 Years of Best Sellers, 1895–1965*. New York: R. R. Bowker, 1967.

Hawes, Elizabeth. *Camus: A Romance.* New York: Grove, 2009.

Haydn, Hiram. *Words & Faces: An Intimate Chronicle of Book and Magazine Publishing.* New York: Harcourt Brace Jovanovich, 1974.

Hayes, Helen, and Anita Loos. *Twice Over Lightly: New York Then and Now.* New York: Harcourt Brace Jovanovich, 1972.

Hellman, Geoffrey T. *AAK: A Profile.* New York: privately printed, 1952.

———. "Publisher" (three-part series), *The New Yorker*: "I—A Very Dignified Pavane," November 20, 1948, 44–57; "II—Flair Is the Word," November 27, 1948, 36–52; "III—The Pleasures, Prides, and Cream," December 4, 1948, 40–53.

Henderson, Cathy, and Dave Oliphant. *The Company They Kept: Alfred A. and Blanche W. Knopf, Publishers: An Exhibition Catalog.* Austin: Harry Ransom Humanities Research Center, University of Texas at Austin, 1995.

Henderson, Cathy, and Richard Oram. *The House of Knopf.* The Dictionary of Literary Biography 355. Detroit: Gale, 2010.

Hergesheimer, Joseph. *Balisand.* New York: Alfred A. Knopf, 1924.

———. *Berlin.* New York: Alfred A. Knopf, 1932.

———. *The Bright Shawl.* New York: Alfred A. Knopf, 1922.

———. *Cytherea.* New York: Alfred A. Knopf, 1922.

———. *The Foolscap Rose.* New York: Alfred A. Knopf, 1934.

———. *From an Old House.* New York: Alfred A. Knopf, 1925.

———. *Gold and Iron.* New York: Alfred A. Knopf, 1918.

———. *The Happy End.* New York: Alfred A. Knopf, 1919.

———. *Java Head.* New York: Alfred A. Knopf, 1919.

———. *The Limestone Tree.* New York: Alfred A. Knopf, 1931.

———. *Linda Condon.* New York: Alfred A. Knopf, 1919.

———. *Mountain Blood.* New York: Alfred A. Knopf, 1919.

———. *The Party Dress.* New York: Alfred A. Knopf, 1930.

———. *The Presbyterian Child.* New York: Alfred A. Knopf, 1923.

———. *Quiet Cities.* New York: Alfred A. Knopf, 1928.

———. *Swords & Roses.* New York: Alfred A. Knopf, 1929.

———. *Tampico.* New York: Alfred A. Knopf, 1926.

———. *The Three Black Pennys.* New York: Alfred A. Knopf, 1917.

———. *Tol'able David.* New York: Alfred A. Knopf, 1923.

———. *Tropical Winter.* New York: Alfred A. Knopf, 1933.

———. *Tubal Cain.* New York: Alfred A. Knopf, 1922.

———. *Wild Oranges.* New York: Alfred A. Knopf, 1922.

Herrmann, Dorothy. *With Malice Toward All: The Quips, Lives and Loves of Some Celebrated 20th-Century American Wits.* New York: Putnam, 1982.

Huggins, Nathan Irvin. *Harlem Renaissance.* New York: Oxford University Press, 1971.

Hughes, Langston. *Ask Your Mama: 12 Moods for Jazz.* New York: Alfred A. Knopf, 1961.

———. *The Big Sea: An Autobiography.* New York: Alfred A. Knopf, 1940.

———. *The Collected Poems of Langston Hughes.* Edited by Arnold Rampersad and David Roessel. New York: Alfred A. Knopf, 1994.

———. *Don't You Turn Back: Poems.* Selected by Lee Bennett Hopkins. New York: Alfred A. Knopf, 1969.

———. *Fine Clothes to the Jew.* New York: Alfred A. Knopf, 1927.

———. *A New Song.* New York: International Workers Order, 1938.

———. *Not Without Laughter.* New York: Alfred A. Knopf, 1930.

———. *One-Way Ticket.* New York: Alfred A. Knopf, 1949.

———. *The Panther & the Lash: Poems of Our Times.* New York: Alfred A. Knopf, 1967.

———. *Shakespeare in Harlem.* New York: Alfred A. Knopf, 1942.

———. *The Ways of White Folks.* New York: Alfred A. Knopf, 1934.

———. *The Weary Blues.* New York: Alfred A. Knopf, 1926.

Hughes, Langston, and Carl Van Vechten. *Remember Me to Harlem: The Letters of Langston Hughes and Carl Van Vechten, 1925–1964.* Edited by Emily Bernard. New York: Alfred A. Knopf, 2001.

Hurst, Fannie. *Anatomy of Me.* New York: Doubleday, 1958.

———. *Appassionata.* New York: Alfred A. Knopf, 1926.

———. *Mannequin.* New York: Alfred A. Knopf, 1926.

———. *Song of Life.* New York: Alfred A. Knopf, 1927.

Johnson, David R. *Conrad Richter: A Writer's Life.* University Park: Pennsylvania State University Press, 2001.

Johnson, Diane. *Dashiell Hammett: A Life.* New York: Random House, 1983.

Jones, Ernest. *The Life and Work of Sigmund Freud.* New York: Basic Books, 1953.

Josephy, Robert. *Taking Part: A Twentieth-Century Life.* Iowa City: University of Iowa Press, 1993.

Kantor, Tim. *My Father's Voice: MacKinlay Kantor Long Remembered.* New York: McGraw-Hill, 1988.

Kaplan, Alice Y. *Dreaming in French: The Paris Years of Jacqueline Bouvier Kennedy, Susan Sontag, and Angela Davis.* Chicago: University of Chicago Press, 2012.

Kellner, Bruce. *Carl Van Vechten and the Irreverent Decades.* Norman: University of Oklahoma Press, 1968.

———. *The Last Dandy, Ralph Barton: American Artist, 1891–1931.* Columbia: University of Missouri Press, 1991.

Knopf, Alfred A., ed. *The Borzoi 1920: Being a Sort of Record of Five Years' Publishing.* New York: Alfred A. Knopf, 1920.

———. *Portrait of a Publisher 1915–1965.* New York: The Typophiles, 1965.

———. *Publishing Then and Now: 1912–1964.* New York: New York Public Library, 1964.

———. *Some Random Recollections: An Informal Talk Made at the Grolier Club, New York, 21 October 1948.* New York: Typophiles, 1949.

Knopf, Alfred A., ed. "Blanche Wolf Knopf Reminiscences." *The Borzoi Quarterly* 15, no. 3 (1966).

Knopf, Blanche. "An American Publisher Tours South America." *The Saturday Review,* April 10, 1943.

Koestenbaum, Wayne. *Jackie Under My Skin: Interpreting an Icon.* New York: Farrar, Straus and Giroux, 1995.

Kolodin, Irving. *In Quest of Music: A Journey in Time.* Garden City, NY: Doubleday, 1980.

Korda, Michael. *Another Life: A Memoir of Other People.* New York: Random House, 1999.

———. *Making the List: A Cultural History of the American Bestseller, 1900–1999.* New York: Barnes & Noble, 2001.

Kraft, James. *Who Is Witter Bynner?: A Biography.* Albuquerque: University of New Mexico Press, 1995.

Kroch, Adolph. "To Alfred Knopf," in Knopf, *Portrait of a Publisher,* vol. 2.

Lee, Hermione. *Willa Cather: Double Lives.* New York: Pantheon Books, 1989.

Lemay, Harding. *Inside, Looking Out: A Personal Memoir.* New York: Harper's Magazine Press, 1971.

Lewis, Edith. *Willa Cather Living: A Personal Record.* New York: Alfred A. Knopf, 1953.

Lingeman, Richard R. *Sinclair Lewis: Rebel from Main Street.* New York: Random House, 2002.

Lovegren, Sylvia. *Fashionable Food: Seven Decades of Food Fads.* New York: Macmillan, 1995.

Mann, Thomas. *The Beloved Returns: Lotte in Weimar.* Translated by H. T. Lowe-Porter. New York: Alfred A. Knopf, 1940.

———. *The Black Swan.* Translated by Willard R. Trask. New York: Alfred A. Knopf, 1954.

———. *Buddenbrooks: The Decline of a Family.* Translated by H. T. Lowe-Porter. New York: Alfred A. Knopf, 1924.

———. *The Coming Victory of Democracy.* Translated by Agnes E. E. Meyer. New York: Alfred A. Knopf, 1938.

———. *Confessions of Felix Krull, Confidence Man: The Early Years.* Translated by Denver Lindley. New York: Alfred A. Knopf, 1955.

———. *Death in Venice and Other Stories.* Translated by Kenneth Burke. New York: Alfred A. Knopf, 1925.

———. *Doctor Faustus: The Life of the German Composer, Adrian Leverkühn.* Translated by H. T. Lowe-Porter. New York: Alfred A. Knopf, 1948.

———. *The Holy Sinner.* Translated by H. T. Lowe-Porter. New York: Alfred A. Knopf, 1951.

———. *Joseph and His Brothers.* Translated by H. T. Lowe-Porter. New York: Alfred A. Knopf, 1948.

———. *Joseph in Egypt.* Translated by H. T. Lowe-Porter. New York: Alfred A. Knopf, 1938.

———. *Joseph the Provider.* Translated by H. T. Lowe-Porter. New York: Alfred A. Knopf, 1944.

———. *Last Essays.* Translated by Richard Winston and Clara Winston. New York: Alfred A. Knopf, 1959.

———. *The Magic Mountain.* Translated by John E. Woods. New York: Alfred A. Knopf, 1995.

———. *Royal Highness.* Translated by A. Cecil Curtis. New York: Alfred A. Knopf, 1965.

———. *A Sketch of My Life.* Translated by H. T. Lowe-Porter. New York: Alfred A. Knopf, 1960.

———. *The Tables of the Law.* Translated by H. T. Lowe-Porter. New York: Alfred A. Knopf, 1964.

———. *Young Joseph.* Translated by H. T. Lowe-Porter. New York: Alfred A. Knopf, 1935.

Mayfield, Sara. *The Constant Circle: H. L. Mencken and His Friends.* New York: Delacorte Press, 1968.

Mencken, H. L. *The American Language: An Inquiry into the Development of English in the United States.* New York: Alfred A. Knopf, 1936.

——. *The Bathtub Hoax, and Other Blasts & Bravos from the "Chicago Tribune."* New York: Alfred A. Knopf, 1958.

——. *The Diary of H. L. Mencken.* Edited by Charles A. Fecher. New York: Alfred A. Knopf, 1989.

——. *Happy Days, 1880–1892.* New York: Alfred A. Knopf, 1940.

——. *Heathen Days, 1890–1936.* New York: Alfred A. Knopf, 1943.

——. *Heliogabalus: A Buffoonery in Three Acts.* New York: Alfred A. Knopf, 1920.

——. *In Defense of Women.* New York: Alfred A. Knopf, 1922.

——. *Letters of H. L. Mencken.* Edited by Guy J. Forgue. Boston: Northeastern University Press, 1981.

——. *A Mencken Chrestomathy: His Own Selection of His Choicest Writing.* New York: Alfred A. Knopf, 1949.

——. *My Life as Author and Editor.* Edited by Jonathan Yardley. New York: Alfred A. Knopf, 1993.

——. *The New Mencken Letters.* Edited by Carl Bode. New York: Dial Press, 1977.

——. *A Second Mencken Chrestomathy.* Edited by Terry Teachout. New York: Alfred A. Knopf, 1995.

——. *Treatise on the Gods.* New York: Alfred A. Knopf, 1946.

Mencken, H. L., and Sara Haardt Mencken. *Mencken and Sara: A Life in Letters; The Private Correspondence of H. L. Mencken and Sara Haardt.* Edited by Marion E. Rodgers. New York: McGraw-Hill, 1987.

Moiseiwitsch, Maurice. *Moiseiwitsch: Biography of a Concert Pianist.* London: Frederick Muller, 1965.

Nasaw, David. *The Patriarch: The Remarkable Life and Turbulent Times of Joseph P. Kennedy.* New York: Penguin Press, 2012.

Neihart, Ben. *Rough Amusements: The True Story of A'lelia Walker, Patroness of the Harlem Renaissance's Down-Low Culture; An Urban Historical.* New York: Bloomsbury, 2003.

Okrent, Daniel. *Last Call: The Rise and Fall of Prohibition.* New York: Scribner, 2010.

Peters, Margot. *May Sarton: A Biography.* New York: Alfred A. Knopf, 1997.

Pollack, Howard. *George Gershwin: His Life and Work.* Berkeley: University of California Press, 2006.

Radway, Janice A. *A Feeling for Books: The Book-of-the-Month Club, Literary Taste, and Middle-Class Desire.* Chapel Hill: University of North Carolina Press, 1997.

Rampersad, Arnold. *The Life of Langston Hughes.* 2 vols. New York: Oxford University Press, 1986–88.

Rascoe, Burton. *Before I Forget.* Garden City, NY: Doubleday, Doran, 1937.

——. *A Bookman's Daybook.* Edited by C. H. Grattan. New York: H. Liveright, 1929.

Reston, James. *Prelude to Victory.* New York: Alfred A. Knopf, 1942.

——. *Sketches in the Sand.* New York: Alfred A. Knopf, 1967.

Robinson, Phyllis C. *Willa: The Life of Willa Cather.* Garden City, NY: Doubleday, 1983.

Rodgers, Marion Elizabeth. *Mencken: The American Iconoclast; The Life and Times of the Bad Boy of Baltimore.* Oxford; New York: Oxford University Press, 2005.

Rogers, Bruce, ed. *Alfred A. Knopf: Quarter Century*. New York: Plimpton, 1940.

Rollyson, Carl E. *Rebecca West: A Life*. New York: Scribner, 1996.

Rubin, Joan Shelby. *The Making of Middlebrow Culture*. Chapel Hill: University of North Carolina Press, 1992.

Rubinstein, Arthur. *My Many Years*. New York: Alfred A. Knopf, 1980.

Sachs, Harvey. *Arthur Rubenstein: A Life*. London: Weidenfeld & Nicolson, 1995.

Sandelin, Clarence K. *Robert Nathan*. New York: Twayne, 1968.

Sartre, Jean-Paul. *The Age of Reason*. Translated by Eric Sutton. New York: Alfred A. Knopf, 1947.

———. *The Condemned of Altona: A Play in Five Acts*. Translated by Sylvia and George Lesson. New York: Alfred A. Knopf, 1961.

———. *The Devil & the Good Lord, and Two Other Plays*. Translated by Kitty Black. New York: Alfred A. Knopf, 1960.

———. *No Exit (Huis Clos): A Play in One Act, & the Flies (Les Mouches): A Play in Three Acts*. Translated by Stuart Gilbert. New York: Alfred A. Knopf, 1947.

———. *The Reprieve*. Translated by Eric Sutton. New York: Alfred A. Knopf, 1947.

———. *Search for a Method*. Translated by Hazel E. Barnes. New York: Alfred A. Knopf, 1963.

———. *Troubled Sleep*. Translated by Gerard Hopkins. New York: Alfred A. Knopf, 1964.

Schorer, Mark. *Sinclair Lewis: An American Life*. New York: McGraw-Hill, 1961.

Seabrook, William. *Jungle Ways*. New York: Harcourt, Brace, 1931.

Seaver, Richard, and Jeannette Seaver. *The Tender Hour of Twilight: Paris in the '50s, New York in the '60s; A Memoir of Publishing's Golden Age*. New York: Farrar, Straus and Giroux, 2012.

Secrest, Meryle. *Elsa Schiaparelli: A Biography*. New York: Alfred A. Knopf. 2014.

Shirer, William L. *Berlin Diary: The Journal of a Foreign Correspondent, 1934–1941*. New York: Alfred A. Knopf, 1941.

———. *End of a Berlin Diary*. New York: Alfred A. Knopf, 1947.

———. *Rise and Fall of Adolf Hitler*. New York: Alfred A. Knopf, 1961.

Silverman, Al. *Time of Their Lives: The Golden Age of Great American Publishers, Their Editors and Authors*. New York: Truman Talley Books, 2008.

Sloat, Warren. *1929: America Before the Crash*. New York: Macmillan, 1979.

Souhami, Diana. *Wild Girls: Paris, Sappho, and Art; The Lives and Loves of Natalie Barney and Romaine Brooks*. New York: St. Martin's Press, 2005.

Stannard, Martin. *Muriel Spark: The Biography*. New York: W. W. Norton, 2010.

Stevens, Holly. *Souvenirs and Prophecies: The Young Wallace Stevens*. New York: Alfred A. Knopf, 1977.

Stevens, Wallace. *The Auroras of Autumn: Poems*. New York: Alfred A. Knopf, 1950.

———. *The Collected Poems of Wallace Stevens*. New York: Alfred A. Knopf, 1954.

———. *Harmonium*. New York: Alfred A. Knopf, 1923.

———. *Ideas of Order*. New York: Alfred A. Knopf, 1936.

———. *Letters of Wallace Stevens*. Edited by Holly Stevens. New York: Alfred A. Knopf, 1966.

———. *The Man with the Blue Guitar & Other Poems*. New York: Alfred A. Knopf, 1937.

————. *The Necessary Angel: Essays on Reality and the Imagination*. New York: Alfred A. Knopf, 1951.

————. *Opus Posthumous*. Edited by Milton J. Bates. New York: Alfred A. Knopf, 1989.

————. *Parts of a World*. New York: Alfred A. Knopf, 1942.

————. *Sunday Morning*. Iowa City, IA: Editions Etoile, 1997.

————. *Transport to Summer*. New York: Alfred A. Knopf, 1947.

Suriano, Gregory R. *Gershwin in His Time: A Biographical Scrapbook, 1919–1937*. New York: Gramercy Books, 1998.

Tebbel, John. *A History of Book Publishing in the United States*. Vol. 2: *The Expansion of an Industry, 1865–1919*, and vol. 3, *The Golden Age Between Two Wars, 1920–1940* (New York: R. R. Bowker, 1975–78).

Todd, Olivier. *Albert Camus: A Life*. New York: Alfred A. Knopf, 1997.

Turner, Catherine. *Marketing Modernism Between the Two World Wars*. Amherst: University of Massachusetts Press, 2003.

Van Vechten, Carl. *The Blind Bow-Boy*. New York: Alfred A. Knopf, 1923.

————. *Excavations: A Book of Advocacies*. New York: Alfred A. Knopf, 1926.

————. *Firecrackers: A Realistic Novel*. New York: Alfred A. Knopf, 1925.

————. *Interpreters and Interpretations*. New York: Alfred A. Knopf, 1917.

————. *Letters of Carl Van Vechten*. Edited by Bruce Kellner. New Haven, CT: Yale University Press, 1987.

————. *The Lord of the Sea*. New York: Alfred A. Knopf, 1924.

————. *Lords of the Housetops: Thirteen Cat Tales*. New York: Alfred A. Knopf, 1921.

————. *The Merry-Go-Round*. New York: Alfred A. Knopf, 1918.

————. *Music and Bad Manners*. New York: Alfred A. Knopf, 1916.

————. *The Music of Spain*. New York: Alfred A. Knopf, 1918.

————. *Nigger Heaven*. New York: Alfred A. Knopf, 1926.

————. *Parties: Scenes from Contemporary New York Life*. New York: Alfred A. Knopf, 1930.

————. *Peter Whiffle: His Life and Works*. New York: Alfred A. Knopf, 1922.

————. *Red: Papers on Musical Subjects*. New York: Alfred A. Knopf, 1925.

————. *Sacred and Profane Memories*. New York: Alfred A. Knopf, 1932.

————. *Spider Boy: A Scenario for a Moving Picture*. New York: Alfred A. Knopf, 1928.

————. *The Splendid Drunken Twenties: Selections from the Daybooks, 1922–1930*. Edited by Bruce Kellner. Urbana: University of Illinois Press, 2003.

————. *The Tattooed Countess: A Romantic Novel with a Happy Ending*. New York: Alfred A. Knopf, 1924.

————. *The Tiger in the House*. New York: Alfred A. Knopf, 1936.

West, Rebecca, *The Young Rebecca: Writings of Rebecca West, 1911–17*. Selected and introduced by Jane Marcus. New York: Viking, 1982.

White, Edmund. *The Tastemaker: Carl Van Vechten and the Birth of Modern America*. New York: Farrar, Straus and Giroux, 2014.

Worthen, John. *D. H. Lawrence: The Life of an Outsider*. New York: Counterpoint, 2005.

ACKNOWLEDGMENTS

Blanche Knopf, born at the end of the Gilded Age, was embedded in my life even when I was a student of British Romanticism, though it would be decades before I realized the connection. While a professor, I read and used in the classroom the now classic biography of the poet Percy Bysshe Shelley published by Knopf in 1940—when Blanche, I would discover, had become a good friend of its author, Newman Ivey White. Knopf also published the great Leslie A. Marchand's three-volume biography of Byron in 1957. Yet another of Blanche's writers was the poet Elinor Wylie, who penned a quixotic novel about Shelley that allowed the poet to transcend his real-life drowning.

Mildly interested in Wylie's life, which I'd heard was short but exotic, a decade ago I ended up following the trail that led me to her publisher, whom Wylie had written about enthusiastically. But when I looked up Blanche Knopf, I could find little about her except vague references to her importance in the literary world. Thus was born this biography: her story had not been told. What better time to honor her, as the company she cofounded has just celebrated its hundredth anniversary?

I am especially indebted to two predecessors, the Pulitzer Prize winner Susan Sheehan and the late *Newsweek* critic Peter Prescott, who between them worked for more than thirty years researching and writing about Knopf and its founding in 1915. Sheehan began the project in the early seventies, when Alfred Knopf and the Knopfs' only child, Alfred "Pat" Knopf, Jr., were still alive. After Sheehan chose to write about other subjects, Peter Prescott took over. When he died in 2004, Prescott was just starting to think through his research and plan his book. Peter's wife, Anne

Prescott, a professor and scholar of the English Renaissance at Barnard College, began turning over Peter's material to the Knopf repository at the Harry Ransom Center at the University of Texas at Austin. Anne graciously shared with me the combined Sheehan/Prescott archives still in her husband's office, material not yet available at the Ransom.

As much as the legwork of Susan Sheehan and Peter Prescott made this book possible, even they were fettered by what Pat Knopf considered the plunder of the company's records: "letters stolen for literary value, for intimacy, for incrimination—and sometimes just thrown out." Once, for instance, in 1973, when Alfred realized that Columbia University possessed "inappropriate" files about his personal life, he informed Sheehan of his discovery, saying, "When I wrote you May 31, 1974, I had no knowledge—stupid as I was—of the existences of our early files . . . I do expect you to give me a reasonably full report of what they contain and most particularly matters [that] may show indiscretions on the part of either Blanche or me and that you will submit such material to me before you make any use of it." There is no evidence that Susan acquiesced, though such new strictures may well have encouraged her to give up the project.

Before his death in 1984, Alfred had written at least five partial memoirs, begun in the late 1950s. He would call the "disconnected, partially edited 1000 pages" "those damned reminiscences." Due mostly to the passage of time, each version is different from the previous one. After all, memories fade and change and are overwritten by new ones. I assume (and hope) that "my" Blanche will be imagined differently by another writer in the future, one who is privy to materials that I haven't seen. Inevitably, the records I've inherited from Sheehan and Prescott are at times a palimpsest, references and comments from different periods and two individuals often layered one over the other on thin onionskin paper. The writers, assuming they were constructing notes for their eyes only, named and referred to the pages idiosyncratically. They numbered their pages according to private codes, and Susan's system was eventually absorbed by Peter's, his observations frequently building on her remarks, interviews, and letters. Often he just combined his reflections with hers, the material untitled or given various labels. At times, each used private codes or abbreviations, between them calling a single document by several different names.

The Ransom Center librarians Richard Workman and Richard Oram are responsible for supervising the cataloging of much of the Knopf collection, and both have proved generous with their time and knowledge. Amy Root Clements, with her University of Texas dissertation on Knopf's early years, now published as a book, *The Art of Prestige*, by the University of Massachusetts, Amherst, and John Thompson, a New York writer and publisher who continues to work on an extensive history of the Knopf financial enterprise, have eased my way.

Though Blanche herself is long gone, many connected to her personal and professional life have allowed me to get to know her: Susan Sheehan, Judith Jones, Harding Lemay, Bruce Kellner, Arnold Rampersad, and Bruce Fleming were willing to answer endless questions. Three exceptional research assistants were Evan Scott Edwards, Annette Martinez, and Allegra Hastings-Martinez, all sine qua non. Simon Lea of the Albert Camus Society UK never showed impatience with my desire to "nail it down." On the sidelines were Deirdre Bair, Betty Ballantine, Stephen Bayley, Emily Bernard, Warren Boroson, Scotty Bowers, A'lelia Bundles, Bruce Clayton, Charles Dellheim, Suzanne and Patrick Ford, Stephen Foster, Robert Gaynor, Elizabeth Hawes, Boris Kachka, Howard Kaminsky, Alice Knopf, Susan Knopf, Michael Korda, Megan Marshall, Miriam Medina, Lyonel Nelson, Craig Nolan, Brian Pfremmer, Barbara Pokras, Nora Post, Eric Rayman, Azra Raza, Sughra Raza, Daniel Rigney, Julie Shamrock Rollend, Frank Romano, Jay Rubenstein, Craig Sauter, Martin Stannard, Paul Sugarman, Judith Thurman, Dick Todd, Amanda Vaill, Manda Weintraub, and Fran Yariv.

Institutional support was invaluable, especially for a book about books. Special thanks for their untiring efforts go to Vincent Fitzpatrick at Baltimore's Enoch Pratt Free Library, curator of the H. L Mencken Collection; L. J. Cormier and staff at the Kingston, NY, Library; Katy Chung and Mary Debellis at the Mahopac, NY, Library; David Smith (retired), New York Public Library; Debbi Smith, Adelphi University Library; Melissa Straw, Goucher College Special Collections; Nancy Lyon, Sterling Memorial Library, Yale University; and, far more than required, to Richard Oram at the Ransom Center.

Also contributing, however obscure my request, were Dan Berrett, *The Chronicle of Higher Education*; Michael Boriskin, executive director, Copland House, Peekskill, NY; Bridget P. Carr, archivist, Boston Symphony Orchestra; Katie Martello and Nell Boucher, Mohonk Mountain House, New Paltz, NY; Anne Cooper Albright, Wells Library, Oberlin College, Oberlin, OH; Robert DeSpain and Julia Ehrhardt, Coe Library, Cedar Rapids, IA; Marcia Farabee, principal librarian, National Symphony Orchestra, Kennedy Center, Washington, D.C.; David Frasier, Lilly Library, Indiana University; Kalé Haywood, Department of History, Allegheny College; Amanda Lawrence, University of Illinois Archives, Urbana; Maira Liriano, New York Public Library; Amy McDonald, Duke University Archives; John A. Maltese, Department of Political Science, University of Georgia; Zoe Rhine, Buncombe County Library, NC; Adrienne Leigh Sharpe, Beinecke Rare Book and Manuscript Library, Yale University; Ellen M. Shea, Head of Research Services, Schlesinger Library on the History of Women in America, Radcliffe Institute, Harvard University; Leann Swims, Grove Park Inn, Asheville, NC; Jack W. L. Thomson, executive director, Preservation Society of Asheville & Buncombe County, NC; Matthew Tuni, Manuscripts Special Collection, University of North Carolina, Chapel Hill; Anthony Hopenhajm and Kiera McGill, Seaman Schepps Jewelry, New York; Patti Solosky, Union College; National Library of Scotland, Edinburgh; Abby Yochelson, Library of Congress, Washington, D.C.; anonymous librarians at Firestone Library, Princeton University; Newberry Library, Chicago; University of California, Santa Barbara, Dame Judith Anderson Special Collection.

In addition, my Hudson Valley Writers' group energized this project: Holly George-Warren ruthlessly stomps repetition and promotes clear transitions; Richard Hoffman, a master of tone, forces me to afford just treatment to all characters and to "lose the attitude"; and John Milward, like a dog tracking a flea, redlines even a hint of highfalutin diction.

Marion Ettlinger, with her extraordinary portraiture, helped me better understand

ACKNOWLEDGMENTS

Carl Van Vechten's later passion for photography. My editor, Ileene Smith, who worked with Pat Knopf in the early days of her publishing career, challenged me to weigh each word and justify every supposition—and she "got" Blanche, as did my agent, Carol Mann, both women quick to understand the publisher's importance: they needed no pitch. John Knight, Ileene's assistant, never showed the slightest impatience at the exhaustive and surely exhausting demands of the manuscript (and its author), its nearly eight hundred endnotes only reasonable to someone who realized that a book about books, as I have often called *The Lady with the Borzoi*, would demand such meticulousness. To John goes my deepest gratitude. Jeff Seroy and Stephen Pfau made sure there's a public for *The Lady with the Borzoi*, and Scott Auerbach did the heavy yet delicate lifting of the production editorial work. In addition to the exemplary staff of Farrar, Straus and Giroux, I thank FSG's president and publisher, Jonathan Galassi, for welcoming *The Lady with the Borzoi* into his distinguished house. On January 3, 2010, Galassi outlined in a *New York Times* article how "a publisher . . . does far more than print and sell a book. [A publisher] selects, nurtures, positions and promotes the writer's work."

Too often, as with Blanche, the publisher gets lost in the shuffle. But here we are, more than fifty years after Blanche's death, able to return her to the history of publishing, where she belongs.

INDEX

A NOTE ABOUT THE AUTHOR

Laura Claridge is the author of biographies of Tamara de Lempicka, Emily Post, and Norman Rockwell. A frequent contributor to *The Wall Street Journal*, *Vogue*, *The Boston Globe*, the *Los Angeles Times*, and other publications, she lives in the Hudson Valley.